STORY

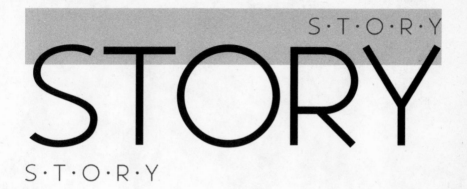

STORY

Substance, Structure, Style,
and the Principles of Screenwriting

ROBERT McKEE

ReganBooks
An Imprint of HarperCollinsPublishers

HarperCollins books may be purchased for educational, business, or sales promotional use. For information please write: Special Markets Department, Harper-Collins Publishers, Inc., 10 East 53rd Street, New York, NY 10022.

FIRST EDITION

Designed by Laura Lindgren

Library of Congress Cataloging-in-Publication Data
McKee, Robert, 1941–
    Story : substance, structure, style, and the principles of screenwriting /
    Robert McKee.
          p. cm.
    Includes bibliographical references and index.
    ISBN: 0-06-039168-5
    1. Motion picture authorship. 2. Motion picture plays—Technique. I. Title.
PN 1996.M465   1997
808.2'3—dc21   97-24139

99 00 01 ❖/RRD 20 19 18 17 16 15 14 13 12

I dedicate this book to the happy memory of my parents who, in their very different ways, taught me the love of story.

When I was first learning to read, but not always behaving appropriately, my father introduced me to the fables of Aesop in the hope that these ancient cautionary tales might improve my deportment. Each evening, after working my way through the likes of "The Fox and the Grapes," he would nod and ask, "And what does this story mean to you, Robert?" As I stared at these texts and their handsome color illustrations, struggling to find my interpretations, I slowly came to realize that stories mean much more than words and pretty pictures.

Later, before entering the university, I deduced that the best possible life includes as many rounds of golf as possible, and therefore, I would become a dentist. "Dentist?!" my mother laughed. "You can't be serious. What happens when they cure all teeth problems? Where will dentists be then? No, Bobby, people will always need entertainment. I'm looking out for your future. You're going into show business."

CONTENTS

Acknowledgments / ix
Notes on the Text / xi

PART 1: THE WRITER AND THE ART OF STORY
Introduction / 3
1. The Story Problem / 11

PART 2: THE ELEMENTS OF STORY
2. The Structure Spectrum / 31
3. Structure and Setting / 67
4. Structure and Genre / 79
5. Structure and Character / 100
6. Structure and Meaning / 110

PART 3: THE PRINCIPLES OF STORY DESIGN
7. The Substance of Story / 135
8. The Inciting Incident / 181
9. Act Design / 208
10. Scene Design / 233
11. Scene Analysis / 252
12. Composition / 288
13. Crisis, Climax, Resolution / 303

PART 4: THE WRITER AT WORK
14. The Principle of Antagonism / 317
15. Exposition / 334
16. Problems and Solutions / 346
17. Character / 374
18. The Text / 388
19. A Writer's Method / 410
Fade Out / 418

Suggested Readings / 421
Filmography / 423
Index / 457

ACKNOWLEDGMENTS

For her sensitivity to the truth, for her unblinking editorial eye and omnivorous will to omit needless words, her unerring logic, optimism, inspiration . . . for her love, I thank my wife, Suzanne Childs.

As the lucky associate of astute accomplices willing to suffer rough drafts, close holes, sand ragged edges, and wisely point out that things don't always mean what their author thinks they mean, I thank Jess Money, Gail McNamara, and my editor, Andrew Albanese.

If it weren't for my agent's uncanny timing, I would have procrastinated this book into the next century. Thank you, Debra Rodman.

If it weren't for my publisher's persistence, I would have procrastinated my agent's promptings into the next century. Thank you, Judith Regan.

If it weren't for the support of the Evans Scholars Foundation and the minds I met at the University of Michigan, my life would have been diminished. I offer my gratitude to Kenneth Rowe, John Arthos, Hugh Norton, Claribel Baird, Donald Hall, and all other professors whose names I've forgotten, but whose brilliant teachings have braced my days.

Lastly, most importantly, my students. Over the years my understanding of the art of story has grown thanks, in great part, to the questions you've asked, questions both perceptive and practical, that have sent me further and deeper in search of answers. This book would not exist without you.

NOTES ON THE TEXT

The hundreds of examples in *Story* are drawn from a century of film writing and filmmaking around the world. Whenever possible, I offer more than one title of the most recent and widely seen works I know. Because it's impossible to select films everyone has seen and remembers in detail, I've leaned toward those readily available on video. But first and foremost, each film has been chosen because it is a clear illustration of the point made in the text.

To deal with the pronoun problem I have avoided constructions that distract the reader's eye, such as the annoying alternation of "she" and "her" with "he" and "him," the repetitious "he and she" and "him and her," the awkward "s/he" and "her/im," and the ungrammatical "they" and "them" as neuter singulars. Rather, I use the nonexclusive "he" and "him" to mean "writer."

PART I

THE WRITER AND THE ART OF STORY

Stories are equipment for living.
—KENNETH BURKE

INTRODUCTION

Story **is about principles, not rules.**

A rule says, "You *must* do it *this way*." A principle says, "This *works* . . . and has through all remembered time." The difference is crucial. Your work needn't be modeled after the "well-made" play; rather, it must be *well made* within the principles that shape our art. Anxious, inexperienced writers obey rules. Rebellious, unschooled writers break rules. Artists master the form.

Story **is about eternal, universal forms, not formulas.**

All notions of paradigms and foolproof story models for commercial success are nonsense. Despite trends, remakes, and sequels, when we survey the totality of Hollywood film, we find an astounding variety of story designs, but no prototype. DIE HARD is no more typical of Hollywood than are PARENTHOOD, POSTCARDS FROM THE EDGE, THE LION KING, THIS IS SPINAL TAP, REVERSAL OF FORTUNE, DANGEROUS LIAISONS, GROUNDHOG DAY, LEAVING LAS VEGAS, or thousands of other excellent films in dozens of genres and subgenres from farce to tragedy.

Story urges the creation of works that will excite audiences on the six continents and live in revival for decades. No one needs yet another recipe book on how to reheat Hollywood leftovers. We need a rediscovery of the underlying tenets of our art, the guiding principles that liberate talent. No matter where a film is made—Hollywood, Paris, Hong Kong—if it's of archetypal quality, it triggers a global and perpetual chain reaction of pleasure that carries it from cinema to cinema, generation to generation.

Story **is about archetypes, not stereotypes.**

The archetypal story unearths a universally human experience, then wraps itself inside a unique, culture-specific expression. A stereotypical story reverses this pattern: It suffers a poverty of both content and form. It confines itself to a narrow, culture-specific experience and dresses in stale, nonspecific generalities.

For example, Spanish custom once dictated that daughters must be married off in order from oldest to youngest. Inside Spanish culture, a film about the nineteenth-century family of a strict patriarch, a powerless mother, an unmarriageable oldest daughter, and a long-suffering youngest daughter may move those who remember this practice, but outside Spanish culture audiences are unlikely to empathize. The writer, fearing his story's limited appeal, resorts to the familiar settings, characters, and actions that have pleased audiences in the past. The result? The world is even less interested in these clichés.

On the other hand, this repressive custom could become material for a worldwide success if the artist were to roll up his sleeves and search for an archetype. An archetypal story creates settings and characters so rare that our eyes feast on every detail, while its telling illuminates conflicts so true to humankind that it journeys from culture to culture.

In Laura Esquivel's LIKE WATER FOR CHOCOLATE, mother and daughter clash over the demands of dependence versus independence, permanence versus change, self versus others—conflicts every family knows. Yet Esquivel's observation of home and society, of relationship and behavior is so rich in never-before-seen detail, we're drawn irresistibly to these characters and fascinated by a realm we've never known, nor could imagine.

Stereotypical stories stay at home, archetypal stories travel. From Charlie Chaplin to Ingmar Bergman, from Satyajit Ray to Woody Allen, the cinema's master storytellers give us the double-edged encounter we crave. First, the discovery of a world we do not know. No matter how intimate or epic, contemporary or historical, concrete or fantasized, the world of an eminent artist always strikes us as somewhat exotic or strange. Like an explorer parting forest leaves, we step wide-eyed into an untouched society, a cliché-free zone where the ordinary becomes extraordinary.

Second, once inside this alien world, we find ourselves. Deep within these characters and their conflicts we discover our own humanity. We go to the movies to enter a new, fascinating world, to inhabit vicariously another human being who at first seems so unlike us and yet at heart *is* like us, to live in a fictional reality that illuminates our daily reality. We do not wish to escape life but to find life, to use our minds in fresh, experimental ways, to flex our emotions, to enjoy, to learn, to add depth to our days. *Story* was written to foster films of archetypal power and beauty that will give the world this dual pleasure.

Story is about thoroughness, not shortcuts.

From inspiration to last draft you may need as much time to write a screenplay as to write a novel. Screen and prose writers create the same density of world, character, and story, but because screenplay pages have so much white on them, we're often mislead into thinking that a screenplay is quicker and easier than a novel. But while scribomaniacs fill pages as fast as they can type, film writers cut and cut again, ruthless in their desire to express the absolute maximum in the fewest possible words. Pascal once wrote a long, drawn-out letter to a friend, then apologized in the postscript that he didn't have time to write a short one. Like Pascal, screenwriters learn that economy is key, that brevity takes time, that excellence means perseverance.

Story is about the realities, not the mysteries of writing.

There's been no conspiracy to keep secret the truths of our art. In the twenty-three centuries since Aristotle wrote *The Poetics*, the "secrets" of story have been as public as the library down the street. Nothing in the craft of storytelling is abstruse. In fact, at first glance telling story for the screen looks deceptively easy. But moving closer and closer to the center, trying scene by scene to make the story work, the task becomes increasingly difficult, as we realize that on the screen there's no place to hide.

If a screenwriter fails to move us with the purity of a dramatized scene, he cannot, like a novelist in authorial voice, or the playwright in soliloquy, hide behind his words. He cannot smooth a coating of explanatory or emotive language over cracks in logic, blotchy motivation, or colorless emotion and simply *tell* us what to think or how to feel.

The camera is the dread X-ray machine of all things false. It magnifies life many times over, then strips naked every weak or phony story turn, until in confusion and frustration we're tempted to quit. Yet, given determination and study, the puzzle yields. Screenwriting is full of wonders but no unsolvable mysteries.

Story is about mastering the art, not second-guessing the marketplace.

No one can teach what will sell, what won't, what will be a smash or a fiasco, because *no one knows*. Hollywood's bombs are made with the same commercial calculation as its hits, whereas darkish dramas that read like a checklist of everything moneyed wisdom says you must never do—ORDINARY PEOPLE, THE ACCIDENTAL TOURIST, TRAINSPOTTING—quietly conquer the domestic and international box office. Nothing in our art is guaranteed. That's why so many agonize over "breaking in," "making it," and "creative interference."

The honest, big-city answer to all these fears is that you'll get an agent, sell your work, and see it realized faithfully on screen when you write with surpassing quality . . . and not until. If you knock out a knockoff of last summer's hit, you'll join the ranks of lesser talents who each year flood Hollywood with thousands of cliché-ridden stories. Rather than agonizing over the odds, put your energies into achieving excellence. If you show a brilliant, original screenplay to agents, they'll fight for the right to represent you. The agent you hire will incite a bidding war among story-starved producers, and the winner will pay you an embarrassing amount of money.

What's more, once in production, your *finished* screenplay will meet with surprisingly little interference. No one can promise that unfortunate conjunctions of personalities won't spoil good work, but be certain that Hollywood's best acting and directing talents are acutely aware that their careers depend on working within quality writing. Yet because of Hollywood's ravenous appetite for story, scripts are often picked before they're ripe, forcing changes on the set. Secure writers don't sell first drafts. They patiently rewrite until the script is as director-ready, as actor-ready as possible. Unfinished work invites tampering, while polished, mature work seals its integrity.

Story is about respect, not disdain, for the audience.

When talented people write badly it's generally for one of two reasons: Either they're blinded by an idea they feel compelled to prove or they're driven by an emotion they must express. When talented people write well, it is generally for this reason: They're moved by a desire to touch the audience.

Night after night, through years of performing and directing, I've stood in awe of the audience, of its capacity for response. As if by magic, masks fall away, faces become vulnerable, receptive. Filmgoers do not defend their emotions, rather they open to the storyteller in ways even their lovers never know, welcoming laughter, tears, terror, rage, compassion, passion, love, hate—the ritual often exhausts them.

The audience is not only amazingly sensitive, but as it settles into a darkened theatre its collective IQ jumps twenty-five points. When you go to the movies, don't you often feel you're more intelligent than what you're watching? That you know what characters are going to do before they do it? That you see the ending coming long before it arrives? The audience is not only smart, it's smarter than most films, and that fact won't change when you move to the other side of the screen. It's all a writer can do, using every bit of craft he's mastered, to keep ahead of the sharp perceptions of a focused audience.

No film can be made to work without an understanding of the reactions and anticipations of the audience. You must shape your story in a way that both expresses your vision and satisfies the audience's desires. The audience is a force as determining of story design as any other element. For without it, the creative act is pointless.

Story **is about originality, not duplication.**

Originality is the confluence of content and form—distinctive choices of subject plus a unique shaping of the telling. Content (setting, characters, ideas) and form (selection and arrangement of events) require, inspire, and mutually influence one another. With content in one hand and a mastery of form in the other, a writer sculpts story. As you rework a story's substance, the telling reshapes itself. As you play with a story's shape, its intellectual and emotional spirit evolves.

A story is not only what you have to say but how you say it. If content is cliché, the telling will be cliché. But if your vision is deep and original, your story design will be unique. Conversely, if the telling is conventional and predictable, it will demand stereotypical roles to act out well-worn behaviors. But if the story design is innovative, then settings, characters, and ideas must be equally fresh to fulfill it. We shape the telling to fit the substance, rework the substance to support the design.

Never, however, mistake eccentricity for originality. Difference for the sake of difference is as empty as slavishly following commercial imperatives. After working for months, perhaps years, to gather facts, memories, and imagination into a treasury of story material, no serious writer would cage his vision inside a formula, or trivialize it into avant-garde fragmentations. The "well-made" formula may choke a story's voice, but "art movie" quirkiness will give it a speech impediment. Just as children break things for fun or throw tantrums to force attention on themselves, too many filmmakers use infantile gimmicks on screen to shout, "Look what I can do!" A mature artist never calls attention to himself, and a wise artist never does anything merely because it breaks convention.

Films by masters such as Horton Foote, Robert Altman, John Cassavetes, Preston Sturges, François Truffaut, and Ingmar Bergman are so idiosyncratic that a three-page synopsis identifies the artist as surely as his DNA. Great screenwriters are distinguished by a personal storytelling style, a style that's not only inseparable from their vision, but in a profound way is their vision. Their formal choices—number of protagonists, rhythm of progressions, levels of conflict, temporal arrangements, and the like—play with and against substantive choices of content—setting, character, idea—until all elements meld into a unique screenplay.

If, however, we were to put the content of their films aside for the moment, and study the pure patterning of their events, we'd see that, like a melody without a lyric, like a silhouette without a matrix, their story designs are powerfully charged with meaning. The storyteller's selection and arrangement of events is his master metaphor for the interconnectedness of all the levels of reality—personal, political, environmental, spiritual. Stripped of its surface of characterization and location, story structure reveals his personal cosmology, his insight into the deepest patterns and motivations for how and why things happen in this world—his map of life's hidden order.

No matter who your heroes may be—Woody Allen, David Mamet, Quentin Tarantino, Ruth Prawer Jhabvala, Oliver Stone, William Goldman, Zhang Yimou, Nora Ephron, Spike Lee, Stanley Kubrick—you admire them because they're unique. Each has stepped out of the crowd because each selects a content like no one else, designs a form like no one else, combining the two into a style unmistakably his own. I want the same for you.

But my hope for you goes beyond competence and skill. I'm starved for great films. Over the last two decades I've seen good films and a few very good films, but rarely, rarely a film of staggering power and beauty. Maybe it's me; maybe I'm jaded. But I don't think so. Not yet. I still believe that art transforms life. But I know that if you can't play all the instruments in the orchestra of story, no matter what music may be in your imagination, you're condemned to hum the same old tune. I've written *Story* to empower your command of the craft, to free you to express an original vision of life, to lift your talent beyond convention to create films of distinctive substance, structure, and style.

1

THE STORY PROBLEM

THE DECLINE OF STORY

Imagine, in one global day, the pages of prose turned, plays performed, films screened, the unending stream of television comedy and drama, twenty-four-hour print and broadcast news, bedtime tales told to children, barroom bragging, back-fence Internet gossip, humankind's insatiable appetite for stories. Story is not only our most prolific art form but rivals all activities—work, play, eating, exercise—for our waking hours. We tell and take in stories as much as we sleep—and even then we dream. Why? Why is so much of our life spent inside stories? Because as critic Kenneth Burke tells us, stories are equipment for living.

Day after day we seek an answer to the ageless question Aristotle posed in *Ethics*: How should a human being lead his life? But the answer eludes us, hiding behind a blur of racing hours as we struggle to fit our means to our dreams, fuse idea with passion, turn desire into reality. We're swept along on a risk-ridden shuttle through time. If we pull back to grasp pattern and meaning, life, like a Gestalt, does flips: first serious, then comic; static, frantic; meaningful, meaningless. Momentous world events are beyond our control while personal events, despite all effort to keep our hands on the wheel, more often than not control us.

Traditionally humankind has sought the answer to Aristotle's question from the four wisdoms—philosophy, science, religion, art—taking insight from each to bolt together a livable meaning.

But today who reads Hegel or Kant without an exam to pass? Science, once the great explicator, garbles life with complexity and perplexity. Who can listen without cynicism to economists, sociologists, politicians? Religion, for many, has become an empty ritual that masks hypocrisy. As our faith in traditional ideologies diminishes, we turn to the source we still believe in: the art of story.

The world now consumes films, novels, theatre, and television in such quantities and with such ravenous hunger that the story arts have become humanity's prime source of inspiration, as it seeks to order chaos and gain insight into life. Our appetite for story is a reflection of the profound human need to grasp the patterns of living, not merely as an intellectual exercise, but within a very personal, emotional experience. In the words of playwright Jean Anouilh, "Fiction gives life its form."

Some see this craving for story as simple entertainment, an escape from life rather than an exploration of it. But what, after all, is entertainment? To be entertained is to be immersed in the ceremony of story to an intellectually and emotionally satisfying end. To the film audience, entertainment is the ritual of sitting in the dark, concentrating on a screen in order to experience the story's meaning and, with that insight, the arousal of strong, at times even painful emotions, and as the meaning deepens, to be carried to the ultimate satisfaction of those emotions.

Whether it's the triumph of crazed entrepreneurs over Hittite demons in GHOSTBUSTERS or the complex resolution of inner demons in SHINE; the integration of character in THE RED DESERT or its disintegration in THE CONVERSATION, all fine films, novels, and plays, through all shades of the comic and tragic, entertain when they give the audience a fresh model of life empowered with an affective meaning. To retreat behind the notion that the audience simply wants to dump its troubles at the door and escape reality is a cowardly abandonment of the artist's responsibility. Story isn't a flight from reality but a vehicle that carries us on our search for reality, our best effort to make sense out of the anarchy of existence.

Yet, while the ever-expanding reach of the media now gives us the opportunity to send stories beyond borders and languages to hundreds of millions, the overall quality of storytelling is eroding. On occasion we read or see works of excellence, but for the most part we weary of searching newspaper ads, video shops, and TV listings for something of quality, of putting down novels half-read, of slipping out of plays at the intermission, of walking out of films soothing our disappointment with "But it was beautifully photographed . . ." The art of story is in decay, and as Aristotle observed twenty-three hundred years ago, when storytelling goes bad, the result is decadence.

Flawed and false storytelling is forced to substitute spectacle for substance, trickery for truth. Weak stories, desperate to hold audience attention, degenerate into multimillion-dollar razzle-dazzle demo reels. In Hollywood imagery becomes more and more extravagant, in Europe more and more decorative. The behavior of actors becomes more and more histrionic, more and more lewd, more and more violent. Music and sound effects become increasingly tumultuous. The total effect transudes into the grotesque. A culture cannot evolve without honest, powerful storytelling. When society repeatedly experiences glossy, hollowed-out, pseudo-stories, it degenerates. We need true satires and tragedies, dramas and comedies that shine a clean light into the dingy corners of the human psyche and society. If not, as Yeats warned, ". . . the centre can not hold."

Each year, Hollywood produces and/or distributes four hundred to five hundred films, virtually a film per day. A few are excellent, but the majority are mediocre or worse. The temptation is to blame this glut of banality on the Babbitt-like figures who approve productions. But recall a moment from THE PLAYER: Tim Robbins's young Hollywood executive explains that he has many enemies because each year his studio accepts over twenty thousand story submissions but only makes twelve films. This is accurate dialogue. The story departments of the major studios pore through thousands upon thousands of scripts, treatments, novels, and plays searching for a great screen story. Or, more likely, something halfway to good that they could develop to better-than-average.

By the 1990s script development in Hollywood climbed to over $500 million per annum, three quarters of which is paid to writers for options and rewrites on films that will never be made. Despite a half-billion dollars and the exhaustive efforts of development personnel, Hollywood cannot find better material than it produces. The hard-to-believe truth is that what we see on the screen each year is a reasonable reflection of the best writing of the last few years.

Many screenwriters, however, cannot face this downtown fact and live in the exurbs of illusion, convinced that Hollywood is blind to their talent. With rare exceptions, unrecognized genius is a myth. First-rate screenplays are at least optioned if not made. For writers who can tell a quality story, it's a seller's market—always has been, always will be. Hollywood has a secure international business for hundreds of films each year, and they will be made. Most will open, run a few weeks, close, and be mercifully forgotten.

Yet Hollywood not only survives, it thrives, because it has virtually no competition. This wasn't always the case. From the rise of Neo-realism to the high tide of the New Wave, North American cinemas were crowded with works by brilliant Continental filmmakers that challenged Hollywood's dominance. But with the death or retirement of these masters, the last twenty-five years have seen a slow decay in the quality of European films.

Today European filmmakers blame their failure to attract audience on a conspiracy of distributors. Yet the films of their predecessors—Renoir, Bergman, Fellini, Buñuel, Wajda, Clouzot, Antonioni, Resnais—were screened throughout the world. The system hasn't changed. The audience for non-Hollywood film is still vast and loyal. Distributors have the same motivation now they had then: money. What's changed is that contemporary "auteurs" cannot tell story with the power of the previous generation. Like pretentious interior decorators, they make films that strike the eye, and nothing more. As a result, the storm of European genius has become a slough of arid films that leave a vacuum for Hollywood to fill.

Asian works, however, now travel throughout North America and the world, moving and delighting millions, seizing the international spotlight with ease for one reason: Asian filmmakers tell superb stories. Rather than scapegoating distributors, non-Hollywood filmmakers would do well to look to the East, where artists have the passion to tell stories and the craft to tell them beautifully.

THE LOSS OF CRAFT

The art of story is the dominant cultural force in the world, and the art of film is the dominant medium of this grand enterprise. The world audience is devoted but thirsting for story. Why? Not from a poverty of effort. The Writers Guild of America script registration service logs over thirty-five thousand titles yearly. These are only those that are registered. Across America hundreds of thousands of screenplays are attempted each year, but only a handful are *quality* screenplays, for many reasons but this above all: Today's would-be writers rush to the typewriter without first learning their craft.

If your dream were to compose music, would you say to yourself: "I've heard a lot of symphonies . . . I can also play the piano . . . I think I'll knock one out this weekend"? No. But that's exactly how many screenwriters begin: "I've seen a lot of flicks, some good and some bad . . . I got A's in English . . . vacation time's coming . . . "

If you hoped to compose, you'd head for music school to study both theory and practice, focusing on the genre of symphony. After years of diligence, you'd merge your knowledge with your creativity, flex your courage, and venture to compose. Too many struggling writers never suspect that the creation of a fine screenplay is as difficult as the creation of a symphony, and in some ways more so. For while the composer scores with the mathematical purity of notes, we dip into the messy stuff known as human nature.

The novice plunges ahead, counting solely on experience, thinking that the life he's lived and the films he's seen give him something to say and the way to say it. Experience, however, is overrated. Of course we want writers who don't hide from life, who live deeply, observe closely. This is vital but never enough. For most writers, the knowledge they gain from reading and study equals or outweighs experience, especially if that experience goes unexamined. *Self-knowledge* is the key—life *plus* deep reflection on our reactions to life.

As for technique, what the novice mistakes for craft is simply his unconscious absorption of story elements from every novel, film, or play he's ever encountered. As he writes, he matches his work by trial and error against a model built up from accumulated reading and watching. The unschooled writer calls this "instinct," but it's merely habit and it's rigidly limiting. He either imitates his mental prototype or imagines himself in the avant-garde and rebels against it. But the haphazard groping toward or revolt against the sum of unconsciously ingrained repetitions is not, in any sense, technique, and leads to screenplays clogged with clichés of either the commercial or the art house variety.

This hit-or-miss struggle wasn't always the case. In decades past screenwriters learned their craft either through university study or on their own in a library, through experience in the theatre or in writing novels, through apprenticeship to the Hollywood studio system, or through a combination of these means.

Early in this century a number of American universities came to believe that, like musicians and painters, writers need the equivalent of music or art school to learn the principles of their craft. To that end scholars such as William Archer, Kenneth Rowe, and John Howard Lawson wrote excellent books on dramaturgy and the prose arts. Their method was intrinsic, drawing strength from the big-muscle movements of desire, forces of antagonism, turning points, spine, progression, crisis, climax—*story seen from the inside out.* Working writers, with or without formal educations, used these texts to develop their art, turning the half-century from the Roaring Twenties through the protesting sixties into a golden age of the American story on screen, page, and stage.

Over the last twenty-five years, however, the method of teaching creative writing in American universities has shifted from the intrinsic to the extrinsic. Trends in literary theory have drawn professors away from the deep sources of story toward language, codes, text—*story seen from the outside.* As a result, with some notable exceptions, the current generation of writers has been undereducated in the prime principles of story.

Screenwriters abroad have had even less opportunity to study their craft. European academics generally deny that writing can, in any sense, be taught, and as a result, courses in Creative Writing have never been included in the curriculum of Continental universities. Europe does, of course, foster many of the world's most brilliant art and music academies. Why it's felt that one art is teachable, another not, is impossible to say. What's worse, disdain for screenwriting has, until recently, excluded it from study in all European film schools save Moscow and Warsaw.

Much can be said against the old Hollywood studio system, but to its credit it was a system of apprenticeship overseen by seasoned story editors. That day is gone. Every now and then a studio rediscovers apprenticeship, but in its zeal to bring back the golden days it forgets that an apprentice needs a master. Today's executives may recognize ability, but few have the skill or patience to turn a talent into an artist.

The final cause for the decline of story runs very deep. Values, the positive/negative charges of life, are at the soul of our art. The writer shapes story around a perception of what's worth living for, what's worth dying for, what's foolish to pursue, the meaning of justice, truth—the essential values. In decades past, writer and society more or less agreed on these questions, but more and more ours has become an age of moral and ethical cynicism, relativism, and subjectivism—a great confusion of values. As the family disintegrates and sexual antagonisms rise, who, for example, feels he understands the nature of love? And how, if you do have a conviction, do you express it to an ever-more skeptical audience?

This erosion of values has brought with it a corresponding erosion of story. Unlike writers in the past, we can assume nothing. First we must dig deeply into life to uncover new insights, new refinements of value and meaning, then create a story vehicle that expresses our interpretation to an increasingly agnostic world. No small task.

THE STORY IMPERATIVE

When I moved to Los Angeles, I did what many do to keep eating and writing—I read. I worked for UA and NBC, analyzing screen and teleplay submissions. After the first couple hundred analyses, I felt I could write up in advance an all-purpose Hollywood story analyst's coverage and just fill in title and writer. The report I wrote over and over again went like this:

> *Nice description, actable dialogue. Some amusing moments; some sensitive moments. All in all, a script of well-chosen words. The story, however, sucks. The first thirty pages crawl on a fat belly of exposition; the rest never get to their feet. The main plot, what there is of it, is riddled with convenient coincidence and weak motivation. No discernible protagonist. Unrelated tensions that could shape into subplots never do. Characters are never revealed to be more than they seem. Not a moment's insight into the inner lives of these people or their society. It's a lifeless collection of predictable, ill-told, and clichéd episodes that wander off into a pointless haze. PASS ON IT.*

But I never wrote this report:

> *Great story! Grabbed me on page one and held me in its embrace. The first act builds to a sudden climax that spins off into a superb weave of plot and subplot. Sublime revelations of deep character. Amazing insight into this society. Made me laugh, made me cry. Drove to an Act Two climax so moving that I thought the story was over. And yet, out of the ashes of the second act, this writer created a third act of such power, such beauty, such magnificence I'm writing this report from the floor. However, this script is a 270-page grammatical nightmare with every fifth word misspelled. Dialogue's so tangled Olivier couldn't get his tongue around it. Descriptions are stuffed with camera directions, subtextural explanations, and philosophical commentary. It's not even typed in the proper format. Obviously not a professional writer. PASS ON IT.*

If I'd written this report, I'd have lost my job.

The sign on the door doesn't read "Dialogue Department" or "Description Department." It reads "Story Department." A good story makes a good film possible, while failure to make the story work virtually guarantees disaster. A reader who can't grasp this fundamental deserves to be fired. It's surprisingly rare, in fact, to find a beautifully crafted story with bad dialogue or dull description. More often than not, the better the storytelling, the more vivid the images, the sharper the dialogue. But lack of progression, false motivation, redundant characters, empty subtext, holes, and other such story problems are the root causes of a bland, boring text.

Literary talent is not enough. If you cannot tell a story, all those beautiful images and subtleties of dialogue that you spent months and months perfecting waste the paper they're written on. What we create for the world, what it demands of us, is story. Now and forever. Countless writers lavish dressy dialogue and manicured descriptions on anorexic yarns and wonder why their scripts never see production, while others with modest literary talent but great storytelling power have the deep pleasure of watching their dreams living in the light of the screen.

Of the total creative effort represented in a finished work, 75 percent or more of a writer's labor goes into designing story. Who are these characters? What do they want? Why do they want it? How do they go about getting it? What stops them? What are the consequences? Finding the answers to these grand questions and shaping them into story is our overwhelming creative task.

Designing story tests the maturity and insight of the writer, his knowledge of society, nature, and the human heart. Story demands both vivid imagination and powerful analytic thought. Self-expression is never an issue, for, wittingly or unwittingly, all stories, honest and dishonest, wise and foolish, faithfully mirror their maker, exposing his humanity . . . or lack of it. Compared to this terror, writing dialogue is a sweet diversion.

So the writer embraces the principle, *Tell Story* . . . then freezes. For what is story? The idea of story is like the idea of music. We've heard tunes all our lives. We can dance and sing along. We think we understand music until we try to compose it and what comes out of the piano scares the cat.

If both TENDER MERCIES and RAIDERS OF THE LOST ARK are wonderful stories beautifully told for the screen—and they are— what on earth do they have in common? If HANNAH AND HER SISTERS and MONTY PYTHON AND THE HOLY GRAIL are both brilliant comic stories delightfully told, and they are, where do they touch? Compare THE CRYING GAME to PARENTHOOD, TERMINATOR to REVERSAL OF FORTUNE, UNFORGIVEN to EAT DRINK MAN WOMAN. Or A FISH CALLED WANDA to MAN BITES DOG, WHO FRAMED ROGER RABBIT to RESERVOIR DOGS. Moving back through the decades, compare VERTIGO to $8^1/_2$ to PERSONA to RASHOMON to CASABLANCA to GREED to MODERN TIMES to THE BATTLESHIP POTEMKIN—all superb screen stories, all vastly different, yet all produce the same result: an audience leaving the theatre exclaiming, "What a great story!"

Drowning in a sea of genres and styles, the writer may come to believe that if all these films tell story, then anything can be a story. But if we look deeply, if we strip away the surface, we find that at heart all are the same thing. Each is an embodiment of the universal form of story. Each articulates this form to the screen in a unique way, but in each the essential form is identical, and it is to this deep form that the audience is responding when it reacts with, "What a good story!"

Each of the arts is defined by its essential form. From symphony to hip-hop, the underlying form of music makes a piece music and not noise. Whether representational or abstract, the cardinal principles of visual art make a canvas a painting, not a doodle. Equally, from Homer to Ingmar Bergman, the universal form of story shapes a work into story, not portraiture or collage. Across all cultures and through all ages, this innate form has been endlessly variable but changeless.

Yet form does not mean "formula." There is no screenplay-writing recipe that guarantees your cake will rise. Story is far too rich in mystery, complexity, and flexibility to be reduced to a formula. Only a fool would try. Rather, a writer must grasp story *form*. This is inescapable.

GOOD STORY *WELL TOLD*

"Good story" means something worth telling that the world wants to hear. Finding this is your lonely task. It begins with talent. You must be born with the creative power to put things together in a way no one has ever dreamed. Then you must bring to the work a vision that's driven by fresh insights into human nature and society, coupled with in-depth knowledge of your characters and your world. All that . . . and, as Hallie and Whit Burnett reveal in their excellent little book, a lot of love.

The love of story—the belief that your vision can be expressed only through story, that characters can be more "real" than people, that the fictional world is more profound than the concrete. The love of the dramatic—a fascination with the sudden surprises and revelations that bring sea-changes in life. The love of truth—the belief that lies cripple the artist, that every truth in life must be questioned, down to one's own secret motives. The love of humanity—a willingness to empathize with suffering souls, to crawl inside their skins and see the world through their eyes. The love of sensation—the desire to indulge not only the physical but the inner senses. The love of dreaming—the pleasure in taking leisurely rides on your imagination just to see where it leads. The love of humor—a joy in the saving grace that restores the balance of life. The love of language—the delight in sound and sense, syntax and semantics. The love of duality—a feel for life's hidden contradictions, a healthy suspicion that things are not what they seem. The love of perfection—the passion to write and rewrite in pursuit of the perfect moment. The love of uniqueness—the thrill of audacity and a stone-faced calm when it is met by ridicule. The love of beauty—an innate sense that treasures good writing, hates bad writing, and knows the difference. The love of self—a strength that doesn't need to be constantly reassured, that never doubts that you are indeed a writer. You must love to write and bear the loneliness.

But the love of a good story, of terrific characters and a world driven by your passion, courage, and creative gifts is still not enough. Your goal must be a good story *well told*.

Just as a composer must excel in the principles of musical composition, so you must master the corresponding principles of story composition. This craft is neither mechanics nor gimmicks. It is the concert of techniques by which we create a conspiracy of interest between ourselves and the audience. Craft is the sum total of all means used to draw the audience into deep involvement, to hold that involvement, and ultimately to reward it with a moving and meaningful experience.

Without craft, the best a writer can do is snatch the first idea off the top of his head, then sit helpless in front of his own work, unable to answer the dreaded questions: *Is it good? Or is it sewage? If sewage, what do I do?* The conscious mind, fixated on these terrible questions, blocks the subconscious. But when the conscious mind is put to work on the objective task of executing the craft, the spontaneous surfaces. Mastery of craft frees the subconscious.

What is the rhythm of a writer's day? First, you enter your imagined world. As characters speak and act, you write. What's the next thing you do? You step out of your fantasy and read what you've written. And what do you do as you read? You analyze. "Is it good? Does it work? Why not? Should I cut? Add? Reorder?" You write, you read; create, critique; impulse, logic; right brain, left brain; re-imagine, rewrite. And the quality of your rewriting, the possibility of perfection, depends on a command of the craft that guides you to correct imperfection. An artist is never at the mercy of the whims of impulse; he willfully exercises his craft to create harmonies of instinct and idea.

STORY AND LIFE

Over the years I've observed two typical and persistent kinds of failed screenplay. The first is the "personal story" bad script:

> *In an office setting we meet a protagonist with a problem: She deserves a promotion but she's being passed over. Angry, she heads for her parents' home to discover that Dad's gone senile and Mom can't cope. Home to her apartment and a fight with her slobbish, conniving roommate. Now out on a date and smack into a failure to communicate: Her insensitive lover takes her to an expensive French restaurant, completely forgetting that she's on a diet. Back to the office where, amazingly, she gets her promotion ... but new pres-*

sures arise. Back at her parents' place, where just as she solves Dad's problem, Mom goes over the edge. Coming home she discovers that her roommate has stolen her TV and vanished without paying the rent. She breaks up with her lover, raids the refrigerator, and gains five pounds. But chin up, she turns her promotion into a triumph. A nostalgic heart-to-heart over a dinner with her folks cures Mom's woes. Her new roommate not only turns out to be an anal-retentive gem who pays the rent weeks ahead with cashier's checks, but introduces her to Someone New. We're now on page ninety-five. She sticks to her diet and looks great for the last twenty-five pages, which are the literary equivalent of running in slow-mo through daisies as the romance with Someone New blossoms. At last she confronts her Crisis Decision: whether or not to commit? The screenplay ends on a tearful Climax as she decides she needs her space.

Second is the "guaranteed commercial success" bad script:

Through a luggage mix-up at the airport, a software salesman comes into possession of the-thing-that-will-end-civilization-as-we-know-it-today. The-thing-that-will-end-civilization-as-we-know-it-today is quite small. In fact, it's concealed inside a ballpoint pen unwittingly in the pocket of this hapless protagonist, who becomes the target of a cast of three dozen characters, all of whom have double or triple identities, all of whom have worked on both sides of the Iron Curtain, all of whom have known one another since the Cold War, all of whom are trying to kill the guy. This script is stuffed with car chases, shoot-outs, hair-raising escapes, and explosions. When not blowing things up or shooting folks down, it halts for dialogue-thick scenes as the hero tries to sort through these duplicitous people and find out just whom he can trust. It ends with a cacophony of violence and multimillion-dollar effects, during which the hero manages to destroy the-thing-that-will-end-civilization-as-we-know-it-today and thus save humanity.

The "personal story" is understructured, slice-of-life portraiture that mistakes verisimilitude for truth. This writer believes that the more precise his observation of day-to-day facts, the more accurate his reportage of what actually happens, the more truth he tells. But fact, no matter how minutely observed, is truth with a small "t." Big "T" Truth is located behind, beyond, inside, below the surface of things, holding reality together or tearing it apart, and cannot be directly observed. Because this writer sees only what is visible and factual, he is blind to the truth of life.

The "guaranteed commercial success," on the other hand, is an overstructured, overcomplicated, overpopulated assault on the physical senses that bears no relationship to life whatsoever. This writer is mistaking kinesis for entertainment. He hopes that, regardless of story, if he calls for enough high-speed action and dazzling visuals, the audience will be excited. And given the Computer Generated Image phenomenon that drives so many summer releases, he would not be altogether wrong.

Spectacles of this kind replace imagination with simulated actuality. They use story as an excuse for heretofore unseen effects that carry us into a tornado, the jaws of a dinosaur, or futuristic holocausts. And make no mistake, these razzle-dazzle spectacles can deliver a circus of excitement. But like amusement park rides, their pleasures are short-lived. For the history of filmmaking has shown again and again that as fast as new kinetic thrills rise to popularity, they sink under a "been there, done that" apathy.

Every decade or so technical innovation spawns a swarm of ill-told movies, for the sole purpose of exploiting spectacle. The invention of film itself, a startling simulation of actuality, caused great public excitement, followed by years of vapid stories. In time, however, the silent film evolved into a magnificent art form, only to be destroyed by the advent of sound, a yet more realistic simulation of actuality. Films of the early 1930s took a step backward as audiences willingly suffered bland stories for the pleasure of hearing actors talk. The talkie then grew in power and beauty, only to be knocked off stride by the inventions of color, 3-D, wide-screen, and now Computer Generated Images, or CGI.

CGI is neither a curse nor a panacea. It simply adds fresh hues to the story pallet. Thanks to CGI, anything we can imagine can be done, and done with subtle satisfaction. When CGIs are motivated by a strong story, such as FORREST GUMP or MEN IN BLACK, the effect vanishes behind the story it's telling, enriching the moment without calling attention to itself. The "commercial" writer, however, is often dazzled by the glare of spectacle and cannot see that lasting entertainment is found only in the charged human truths beneath the image.

The writers of portraiture and spectacle, indeed all writers, must come to understand the relationship of story to life: *Story is metaphor for life.*

A storyteller is a life poet, an artist who transforms day-to-day living, inner life and outer life, dream and actuality into a poem whose rhyme scheme is events rather than words—a two-hour metaphor that says: Life is like *this*! Therefore, a story must abstract from life to discover its essences, but not become an abstraction that loses all sense of life-as-lived. A story must be *like* life, but not so verbatim that it has no depth or meaning beyond what's obvious to everyone on the street.

Writers of portraiture must realize that facts are neutral. The weakest possible excuse to include anything in a story is: "But it actually happened." Everything happens; everything imaginable happens. Indeed, the unimaginable happens. But story is not life in actuality. Mere occurrence brings us nowhere near the truth. What happens is fact, not truth. Truth is what we *think about* what happens.

Consider a set of facts known as "The Life of Joan of Arc." For centuries celebrated writers have brought this woman to the stage, page, and screen, and each Joan is unique—Anouilh's spiritual Joan, Shaw's witty Joan, Brecht's political Joan, Dreyer's suffering Joan, Hollywood's romantic warrior. In Shakespeare's hands she became the lunatic Joan, a distinctly British point of view. Each Joan is divinely inspired, raises an army, defeats the English, burns at the stake. Joan's facts are always the same, but whole genres shift while the "truth" of her life waits for the writer to find its meaning.

Likewise, writers of spectacle must realize that abstractions are neutral. By abstractions I mean strategies of graphic design, visual effects, color saturation, sound perspective, editing rhythm, and the like. These have no meaning in and of themselves. The identical editing pattern applied to six different scenes results in six distinctively different interpretations. The aesthetics of film are the means to express the living content of story, but must *never* become an end in themselves.

POWERS AND TALENTS

Although the authors of portraiture or spectacle are weak in story, they may be blessed with one of two essential powers. Writers who lean toward reportage often have the power of the senses, the power to transport corporal sensations into the reader. They see and hear with such acuity and sensitivity that the reader's heart jumps when struck by the lucid beauty of their images. Writers of action extravaganzas, on the other hand, often have the imaginative power to lift audiences beyond what is to what could be. They can take presumed impossibilities and turn them into shocking certainties. They also make hearts jump. Both sensory perception and a lively imagination are enviable gifts, but, like a good marriage, one complements the other. Alone they are diminished.

At one end of reality is pure fact; at the other end, pure imagination. Spanning these two poles is the infinitely varied spectrum of fiction. Strong storytelling strikes a balance along this spectrum. If your writing drifts to one extreme or the other, you must learn to draw all aspects of your humanity into harmony. You must place yourself along the creative spectrum: sensitive to sight, sound, and feeling, yet balancing that with the power to imagine. Dig in a two-handed way, using your insight and instinct to move us, to express your vision of how and why human beings do the things they do.

Last, not only are sensory and imaginative powers prerequisite to creativity, writing also demands two singular and essential talents. These talents, however, have no necessary connection. A mountain of one does not mean a grain of the other.

The first is literary talent—the creative conversion of ordinary language into a higher, more expressive form, vividly describing the world and capturing its human voices. Literary talent is, however, common. In every literate community in the world, hundreds, if not thousands of people can, to one degree or another, begin with the ordinary language of their culture and end with something extraordinary. They write beautifully, a few magnificently, in the literary sense.

The second is story talent—the creative conversion of life itself to a more powerful, clearer, more meaningful experience. It seeks out the inscape of our days and reshapes it into a telling that enriches life. Pure story talent is rare. What writer, on instinct alone, creates brilliantly told stories year after year and never gives a moment's thought to how he does what he does or could do it better? Instinctive genius may produce a work of quality once, but perfection and prolificness do not flow from the spontaneous and untutored.

Literary and story talent are not only distinctively different but are unrelated, for stories do not need to be written to be told. Stories can be expressed any way human beings can communicate. Theatre, prose, film, opera, mime, poetry, dance are all magnificent forms of the story ritual, each with its own delights. At different times in history, however, one of these steps to the fore. In the sixteenth century it was the theatre; in the nineteenth century, the novel; in the twentieth century, the cinema, the grand concert of all the arts. The most powerful, eloquent moments on screen require no verbal description to create them, no dialogue to act them. They are image, pure and silent. The material of literary talent is words; the material of story talent is *life itself*.

CRAFT MAXIMIZES TALENT

Rare as story talent is, we often meet people who seem to have it by nature, those street-corner raconteurs for whom storytelling is as easy as a smile. When, for example, coworkers gather around the coffee machine, the storytelling begins. It's the currency of human contact. And whenever a half-dozen souls gather for this mid-morning ritual, there will always be at least one who has the gift.

Let's say that this morning our storyteller tells her friends the story of "How I Put My Kids on the School Bus." Like Coleridge's Ancient Mariner, she hooks everyone's attention. She draws them into her spell, holding them slack-jawed over their coffee cups. She spins her tale, building them up, easing them down, making them laugh, maybe cry, holding all in high suspense until she pays it off with a dynamite last scene: "And that's how I got the little nosepickers on the bus this morning." Her coworkers lean back satisfied, muttering, "God, yes, Helen, my kids are just like that."

Now let's say the storytelling passes to the guy next to her who tells the others the heartrending tale of how his mother died over the weekend . . . and bores the hell out of everyone. His story is all on the surface, repetitious rambling from trivial detail to cliché: "She looked so good in her coffin." Halfway through his rendition, the rest head back to the coffee pot for another cup, turning a deaf ear to his tale of grief.

Given the choice between trivial material brilliantly told versus profound material badly told, an audience will always choose the trivial told brilliantly. Master storytellers know how to squeeze life out of the least of things, while poor storytellers reduce the profound to the banal. You may have the insight of a Buddha, but if you cannot tell story, your ideas turn dry as chalk.

Story talent is primary, literary talent secondary but essential. This principle is absolute in film and television, and truer for stage and page than most playwrights and novelists wish to admit. Rare as story talent is, you must have some or you wouldn't be itching to write. Your task is to wring from it all possible creativity. Only by using everything and anything you know about the craft of storytelling can you make your talent forge story. For talent without craft is like fuel without an engine. It burns wildly but accomplishes nothing.

PART 2

THE ELEMENTS OF STORY

A beautifully told story is a symphonic unity in which structure, setting, character, genre, and idea meld seamlessly. To find their harmony, the writer must study the elements of story as if they were instruments of an orchestra—first separately, then in concert.

2

THE STRUCTURE SPECTRUM

THE TERMINOLOGY OF STORY DESIGN

When a character steps into your imagination, he brings an abundance of story possibilities. If you wish, you could start the telling before the character is born, then follow him day after day, decade after decade until dead and gone. A character's life encompasses hundreds of thousands of living hours, hours both complex and multileveled.

From an instant to eternity, from the intracranial to the intergalactic, the life story of each and every character offers encyclopedic possibilities. The mark of a master is to select only a few moments but give us a lifetime.

Starting at the deepest level, you might set the story within the protagonist's inner life and tell the whole tale inside his thoughts and feelings, awake or dreaming. Or you could shift up to the level of personal conflict between protagonist and family, friends, lovers. Or expand into social institutions, setting the character at odds with school, career, church, the justice system. Or wider still, you could pit the character against the environment—dangerous city streets, lethal diseases, the car that won't start, time running out. Or any combination of all these levels.

But this complex expanse of *life story* must become *the story told*. To design a feature film, you must reduce the seething mass and rush of *life story* to just two little hours, more or less, that somehow express everything you left out. And when a story is well told, isn't that the effect? When friends come back from a film and you ask them what it was about, have you noticed they often put *the story told* inside *life story*?

"Great! About a guy raised on a sharecropper's farm. As a kid he toiled with his family under the hot sun. He went to school but didn't do too well because he had to get up at dawn, all that weeding and hoeing. But somebody gave him a guitar and he learned to play, write his own songs . . . finally, fed up with this backbreaking life, he ran away, living hand to mouth playing in honky-tonk bars. Then he met a beautiful gal with a great voice. They fell in love, teamed up, and, bang, their careers skyrocketed. But the trouble was the spotlight was always on her. He wrote their songs, arranged, backed her up, but people only came to see her. Living in her shadow, he turned to drink. Finally she throws him out, and there he is back on the road again, until he hits rock bottom. He wakes up in a cheap motel in a dusty Midwest town, middle of nowhere, penniless, friendless, a hopeless drunk, not a dime for the phone and no one to call if he had one."

In other words, TENDER MERCIES told from birth. But nothing of the above is in the film. TENDER MERCIES begins the morning Robert Duvall's Mac Sledge wakes up at rock bottom. The next two hours cover the next year in Sledge's life. Yet, in and between scenes, we come to know all of his past, everything of significance that happens to Sledge in that year, until the last image gives us a vision of his future. A man's life, virtually from birth to death, is captured between the FADE IN and FADE OUT of Horton Foote's Oscar-winning screenplay.

Structure

From the vast flux of *life story* the writer must make choices. Fictional worlds are not daydreams but sweatshops where we labor in search of material to tailor a film. Yet when asked "What do you choose?" no two writers agree. Some look for character, others for action or strife, perhaps mood, images, dialogue. But no one element, in and of itself, will build a story. A film isn't just moments of conflict or activity, personality or emotionality, witty talk or symbols. What the writer seeks are *events*, for an event contains all the above and more.

> **STRUCTURE is a selection of events from the characters' life stories that is composed into a strategic sequence to arouse specific emotions and to express a specific view of life.**

An event is caused by or affects people, thus delineating characters; it takes place in a setting, generating image, action, and dialogue; it draws energy from conflict producing emotion in characters and audience alike. But event choices cannot be displayed randomly or indifferently; they must be composed, and "to compose" in story means much the same thing it does in music. What to include? To exclude? To put before and after what?

To answer these questions you must know your purpose. Events composed to do what? One purpose may be to express your feelings, but this becomes self-indulgence if it doesn't result in arousing emotions in the audience. A second purpose may be to express ideas, but this risks solipsism if the audience cannot follow. So the design of events needs a dual strategy.

Event

"Event" means *change*. If the streets outside your window are dry, but after a nap you see they're wet, you assume an event has taken place, called rain. The world's changed from dry to wet. You cannot, however, build a film out of nothing but changes in weather—although there are those who have tried. *Story Events* are meaningful, not trivial. To make change meaningful it must, to begin with, happen to a character. If you see someone drenched in a downpour, this has somewhat more meaning than a damp street.

> **A STORY EVENT creates meaningful change in the life situation of a character that is expressed and experienced in terms of a VALUE.**

To make change meaningful you must express it, and the audience must react to it, in terms of a value. By values I don't mean virtues or the narrow, moralizing "family values" use of the word. Rather, *Story Values* refers to the broadest sense of the idea. Values are the soul of storytelling. Ultimately ours is the art of expressing to the world a perception of values.

STORY VALUES are the universal qualities of human experience that may shift from positive to negative, or negative to positive, from one moment to the next.

For example: alive/dead (positive/negative) is a story value, as are love/hate, freedom/slavery, truth/lie, courage/cowardice, loyalty/betrayal, wisdom/stupidity, strength/weakness, excitement/boredom and so on. All such binary qualities of experience that can reverse their charge at any moment are Story Values. They may be moral, good/evil; ethical, right/wrong; or simply charged with value. Hope/despair is neither moral nor ethical, but we certainly know when we are at one end of the experience or the other.

Imagine that outside your window is 1980s East Africa, a realm of drought. Now we have a value at stake: survival, life/death. We begin at the negative: This terrible famine is taking lives by the thousands. If then it should rain, a monsoon that brings the earth back to green, animals to pasture, and people to survival, this rain would be deeply meaningful because it switches the value from negative to positive, from death to life.

However, as powerful as this event would be, it still does not qualify as a Story Event because it happened by coincidence. Rain finally fell in East Africa. Although there's a place for coincidence in storytelling, a story cannot be built out of nothing but accidental events, no matter how charged with value.

A Story Event creates meaningful change in the life situation of a character that is expressed and experienced in terms of a value and ACHIEVED THROUGH CONFLICT.

Again, a world of drought. Into it comes a man who imagines himself a "rainmaker." This character has deep inner conflict between his passionate belief that he can bring rain, although he has never been able to do it, and his terrible fear that he's a fool or mad. He meets a woman, falls in love, then suffers as she tries to believe in him, but turns away, convinced he's a charlatan or worse. He has a strong conflict with society—some follow him as if he's a messiah; others want to stone him out of town. Lastly, he faces implacable conflict with the physical world—the hot winds, empty skies, parched earth. If this man can struggle through all his inner and personal conflicts, against social and environmental forces and finally coax rain out of a cloudless sky, that storm would be majestic and sublimely meaningful—for it is *change motivated through conflict*. What I have described is THE RAINMAKER, adapted to the screen by Richard Nash from his own play.

Scene

For a typical film, the writer will choose forty to sixty Story Events or, as they're commonly known, scenes. A novelist may want more than sixty, a playwright rarely as many as forty.

> **A SCENE is an action through conflict in more or less continuous time and space that turns the value-charged condition of a character's life on at least one value with a degree of perceptible significance. Ideally, every scene is a STORY EVENT.**

Look closely at each scene you've written and ask: What value is at stake in my character's life at this moment? Love? Truth? What? How is that value charged at the top of the scene? Positive? Negative? Some of both? Make a note. Next turn to the close of the scene and ask, Where is this value now? Positive? Negative? Both? Make a note and compare. If the answer you write down at the end of the scene is the same note you made at the opening, you now have another important question to ask: Why is this scene in my script?

If the value-charged condition of the character's life stays unchanged from one end of a scene to the other, nothing meaningful happens. The scene has activity—talking about this, doing that—but nothing changes in value. It is a nonevent.

Why then is the scene in the story? The answer is almost certain to be "exposition." It's there to convey information about characters, world, or history to the eavesdropping audience. If exposition is a scene's sole justification, a disciplined writer will trash it and weave its information into the film elsewhere.

No scene that doesn't turn. This is our ideal. We work to round every scene from beginning to end by turning a value at stake in a character's life from the positive to the negative or the negative to the positive. Adherence to this principle may be difficult, but it's by no means impossible.

DIE HARD, THE FUGITIVE, and STRAW DOGS clearly meet this test, but the ideal is also kept in subtler, though no less rigorous ways, in REMAINS OF THE DAY and THE ACCIDENTAL TOURIST. The difference is that *Action* genres turn on public values such as freedom/slavery or justice/injustice; the *Education* genre turns on interior values such as self-awareness/self-deception or life as meaningful/meaningless. Regardless of genre, the principle is universal: If a scene is not a true event, cut it.

For example:

> *Chris and Andy are in love and live together. They wake up one morning and start to squabble. Their spat builds in the kitchen as they hurry to make breakfast. In the garage, the fight becomes nastier as they climb into their car to drive to work together. Finally words explode into violence on the highway. Andy wrenches the car to the shoulder and jumps out, ending their relationship. This series of actions and locations creates a scene: It takes the couple from the positive (in love and together) to the negative (in hate and apart).*

The four shifts of place—bedroom to kitchen to garage to highway—are camera setups but not true scenes. Although they intensify behavior and make the critical moment credible, they do not change the values at stake. As the argument moves through the morning, the couple is still together and presumably in love. But when the action reaches its Turning Point—a slamming car door and Andy's declaration, "It's over!"—life turns upside down for the lovers, activity changes to action, and the sketch becomes a complete scene, a **Story Event.**

Generally the test of whether a series of activities constitutes a true scene is this: Could it have been written "in one," in a unity of time and place? In this case the answer is yes. Their argument could begin in a bedroom, build in the bedroom, and end the relationship in the bedroom. Countless relationships have ended in bedrooms. Or the kitchen. Or the garage. Or not on the highway but in the office elevator. A playwright might write the scene "in one" because the staging limitations of the theatre often force us to keep the unities of time and place; the novelist or screenwriter, on the other hand, might travel the scene, parsing it out in time and space to establish future locations, Chris's taste in furniture, Andy's driving habits—for any number of reasons. This scene could even cross-cut with another scene, perhaps involving another couple. The variations are endless, but in all cases this is a single Story Event, the "lovers break up" scene.

Beat

Inside the scene is the smallest element of structure, the *Beat*. (Not to be confused with [beat], an indication within a column of dialogue meaning "short pause".)

> **A BEAT is an exchange of behavior in action/reaction. Beat by Beat these changing behaviors shape the turning of a scene.**

Taking a closer look at the "lovers break up" scene: As the alarm goes off, Chris teases Andy and he reacts in kind. As they dress, teasing turns to sarcasm and they throw insults back and forth. Now in the kitchen Chris threatens Andy with: "If I left you, baby, you'd be so miserable . . ." but he calls her bluff with "That's a misery I'd love." In the garage Chris, afraid she's losing him, begs Andy to stay, but he laughs and ridicules her plea. Finally, in the speeding car, Chris doubles her fist and punches Andy. A fight, a squeal of brakes. Andy jumps out with a bloody nose, slams the door and shouts, "It's over," leaving her in shock.

This scene is built around six beats, six distinctively different behaviors, six clear changes of action/reaction: teasing each other, followed by a give-and-take of insults, then threatening and daring each other, next pleading and ridiculing, and finally exchanges of violence that lead to the last Beat and Turning Point: Andy's decision and action that ends the relationship, and Chris's dumbfounded surprise.

Sequence

Beats build scenes. Scenes then build the next largest movement of story design, the *Sequence*. Every true scene turns the value-charged condition of the character's life, but from event to event the degree of change can differ greatly. Scenes cause relatively minor yet significant change. The capping scene of a sequence, however, delivers a more powerful, determinant change.

A SEQUENCE is a series of scenes—generally two to five—that culminates with greater impact than any previous scene.

For example, this three-scene sequence:

Setup: A young business woman who's had a notable career in the Midwest has been approached by headhunters and interviewed for a position with a New York corporation. If she wins this post, it'll be a huge step up in her career. She wants the job very much but hasn't won it yet (negative). She is one of six finalists. The corporate heads realize that this position has a vital public dimension to it, so they want to see these applicants on their feet in an informal setting before making the final decision. They invite all six to a party on Manhattan's East Side.

Scene One: A West Side Hotel where our protagonist prepares for the evening. The value at stake is self-confidence/self-doubt. She'll need all her confidence to pull off this evening successfully, but she's filled with doubts (negative). Fear knots her middle as she paces the room, telling herself she was a fool to come East, these New Yorkers will eat her alive. She flings clothes out of her suitcase, trying on this, trying on that, but each outfit looks worse than the one before. Her hair is an uncombable tangle of frizz. As she grapples with her clothes and hair, she decides to pack it in and save herself the humiliation.

Suddenly, the phone rings. It's her mother, calling to lace a good-luck toast with guilt trips about loneliness and her fear of abandonment. Barbara hangs up, realizing that the piranhas of Manhattan are no match for the great white shark at home. *She needs this job!* She then amazes herself with a combination of clothes and accessories she's never tried before. Her hair falls magically into place. She plants herself in front of the mirror, looking great, eyes bright, glowing with confidence (positive).

Scene Two: Under the hotel marquee. Thunder, lightning, pelting rain. Because Barbara's from Terre Haute, she didn't know to tip the doorman five bucks when she registered, so he won't go out into the storm to find a cab for a stiff. Besides, when it rains in New York there are no cabs. So she studies her visitors' map, pondering what to do. She realizes if she tries to run from the West Eighties over to Central Park West, then all the way down CPW to Fifty-ninth Street, across Central Park South to Park Avenue, and up into the East Eighties, she'll never get to the party on time. So she decides to do what they warn never, ever to do—to run through Central Park at night. This scene takes on a new value: life/death.

She covers her hair with a newspaper and darts into the night, daring death (negative). A lightning flash and, bang, she's surrounded by that gang that is always out there, rain or shine, waiting for the fools who run through the park at night. But she didn't take karate classes for nothing. She kick-fights her way through the gang, breaking jaws, scattering teeth on the concrete, until she stumbles out of the park, alive (positive).

Scene Three: Mirrored lobby—Park Avenue apartment building. The value at stake now switches to social success/social failure. She's survived. But then she looks in the mirror and sees a drowned rat: newspaper shredded in her hair; blood all over her clothes—the gang's blood—but blood nonetheless. Her self-confidence plummets past doubt and fear until she bows in personal defeat (negative), crushed by her social disaster (negative).

Taxis pull up with the other applicants. All found cabs; all get out looking New York chic. They take pity on the poor loser from the Midwest and usher her into an elevator.

In the penthouse they towel off her hair and find mismatched clothes for her to wear, and because she looks like this, the spotlight's on her all night. Because she knows she has lost anyway, she relaxes into her natural self and from deep within comes a chutzpah she never knew she had; she not only tells them about her battle in the park but makes jokes about it. Mouths go slack with awe or wide with laughter. At end of the evening, all the executives know exactly who they want for the job: Anyone who can go through that terror in the park and display this kind of cool is clearly the person for them. The evening ends on her personal and social triumphs as she is given the job (doubly positive).

Each scene turns on its own value or values. Scene One: self-doubt to self-confidence. Scene Two: death to life; self-confidence to defeat. Scene Three: social disaster to social triumph. But the three scenes become a sequence of another, greater value that overrides and subordinates the others, and that is THE JOB. At the beginning of the sequence she has NO JOB. The third scene becomes a Sequence Climax because here social success wins her

THE JOB. From her point of view *THE JOB* is a value of such magnitude she risked her life for it.

It's useful to title each sequence to make clear to yourself why it's in the film. The story purpose of this "getting the job" sequence is to take her from *NO JOB* to *JOB*. It could have been accomplished in a single scene with a personnel officer. But to say more than "she's qualified," we might create a full sequence that not only gets her the job but dramatizes her inner character and relationship to her mother, along with insights into New York City and the corporation.

Act

Scenes turn in *minor* but significant ways; a series of scenes builds a sequence that turns in a *moderate*, more impactful way; a series of sequences builds the next largest structure, the *Act*, a movement that turns on a *major* reversal in the value-charged condition of the character's life. The difference between a basic scene, a scene that climaxes a sequence, and a scene that climaxes an act is the degree of change, or, more precisely, the degree of impact that change has, for better or worse, on the character—on the character's inner life, personal relationships, fortunes in the world, or some combination of all these.

An ACT is a series of sequences that peaks in a climactic scene which causes a major reversal of values, more powerful in its impact than any previous sequence or scene.

Story

A series of acts builds the largest structure of all: the *Story*. A story is simply one huge master event. When you look at the value-charged situation in the life of the character at the beginning of the story, then compare it to the value-charge at the end of the story, you should see the *arc of the film*, the great sweep of change that takes life from one condition at the opening to a changed condition at the end. This final condition, this end change, must be *absolute* and *irreversible*.

Change caused by a scene could be reversed: The lovers in the previous sketch could get back together; people fall in and out and back in love again every day. A sequence could be reversed: The Midwest businesswoman could win her job only to discover that she reports to a boss she hates and wishes she were back in Terre Haute. An act climax could be reversed: A character could die, as in the Act Two climax of E.T., and then come back to life. Why not? In a modern hospital, reviving the dead is commonplace. So, scene by sequence by act, the writer creates minor, moderate, and major change, but conceivably, each of those changes could be reversed. This is not, however, the case in the climax of the last act.

STORY CLIMAX: A story is a series of acts that build to a last act climax or story climax which brings about absolute and irreversible change.

If you make the smallest element do its job, the deep purpose of the telling will be served. Let every phrase of dialogue or line of description either turn behavior and action or set up the conditions for change. Make your beats build scenes, scenes build sequences, sequences build acts, acts build story to its climax.

The scenes that turn the life of the Terre Haute protagonist from self-doubt to self-confidence, from danger to survival, from social disaster to success combine into a sequence that takes her from *NO JOB* to JOB. To arc the telling to a Story Climax, perhaps this opening sequence sets up a series of sequences that takes her from *NO JOB* to *PRESIDENT OF THE CORPORATION* at the Act One climax. This Act One climax sets up an Act Two in which internecine corporate wars lead to her betrayal by friends and associates. At the Act Two climax she's fired by the board of directors and *out on the street.* This major reversal sends her to a rival corporation where, armed with business secrets gleaned while she was president, she quickly reaches the top again so she can enjoy *destroying her previous employers.* These acts arc her from the *hardworking, optimistic,* and *honest* young professional who opens the film to the *ruthless, cynical,* and *corrupt* veteran of corporate wars who ends the film—absolute, irreversible change.

THE STORY TRIANGLE

In some literary circles "plot" has become a dirty word, tarred with a connotation of hack commercialism. The loss is ours, for plot is an accurate term that names the internally consistent, inter-related pattern of events that move through time to shape and design a story. While no fine film was ever written without flashes of fortuitous inspiration, a screenplay is not an accident. Material that pops up willy-nilly cannot remain willy-nilly. The writer redrafts inspiration again and again, making it look as if an instinc-tive spontaneity created the film, yet knowing how much effort and unnaturalness went into making it look natural and effortless.

To PLOT means to navigate through the dangerous ter-rain of story and when confronted by a dozen branching possibilities to choose the correct path. Plot is the writer's choice of events and their design in time.

Again, what to include? Exclude? Put before and after what? Event choices must be made; the writer chooses either well or ill; the result is plot.

When TENDER MERCIES premiered, some reviewers described it as "plotless," then praised it for that. TENDER MERCIES not only has a plot, it is exquisitely plotted through some of the most difficult film terrain of all: a story in which the arc of the film takes place within the mind of the protagonist. Here the protagonist experiences a deep and irreversible revolution in his attitude toward life and/or toward himself.

For the novelist such stories are natural and facile. In either third-person or first-person, the novelist can directly invade thought and feeling to dramatize the tale entirely on the landscape of the protagonist's inner life. For the screenwriter such stories are by far the most fragile and difficult. We cannot drive a camera lens through an actor's forehead and photograph his thoughts, although there are those who would try. Somehow we must lead the audi-ence to interpret the inner life from outer behavior without loading the soundtrack with expositional narration or stuffing the mouths of characters with self-explanatory dialogue. As John Carpenter said, "Movies are about making mental things physical."

To begin the great sweep of change within his protagonist, Horton Foote opens TENDER MERCIES with Sledge drowning in the meaninglessness of his life. He is committing slow suicide with alcohol because he no longer believes in anything—neither family, nor work, nor this world, nor the hereafter. As Foote progresses the film, he avoids the cliché of finding meaning in one overwhelming experience of great romance, brilliant success, or religious inspiration. Instead he shows us a man weaving together a simple yet meaningful life from the many delicate threads of love, music, and spirit. At last Sledge undergoes a quiet transformation and finds a life worth living.

We can only imagine the sweat and pains Horton Foote invested in plotting this precarious film. A single misstep—one missing scene, one superfluous scene, a slight misordering of incident—and like a castle of cards, the riveting inner journey of Mac Sledge collapses into portraiture. Plot, therefore, doesn't mean ham-handed twists and turns, or high-pressure suspense and shocking surprise. Rather, events must be selected and their patterning displayed through time. In this sense of composition or design, all stories are plotted.

Archplot, Miniplot, Antiplot

Although the variations of event design are innumerable, they are not without limits. The far corners of the art create a triangle of formal possibilities that maps the universe of stories. Within this triangle is the totality of writers' cosmologies, all their multitudinous visions of reality and how life is lived within it. To understand your place in this universe, study the coordinates of this map, compare them to your work-in-progress, and let them guide you to that point you share with other writers of a similar vision.

At the top of the story triangle are the principles that constitute *Classical Design*. These principles are "classical" in the truest sense:

timeless and transcultural, fundamental to every earthly society, civilized and primitive, reaching back through millennia of oral storytelling into the shadows of time. When the epic *Gilgamesh* was carved in cuneiform on twelve clay tablets 4,000 years ago, converting story to the written word for the first time, the principles of Classical Design were already fully and beautifully in place.

CLASSICAL DESIGN means a story built around an active protagonist who struggles against primarily external forces of antagonism to pursue his or her desire, through continuous time, within a consistent and causally connected fictional reality, to a closed ending of absolute, irreversible change.

This collection of timeless principles I call the Archplot: Arch (pronounced "ark" as in archangel) in the dictionary sense of "eminent above others of the same kind."

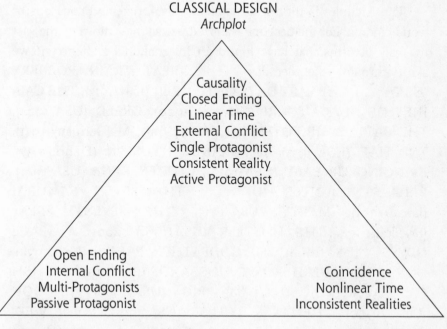

CLASSICAL DESIGN
Archplot

Causality
Closed Ending
Linear Time
External Conflict
Single Protagonist
Consistent Reality
Active Protagonist

Open Ending
Internal Conflict
Multi-Protagonists
Passive Protagonist

Coincidence
Nonlinear Time
Inconsistent Realities

MINIMALISM
Miniplot

ANTI-STRUCTURE
Antiplot

The Archplot, however, is not the limit of storytelling shapes. In the left corner, I place all examples of minimalism. As the word suggests, minimalism means that the writer begins with the elements of Classical Design but then reduces them—shrinking or compressing, trimming or truncating the prominent features of the Archplot. I call this set of minimalist variations *Miniplot*. Miniplot does not mean *no plot*, for its story must be as beautifully executed as an Archplot. Rather, minimalism strives for simplicity and economy while retaining enough of the classical that the film will still satisfy the audience, sending them out of the cinema thinking, "What a good story!"

In the right corner is *Antiplot*, the cinema counterpart to the antinovel or Nouveau Roman and Theatre of the Absurd. This set of antistructure variations doesn't reduce the Classical but reverses it, contradicting traditional forms to exploit, perhaps ridicule the very idea of formal principles. The Antiplot-maker is rarely interested in understatement or quiet austerity; rather, to make clear his "revolutionary" ambitions, his films tend toward extravagance and self-conscious overstatement.

The Archplot is the meat, potatoes, pasta, rice, and couscous of world cinema. For the past one hundred years it has informed the vast majority of films that have found an international audience. If we skim through the decades—THE GREAT TRAIN ROBBERY (USA/1904), THE LAST DAYS OF POMPEII (Italy/1913), THE CABINET OF DR. CALIGARI (Germany/1920), GREED (USA/1924), THE BATTLESHIP POTEMKIN (USSR/1925), M (Germany/1931), TOP HAT (USA/1935), LA GRANDE ILLUSION (France/1937), BRINGING UP BABY (USA/1938), CITIZEN KANE (USA/1941), BRIEF ENCOUNTER (UK/1945), THE SEVEN SAMURAI (Japan/1954), MARTY (USA/1955), THE SEVENTH SEAL (Sweden/1957), THE HUSTLER (USA/1961), 2001: A SPACE ODYSSEY (USA/1968), THE GODFATHER, PART II (USA/1974), DONA FLOR AND HER TWO HUSBANDS (Brazil/1978), A FISH CALLED WANDA (UK/1988), BIG (USA/1988), JU DOU (China/1990), THELMA & LOUISE (USA/1991), FOUR WEDDINGS AND A FUNERAL (UK/1994), SHINE (Australia/1996)—we glimpse the staggering variety of story embraced within the Archplot.

Miniplot, though less various, is equally international: NANOOK OF THE NORTH (USA/1922), LA PASSION DE JEANNE D'ARC (France/1928), ZERO DE CONDUITE (France/1933), PAISAN (Italy/1946), WILD STRAWBERRIES (Sweden/1957), THE MUSIC ROOM (India/1964), THE RED DESERT (Italy/1964), FIVE EASY PIECES (USA/1970), CLAIRE'S KNEE (France/1970), IN THE REALM OF THE SENSES (Japan/1976), TENDER MERCIES (USA/1983), PARIS, TEXAS (West Germany/France/1984), THE SACRIFICE (Sweden/France/1986), PELLE THE CONQUEROR (Denmark/1987), STOLEN CHILDREN (Italy/1992), A RIVER RUNS THROUGH IT (USA/1993), TO LIVE (China/1994), and SHALL WE DANCE (Japan/1997). Miniplot also embraces narrative documentaries such as WELFARE (USA/1975).

Examples of Antiplot are less common, predominantly European, and post-World War II: UN CHIEN ANDALOU (France/1928), BLOOD OF THE POET (France/1932), MESHES OF THE AFTER-NOON (USA/1943), THE RUNNING, JUMPING AND STANDING STILL FILM (UK/1959), LAST YEAR AT MARIENBAD (France/1960), 8^1/$_2$ (Italy/1963), PERSONA (Sweden/1966), WEEKEND (France/1967), DEATH BY HANGING (Japan/1968), CLOWNS (Italy/1970), MONTY PYTHON AND THE HOLY GRAIL (UK/1975), THAT OBSCURE OBJECT OF DESIRE (France/Spain/1977), BAD TIMING (UK/1980), STRANGER THAN PARADISE (USA/1984), AFTER HOURS (USA/1985), A ZED & TWO NOUGHTS (UK/Netherlands/1985), WAYNE'S WORLD (USA/1993), CHUNGKING EXPRESS (Hong Kong/1994), LOST HIGHWAY (USA/1997). Antiplot also includes the documentary-cum-collage such as Alain Resnais's NIGHT AND FOG (France/1955) and KOYAANISQATSI (USA/1983).

FORMAL DIFFERENCES WITHIN THE STORY TRIANGLE

Closed Versus Open Endings

The Archplot delivers a closed ending—all questions raised by the story are answered; all emotions evoked are satisfied. The audience leaves with a rounded, closed experience—nothing in doubt, nothing unsated.

Miniplot, on the other hand, often leaves the ending somewhat open. Most of the questions raised by the telling are answered, but an unanswered question or two may trail out of the film, leaving the audience to supply it subsequent to the viewing. Most of the emotion evoked by the film will be satisfied, but an emotional residue may be left for the audience to satisfy. Although Miniplot may end on a question mark of thought and feeling, "open" doesn't mean the film quits in the middle, leaving everything hanging. The question must be answerable, the emotion resolvable. All that has gone before leads to clear and limited alternatives that make a degree of closure possible.

A Story Climax of absolute, irreversible change that answers all questions raised by the telling and satisfies all audience emotion is a CLOSED ENDING.

A Story Climax that leaves a question or two unanswered and some emotion unfulfilled is an OPEN ENDING.

At the climax of PARIS, TEXAS father and son are reconciled; their future is set and our hope for their happiness satisfied. But the husband/wife, mother/son relationships are left unresolved. The questions "Will this family have a future together? If so, what kind of future will it be?" are open. The answers will be found in the privacy of postfilm thoughts: If you want this family to get together, but your heart tells you they aren't going to make it, it's a sad evening. If you can convince yourself that they will live happily ever after, you walk out pleased. The minimalist storyteller deliberately gives this last critical bit of work to the audience.

External Versus Internal Conflict

The Archplot puts emphasis on external conflict. Although characters often have strong inner conflicts, the emphasis falls on their struggles with personal relationships, with social institutions, or with forces in the physical world. In Miniplot, to the contrary, the protagonist may have strong external conflicts with family, society, and environment, but emphasis will fall on the battles within his own thoughts and feelings, conscious or unconscious.

Compare the journeys of the protagonists in THE ROAD WARRIOR and THE ACCIDENTAL TOURIST. In the former, Mel Gibson's Mad Max undergoes an inner transformation from self-sufficient loner to self-sacrificing hero, but the emphasis of the story falls on the survival of the clan. In the latter, the life of William Hurt's travel writer changes as he remarries and becomes the much-needed father to a lonely boy, but the emphasis of the film falls on the resurrection of this man's spirit. His transformation from a man suffering a paralysis of emotions to a man free to love and feel is the film's dominant arc of change.

Single Versus Multiple Protagonists

The classically told story usually places a single protagonist—man, woman, or child—at the heart of the telling. One major story dominates screentime and its protagonist is the star role. However, if the writer splinters the film into a number of relatively small, subplot-sized stories, each with a separate protagonist, the result minimalizes the roller-coaster dynamic of the Archplot and creates the Multiplot variation of Miniplot that's grown in popularity since the 1980s.

In THE FUGITIVE's highly charged Archplot the camera never loses sight of Harrison Ford's protagonist: no glances sideways, not even a hint of a subplot. PARENTHOOD, on the other hand, is a tempered weave of no fewer than six tales of six protagonists. As in an Archplot, the conflicts of these six characters are predominantly external; none of them undergoes the deep suffering and inner change of THE ACCIDENTAL TOURIST. But because these family battles draw our feelings in so many directions and because each story receives a brief fifteen or twenty minutes of screentime, their multiple design softens the telling.

The Multiplot dates from INTOLERANCE (USA/1916), GRAND HOTEL (USA/1932), THROUGH A GLASS DARKLY (Sweden/1961), and SHIP OF FOOLS (USA/1965) to its common use today—SHORT CUTS, PULP FICTION, DO THE RIGHT THING, and EAT DRINK MAN WOMAN.

Active Versus Passive Protagonist

The single protagonist of an Archplot tends to be active and dynamic, willfully pursuing desire through ever-escalating conflict and change. The protagonist of a Miniplot design, although not inert, is relatively reactive and passive. Generally this passivity is compensated for either by giving the protagonist a powerful inner struggle as in THE ACCIDENTAL TOURIST or by surrounding him with dramatic events as in the Multiplot design of PELLE THE CONQUEROR.

An ACTIVE PROTAGONIST, in the pursuit of desire, takes action in direct conflict with the people and the world around him.

A PASSIVE PROTAGONIST is outwardly inactive while pursuing desire inwardly, in conflict with aspects of his or her own nature.

The title character of PELLE THE CONQUEROR is an adolescent under the control of the adult world and therefore has little choice but to be reactive. Writer Bille August, however, takes advantage of Pelle's alienation to make him the passive observer of tragic stories around him: Illicit lovers commit infanticide, a woman castrates her husband for adultery, the leader of a workers' revolt is bludgeoned into a cretin. Because August controls the telling from the child's point of view, these violent events are kept offscreen or at a distance, so that we rarely see the cause, only the aftermath. The design softens or minimalizes what could have been melodramatic, even distasteful.

Linear Versus Nonlinear Time

An Archplot begins at a certain point in time, moves elliptically through more or less continuous time, and ends at a later date. If flashbacks are used, they are handled so that the audience can place the story's events in their temporal order. An antiplot, on the other hand, is often disjunctive, scrambling or fragmenting time to make it difficult, if not impossible, to sort what happened into any linear sequence. Godard once remarked that in his aesthetic a film must have a beginning, middle, and end . . . but not necessarily in that order.

A story with or without flashbacks and arranged into a temporal order of events that the audience can follow is told in LINEAR TIME.

A story that either skips helter-skelter through time or so blurs temporal continuity that the audience cannot sort out what happens before and after what is told in NONLINEAR TIME.

In the aptly titled Antiplot BAD TIMING a psychoanalyst (Art Garfunkel) meets a woman (Theresa Russell) while vacationing in Austria. The first third of the film contains scenes that seem to come from the early going of the affair, but between them flash-forwards leap to scenes from the relationship's middle and late stages. The center third of the film is spattered with scenes that we assume are from their middle period, but interspersed with flashbacks to the beginning and flash-forwards to the end. The last third is dominated by scenes that seem to come from the couple's final days but are spliced with flashbacks to middle and beginning. The film ends on an act of necrophilia.

BAD TIMING is a contemporary reworking of the ancient idea of "character as destiny"—the notion that your fate equals who you are, that the final consequences of your life will be determined by the unique nature of your character and nothing else—not family, society, environment, or chance. By tossing time like a salad, BAD TIMING's antistructure design disconnects the characters from the world around them. What difference does it make whether they went to Salzburg one weekend or Vienna the next; whether they had lunch here or dinner there; quarreled over this or that or didn't? What matters is the poisonous alchemy of their personalities. The moment this couple met they stepped on a bullet train to their grotesque fate.

Causality Versus Coincidence

The Archplot stresses how things happen in the world, how a cause creates an effect, how this effect becomes a cause that triggers yet another effect. Classical story design charts the vast interconnectedness of life from the obvious to the impenetrable, from the intimate to the epic, from individual identity to the international infosphere. It lays bare the network of chain-linked causalities that, when understood, gives life meaning. The Antiplot, on the other hand, often substitutes coincidence for causality, putting emphasis on the random collisions of things in the universe that break the chains of causality and lead to fragmentation, meaninglessness, and absurdity.

CAUSALITY drives a story in which motivated actions cause effects that in turn become the causes of yet other effects, thereby interlinking the various levels of conflict in a chain reaction of episodes to the Story Climax, expressing the interconnectedness of reality.

COINCIDENCE drives a fictional world in which unmotivated actions trigger events that do not cause further effects, and therefore fragment the story into divergent episodes and an open ending, expressing the disconnectedness of existence.

In AFTER HOURS a young man (Griffin Dunne) makes a date with a woman he meets by chance in a Manhattan coffee shop. On the trip to her Soho apartment his last twenty bucks is blown out the taxi window. He then seems to find his money stapled to a bizarre statue-in-progress in her loft. His date suddenly commits a well-planned suicide. Trapped in Soho without money for the subway, he's mistaken for a burglar and hunted by a vigilante mob. Lunatic characters and an overflowing toilet block his escape, until he's hidden inside a statue, stolen by real burglars, and finally falls out of their getaway truck, smack onto the steps of the building where he works, right on time for his day at the word processor. He's a pool ball on the table of God, randomly bouncing around until he drops into a pocket.

Consistent Versus Inconsistent Realities

Story is a metaphor for life. It takes us beyond the factual to the essential. Therefore, it's a mistake to apply a one-for-one standard from reality to story. The worlds we create obey their own internal rules of causality. An Archplot unfolds within a consistent reality . . . but reality, in this case, doesn't mean actuality. Even the most naturalistic, "life as lived" Miniplot is an abstracted and rarefied existence. Each fictional reality uniquely establishes how things happen within it. In an Archplot these rules cannot be broken— even if they are bizarre.

> **CONSISTENT REALITIES** are fictional settings that establish modes of interaction between characters and their world that are kept consistently throughout the telling to create meaning.

Virtually all works in the *Fantasy* genre, for example, are Archplots in which whimsical rules of "reality" are strictly obeyed. Suppose that in WHO FRAMED ROGER RABBIT a human character were to chase Roger, a cartoon character, toward a locked door. Suddenly Roger flattens into two dimensions, slides under the sill, and escapes. The human slams into the door. Fine. But now this becomes a story rule: No human can catch Roger because he can switch to two dimensions and escape. Should the writer want Roger caught in a future scene, he would have to devise a non-human agent or go back to rewrite the previous chase. Having created story rules of causality, the writer of an Archplot must work within his self-created discipline. Consistent Reality, therefore, means an internally consistent world, true to itself.

> **INCONSISTENT REALITIES are settings that mix modes of interaction so that the story's episodes jump inconsistently from one "reality" to another to create a sense of absurdity.**

In an Antiplot, however, the only rule is to break rules: In Jean-Luc Godard's WEEKEND a Parisian couple decides to murder an elderly aunt for her insurance money. On the way to the aunt's country home an accident, more hallucinatory than real, destroys their red sports car. Later, as the couple trudges on foot down a lovely shaded lane, Emily Brontë suddenly appears, plucked out of nineteenth-century England and dropped onto a twentieth-century French path, reading her novel *Wuthering Heights*. The Parisians hate Emily on sight, whip out a Zippo lighter, set her crinoline skirts on fire, burn her to a crisp . . . and walk on.

A slap in the face for classical literature? Perhaps, but it doesn't happen again. This isn't a time-travel movie. Nobody else shows up out of the past or future; just Emily; just once. A rule made to be broken.

The desire to turn the Archplot on its head began early in this century. Writers such as August Strindberg, Ernst Toller, Virginia Woolf, James Joyce, Samuel Beckett, and William S. Burroughs felt the need to sever the links between the artist and external reality, and with it, between the artist and the greater part of the audience. Expressionism, Dadaism, Surrealism, Stream of Consciousness, Theatre of the Absurd, the antinovel, and cinematic antistructure may differ in technique but share the same result: a retreat inside the artist's private world to which the audience is admitted at the artist's discretion. These are worlds in which not only are events atemporal, coincidental, fragmented, and chaotic, but characters do not operate within a recognizable psychology. Neither sane nor insane, they are either deliberately inconsistent or overtly symbolic.

Films in this mode are not metaphors for "life as lived," but for "life as thought about." They reflect not reality, but the solipsism of the filmmaker, and in doing so, stretch the limits of story design toward didactic and ideational structures. However, the inconsistent reality of an Antiplot such as WEEKEND has a unity of sorts. When done well, it's felt to be an expression of the subjective state of mind of the filmmaker. This sense of a single perception, no matter how incoherent, holds the work together for audiences willing to venture into its distortions.

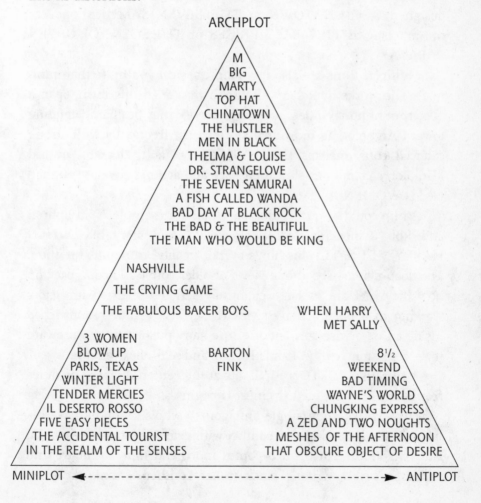

ARCHPLOT

M
BIG
MARTY
TOP HAT
CHINATOWN
THE HUSTLER
MEN IN BLACK
THELMA & LOUISE
DR. STRANGELOVE
THE SEVEN SAMURAI
A FISH CALLED WANDA
BAD DAY AT BLACK ROCK
THE BAD & THE BEAUTIFUL
THE MAN WHO WOULD BE KING

NASHVILLE

THE CRYING GAME

THE FABULOUS BAKER BOYS   WHEN HARRY
                                           MET SALLY

3 WOMEN
BLOW UP   BARTON   8½
PARIS, TEXAS   FINK   WEEKEND
WINTER LIGHT   BAD TIMING
TENDER MERCIES   WAYNE'S WORLD
IL DESERTO ROSSO   CHUNGKING EXPRESS
FIVE EASY PIECES   A ZED AND TWO NOUGHTS
THE ACCIDENTAL TOURIST   MESHES OF THE AFTERNOON
IN THE REALM OF THE SENSES   THAT OBSCURE OBJECT OF DESIRE

MINIPLOT ◄- -► ANTIPLOT

The seven formal contradictions and contrasts listed above are not hard and fast. There are unlimited shades and degrees of openness/closedness, passivity/activity, consistent/inconsistent reality, and the like. All storytelling possibilities are distributed inside the story design triangle, but very few films are of such purity of form that they settle at its extreme corners. Each side of the triangle is a spectrum of structural choices, and writers slide their stories along these lines, blending or borrowing from each extreme.

THE FABULOUS BAKER BOYS and THE CRYING GAME fall halfway between Archplot and Miniplot. Each tells the tale of a rather passive isolate; each leaves its ending open as the future of the subplot's love story goes unanswered. Neither is as classically designed as CHINATOWN or THE SEVEN SAMURAI, nor as minimalistic as FIVE EASY PIECES or THE SCENT OF GREEN PAPAYA.

Multiplot films are also less than classical and more than minimal. The works of Robert Altman, a master of this form, span a spectrum of possibilities. A Multiplot work may be "hard," tending toward Archplot, as individual stories turn frequently with strong external consequences (NASHVILLE), or "soft," leaning toward Miniplot, as plot lines slow their pace and action becomes internalized (3 WOMEN).

A film could be quasi-Antiplot. When, for example, Nora Ephron and Rob Reiner inserted scenes of *Mockumentary* into WHEN HARRY MET SALLY, his film's overall "reality" came into question. The documentary-styled interviews of older couples looking back on how they met are in fact delightfully scripted scenes with actors working in a documentary style. These false realities sandwiched inside an otherwise conventional love story pushed the film toward the inconsistent reality of antistructure and self-reflexive satire.

A film like BARTON FINK sits at the center, drawing qualities from each of the three extremes. It begins as the story of a young New York playwright (single protagonist) who's trying to make his mark in Hollywood (active conflict with external forces)—*Archplot*. But Fink (John Turturro) becomes more and more reclusive and suffers a severe writer's block (inner conflict)—*Miniplot*. When that progresses into hallucination, we grow less and less sure of what's real, what's fantasy (inconsistent realities), until nothing can be trusted (fractured temporal and causal order)—*Antiplot*. The ending is rather open, with Fink staring out to sea, but it's fairly certain he'll never write in that town again.

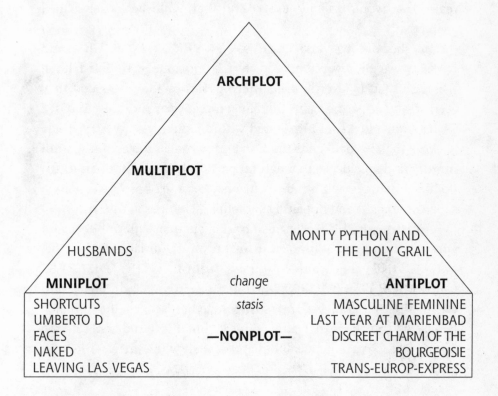

Change Versus Stasis

Above the line drawn between Miniplot and Antiplot are stories in which life clearly changes. At the limits of Miniplot, however, change may be virtually invisible because it occurs at the deepest level of inner conflict: HUSBANDS. Change at the limits of Antiplot may explode into a cosmic joke: MONTY PYTHON AND THE HOLY GRAIL. But in both cases stories arc and life changes for better or worse.

Below this line stories remain in stasis and do not arc. The value-charged condition of the character's life at the end of the film is virtually identical to that at the opening. Story dissolves into portraiture, either a portrait of verisimilitude or one of absurdity. I term these films *Nonplot*. Although they inform us, touch us, and have their own rhetorical or formal structures, they do not tell story. Therefore, they fall outside the story triangle and into a realm that would include everything that could be loosely called "narrative."

In slice-of-life works such as UMBERTO D, FACES, and NAKED, we discover protagonists leading lonely, troubled lives. They're tested by even more suffering, but by the film's end they seem resigned to the pain of life, even ready for more. In SHORT CUTS, individual lives are altered within its many story lines, but a soulless malaise bookends the film and permeates everything, until murder and suicide seem a natural part of the landscape. Although nothing changes within the universe of a Nonplot, we gain a sobering insight and hopefully something changes within us.

Antistructured Nonplots also trace a circular pattern but turn it with absurdity and satire done in an supra-unnaturalistic style. MASCULINE FEMININE (France/1966), THE DISCREET CHARM OF THE BOURGEOISIE (France/1972), and PHANTOM OF LIBERTY (France/1974) string together scenes that ridicule bourgeois antics, sexual and political, but the blind fools of the opening scenes are just as blind and foolish when the closing titles roll.

THE POLITICS OF STORY DESIGN

In an ideal world art and politics would never touch. In reality they can't keep their hands off each other. So as in all things, politics lurks inside the story triangle: the politics of taste, the politics of festivals and awards, and, most important, the politics of artistic versus commercial success. And as in all things political, the distortion of truth is greatest at the extremes. Each of us has a natural address somewhere on the story triangle. The danger is that for reasons more ideological than personal, you may feel compelled to leave home and work in a distant corner, trapping yourself into designing stories you don't in your heart believe. But if you take an honest look at film's often specious polemics, you won't lose your way.

Over the years the primary political issue in cinema has been "Hollywood film" versus "art film." Although the terms seem dated, their partisans are very contemporary and vocal. Traditionally, their arguments have been framed in terms of big budget versus low budget, special effects versus painterly composition, the star system versus ensemble acting, private finance versus government support, and auteurs versus guns-for-hire. But hiding inside these debates are two diametrically opposed visions of life. The crucial frontier stretches across the bottom of story triangle: stasis versus change, a philosophical contradiction with profound implications for the writer. Let's begin by defining terms:

The concept "Hollywood film" does not include REVERSAL OF FORTUNE, Q & A, DRUGSTORE COWBOY, POSTCARDS FROM THE EDGE, SALVADOR, RUNNING ON EMPTY, BLUE VELVET, BOB ROBERTS, JFK, DANGEROUS LIAISONS, THE FISHER KING, DO THE RIGHT THING, or EVERYBODY SAYS I LOVE YOU. These films, and many more like them, are acclaimed international successes produced by Hollywood studios. THE ACCIDENTAL TOURIST made more than $250 million worldwide, surpassing most *Action* films, but doesn't fall within the definition. The political meaning of "Hollywood film" is narrowed to thirty or forty special effects–dominated flicks and an equal number of farces and romances that Hollywood makes each year— far less than half of the town's output.

"Art film," in the broadest sense, means non-Hollywood, more specifically foreign film, even more specifically European film. Each year western Europe produces over four hundred films, generally more than Hollywood. "Art film," however, doesn't refer to the large number of European productions that are blood-spattered action, hard-core pornography, or slapstick farce. In the language of cafe criticism "art film" (a silly phrase—imagine "art novel" or "art theatre") is restricted to that trickle of excellent films, like BABETTE'S FEAST, IL POSTINO, or MAN BITES DOG, that manage to cross the Atlantic.

These terms were coined in the wars of cultural politics and point to vastly different, if not contradictory, views of reality. Hollywood filmmakers tend to be overly (some would say foolishly) optimistic about the capacity of life to change—especially for the better. Consequently, to express this vision they rely on the Archplot and an inordinately high percentage of positive endings. Non-Hollywood filmmakers tend to be overly (some would say chicly) pessimistic about change, professing that the more life changes, the more it stays the same, or, worse, that change brings suffering. Consequently, to express the futility, meaninglessness, or destructiveness of change, they tend to make static, Nonplot portraiture or extreme Miniplots and Antiplots with negative endings.

These are tendencies, of course, with exceptions on both sides of the Atlantic, but the dichotomy is real and deeper than the seas that separate the Old World from the New. Americans are escapees from prisons of stagnant culture and rigid class who crave change. We change and change again, trying to find what, if anything, works. After weaving the trillion-dollar safety net of the Great Society, we're now shredding it. The Old World, on the other hand, has learned through centuries of hard experience to fear such change, that social transformations inevitably bring war, famine, chaos.

The result is our polarized attitude toward story: The ingenuous optimism of Hollywood (not naive about change but about its insistence on positive change) versus the equally ingenuous pessimism of the *art film* (not naive about the human condition but about its insistence that it will never be other than negative or static). Too often Hollywood films force an up-ending for reasons more commercial than truthful; too often non-Hollywood films cling to the dark side for reasons more fashionable than truthful. The truth, as always, sits somewhere in the middle.

The art film's focus on inner conflict draws the interest of those with advanced degrees, because the inner world is where the highly educated spend a large amount of time. Minimalists, however, often overestimate the appetite of even the most self-absorbed minds for a diet of nothing but inner conflict. Worse, they also overestimate their talent to express the unseeable on screen. By the same token, Hollywood's action filmmakers underestimate the interest of their audience in character, thought, and feeling, and, worse, overestimate their ability to avoid *Action* genre clichés.

Because story in Hollywood film is often forced and clichéd, directors must compensate with something else to hold the audience's attention, resorting to transformation effects and cacophonous derring-do: THE FIFTH ELEMENT. In the same vein, because story is often thin or absent in the art film, again, directors must compensate. In this case, with one of two possibilities: information or sensory stimulation. Either dialogue-heavy scenes of political argument, philosophical musing, and characters' self-conscious descriptions of their emotions; or lush production design and photography or musical scores to pleasure the audience's senses: THE ENGLISH PATIENT.

The sad truth of the political wars of contemporary cinema is that the excesses of both "art film" and "Hollywood film" are the mirror images of each other: The telling is forced to become a dazzling surface of spectacle and sound to distract the audience from the vacancy and falsity of the story . . . and in both boredom follows as night the day.

Behind the political squabbling over finance, distribution, and awards lies a deep cultural divide, reflected in the opposing worldviews of Archplot versus Miniplot and Antiplot. From story to story the writer may move anywhere within the triangle, but most of us feel more at home in one place or another. You must make your own "political" choices and decide where you reside. As you do, let me offer these points for you to weigh:

The Writer Must Earn His Living Writing

Writing while holding down a forty-hour-a-week job is possible. Thousands have done it. But in time, exhaustion sets in, concentration wanders, creativity crumbles, and you're tempted to quit. Before you do, you must find a way to earn your living from your writing. A talented writer's survival in the real world of film and television, theatre, and publishing begins with his recognition of this fact: As story design moves away from the Archplot and down the triangle toward the far reaches of Miniplot, Antiplot, and Non-plot, *the audience shrinks.*

This atrophy has nothing to do with quality or a lack of it. All three corners of the story triangle gleam with masterworks that the world treasures, pieces of perfection for our imperfect world. Rather, the audience shrinks for this reason: Most human beings believe that life brings closed experiences of absolute, irreversible change; that their greatest sources of conflict are external to themselves; that they are the single and active protagonists of their own existence; that their existence operates through continuous time within a consistent, causally interconnected reality; and that inside this reality events happen for explainable and meaningful reasons. Since our first ancestor stared into a fire of his own making and thought the thought, "I am," this is how human beings have seen the world and themselves in it. Classical design is a mirror of the human mind.

Classical design is a model of memory and anticipation. When we think back to the past, do we piece events together antistruc-tured? Minimalistically? No. We collect and shape memories around an Archplot to bring the past back vividly. When we day-dream about the future, what we dread or pray will happen, is our vision minimalistic? Antistructured? No, we mold our fantasies and hopes into an Archplot. Classical design displays the temporal, spatial, and causal patterns of human perception, outside which the mind rebels.

Classical design is not a Western view of life. For thousands of years, from the Levant to Java to Japan, the storytellers of Asia have framed their works within the Archplot, spinning yarns of high adventure and great passion. As the rise of Asian film has shown, Eastern screenwriters draw on the same principles of classical design used in the West, enriching their tellings with a unique wit and irony. The Archplot is neither ancient nor modern, Western nor Eastern; it is human.

When the audience senses that a story is drifting too close to fictional realities it finds tedious or meaningless, it feels alienated and turns away. This is true of intelligent, sensitive people of all incomes and backgrounds. The vast majority of human beings cannot endorse the inconsistent realities of Antiplot, the internalized passivity of Miniplot, and the static circularity of Nonplot as metaphors for life as they live it. As story reaches the bottom of the triangle the audience has shrunk to those loyal, cinephile intellectuals who like to have their realities twisted once in a while. This is an enthusiastic, challenging audience . . . but a very small audience.

If the audience shrinks, the budget must shrink. This is the law. In 1961 Alain Robbe-Grillet wrote LAST YEAR AT MARIENBAD and throughout the seventies and eighties he wrote brilliant Antiplot puzzle pieces—films more about the art of writing than about the act of living. I once asked him how, despite the anticommercial bent of his films, he did it. He said he'd never spent more than $750,000 to make a film and never would. His audience was faithful but meager. At an ultra-low budget his investors doubled their money and kept him in the director's chair. But at $2 million they would lose their shirts and he his seat. Robbe-Grillet was both visionary and pragmatic.

If, like Robbe-Grillet, you wish to write Miniplot or Antiplot, and can find a non-Hollywood producer to work at low budget, and are happy with relatively little money for yourself, good. Do it. But when you write for Hollywood, a low-budget script is no asset. Seasoned professionals who read your minimalist or antistructured piece may applaud your handling of image, but decline to be involved because experience has taught them that if the story is inconsequential, so is the audience.

Even modest Hollywood budgets run into the tens of millions of dollars, and each film must find an audience large enough to repay its cost at a profit greater than the same money would have earned in a secured investment. Why should investors place millions at enormous jeopardy when they can put it into real estate and at least have a building when they're done, not something that's shown in a couple of film festivals, shoved into a refrigerated vault, and forgotten? If a Hollywood studio is going to take this wild ride with you, you must write a film that has at least a chance of recouping its huge risk. In other words, a film that leans toward the Archplot.

The Writer Must Master Classical Form

By instinct or study, fine writers recognize that minimalism and antistructure are not independent forms but reactions to the Classical. Miniplot and Antiplot were born out of the Archplot—one shrinks it, the other contradicts it. The avant-garde exists to oppose the popular and commercial, until it too becomes popular and commercial, then it turns to attack itself. If Nonplot "art films" went hot and were raking in money, the avant-garde would revolt, denounce Hollywood for selling out to portraiture, and seize the Classical for its own.

These cycles between formality/freedom, symmetry/asymmetry are as old as Attic theatre. The history of art is a history of revivals: Establishment icons are shattered by an avant-garde that in time becomes the new establishment to be attacked by a new avant-garde that uses its grandfather's forms of weapons. Rock 'n' roll, which was named after black slang for sex, began as an avant-garde movement against the white-bread sounds of the postwar era. Now it's the definition of musical aristocracy and even used as church music.

The serious use of Antiplot devices not only has gone out of fashion but has become a joke. A vein of dark satire has always run through antistructure works, from UN CHIEN ANDALOU to WEEKEND, but now direct address to camera, inconsistent realities, and alternative endings are the staples of film farce. Antiplot gags that began with Bob Hope and Bing Crosby's THE ROAD TO MOROCCO have been worked into the likes of BLAZING SADDLES, the PYTHON films, and WAYNE'S WORLD. Story techniques that once struck us as dangerous and revolutionary now seem toothless but charming.

Respecting these cycles, great storytellers have always known that, regardless of background or education, everyone, consciously or instinctively, enters the story ritual with Classical anticipation. Therefore, to make Miniplot and Antiplot work the writer must play with or against this expectancy. Only by carefully and creatively shattering or bending the Classical form can the artist lead the audience to perceive the inner life hidden in a Miniplot or to accept the chilling absurdity of an Antiplot. But how can a writer creatively reduce or reverse that which he does not understand?

Writers who found success in the deep corners of the story triangle knew that the starting point of understanding was at the top and began their careers in the Classical. Bergman wrote and directed love stories and social and historical dramas for twenty years before he dared venture into the minimalism of THE SILENCE or the antistructure of PERSONA. Fellini made I VITIONI and LA STRADA before he risked the Miniplot of AMARCORD or the Antiplot of 8$^{1}/_{2}$. Godard made BREATHLESS before WEEKEND. Robert Altman perfected his story talents in the TV series *Bonanza* and *Alfred Hitchcock Presents*. First, the masters mastered the Archplot.

I sympathize with the youthful desire to make a first screenplay read like PERSONA. But the dream of joining the avant-garde must wait while, like the artists before you, you too gain mastery of Classical form. Don't kid yourself into thinking that you understand Archplot because you've seen the movies. You'll know you understand it *when you can do it*. The writer works at his skills until knowledge shifts from the left side of the brain to the right, until intellectual awareness becomes living craft.

The Writer Must Believe in What He Writes

Stanislavski asked his actors: Are you in love with the art in yourself or yourself in the art? You too must examine your motives for wanting to write the way you write. Why do your screenplays find their way to one corner of the triangle or the other? What is your vision?

Each tale you create says to the audience: "I believe life is like *this*." Every moment must be filled with your passionate conviction or we smell a phony. If you write minimalism, do you believe in the meanings of this form? Has experience convinced you that life brings little or no change? If your ambition is anticlassicism, are you convinced of the random meaninglessness of life? If your answer is a passionate yes, then write your Miniplot or Antiplot and do everything possible to see it made.

For the vast majority, however, the honest answer to these questions is no. Yet antistructure and, in particular, minimalism still attract young writers like a Pied Piper. Why? I suspect that for many it isn't the intrinsic meanings of such forms that draw their interest. Rather, it's what these forms represent extrinsically. In other words, politics. It isn't what Antiplot and Miniplot are, it's what they're *not*: They're not Hollywood.

The young are taught that Hollywood and art are antithetical. The novice, therefore, wanting to be recognized as an artist, falls into the trap of writing a screenplay not for what it *is*, but for what it's *not*. He avoids closure, active characters, chronology, and causality to avoid the taint of commercialism. As a result, pretentiousness poisons his work.

A story is the embodiment of our ideas and passions in Edmund Husserl's phrase, "an objective correlative" for the feelings and insights we wish to instill in the audience. When you work with one eye on your script and the other on Hollywood, making eccentric choices to avoid the taint of commercialism, you produce the literary equivalent of a temper tantrum. Like a child living in the shadow of a powerful father, you break Hollywood's "rules" because it makes you feel free. But angry contradiction of the patriarch is not creativity; it's delinquency calling for attention. Difference for the sake of difference is as empty an achievement as slavishly following the commercial imperative. Write only what you believe.

3

STRUCTURE AND SETTING

THE WAR ON CLICHÉ

This may be the most demanding time in history to be a writer. Compare the story-saturated audience of today to that of centuries past. How many times a year did educated Victorians go to the theatre? In a era of huge families and no automatic dishwashers, how much time did they have for fiction? In a typical week our great-great-grandparents may have read or seen five or six hours of story—what many of us now consume per day. By the time modern filmgoers sit down to your work, they've absorbed tens of thousands of hours of TV, movies, prose, and theatre. What will you create that they haven't seen before? Where will you find a truly original story? How will you win the war on cliché?

Cliché is at the root of audience dissatisfaction, and like a plague spread through ignorance, it now infects all story media. Too often we close novels or exit theatres bored by an ending that was obvious from the beginning, disgruntled because we've seen these clichéd scenes and characters too many times before. The cause of this worldwide epidemic is simple and clear; the source of all clichés can be traced to one thing and one thing alone: *The writer does not know the world of his story.*

Such writers select a setting and launch a screenplay assuming a knowledge of their fictional world that they don't have. As they reach into their minds for material, they come up empty. So where do they run? To films and TV, novels and plays with similar settings. From the works of other writers they crib scenes we've seen before, paraphrase dialogue we've heard before, disguise characters we've met before, and pass them off as their own. They reheat literary leftovers and serve up plates of boredom because, regardless of their talents, they lack an in-depth understanding of their story's setting and all it contains. Knowledge of and insight into the world of your story is fundamental to the achievement of originality and excellence.

SETTING

A story's SETTING is four-dimensional—*Period, Duration, Location, Level of Conflict.*

The first dimension of time is Period. Is the story set in the contemporary world? In history? A hypothetical future? Or is it that rare fantasy, such as ANIMAL FARM or WATERSHIP DOWN, in which location in time is unknowable and irrelevant?

PERIOD is a story's place in time.

Duration is the second dimension of time. How much time does the story span within the lives of your characters? Decades? Years? Months? Days? Is it that rare work in which storytime equals screentime, such as MY DINNER WITH ANDRE, a two-hour movie about a two-hour dinner?

Or rarer still, LAST YEAR AT MARIENBAD, a film that liquefies time into timelessness? It's conceivable, through cross-cutting, overlap, repetition, and/or slow motion, for screentime to surpass storytime. Although no feature-length film has attempted this, a few sequences have done it brilliantly—most famous of all, the "Odessa Steps" sequence of THE BATTLESHIP POTEMKIN. The actual assault by the Tsar's army on the Odessa protesters took no more than two or three minutes, the time needed for jack-booted feet to march down the steps from top to bottom. Onscreen the terror expands to five times this length.

DURATION is a story's length through time.

Location is the story's physical dimension. What is the story's specific geography? In what town? On what streets? What buildings on those streets? What rooms inside those buildings? Up what mountain? Across what desert? A voyage to what planet?

LOCATION is a story's place in space.

Level of Conflict is the human dimension. A setting includes not only itsphysical and temporal domain, but social as well. This dimension becomes vertical in this sense: At what Level of Conflict do you pitch your telling? No matter how externalized in institutions or internalized in individuals, the political, economic, ideological, biological, and psychological forces of society shape events as much as period, landscape, or costume. Therefore, the cast of characters, containing its various levels of conflict, is part of a story's setting.

Does your story focus on the inner, even unconscious conflicts within your characters? Or coming up a level, on personal conflicts? Or higher and wider, on battles with institutions in society? Wider still, on struggles against forces of the environment? From the subconscious to the stars, through all the multilayered experiences of life, your story may be set at any one or any combination of these levels.

LEVEL OF CONFLICT is the story's position on the hierarchy of human struggles.

The Relationship Between Structure and Setting

A story's setting sharply defines and confines its possibilities.

Although your setting is a fiction, not everything that comes to mind may be allowed to happen in it. Within any world, no matter how imaginary, only certain events are possible or probable.

If your drama is set among the gated estates of West L.A., we won't see homeowners protesting social injustice by rioting in their tree-lined streets, although they might throw a thousand-dollar-a-plate fund-raiser. If your setting is the housing projects of East

L.A.'s ghetto, these citizens won't dine at thousand-dollar-a-plate galas, but they might hit the streets to demand change.

A STORY must obey its own internal laws of probability. The event choices of the writer, therefore, are limited to the possibilities and probabilities within the world he creates.

Each fictional world creates a unique cosmology and makes its own "rules" for how and why things happen within it. No matter how realistic or bizarre the setting, once its causal principles are established, they cannot change. In fact, of all genres *Fantasy* is the most rigid and structurally conventional. We give the fantasy writer one great leap away from reality, then demand tight-knit probabilities and no coincidence—the strict Archplot of THE WIZARD OF OZ, for example. On the other hand, a gritty realism often allows leaps in logic. In THE USUAL SUSPECTS, for example, screenwriter Christopher McQuarrie arrests his wild improbabilities inside the "law" of free association.

Stories do not materialize from a void but grow out of materials already in history and human experience. From its first glimpse of the first image, the audience inspects your fictional universe, sorting the possible from the impossible, the likely from the unlikely. Consciously and unconsciously, it wants to know your "laws," to learn how and why things happen in your specific world. You create these possibilities and limitations through your personal choice of setting and the way you work within it. Having invented these strictures, you're bound to a contract you must keep. For once the audience grasps the laws of your reality, it feels violated if you break them and rejects your work as illogical and unconvincing.

Seen this way, the setting may feel like a straitjacket to the imagination. When working in development, I'm often struck by how writers try to wriggle out of its restraints by refusing to be specific. "What's your setting?" I'll ask. "America," the writer cheerfully answers. "Sounds a bit vast. Got any particular neighborhood in mind?" "Bob, it won't matter. This is your quintessential American story. It's about divorce. What could be more American? We can set it in Louisiana, New York, or Idaho. Won't matter." But it matters absolutely. Breakup in the Bayou bears little resemblance to a multi-million-dollar Park Avenue litigation, and neither looks like infidelity on a potato farm. There is no such thing as a portable story. An honest story is at home in one, and only one, place and time.

THE PRINCIPLE OF CREATIVE LIMITATION

Limitation is vital. The first step toward a well-told story is to create a small, *knowable* world. Artists by nature crave freedom, so the principle that the structure/setting relationship restricts creative choices may stir the rebel in you. With a closer look, however, you'll see that this relationship couldn't be more positive. The constraint that setting imposes on story design doesn't inhibit creativity; it inspires it.

All fine stories take place within a limited, knowable world. No matter how grand a fictional world may seem, with a close look you'll discover that it's remarkably small. CRIME AND PUNISHMENT is microscopic. WAR AND PEACE, although played against a landscape of Russia in turmoil, is the focused tale of a handful of characters and their interrelated families. DR. STRANGELOVE is set in the office of General Jack D. Ripper, a Flying Fortress heading for Russia, and the War Room of the Pentagon. It climaxes in planetary nuclear annihilation, but the telling is limited to three sets and eight principal characters.

The world of a story must be small enough that the mind of a single artist can surround the fictional universe it creates and come to know it in the same depth and detail that God knows the one He created. As my mother used to say, "Not a sparrow falls that God does not know." Not a sparrow should fall in the world of a writer that he wouldn't know. By the time you finish your last draft, you must possess a commanding knowledge of your setting in such depth and detail that no one could raise a question about your world—from the eating habits of your characters to the weather in September—that you couldn't answer instantly.

A "small" world, however, does not mean a trivial world. Art consists of separating one tiny piece from the rest of the universe and holding it up in such a way that it appears to be the most important, fascinating thing of this moment. "Small," in this case, means knowable.

"Commanding knowledge" does not mean an extended awareness into every crevice of existence. It means knowledge of all that's germane. This may seem an impossible ideal, but the best writers attain it every day. What relevant question about the time, place, and characters of CRIES AND WHISPERS would elude Ingmar Bergman? Or David Mamet of GLENGARRY GLEN ROSS? Or John Cleese of A FISH CALLED WANDA? It's not that fine artists give deliberate, conscious thought to each and every aspect of life implied by their stories, but at some level they absorb it all. Great writers *know*. Therefore, work within what's knowable. A vast, populous world stretches the mind so thinly that knowledge must be superficial. A limited world and restricted cast offer the possibility of knowledge in depth and breadth.

The irony of setting versus story is this: The larger the world, the more diluted the knowledge of the writer, therefore the fewer his creative choices and the more clichéd the story. The smaller the world, the more complete the knowledge of the writer, therefore the greater his creative choices. Result: a fully original story and victory in the war on cliché.

RESEARCH

The key to winning this war is research, taking the time and effort to acquire knowledge. I suggest these specific methods: research of memory, research of imagination, research of fact. Generally, a story needs all three.

Memory

Lean back from your desk and ask, "What do I know from personal experience that touches on my characters' lives?"

You're writing, let's say, about a middle-aged executive who faces a career-making/career-destroying presentation. His personal and professional life hangs in the balance. He's afraid. How does fear feel? Slowly, memory takes you back to the day your mother, for reasons you'll never understand, locked you in a closet, left the house, and didn't come back until the next day. Bring back those long, fright-filled hours when the dark smothered you. Could your character feel the same? If so, vividly describe your day and night in the closet. You may think you know, but you don't know you know until you can write it down. Research is not daydreaming. Explore your past, relive it, then write it down. In your head it's only memory, but written down it becomes working knowledge. Now with the bile of fear in your belly, write an honest, one-of-a-kind scene.

Imagination

Lean back and ask, "What would it be like to live my character's life hour by hour, day by day?"

In vivid detail sketch how your characters shop, make love, pray—scenes that may or may not find their way into your story, but draw you into your imagined world until it feels like déjà vu. While memory gives us whole chunks of life, imagination takes fragments, slivers of dream, and chips of experience that seem unrelated, then seeks their hidden connections and merges them into a whole. Having found these links and envisioned the scenes, write them down. A working imagination is research.

Fact

Have you ever had writer's block? Scary, isn't it? Days drag by and nothing gets written. Cleaning the garage looks like fun. You rearrange your desk over and over and over until you think you're losing your mind. I know a cure, but it isn't a trip to your psychiatrist. It's a trip to the library.

You're blocked because you have nothing to say. Your talent didn't abandon you. If you had something to say, you couldn't stop yourself from writing. You can't kill your talent, but you can starve it into a coma through ignorance. For no matter how talented, the ignorant cannot write. Talent must be stimulated by facts and ideas. Do research. Feed your talent. Research not only wins the war on cliché, it's the key to victory over fear and its cousin, depression.

Suppose, for example, you're writing in the genre of *Domestic Drama*. You were raised in a family, perhaps you've raised a family, you've seen families, you can imagine families. But if you were go to the library and read respected works on the dynamics of family life, two very important things would happen:

1. Everything life has taught you would be powerfully confirmed. On page after page you'll recognize your own family. This discovery, that your personal experience is universal, is critical. It means you'll have an audience. You'll write in a singular way, but audiences everywhere will understand because the patterns of family are ubiquitous. What you've experienced in your domestic life is analogous to all others—the rivalries and alliances, loyalties and betrayals, pains and joys. As you express emotions you feel are yours and yours alone, each member of the audience will recognize them as his and his alone.

2. No matter how many families you live in, how many you observe, or how vivid your imagination, your knowledge of the nature of family is limited to the finite circle of your experience. But as you take notes in the library, your solid, factual research will expand that circle globally. You'll be struck by sudden and powerful insights and reach a depth of understanding you couldn't have gained any other way.

Research from memory, imagination, and fact is often followed by a phenomenon that authors love to describe in mystical terms: Characters suddenly spring to life and of their own free will make choices and take actions that create Turning Points that twist, build, and turn again until the writer can hardly type fast enough to keep up with the outpourings.

This "virgin birth" is a charming self-deception writers love to indulge in, but the sudden impression that the story is writing itself simply marks the moment when a writer's knowledge of the subject has reached the saturation point. The writer becomes the god of his little universe and is amazed by what seems to be spontaneous creation, but is in fact the reward for hard work.

Be warned, however. While research provides material, it's no substitute for creativity. Biographical, psychological, physical, political, and historical research of the setting and cast is essential but pointless if it doesn't lead to the creation of events. A story is not an accumulation of information strung into a narrative, but a design of events to carry us to a meaningful climax.

What's more, research must not become procrastination. Too many insecure talents spend years in study and never actually write anything. Research is meat to feed the beasts of imagination and invention, never an end in itself. Nor is there a necessary sequence to research. We do not first fill notebooks full of social, biographical, and historical studies, and once all this work is done, begin to compose a story. Creativity is rarely so rational. Origination and exploration go on alternatively.

Imagine writing a *Psycho-Thriller*. You begin perhaps with a "What if . . ." What would happen if a psychiatrist violated her professional ethics and began an affair with her patient? Intrigued, you wonder, Who is this doctor? Patient? Perhaps he's a soldier, shell-shocked, catatonic. Why does she fall for him? You analyze and explore until growing knowledge leads to wild speculation: Suppose she falls when her treatment seems to work a miracle: Under hypnosis his wide-eyed paralysis melts away to reveal a beautiful, almost angelic personality.

That turn seems too sweet to be true, so you go on a hunt in the other direction, and deep in your studies you come across the concept of *successful schizophrenia*: Some psychotics possess such extreme intelligence and willpower they can easily hide their madness from everyone around them, even their psychiatrists. Could your patient be one of these? Could your doctor be in love with a madman she thinks she's cured?

As new ideas seed your story, story and characters grow; as your story grows, questions are raised and it hungers for more research. Creation and investigation go back and forth, making demands on each other, pushing and pulling this way or that until the story shakes itself out, complete and alive.

CREATIVE CHOICES

Fine writing is never one to one, never a matter of devising the exact number of events necessary to fill a story, then penciling in dialogue. Creativity is five to one, perhaps ten or twenty to one. The craft demands the invention of far more material than you can possibly use, then the astute selection from this quantity of quality events, moments of originality that are true to character and true to world. When actors compliment each other, for example, they often say, "I like your choices." They know that if a colleague has arrived at a beautiful moment, it's because in rehearsal the actor tried it twenty different ways, then chose the one perfect moment. The same is true for us.

CREATIVITY means creative choices of inclusion and exclusion.

Imagine writing a romantic comedy set on the East Side of Manhattan. Your thoughts meander back and forth between the separate lives of your characters, searching for that perfect moment when the lovers meet. Then sudden inspiration: "A singles bar! That's it! They meet at P. J. Clarke's!" And why not? Given the affluent New Yorkers of your imagining, meeting in a singles bar is certainly possible. Why not? Because it's a dreadful cliché. It was a fresh idea when Dustin Hoffman met Mia Farrow in JOHN AND MARY, but since then, yuppie lovers have bumped into each other in a singles bar in film after film, soap operas, and sitcoms.

But if you know the craft, you know how to cure clichés: Sketch a list of five, ten, fifteen different "East Side lovers meet" scenes. Why? Because experienced writers never trust so-called inspiration. More often than not, inspiration is the first idea picked off the top of your head, and sitting on the top of your head is every film you've ever seen, every novel you've ever read, offering clichés to pluck. This is why we fall in love with an idea on Monday, sleep on it, then reread it with disgust on Tuesday as we realize we've seen this cliché in a dozen other works. True inspiration comes from a deeper source, so let loose your imagination and experiment:

1. *Singles Bar.* Cliché, but a choice. Don't throw it away yet.
2. *Park Avenue.* A tire blows out on his BMW. He stands at the curb, helpless in his three-piece suit. She comes along on her motorcycle and takes pity on him. She gets out the spare, and as she doctors the car, he plays nurse, handing her jack handle, lug nuts, wheel cover . . . until suddenly eyes meet and sparks fly.
3. *Toilet.* She's so drunk at the office Christmas party that she stumbles into the men's room to throw up. He finds her collapsed on the floor. Quickly, before others enter, he locks the stall door and helps her through her illness. When the coast is clear he sneaks her out, saving her embarrassment.

On and on the list grows. You needn't write out these scenes in full. You're on a search for ideas, so simply sketch the bold strokes of what happens. If you know your characters and world in depth, a dozen or more such scenes won't be a difficult task. Once you've exhausted your best ideas, survey your list, asking these questions: Which scene is truest to my characters? Truest to their world? *And has never been on the screen quite this way before?* This is the one you write into the screenplay.

Suppose, however, as you question the meeting-cute scenes on your list, deep in your gut you realize that, while all have their virtues, your first impression was right. Cliché or not, these lovers would meet in a singles bar; nothing could be more expressive of their natures and milieu. Now what do you do? Follow your instincts and start a new list: a dozen different ways to meet in a singles bar. Research this world, hang out, observe the crowd, get involved, until you know the singles bar scene like no writer before you.

Scanning your new list you ask the same questions: Which variation is truest to character and world? Which has never been onscreen before? When your script becomes a film and the camera dollies toward a singles bar, the audience's first reaction may be, "Oh man, not another singles bar scene." But then you take them through the door, show them what really goes on in those meat racks. If you've done your task well, jaws will drop and heads will nod: "That's right! It's not 'What's your astrological sign? Read any good books lately?' That's the embarrassment, danger. That's the truth."

If your finished screenplay contains every scene you've ever written, if you've never thrown an idea away, if your rewriting is little more than tinkering with dialogue, your work will almost certainly fail. No matter our talent, we all know in the midnight of our souls that 90 percent of what we do is less than our best. If, however, research inspires a pace of ten to one, even twenty to one, and if you then make brilliant choices to find that 10 percent of excellence and burn the rest, every scene will fascinate and the world will sit in awe of your genius.

No one has to see your failures unless you add vanity to folly and exhibit them. Genius consists not only of the power to create expressive beats and scenes, but of the taste, judgment, and will to weed out and destroy banalities, conceits, false notes, and lies.

4

STRUCTURE AND GENRE

THE FILM GENRES

Through tens of thousands of years of tales told at fireside, four millennia of the written word, twenty-five hundred years of theatre, a century of film, and eight decades of broadcasting, countless generations of storytellers have spun story into an astonishing diversity of patterns. To make sense of this outpouring, various systems have been devised to sort stories according to shared elements, classifying them by *genre*. No two systems, however, have ever agreed on which story elements to use in the sorting, and, therefore, no two agree on the number and kind of genres.

Aristotle gave us the first genres by dividing dramas according to the value-charge of their ending versus their story design. A story, he noted, could end on either a positive or a negative charge. Then each of these two types could be either a Simple design (ending flat with no turning point or surprise) or a Complex design (climaxing around a major reversal in the protagonist's life). The result is his four basic genres: Simple Tragic, Simple Fortunate, Complex Tragic, Complex Fortunate.

Over the centuries, however, the lucidity of Aristotle was lost as genre systems became more and more blurred and bloated. Goethe listed seven types by subject matter—love, revenge, and so on. Schiller argued that there must be more but couldn't name them. Polti inventoried no less than three dozen different emotions from which he deduced "Thirty-Six Dramatic Situations," but his categories such as "An Involuntary Crime Committed for Love" or "Self-Sacrifice for an Ideal" are vague beyond use. The semiologist Metz reduced all film edits to eight possibilities he called "syntagmas," then tried to schematize all of cinema inside "La Gran Syntagma," but his effort to turn art into science crumbled like the Tower of Babel.

The neo-Aristotelian critic Norman Friedman, on the other hand, developed a system that once again delineates genres by structure and values. We're indebted to Friedman for distinctions such as the *Education Plot, Redemption Plot,* and *Disillusionment Plot*—subtle forms in which story arcs at the level of inner conflict to bring about deep changes within the mind or moral nature of the protagonist.

While scholars dispute definitions and systems, the audience is already a genre expert. It enters each film armed with a complex set of anticipations learned through a lifetime of moviegoing. The genre sophistication of filmgoers presents the writer with this critical challenge: He must not only fulfill audience anticipations, or risk their confusion and disappointment, but he must lead their expectations to fresh, unexpected moments, or risk boring them. This two-handed trick is impossible without a knowledge of genre that surpasses the audience's.

Below is the genre and subgenre system used by screenwriters—a system that's evolved from practice, not theory, and that turns on differences of subject, setting, role, event, and values.

1. **LOVE STORY.** Its subgenre, **Buddy Salvation,** substitutes friendship for romantic love: MEAN STREETS, PASSION FISH, ROMY AND MICHELE'S HIGH SCHOOL REUNION.
2. **HORROR FILM.** This genre divides into three subgenres: the **Uncanny,** in which the source of horror is astounding but subject to "rational" explanation, such as beings from outer space, science-made monsters, or a maniac; the **Supernatural,** in which the source of horror is an "irrational" phenomenon from the spirit realm; and the **Super-Uncanny,** in which the audience is kept guessing between the other two possibilities—THE TENANT, HOUR OF THE WOLF, THE SHINING.

3. **MODERN EPIC** (the individual versus the state): SPAR-
TACUS, MR. SMITH GOES TO WASHINGTON, VIVA
ZAPATA!, 1984, THE PEOPLE VS. LARRY FLINT.

4. **WESTERN.** The evolution of this genre and its subgenres is
brilliantly traced in Will Wright's *Six Guns and Society*.

5. **WAR GENRE.** Although war is often the setting for another
genre, such as the **Love Story,** the **WAR GENRE** is
specifically about combat. **Pro-war** versus **Antiwar** are its
primary subgenres. Contemporary films generally oppose
war, but for decades the majority covertly glorified it, even
in its most grisly form.

6. **MATURATION PLOT** or the coming-of-age story: STAND
BY ME, SATURDAY NIGHT FEVER, RISKY BUSINESS,
BIG, BAMBI, MURIEL'S WEDDING.

7. **REDEMPTION PLOT.** Here the film arcs on a moral
change within the protagonist from bad to good: THE
HUSTLER, LORD JIM, DRUGSTORE COWBOY,
SCHINDLER'S LIST, LA PROMESSE.

8. **PUNITIVE PLOT.** In these the good guy turns bad and is
punished: GREED, THE TREASURE OF THE SIERRA
MADRE, MEPHISTO, WALL STREET, FALLING DOWN.

9. **TESTING PLOT.** Stories of willpower versus temptation to
surrender: THE OLD MAN AND THE SEA, COOL HAND
LUKE, FITZCARRALDO, FORREST GUMP.

10. **EDUCATION PLOT.** This genre arcs on a deep change within
the protagonist's view of life, people, or self from the negative
(naive, distrustful, fatalistic, self-hating) to the positive (wise,
trusting, optimistic, self-possessed): HAROLD AND
MAUDE, TENDER MERCIES, WINTER LIGHT, IL
POSTINO, GROSS POINTE BLANK, MY BEST FRIEND'S
WEDDING, SHALL WE DANCE.

11. **DISILLUSIONMENT PLOT.** A deep change of worldview
from the positive to the negative: MRS. PARKER AND
THE VICIOUS CIRCLE, L'ECLISSE, LE FEU FOLLET,
THE GREAT GATSBY, MACBETH.

Some genres are mega-genres, so large and complex that they're filled with numerous subgenre variations:

12. **COMEDY.** Subgenres range from **Parody** to **Satire** to **Sitcom** to **Romantic** to **Screwball** to **Farce** to **Black Comedy,** all differing by the focus of comic attack (bureaucratic folly, upper-class manners, teenage courtship, etc.) and the degree of ridicule (gentle, caustic, lethal).

13. **CRIME.** Subgenres vary chiefly by the answer to this question: From whose point of view do we regard the crime? **Murder Mystery** (master detective's POV); **Caper** (master criminal's POV); **Detective** (cop's POV); **Gangster** (crook's POV); **Thriller** or **Revenge Tale** (victim's POV); **Courtroom** (lawyer's POV); **Newspaper** (reporter's POV); **Espionage** (spy's POV); **Prison Drama** (inmate's POV); **Film Noir** (POV of a protagonist who may be part criminal, part detective, part victim of a femme fatale).

14. **SOCIAL DRAMA.** This genre identifies problems in society—poverty, the education system, communicable diseases, the disadvantaged, antisocial rebellion, and the like—then constructs a story demonstrating a cure. It has a number of sharply focused subgenres: **Domestic Drama** (problems within the family), the **Woman's Film** (dilemmas such as career versus family, lover versus children), **Political Drama** (corruption in politics), **Eco-Drama** (battles to save the environment), **Medical Drama** (struggles with physical illness), and **Psycho-Drama** (struggles with mental illness).

15. **ACTION/ADVENTURE**. This often borrows aspects from other genres such as **War** or **Political Drama** to use as motivation for explosive action and derring-do. If **ACTION/ADVENTURE** incorporates ideas such as destiny, hubris, or the spiritual, it becomes the subgenre **High Adventure:** THE MAN WHO WOULD BE KING. If Mother Nature is the source of antagonism, it's a **Disaster/Survival Film:** ALIVE, THE POSEIDON ADVENTURE.

Taking a still wider view, supra-genres are created out of settings, performance styles, or filmmaking techniques that contain a host of autonomous genres. They are like mansions of many rooms where one of the basic genres, subgenres, or any combination might find a home:

16. **HISTORICAL DRAMA.** History is an inexhaustible source of story material and embraces every type of story imaginable. The treasure chest of history, however, is sealed with this warning: What is past must be present. A screenwriter isn't a poet hoping to be discovered after he's dead. He must find an audience today. Therefore, the best use of history, and the only legitimate excuse to set a film in the past and thereby add untold millions to the budget, is anachronism—to use the past as a clear glass through which you show us the present.

   Many contemporary antagonisms are so distressing or loaded with controversy that it's difficult to dramatize them in a present-day setting without alienating the audience. Such dilemmas are often best viewed at a safe distance in time. **HISTORICAL DRAMA** polishes the past into a mirror of the present, making clear and bearable the painful problems of racism in GLORY, religious strife in MICHAEL COLLINS, or violence of all kinds, especially against women, in UNFORGIVEN.

   Christopher Hampton's DANGEROUS LIAISONS: Setting a down ending, love/hate story in the France of lace cuffs and piquant repartee seemed like protocol for commercial disaster. But the film found a huge audience by turning a scalding light on a mode of modern hostility too politically sensitive to be addressed directly: courtship as combat. Hampton stepped back two centuries to an age in which sexual politics exploded into a war for sexual supremacy, where the ascendant emotion was not love but fear and suspicion of the opposite sex. Despite the antiquated setting, within minutes the audience felt intimately at home with its corrupted aristocrats—they are us.

17. **BIOGRAPHY.** This cousin to **Historical Drama** focuses on a person rather than an era. **BIOGRAPHY,** however, must never become a simple chronicle. That someone lived, died, and did interesting things in between is of scholarly interest and no more. The biographer must interpret facts as if they were fiction, find the meaning of the subject's life, and then cast him as the protagonist of his life's genre: YOUNG MR. LINCOLN defends the innocent in a **Courtroom Drama;** GANDHI becomes the hero of a **Modern Epic;** ISADORA succumbs to a **Disillusionment Plot;** NIXON suffers in a **Punitive Plot.**

These caveats apply equally to the subgenre **Autobiography.** This idiom is popular with filmmakers who feel that they should write a film about a subject they know. And rightly so. But autobiographical films often lack the very virtue they promise: self-knowledge. For while it's true that the unexamined life is not worth living, it's also the case that the unlived life isn't worth examining. BIG WEDNESDAY, for example.

18. **DOCU-DRAMA.** A second cousin to **Historical Drama,** **DOCU-DRAMA** centers on recent rather than past events. Once invigorated by cinema verité—BATTLE OF ALGIERS—it's become a popular TV genre, sometimes powerful, but often with little documentary value.

19. **MOCKUMENTARY.** This genre pretends to be rooted in actuality or memory, behaves like documentary or autobiography, but is utter fiction. It subverts fact-based filmmaking to satirize hypocritical institutions: the backstage world of rock 'n' roll in THIS IS SPINAL TAP; the Catholic Church in ROMA; middle-class mores in ZELIG; TV journalism in MAN BITES DOG; politics in BOB ROBERTS; crass American values in TO DIE FOR.

20. **MUSICAL.** Descended from opera, this genre presents a "reality" in which characters sing and dance their stories. It's often a **Love Story,** but it can be **Film Noir:** the stage adaptation of SUNSET BOULEVARD; **Social Drama:**

WEST SIDE STORY; **Punitive Plot:** ALL THAT JAZZ; **Biography:** EVITA. Indeed, any genre can work in musical form and all can be satirized in **Musical Comedy.**

21. **SCIENCE FICTION.** In hypothetical futures that are typically technological dystopias of tyranny and chaos, the **SCIENCE FICTION** writer often marries the man-against-state **Modern Epic** with **Action/Adventure:** the STAR WARS trilogy and TOTAL RECALL. But, like history, the future is a setting in which any genre may play. In SOLARIS, for example, Andrei Tarkovsky used sci-fi to act out the inner conflicts of a **Disillusionment Plot.**

22. **SPORTS GENRE.** Sport is a crucible for character change. This genre is a natural home for the **Maturation Plot:** NORTH DALLAS FORTY; the **Redemption Plot:** SOME- BODY UP THERE LIKES ME; the **Education Plot:** BULL DURHAM; the **Punitive Plot:** RAGING BULL; the **Testing Plot:** CHARIOTS OF FIRE; the **Disillusionment Plot:** THE LONELINESS OF THE LONG DISTANCE RUNNER; **Buddy Salvation:** WHITE MEN CAN'T JUMP; **Social Drama:** A LEAGUE OF THEIR OWN.

23. **FANTASY.** Here the writer plays with time, space, and the physical, bending and mixing the laws of nature and the supernatural. The extra-realities of **FANTASY** attract the **Action** genres but also welcome others such as the **Love Story:** SOMEWHERE IN TIME; **Political Drama/ Allegory:** ANIMAL FARM; **Social Drama:** IF . . . ; **Maturation Plot:** ALICE IN WONDERLAND.

24. **ANIMATION.** Here the law of universal metamorphism rules: Anything can become something else. Like **Fantasy** and **Science Fiction, ANIMATION** leans toward the **Action** genres of cartoon **Farce:** BUGS BUNNY; or **High Adventure:** THE SWORD IN THE STONE, THE YELLOW SUBMARINE; and because the youth audience is its natural market, many **Maturation Plots:** THE LION KING, THE LITTLE MERMAID; but as the animators of Eastern Europe and Japan have shown, there are no restraints.

Lastly, for those who believe that genres and their conventions are concerns of "commercial" writers only, and that serious art is nongeneric, let me add one last name to the list:

25. **ART FILM.** The avant-garde notion of writing outside the genres is naive. No one writes in a vacuum. After thousands of years of storytelling no story is so different that it has no similarity to anything else ever written. The **ART FILM** has become a traditional genre, divisible into two subgenres, **Minimalism** and **Antistructure,** each with its own complex of formal conventions of structure and cosmology. Like **Historical Drama,** the **ART FILM** is a supra-genre that embraces other basic genres: **Love Story, Political Drama,** and the like.

Although this slate is reasonably comprehensive, no list can ever be definitive or exhaustive because the lines between genres often overlap as they influence and merge with one another. Genres are not static or rigid, but evolving and flexible, yet firm and stable enough to be identified and worked with, much as a composer plays with the malleable movements of musical genres.

Each writer's homework is first to identify his genre, then research its governing practices. And there's no escaping these tasks. We're all genre writers.

THE RELATIONSHIP BETWEEN STRUCTURE AND GENRE

Each genre imposes conventions on story design: conventional value-charges at climax such as the down-ending of the *Disillusionment Plot;* conventional settings such as the *Western;* conventional events such as boy-meets-girl in the *Love Story;* conventional roles such as the criminal in a *Crime Story.* The audience knows these conventions and expects to see them fulfilled. Consequently, the choice of genre sharply determines and limits what's possible within a story, as its design must envision the audience's knowledge and anticipations.

GENRE CONVENTIONS are specific settings, roles, events, and values that define individual genres and their sub-genres.

Each genre has unique conventions, but in some these are relatively uncomplicated and pliable. The primary convention of the *Disillusionment Plot* is a protagonist who opens the story filled with optimism, who holds high ideals or beliefs, whose view of life is positive. Its second convention is a pattern of repeatedly negative story turns that may at first raise his hopes, but ultimately poison his dreams and values, leaving him deeply cynical and disillusioned. The protagonist of THE CONVERSATION, for example, begins with an orderly, secure hold on life and ends in a paranoid nightmare. This simple set of conventions offers uncountable possibilities, for life knows a thousand paths to hopelessness. Among the many memorable films in this genre are THE MISFITS, LA DOLCE VITA, and LENNY.

Other genres are relatively inflexible and filled with a complex of rigid conventions. In the *Crime Genre* there must be a crime; it must happen early in the telling. There must be a detective character, professional or amateur, who discovers clues and suspects. In the *Thriller* the criminal must "make it personal." Although the story may start with a cop who works for a paycheck, to deepen the drama, at some point, the criminal goes over the line. Clichés grow like fungus around this convention: The criminal menaces the family of the cop or turns the cop himself into a suspect; or, cliché of clichés with roots back to THE MALTESE FALCON, he kills the detective's partner. Ultimately, the cop must identify, apprehend, and punish the criminal.

Comedy contains myriad subgenres as well, each with its own conventions, but one overriding convention unites this mega-genre and distinguishes it from drama: *Nobody gets hurt.* In *Comedy*, the audience must feel that no matter how characters bounce off walls, no matter how they scream and writhe under the whips of life, it doesn't really hurt. Buildings may fall on Laurel and Hardy, but they get up out of the rubble, dust themselves off, mutter, "Now, what a fine mess . . ." and on they go.

In A FISH CALLED WANDA Ken (Michael Palin), a character with an obsessive love of animals, tries to kill an old lady but accidentally kills her pet terriers instead. The last dog dies under a massive construction block with his little paw left sticking out. Charles Crichton, the director, shot two versions of this moment: one showing only the paw, but for the second he sent to a butcher's shop for a bag of entrails and added a trail of gore draining away from the squashed terrier. When this gory image flashed in front of preview audiences, the theatre fell dead quiet. The blood and guts said: "It hurt." For general release Crichton switched to the sanitized shot and got his laugh. By genre convention, the comedy writer walks the line between putting characters through the torments of hell while safely reassuring the audience that the flames don't really burn.

Across that line waits the subgenre of *Black Comedy*. Here the writer bends comic convention and allows his audience to feel sharp, but not unbearable, pain: THE LOVED ONE, THE WAR OF THE ROSES, PRIZZI'S HONOR—films in which laughter often chokes us.

Art Films are conventionalized by a number of external practices such as the absence of stars (or stars' salaries), production outside the Hollywood system, generally in a language other than English—all of which become sales points as the marketing team encourages critics to champion the film as an underdog. Its primary internal conventions are, first, a celebration of the cerebral. The *Art Film* favors the intellect by smothering strong emotion under a blanket of mood, while through enigma, symbolism, or unresolved tensions it invites interpretation and analysis in the postfilm ritual of cafe criticism. Secondly and essentially, the story design of an *Art Film* depends on one grand convention: unconventionality. *Minimalist* and/or *Antistructure* unconventionality is the *Art Film*'s distinguishing convention.

Success in the *Art Film* genre usually results in instant, though often temporary, recognition as an artist. On the other hand, the durable Alfred Hitchcock worked solely within the Archplot and genre convention, always aimed for a mass audience, and habitually found it. Yet today he stands atop the pantheon of filmmakers, worshipped worldwide as one of the century's major artists, a film poet whose works resonate with sublime images of sexuality, religiosity, and subtleties of point of view. Hitchcock knew that *there is no necessary contradiction between art and popular success, nor a necessary connection between art and Art Film.*

MASTERY OF GENRE

Each of us owes an enormous debt to the great story traditions. You must not only respect but master your genre and its conventions. Never assume that because you've seen films in your genre you know it. This is like assuming you could compose a symphony because you have heard all nine of Beethoven's. You must study the form. Books of genre criticism may help, but few are current and none is complete. Read everything, nonetheless, for we need all possible help from wherever we can get it. The most valuable insights, however, come from self-discovery; nothing ignites the imagination like the unearthing of buried treasure.

Genre study is best done in this fashion: First, list all those works you feel are like yours, both successes and failures. (The study of failures is illuminating . . . and humbling.) Next, rent the films on video and purchase the screenplays if possible. Then study the films stop and go, turning pages with the screen, breaking each film down into elements of setting, role, event, and value. Lastly, stack, so to speak, these analyses one atop the other and look down through them all asking: What do the stories in my genre always do? What are its conventions of time, place, character, and action? Until you discover answers, the audience will always be ahead of you.

To anticipate the anticipations of the audience you must master your genre and its conventions.

If a film has been properly promoted, the audience arrives filled with expectancy. In the jargon of marketing pros, it's been "positioned." "Positioning the audience" means this: We don't want people coming to our work cold and vague, not knowing what to expect, forcing us to spend the first twenty minutes of screentime clueing them toward the necessary story attitude. We want them to settle into their seats, warm and focused with an appetite we intend to satisfy.

Positioning of the audience is nothing new. Shakespeare didn't call his play *Hamlet*; he called it *The Tragedy of Hamlet, Prince of Denmark*. He gave comedies titles such as *Much Ado About Nothing* and *All's Well That Ends Well*, so that each afternoon at the Globe Theatre his Elizabethan audience was psychologically set to cry or laugh.

Skillful marketing creates genre expectation. From the title to the poster through print and TV ads, promotion seeks to fix the type of story in the mind of the audience. Having told our filmgoers to expect a favorite form, we must deliver as promised. If we botch genre by omitting or misusing conventions, the audience knows instantly and badmouths our work.

For example, the marketing of the unfortunately titled MIKE'S MURDER (USA/1984) positioned the audience to a *Murder Mystery*. The film, however, is in another genre, and for over an hour the audience sat wondering, "Who the hell dies in this movie?" The screenplay is a fresh take on the *Maturation Plot* as it arcs Debra Winger's bank teller from dependency and immaturity to self-possession and maturity. But the sour word-of-mouth of a mispositioned and confused audience cut the "legs" out from under an otherwise good film.

CREATIVE LIMITATIONS

Robert Frost said that writing free verse is like playing tennis with the net down, for it's the self-imposed, indeed artificial demands of poetic conventions that stir the imagination. Let's say a poet arbitrarily imposes this limit: He decides to write in six-line stanzas, rhyming every other line. After rhyming the fourth line with the second line he reaches the end of a stanza. Backed into this corner, his struggle to rhyme the sixth line with the fourth and second may inspire him to imagine a word that has no relationship to his poem whatsoever—it just happens to rhyme—but this random word then springs loose a phrase that in turn brings an image to mind, an image that in turn resonates back through the first five lines, triggering a whole new sense and feeling, twisting and driving the poem to a richer meaning and emotion. Thanks to the poet's Creative Limitation of this rhyme scheme, the poem achieves an intensity it would have lacked had the poet allowed himself the freedom to choose any word he wished.

The principle of Creative Limitation calls for freedom within a circle of obstacles. Talent is like a muscle: without something to push against, it atrophies. So we deliberately put rocks in our path, barriers that inspire. We discipline ourselves as to what to do, while we're boundless as to how to do it. One of our first steps, therefore, is to identify the genre or combination of genres that govern our work, for the stony ground that grows the most fruitful ideas is genre convention.

Genre conventions are the rhyme scheme of a storyteller's "poem." They do not inhibit creativity, they inspire it. The challenge is to keep convention but avoid cliché. That boy meets girl in a *Love Story* is not a cliché but a necessary element of form—a convention. The cliché is that they meet as *Love Story* lovers have always met: Two dynamic individualists are forced to share an adventure and seem to hate each other on sight; or two shy souls, each carrying the torch for someone who won't give them the time of day, find themselves shunted to the edge of a party with no one else to talk to, and so on.

Genre convention is a *Creative Limitation* that forces the writer's imagination to rise to the occasion. Rather than deny convention and flatten the story, the fine writer calls on conventions like old friends, knowing that in the struggle to fulfill them in a unique way, he may find inspiration for the scene that will lift his story above the ordinary. With mastery of genre we can guide audiences through rich, creative variations on convention to reshape and exceed expectations by giving the audience not only what it had hoped for but, if we're very good, more than it could have imagined.

Consider *Action/Adventure*. Often dismissed as mindless fare, it is in fact the single most difficult genre in which to write today . . . simply because it's been done to death. What is an *Action* writer to do that the audience hasn't seen a thousand times before? For example, chief among its many conventions is this scene: *The hero is at the mercy of the villain.* The hero, from a position of helplessness, must turn the tables on the villain. This scene is imperative. It tests and expresses in absolute terms the protagonist's ingenuity, strength of will, and cool under pressure. Without it both the protagonist and his story are diminished; the audience leaves dissatisfied. Clichés grow on this convention like mold on bread, but when its solution is fresh, the telling is much enhanced.

In RAIDERS OF THE LOST ARK, Indiana Jones comes face to face with an Egyptian giant wielding a massive scimitar. A look of terror, then a shrug and a quick bullet as Jones remembers he is carrying a gun. The behind-the-screen legend is that Harrison Ford suggested this much-loved solution because he was too sick with dysentery to take on the acrobatic fight Lawrence Kasdan had scripted.

DIE HARD climaxes around this graceful execution of the convention: John McClane (Bruce Willis), stripped to the waist, weaponless, his hands in the air, is face to face with the sadistic and well-armed Hans Gruber (Alan Rickman). Slowly, however, as the camera tracks around McClane we discover that he's duct-taped a gun to his naked back. He distracts Gruber with a joke, snatches the gun from his back, and kills him.

Of all the hero-at-the-mercy-of-the-villain clichés, "Look out! There's somebody behind you!" is the most archaic. But in MIDNIGHT RUN screenwriter George Gallo gave it new life and delight by riffing lunatic variations in scene after scene.

MIXING GENRES

Genres are frequently combined to resonate with meaning, to enrich character, and to create varieties of mood and emotion. A *Love Story* subplot, for example, finds its way inside almost any *Crime Story.* THE FISHER KING wove five threads—*Redemption Plot, Psycho-Drama, Love Story, Social Drama, Comedy*—into an excellent film. The *Musical Horror Film* was a delicious invention. Given over two dozen principal genres, possibilities for inventive cross-breeding are endless. In this way the writer in command of genre may create a type of film the world has never seen.

REINVENTING GENRES

Equally, mastery of genre keeps the screenwriter contemporary. For the genre conventions are not carved in stone; they evolve, grow, adapt, modify, and break apace with the changes in society. Society changes slowly, but it does change, and as society enters each new phase, the genres transform with it. For genres are simply windows on reality, various ways for the writer to look at life. When the reality outside the window undergoes change, the genres alter with it. If not, if a genre becomes inflexible and cannot bend with the changing world, it petrifies. Below are three examples of genre evolution.

The Western

The *Western* began as morality plays set in the "Old West," a mythical golden age for allegories of good versus evil. But in the cynical atmosphere of the 1970s the genre became dated and stale. When Mel Brooks's BLAZING SADDLES exposed the *Western's* fascist heart, the genre went into virtual hibernation for twenty years before making a comeback by altering its conventions. In the 1980s the *Western* modulated into quasi-*Social Drama*, a corrective to racism and violence: DANCES WITH WOLVES, UNFORGIVEN, POSSE.

The Psycho-Drama

Clinical insanity was first dramatized in the UFA silent THE CABINET OF DR. CALIGARI (Germany/1919). As psychoanalysis grew in reputation, *Psycho-Drama* developed as a kind of a Freudian detective story. In its first stage, a psychiatrist played "detective" to investigate a hidden "crime," a deeply repressed trauma his patient has suffered in the past. Once the psychiatrist exposed this "crime," the victim was either restored to sanity or took a major step toward it: SYBIL, THE SNAKE PIT, THE THREE FACES OF EVE, I

NEVER PROMISED YOU A ROSE GARDEN, THE MARK, DAVID AND LISA, EQUUS.

However, as the serial killer began to haunt society's nightmares, genre evolution took *Psycho-Drama* to its second stage, merging it with the *Detective Genre* into the subgenre known as the *Psycho-Thriller*. In these cops became lay psychiatrists to hunt down psychopaths, and apprehension hinged on the detective's psychoanalysis of the madman: THE FIRST DEADLY SIN, MAN-HUNTER, COP, and, recently, SEVEN.

In the 1980s the *Psycho-Thriller* evolved a third time. In films such as TIGHTROPE, LETHAL WEAPON, ANGEL HEART, and THE MORNING AFTER, the detective himself became the psycho, suffering from a wide variety of modern maladies—sexual obsession, suicidal impulse, traumatic amnesia, alcoholism. In these films the key to justice became the cop's psychoanalysis of himself. Once the detective came to terms with his inner demons, apprehending the criminal was almost an afterthought.

This evolution was a telling statement about our changing society. Gone was the day when we could comfort ourselves with the notion that all the crazy people were locked up, while we sane people were safely outside the asylum walls. Few of us are so naive today. We know that, given a certain conjunction of events, we too could part company with reality. These *Psycho-Thrillers* spoke to this threat, to our realization that our toughest task in life is self-analysis as we try to fathom our humanity and bring peace to the wars within.

By 1990 the genre reached its fourth stage by relocating the psychopath once again, now placing him in your spouse, psychiatrist, surgeon, child, nanny, roommate, neighborhood cop. These films tap communal paranoia, as we discover that the people most intimate in our lives, people we must trust, those we hope will protect us, are maniacs: THE HAND THAT ROCKS THE CRADLE, SLEEPING WITH THE ENEMY, FORCED ENTRY, WHISPERS IN THE DARK, SINGLE WHITE FEMALE, and THE GOOD SON. Most telling of all perhaps is DEAD RINGERS, a film about the ultimate fear: the fear of the person closest to you—yourself.

What horror will crawl up from your unconscious to steal your sanity?

The Love Story

The most important question we ask when writing a *Love Story* is: "What's to stop them?" For where's the story in a *Love Story*? Two people meet, fall in love, marry, raise a family, support each other till death do them part . . . what could be more boring than that? So, for over two thousand years, since the Greek dramatist Menander, writers answered the question with "the parents of the girl." Her parents find the young man unsuitable and become the convention known as Blocking Characters or "the force opposed to love." Shakespeare expanded it to both sets of parents in *Romeo and Juliet*. From 2300 B.C. this essential convention went unchanged . . . until the twentieth century launched the romantic revolution.

The twentieth century has been an Age of Romance like no other. The idea of romantic love (with sex as its implicit partner) dominates popular music, advertising, and Western culture in general. Over the decades, the automobile, telephone, and a thousand other liberating factors have given young lovers greater and greater freedom from parental control. Meanwhile, parents, thanks to the rampant rise in adultery, divorce, and remarriage, have extended romance from a youthful fling to a lifelong pursuit. It's always been the case that young people don't listen to their parents, but today, if a movie Mom and Dad were to object, and the teenage lovers were actually to obey them, the audience would blister the screen with jeers. So, as the-parents-of-the-girl convention faded along with arranged marriages, resourceful writers unearthed a new and amazing array of forces that oppose love.

In THE GRADUATE the Blocking Characters were the conventional parents of the girl but for a very unconventional reason. In WITNESS the force that opposes love is her culture—she's Amish, virtually from another world. In MRS. SOFFEL, Mel Gibson plays an imprisoned murderer condemned to hang and Diane Keaton is the wife of the prison's warden. What is to stop them? All members of "right-thinking" society. In WHEN HARRY MET SALLY, the lovers suffer from the absurd belief that friendship and love are incompatible. In LONE STAR, the blocking force is racism; in THE CRYING GAME, sexual identity; in GHOST, death.

The enthusiasm for romance that opened this century has turned at its close to deep malaise that brings with it a dark, skeptical attitude toward love. In response, we've seen the rise and surprising popularity of down-endings: DANGEROUS LIAISONS, THE BRIDGES OF MADISON COUNTY, THE REMAINS OF THE DAY, HUSBANDS AND WIVES. In LEAVING LAS VEGAS, Ben's a suicidal alcoholic, Sera's a masochistic prostitute, and their love is "star-crossed." These films speak to a growing sense of the hopelessness, if not impossibility, of a lasting love.

To achieve an up-ending some recent films have retooled the genre into the *Longing Story*. Boy-meets-girl has always been an irreducible convention that occurs early in the telling, to be followed by the trials, tribulations, and triumphs of love. But SLEEP-LESS IN SEATTLE and RED end on boy-meets-girl. The audience waits to see how the lovers' "fate" will be shaped in the hands of chance. By cleverly delaying the lovers' meeting to climax, these films avoid the prickly issues of modern love by replacing the difficulty of love with the difficulty of meeting. These aren't love stories but stories of longing, as talk about and desire for love fills the scenes, leaving genuine acts of love and their often troubling consequences to happen in an offscreen future. It may be that the twentieth century gave birth to, then buried, the Age of Romance.

The lesson is this: Social attitudes change. The cultural antenna of the writer must be alert to these movements or risk writing an antique. For example: In FALLING IN LOVE the force that opposes love is that the lovers are each married to someone else. The only tears in the audience came from yawning too hard. One could almost hear their thoughts screaming, "What's your problem? You're married to stiffs. Dump them. Does the word 'divorce' mean anything to you people?"

Through the 1950s, however, a love affair across marriages was seen as a painful betrayal. Many poignant films—STRANGERS

WHEN WE MEET, BRIEF ENCOUNTER—drew their energy from society's antagonism to adultery. But by the 1980s attitudes had shifted, giving rise to the feeling that romance is so precious and life so short, if two married people want to have an affair, let them. Right or wrong, that was the temperament of the time, so that a film with antiquated 1950s values brutally bored the 1980s audience. The audience wants to know how it feels to be alive on the knife edge of the now. What does it mean to be a human being today?

Innovative writers are not only contemporary, they are visionary. They have their ear to the wall of history, and as things change, they can sense the way society is leaning toward the future. They then produce works that break convention and take the genres into their next generation.

This, for example, is one of the many beauties of CHINATOWN. In the climax of all previous *Murder Mysteries* the detective apprehends and punishes the criminal, but CHINATOWN's wealthy and politically powerful killer gets away with it, breaking an honored convention. This film could not have been made, however, until the 1970s when the civil rights movement, Watergate, and the Vietnam War woke America up to the depth of its corruption and the nation realized that indeed the rich were getting away with murder . . . and much more. CHINATOWN rewrote the genre, opening the door to down-ending crime stories such as BODY HEAT, CRIMES AND MISDEMEANORS, Q & A, BASIC INSTINCT, THE LAST SEDUCTION, and SEVEN.

The finest writers are not only visionary, they create classics. Each genre involves crucial human values: love/hate, peace/war, justice/injustice, achievement/failure, good/evil, and the like. Each of these values is an ageless theme that has inspired great writing since the dawn of story. From year to year these values must be reworked to keep them alive and meaningful for the contemporary audience. Yet the greatest stories are always contemporary. They are classics. A classic is reexperienced with pleasure because it can be reinterpreted through the decades, because in it truth and humanity are so abundant that each new generation finds itself mirrored in the story. CHINATOWN is such a work. With an absolute command of genre Towne and Polanski took their talents to a height few have reached before or since.

THE GIFT OF ENDURANCE

Mastery of genre is essential for yet one more reason: Screenwriting is not for sprinters, but for long-distance runners. No matter what you've heard about scripts dashed off over a weekend at poolside, from first inspiration to last polished draft, a quality screenplay consumes six months, nine months, a year, or more. Writing a film demands the same creative labor in terms of world, character, and story as a four-hundred-page novel. The only substantive difference is the number of words used in the telling. A screenplay's painstaking economy of language demands sweat and time, while the freedom to fill pages with prose often makes the task easier, even faster. All writing is discipline, but screenwriting is a drill sergeant. Ask yourself, therefore, what will keep your desire burning over those many months?

Generally, great writers are not eclectic. Each tightly focuses his oeuvre on one idea, a single subject that ignites his passion, a subject he pursues with beautiful variation through a lifetime of work. Hemingway, for example, was fascinated with the question of how to face death. After he witnessed the suicide of his father, it became the central theme, not only of his writing, but of his life. He chased death in war, in sport, on safari, until finally, putting a shotgun in his mouth, he found it. Charles Dickens, whose father was imprisoned for debt, wrote of the lonely child searching for the lost father over and over in *David Copperfield*, *Oliver Twist*, and *Great Expectations*. Molière turned a critical eye on the idiocy and depravity of seventeenth-century France and made a career writing plays whose titles read like a checklist of human vices: *The Miser*, *The Misanthrope*, *The Hypochondriac*. Each of these authors found his subject and it sustained him over the long journey of the writer.

What is yours? Do you, like Hemingway and Dickens, work directly from the life you've lived? Or, like Molière, do you write about your ideas of society and human nature? Whatever your source of inspiration, beware of this: Long before you finish, the love of self will rot and die, the love of ideas sicken and perish. You'll become so tired and bored with writing about yourself or your ideas, you may not finish the race.

So, in addition, ask: What's my favorite genre? Then write in the genre you love. For although the passion for an idea or experience may wither, the love of the movies is forever. Genre should be a constant source of reinspiration. Every time you reread your script, it should excite you, for this is your kind of story, the kind of film you'd stand in line in the rain to see. Do not write something because intellectual friends think it's socially important. Do not write something you think will inspire critical praise in *Film Quarterly*. Be honest in your choice of genre, for of all the reasons for wanting to write, the only one that nurtures us through time is love of the work itself.

5

STRUCTURE
AND CHARACTER

Plot or character? Which is more important? This debate is as old as the art. Aristotle weighed each side and concluded that story is primary, character secondary. His view held sway until, with the evolution of the novel, the pendulum of opinion swung the other way. By the nineteenth century many held that structure is merely an appliance designed to display personality, that what the reader wants is fascinating, complex characters. Today both sides continue the debate without a verdict. The reason for the hung jury is simple: The argument is specious.

We cannot ask which is more important, structure or character, because structure *is* character; character *is* structure. They're the same thing, and therefore one cannot be more important than the other. Yet the argument goes on because of a widely held confusion over two crucial aspects of the fictional role—the difference between *Character* and *Characterization*.

CHARACTER VERSUS CHARACTERIZATION

Characterization is the sum of all observable qualities of a human being, everything knowable through careful scrutiny: age and IQ; sex and sexuality; style of speech and gesture; choices of home, car, and dress; education and occupation; personality and nervosity; values and attitudes—all aspects of humanity we could know by taking notes on someone day in and day out. The totality of these traits

makes each person unique because each of us is a one-of-a-kind combination of genetic givens and accumulated experience. This singular
assemblage of traits is *characterization* . . . but it is not *character*.

> **TRUE CHARACTER** is revealed in the choices a human
> being makes under pressure—the greater the pressure,
> the deeper the revelation, the truer the choice to the
> character's essential nature.

Beneath the surface of characterization, regardless of appearances, who is this person? At the heart of his humanity, what will
we find? Is he loving or cruel? Generous or selfish? Strong or
weak? Truthful or a liar? Courageous or cowardly? The *only* way to
know the truth is to witness him make choices under pressure to
take one action or another in the pursuit of his desire. As he
chooses, he is.

Pressure is essential. Choices made when nothing is at risk
mean little. If a character chooses to tell the truth in a situation
where telling a lie would gain him nothing, the choice is trivial, the
moment expresses nothing. But if the same character insists on
telling the truth when a lie would save his life, then we sense that
honesty is at the core of his nature.

Consider this scene: Two cars motor down a highway. One is a
rusted-out station wagon with buckets, mops, and brooms in the
back. Driving it is an illegal alien—a quiet, shy woman working as
a domestic for under-the-table cash, sole support of her family.
Alongside her is a glistening new Porsche driven by a brilliant and
wealthy neurosurgeon. Two people who have utterly different backgrounds, beliefs, personalities, languages—in every way imaginable their *characterizations* are the opposite of each other.

Suddenly, in front of them, a school bus full of children flips
out of control, smashes against an underpass, bursting into flames,
trapping the children inside. Now, under this terrible pressure,
we'll find out who these two people really are.

Who chooses to stop? Who chooses to drive by? Each has ratio-
nalizations for driving by. The domestic worries that if she gets

caught up in this, the police might question her, find out she's an illegal, throw her back across the border, and her family will starve. The surgeon fears that if he's injured and his hands burned, hands that perform miraculous microsurgeries, the lives of thousands of future patients will be lost. But let's say they both hit the brakes and stop.

This choice gives us a clue to character, but who's stopping to help, and who's become too hysterical to drive any farther? Let's say they both choose to help. This tells us more. But who chooses to help by calling for an ambulance and waiting? Who chooses to help by dashing into the burning bus? Let's say they both rush for the bus—a choice that reveals character in even greater depth.

Now doctor and housekeeper smash windows, crawl inside the blazing bus, grab screaming children, and push them to safety. But their choices aren't over. Soon the flames surge into a blistering inferno, skin peels from their faces. They can't take another breath without searing their lungs. In the midst of this horror each realizes there's only a second left to rescue one of the many children still inside. How does the doctor react? In a sudden reflex does he reach for a white child or the black child closer to him? Which way do the housekeeper's instincts take her? Does she save the little boy? Or the little girl cowering at her feet? How does she make "Sophie's choice"?

We may discover that deep within these utterly different characterizations is an identical humanity—both willing to give their lives in a heartbeat for strangers. Or it may turn out that the person we thought would act heroically is a coward. Or the one we thought would act cowardly is a hero. Or at rock bottom, we may discover that selfless heroism is not the limit of true character in either of them. For the unseen power of their acculturation may force each to a spontaneous choice that exposes unconscious prejudices of gender or ethnicity . . . even while they are performing acts of saintlike courage. Whichever way the scene's written, choice under pressure will strip away the mask of characterization, we'll peer into their inner natures and with a flash of insight grasp their true characters.

CHARACTER REVELATION

The revelation of true character in contrast or contradiction to characterization is fundamental to all fine storytelling. Life teaches this grand principle: What *seems* is not what *is*. People are not what they appear to be. A hidden nature waits concealed behind a facade of traits. No matter what they say, no matter how they comport themselves, the only way we ever come to know characters in depth is through their choices under pressure.

If we're introduced to a character whose demeanor is "loving husband," and by the end of the tale he's still what he first appeared to be, a loving husband with no secrets, no unfulfilled dreams, no hidden passions, we'll be very disappointed. When characterization and true character match, when inner life and outer appearance are, like a block of cement, of one substance, the role becomes a list of repetitious, predictable behaviors. It's not as if such a character isn't credible. Shallow, nondimensional people exist . . . but they are boring.

For example: What went wrong with Rambo? In FIRST BLOOD he was a compelling character—a Vietnam burnout, a loner hiking through the mountains, seeking solitude (characterization). Then a sheriff, for no reason other than wickedly high levels of testosterone, provoked him, and out came Rambo, a ruthless and unstoppable killer (true character). But once Rambo came out, he wouldn't go back in. For the sequels, he strapped bandoleers of bullets across his oiled, pumped muscles, coiffed his locks with a red bandanna until super-hero characterization and true character merged into a figure with less dimension than a Saturday morning cartoon.

Compare that flat pattern to James Bond. Three seems to be the limit on Rambos, but there have been nearly twenty Bond films. Bond goes on and on because the world delights in the repeated revelation of a deep character that contradicts characterization. Bond enjoys playing the lounge lizard: Dressed in a tuxedo, he graces posh parties, a cocktail glass dangling from his fingertips as he chats up beautiful women. But then story pressure builds and Bond's choices reveal that underneath his lounge lizard exterior is a thinking man's Rambo. This exposé of witty super-hero in contradiction to playboy characterization has become a seemingly endless pleasure.

Taking the principle further: The revelation of deep character in contrast or contradiction to characterization is fundamental in major characters. Minor roles may or may not need hidden dimensions, but principals must be written in depth—they cannot be at heart what they seem to be at face.

CHARACTER ARC

Taking the principle further yet: The finest writing not only reveals true character, but arcs or changes that inner nature, for better or worse, over the course of the telling.

In THE VERDICT, protagonist Frank Galvin first appears as a Boston attorney, dressed in a three-piece suit and looking like Paul Newman . . . unfairly handsome. David Mamet's screenplay then peels back this characterization to reveal a corrupt, bankrupt, self-destructive, irretrievable drunk who hasn't won a case for years. Divorce and disgrace have broken his spirit. We see him searching obituaries for people who have died in automobile or industrial accidents, then going to the funerals of these unfortunates to pass out his business card to grieving relatives, hoping to drum up some insurance litigation. This sequence culminates in a rage of drunken self-loathing as he trashes his office, rips the diplomas off the walls, and smashes them before collapsing in a heap. But then comes the case.

He's offered a medical malpractice suit to defend a woman lost in a coma. With a quick settlement, he'd make seventy thousand dollars. But as he looks at his client in her helpless state, he senses that what this case offers is not a fat, easy fee, but his last chance for salvation. He chooses to take on the Catholic Church and the political establishment, fighting not only for his client but for his own soul. With victory comes resurrection. The legal battle changes him into a sober, ethical, and excellent attorney—the kind of man he once was before he lost his will to live.

This is the play between character and structure seen throughout the history of fiction. First, the story lays out the protagonist's characterization: Home from the university for the funeral of his father, Hamlet is melancholy and confused, wishing he were dead: "Oh, that this too too solid flesh would melt . . . "

Second, we're soon led into the heart of the character. His true nature is revealed as he chooses to take one action over another: The ghost of Hamlet's father claims he was murdered by Hamlet's uncle, Claudius, who has now become king. Hamlet's choices expose a highly intelligent and cautious nature battling to restrain his rash, passionate immaturity. He decides to seek revenge, but not until he can prove the King's guilt: "I will speak daggers . . . but use none."

Third, this deep nature is at odds with the outer countenance of the character, contrasting with it, if not contradicting it. We sense that he is not what he appears to be. He's not merely sad, sensitive, and cautious. Other qualities wait hidden beneath his persona. Hamlet: "I am but mad north-north-west; when the wind is southerly I know a hawk from a handsaw."

Fourth, having exposed the character's inner nature, the story puts greater and greater pressure on him to make more and more difficult choices: Hamlet hunts for his father's killer and finds him on his knees in prayer. He could easily kill the King, but Hamlet realizes that if Claudius dies in prayer, his soul might go to heaven. So Hamlet forces himself to wait and kill Claudius when the King's soul is "as damned and black as Hell whereto it goes."

Fifth, by the climax of the story, these choices have profoundly changed the humanity of the character: Hamlet's wars, known and unknown, come to an end. He reaches a peaceful maturity as his lively intelligence ripens into wisdom: "The rest is silence."

STRUCTURE AND CHARACTER FUNCTIONS

The function of STRUCTURE is to provide progressively building pressures that force characters into more and more difficult dilemmas where they must make more and more difficult risk-taking choices and actions, grad-

ually revealing their true natures, even down to the unconscious self.

The function of CHARACTER is to bring to the story the qualities of characterization necessary to convincingly act out choices. Put simply, a character must be credible: young enough or old enough, strong or weak, worldly or naive, educated or ignorant, generous or selfish, witty or dull, in the right proportions. Each must bring to the story the combination of qualities that allows an audience to believe that the character could and would do what he does.

Structure and character are interlocked. The event structure of a story is created out of the choices that characters make under pressure and the actions they choose to take, while characters are the creatures who are revealed and changed by how they choose to act under pressure. If you change one, you change the other. If you change event design, you have also changed character; if you change deep character, you must reinvent the structure to express the character's changed nature.

Suppose a story contains a pivotal event in which the protagonist, at serious risk, chooses to tell the truth. But the writer feels the first draft doesn't work. While studying this scene in the rewrite, he decides that his character would lie and changes his story design by reversing that action. From one draft to the next the protagonist's characterization remains intact—he dresses the same, works the same job, laughs at the same jokes. But in the first draft he's an honest man. In the second, a liar. With the inversion of an event the writer creates a wholly new character.

Suppose, on the other hand, the process takes this path: The writer has a sudden insight into his protagonist's nature, inspiring him to sketch out a radically new psychological profile, transforming an honest man into a liar. To express a wholly changed nature the writer will have to do far more than rework the character's traits. A dark sense of humor might add texture but would never be enough. If story stays the same, character stays the same. If the writer reinvents character, he must reinvent story. A changed character must make new choices, take different actions, and live another story—his story. Whether our instincts work through character or structure, they ultimately meet at the same place.

For this reason the phrase "character-driven story" is redundant. All stories are "character-driven." Event design and character design mirror each other. Character cannot be expressed in depth except through the design of story.

The key is *appropriateness*.

The relative complexity of character must be adjusted to genre. *Action/Adventure* and *Farce* demand simplicity of character because complexity would distract us from the derring-do or pratfalls indispensable to those genres. Stories of personal and inner conflict, such as *Education* and *Redemption Plots*, demand complexity of character because simplicity would rob us of the insight into human nature requisite to those genres. This is common sense. So what does "character-driven" really mean? For too many writers it means "characterization driven," tissue-thin portraiture in which the mask may be well drawn but deep character is left underdeveloped and unexpressed.

CLIMAX AND CHARACTER

The interlock of structure and character seems neatly symmetrical until we come to the problem of endings. A revered Hollywood axiom warns: "Movies are about their last twenty minutes." In other words, for a film to have a chance in the world, the last act and its climax must be the most satisfying experience of all. For no matter what the first ninety minutes have achieved, if the final movement fails, the film will die over its opening weekend.

Compare two films: For the first eighty minutes of BLIND DATE Kim Basinger and Bruce Willis careened through this farce, exploding laugh after laugh. But with the Act Two climax all laughter ceased, Act Three fell flat, and what should have been a hit went south. KISS OF THE SPIDER WOMAN, on the other hand, opened with a tedious thirty or forty minutes, but gradually the film drew us into deep involvement and built pace until the Story Cimax moved us as few dramas do. Audiences who were bored at eight o'clock were elated at ten o'clock. Word-of-mouth gave the film legs; the Academy of Motion Picture Arts and Sciences voted William Hurt an Oscar.

Story is metaphor for life and life is lived in time. Film, therefore, is temporal art, not plastic art. Our cousins are not the spacial media of painting, sculpture, architecture, or still photography, but the temporal forms of music, dance, poetry, and song. And the first commandment of all temporal art is: Thou shalt save the best for last. The final movement of a ballet, the coda of a symphony, the couplet of a sonnet, the last act and its Story Climax—these culminating moments must be the most gratifying, meaningful experiences of all.

A finished screenplay represents, obviously, 100 percent of its author's creative labor. The vast majority of this work, 75 percent or more of our struggles, goes into designing the interlock of deep character to the invention and arrangement of events. The writing of dialogue and description consumes what's left. And of the overwhelming effort that goes into designing story, 75 percent of that is focused on creating the climax of the last act. The story's ultimate event is the writer's ultimate task.

Gene Fowler once said that writing is easy, just a matter of staring at the blank page until your forehead bleeds. And if anything will draw blood from your forehead, it's creating the climax of the last act—the pinnacle and concentration of all meaning and emotion, the fulfillment for which all else is preparation, the decisive center of audience satisfaction. If this scene fails, the story fails. Until you have created it, you don't have a story. If you fail to make the poetic leap to a brilliant culminating climax, all previous scenes, characters, dialogue, and description become an elaborate typing exercise.

Suppose you were to wake up one morning with the inspiration to write this Story Climax: "Hero and villain pursue each other on foot for three days and three nights across the Mojave Desert. On the brink of dehydration, exhaustion, and delirium, a hundred miles from the nearest water, they fight it out and one kills the other." It's thrilling . . . until you look back at your protagonist and remember that he's a seventy-five-year-old retired accountant, hobbled on crutches and allergic to dust. He'd turn your tragic climax into a joke. What's worse, your agent tells you Walter Matthau wants to play him as soon as you get the ending sorted out. What do you do?

Find the page where the protagonist is introduced, on it locate the phrase of description that reads "Jake (75)", then delete 7, insert 3. In other words, rework characterization. Deep character remains unchanged because whether Jake is thirty-five or seventy-five, he still has the will and tenacity to go to the limit in the Mojave. But you must make him credible.

In 1924 Erich von Stroheim made GREED. Its climax plays out over three days and three nights, hero and villain, across the Mojave Desert. Von Stroheim shot this sequence in the Mojave in high summer with temperatures rising to over 130 degrees Fahrenheit. He almost killed his cast and crew, but he got what he wanted: a white-on-white landscape of vast salt wastes extending to the horizon. Under the scorching sun, hero and villain, skin cracked and parched like the desert floor, grapple. In the struggle the villain grabs a rock and smashes in the skull of the hero. But as the hero dies, in his last moment of consciousness, he manages to reach up and handcuff himself to his killer. In the final image the villain collapses in the dust chained to the corpse he just killed.

GREED's brilliant ending is created out of ultimate choices that profoundly delineate its characters. Any aspect of characterization that undermines the credibility of such an action must be sacrificed. Plot, as Aristotle noted, is more important than characterization, but story structure and true character are one phenomenon seen from two points of view. The choices that characters make from behind their outer masks simultaneously shape their inner natures and propel the story. From Oedipus Rex to Falstaff, from Anna Karenina to Lord Jim, from Zorba the Greek to Thelma and Louise, this is the character/structure dynamic of consummate storytelling.

6

STRUCTURE AND MEANING

AESTHETIC EMOTION

Aristotle approached the question of story and meaning in this way: Why is it, he asked, when we see a dead body in the street we have one reaction, but when we read of death in Homer, or see it in the theatre, we have another? Because in life idea and emotion come separately. Mind and passions revolve in different spheres of our humanity, rarely coordinated, usually at odds.

In life, if you see a dead body in the street, you're struck by a rush of adrenaline: "My God, he's dead!" Perhaps you drive away in fear. Later, in the coolness of time, you may reflect on the meaning of this stranger's demise, on your own mortality, on life in the shadow of death. This contemplation may change you within so that the next time you are confronted with death, you have a new, perhaps more compassionate reaction. Or, reversing the pattern, you may, in youth, think deeply but not wisely about love, embracing an idealistic vision that trips you into a poignant but very painful romance. This may harden the heart, creating a cynic who in later years finds bitter what the young still think sweet.

Your intellectual life prepares you for emotional experiences that then urge you toward fresh perceptions that in turn remix the chemistry of new encounters. The two realms influence each other, but first one, then the other. In fact, in life, moments that blaze with a fusion of idea and emotion are so rare, when they happen you think you're having a religious experience. But whereas life separates meaning from emotion, art unites them. Story is an instrument by which you create such epiphanies at will, the phenomenon known as *aesthetic emotion*.

The source of all art is the human psyche's primal, prelinguistic need for the resolution of stress and discord through beauty and harmony, for the use of creativity to revive a life deadened by routine, for a link to reality through our instinctive, sensory feel for the truth. Like music and dance, painting and sculpture, poetry and song, story is first, last, and always the experience of aesthetic emotion—the simultaneous encounter of thought and feeling.

When an idea wraps itself around an emotional charge, it becomes all the more powerful, all the more profound, all the more memorable. You might forget the day you saw a dead body in the street, but the death of Hamlet haunts you forever. Life on its own, without art to shape it, leaves you in confusion and chaos, but aesthetic emotion harmonizes what you know with what you feel to give you a heightened awareness and a sureness of your place in reality. In short, a story well told gives you the very thing you cannot get from life: meaningful emotional experience. In life, experiences become meaningful *with reflection in time*. In art, they are meaningful *now, at the instant they happen*.

In this sense, story is, at heart, nonintellectual. It does not express ideas in the dry, intellectual arguments of an essay. But this is not to say story is anti-intellectual. We pray that the writer has ideas of import and insight. Rather, the exchange between artist and audience expresses idea directly through the senses and perceptions, intuition and emotion. It requires no mediator, no critic to rationalize the transaction, to replace the ineffable and the sentient with explanation and abstraction. Scholarly acumen sharpens taste and judgment, but we must never mistake criticism for art. Intellectual analysis, however heady, will not nourish the soul.

A well-told story neither expresses the clockwork reasonings of a thesis nor vents raging inchoate emotions. It triumphs in the marriage of the rational with the irrational. For a work that's either essentially emotional or essentially intellectual cannot have the validity of one that calls upon our subtler faculties of sympathy, empathy, premonition, discernment . . . our innate sensitivity to the truth.

PREMISE

Two ideas bracket the creative process: *Premise*, the idea that inspires the writer's desire to create a story, and *Controlling Idea*, the story's ultimate meaning expressed through the action and aesthetic emotion of the last act's climax. A Premise, however, unlike a Controlling Idea, is rarely a closed statement. More likely, it's an open-ended question: What would happen if . . . ? What would happen if a shark swam into a beach resort and devoured a vacationer? JAWS. What would happen if a wife walked out on her husband and child? KRAMER VS. KRAMER. Stanislavski called this the "Magic if . . . ," the daydreamy hypothetical that floats through the mind, opening the door to the imagination where everything and anything seems possible.

But "What would happen if . . ." is only one kind of Premise. Writers find inspiration wherever they turn—in a friend's light-hearted confession of a dark desire, the jibe of a legless beggar, a nightmare or daydream, a newspaper fact, a child's fantasy. Even the craft itself may inspire. Purely technical exercises, such as linking a smooth transition from one scene to the next or editing dialogue to avoid repetition, may trigger a burst of imagination. Anything may premise the writing, even, for example, a glance out a window.

In 1965 Ingmar Bergman contracted labyrinthitis, a viral infection of the inner ear that keeps its victims in a ceaselessly swirling vertigo, even while sleeping. For weeks Bergman was bedridden, his head in a brace, trying to keep vertigo at bay by staring at a spot his doctor had painted on the ceiling, but with each glance away the room spun like a whirligig. Concentrating on the spot, he began to imagine two faces intermingled. Days later, as he recovered, he glanced through a window and saw a nurse and a patient sitting comparing hands. Those images, the nurse/patient relationship and merging faces, were the genesis for Bergman's masterpiece PERSONA.

Flashes of inspiration or intuition that seem so random and spontaneous are in fact serendipitous. For what may inspire one writer will be ignored by another. The Premise awakens what waits within, the visions or convictions nascent in the writer. The sum total of his experience has prepared him for this moment and he reacts to it as only he would. Now the work begins. Along the way he interprets, chooses, and makes judgments. If, to some people, a writer's final statement about life appears dogmatic and opinionated, so be it. Bland and pacifying writers are a bore. We want unfettered souls with the courage to take a point of view, artists whose insights startle and excite.

Finally, it's important to realize that whatever inspires the writing need not stay in the writing. A Premise is not precious. As long as it contributes to the growth of story, keep it, but should the telling take a left turn, abandon the original inspiration to follow the evolving story. The problem is not to start writing, but to keep writing and renewing inspiration. We rarely know where we're going; writing is discovery.

STRUCTURE AS RHETORIC

Make no mistake: While a story's inspiration may be a dream and its final effect aesthetic emotion, a work moves from an open premise to a fulfilling climax only when the writer is possessed by serious thought. For an artist must have not only ideas to express, but ideas *to prove*. Expressing an idea, in the sense of exposing it, is never enough. The audience must not just understand; it must believe. You want the world to leave your story convinced that yours is a truthful metaphor for life. And the means by which you bring the audience to your point of view resides in the very design you give your telling. As you create your story, you create your proof; idea and structure intertwine in a rhetorical relationship.

STORYTELLING is the creative demonstration of truth. A story is the living proof of an idea, the conversion of idea to action. A story's event structure is the means by which you first express, then prove your idea . . . without explanation.

Master storytellers never explain. They do the hard, painfully creative thing—they dramatize. Audiences are rarely interested, and certainly never convinced, when forced to listen to the discussion of ideas. Dialogue, the natural talk of characters pursuing desire, is not a platform for the filmmaker's philosophy. Explanations of authorial ideas, whether in dialogue or narration, seriously diminish a film's quality. A great story authenticates its ideas solely within the dynamics of its events; failure to express a view of life through the pure, honest consequences of human choice and action is a creative defeat no amount of clever language can salvage.

To illustrate, consider that prolific genre, *Crime*. What idea is expressed by virtually all detective fiction? "Crime doesn't pay." How do we come to understand that? Hopefully without one character musing to another, "There! What'd I tell ya? Crime doesn't pay. Nope, it looked like they'd get away with it, but the wheels of justice turned unrelentingly . . ." No, we see the idea acted out in front of us: A crime is committed; for a while the criminal goes free; eventually he's apprehended and punished. In the act of punishment—imprisoning him for life or shooting him dead on the street—an emotionally charged idea runs through the audience. And if we could put words to this idea, they wouldn't be as polite as "Crime does not pay." Rather: "They got the bastard!" An electrifying triumph of justice and social revenge.

The kind and quality of aesthetic emotion is relative. The *Psycho-Thriller* strives for very strong effects; other forms, like the *Disillusionment* plot or the *Love Story*, want the softer emotions of perhaps sadness or compassion. But regardless of genre, the principle is universal: the story's meaning, whether comic or tragic, must be dramatized in an emotionally expressive Story Climax without the aid of explanatory dialogue.

CONTROLLING IDEA

Theme has become a rather vague term in the writer's vocabulary. "Poverty," "war," and "love," for example, are not themes; they relate to setting or genre. A true theme is not a word but a sentence—one clear, coherent sentence that expresses a story's irreducible meaning. I prefer the phrase *Controlling Idea*, for like theme, it names a story's root or central idea, but it also implies function: The Controlling Idea shapes the writer's strategic choices. It's yet another *Creative Discipline* to guide your aesthetic choices toward what is appropriate or inappropriate in your story, toward what is expressive of your Controlling Idea and may be kept versus what is irrelevant to it and must be cut.

The Controlling Idea of a completed story must be expressible in a single sentence. After the Premise is first imagined and the work is evolving, explore everything and anything that comes to mind. Ultimately, however, the film must be molded around one idea. This is not to say that a story can be reduced to a rubric. Far more is captured within the web of a story that can ever be stated in words— subtleties, subtexts, conceits, double meanings, richness of all kinds. A story becomes a kind of living philosophy that the audience members grasp as a whole, in a flash, without conscious thought—a perception married to their life experiences. But the irony is this:

The more beautifully you shape your work around one clear idea, the more meanings audiences will discover in your film as they take your idea and follow its implications into every aspect of their lives. Conversely, the more ideas you try to pack into a story, the more they implode upon themselves, until the film collapses into a rubble of tangential notions, saying nothing.

A CONTROLLING IDEA may be expressed in a single sentence describing how and why life undergoes change from one condition of existence at the beginning to another at the end.

The Controlling Idea has two components: Value plus Cause. It identifies the positive or negative charge of the story's critical value at the last act's climax, and it identifies the chief reason that this value has changed to its final state. The sentence composed from these two elements, Value plus Cause, expresses the core meaning of the story.

Value means the primary value in its positive or negative charge that comes into the world or life of your character as a result of the final action of the story. For example: An up-ending *Crime Story* (IN THE HEAT OF THE NIGHT) returns an unjust world (negative) to justice (positive), suggesting a phrase such as "Justice is restored . . ." In a down-ending *Political Thriller* (MISSING), the military dictatorship commands the story's world at climax, prompting a negative phrase such as "Tyranny prevails . . ." A positive-ending *Education Plot* (GROUNDHOG DAY) arcs the protagonist from a cynical, self-serving man to someone who's genuinely selfless and loving, leading to "Happiness fills our lives . . ." A negative-ending *Love Story* (DANGEROUS LIAISONS) turns passion into self-loathing, evoking "Hatred destroys . . . "

Cause refers to the primary reason that the life or world of the protagonist has turned to its positive or negative value. Working back from the ending to the beginning, we trace the chief cause deep within the character, society, or environment that has brought this value into existence. A complex story may contain many forces for change, but generally one cause dominates the others. Therefore, in a *Crime Story*, neither "Crime doesn't pay . . . " (justice triumphs . . .) nor "Crime pays . . . " (injustice triumphs . . .) could stand as a full Controlling Idea because each gives us only half a meaning—the ending value. A story of substance also expresses *why* its world or protagonist has ended on its specific value.

If, for example, you were writing for Clint Eastwood's Dirty Harry, your full Controlling Idea of Value plus Cause would be: "Justice triumphs because the protagonist is more violent than the criminals." Dirty Harry manages some minor detective work here and there, but his violence is the dominant cause for change. This insight then guides you to what's appropriate and inappropriate. It tells you it would be inappropriate to write a scene in which Dirty Harry comes upon the murder victim, discovers a ski cap left behind by the fleeing killer, takes out a magnifying glass, examines it, and concludes, "Hmm . . . this man's approximately thirty-five years of age; he has reddish hair; and he comes from the coal-mining regions of Pennsylvania—notice the anthracitic dust." This is Sherlock Holmes, not Dirty Harry.

If, however, you were writing for Peter Falk's Columbo, your Controlling Idea would be: "Justice is restored because the protagonist is more clever than the criminal." The ski cap forensics might be appropriate for Columbo because the dominant cause for change in the *Columbo* series is Sherlock Holmesian deduction. It would be inappropriate, however, for Columbo to reach under his wrinkled raincoat, come up with a .44 Magnum, and start blowing people away.

To complete the previous examples: IN THE HEAT OF THE NIGHT—justice is restored because a perceptive black outsider sees the truth of white perversion. GROUNDHOG DAY—happiness fills our lives when we learn to love unconditionally. MISSING—tyranny prevails because it's supported by a corrupt CIA. DANGEROUS LIAISONS—hatred destroys us when we fear the opposite sex. The Controlling Idea is the purest form of a story's meaning, the how and why of change, the vision of life the audience members carry away into their lives.

Meaning and the Creative Process

How do you find your story's Controlling Idea? The creative process may begin anywhere. You might be prompted by a Premise, a "What would happen if . . . ," or a bit of character, or an image. You might start in the middle, the beginning, near the end. As your fictional world and characters grow, events interlink and the story builds. Then comes that crucial moment when you take the leap and create the Story Climax. This climax of the last act is a final action that excites and moves you, that feels complete and satisfying. The Controlling Idea is now at hand.

Looking at your ending, ask: As a result of this climatic action, what value, positively or negatively charged, is brought into the world of my protagonist? Next, tracing backward from this climax, digging to the bedrock, ask: What is the chief cause, force, or means by which this value is brought into his world? The sentence you compose from the answers to those two questions becomes your Controlling Idea.

In other words, the story tells you its meaning; you do not dictate meaning to the story. You do not draw action from idea, rather idea from action. For no matter your inspiration, ultimately the story embeds its Controlling Idea within the final climax, and when this event speaks its meaning, you will experience one of the most powerful moments in the writing life—*Self-Recognition:* The Story Climax mirrors your inner self, and if your story is from the very best sources within you, more often than not you'll be shocked by what you see reflected in it.

You may think you're a warm, loving human being until you find yourself writing tales of dark, cynical consequence. Or you may think you're a street-wise guy who's been around the block a few times until you find yourself writing warm, compassionate endings. You think you know who you are, but often you're amazed by what's skulking inside in need of expression. In other words, if a plot works out exactly as you first planned, you're not working loosely enough to give room to your imagination and instincts. Your story should surprise you again and again. Beautiful story design is a combination of the subject found, the imagination at work, and the mind loosely but wisely executing the craft.

Idea Versus Counter-Idea

Paddy Chayefsky once told me that when he finally discovered his story's meaning, he'd scratch it out on a scrap of paper and tape it to his typewriter, so that nothing going through the machine wouldn't in one way or another express his central theme. With a clear statement of Value plus Cause staring him in the eye, he could resist intriguing irrelevancies and concentrate on unifying the telling around the story's core meaning. By "one way or another," Chayefsky meant he'd forge the story dynamically, moving it back and forth across the opposing charges of its primary values. His improvisations would be so shaped that sequence after sequence alternately expressed the positive, then negative dimension of his Controlling Idea. In other words, he fashioned his stories by playing *Idea* against *Counter-Idea.*

PROGRESSIONS build by moving dynamically between the positive and negative charges of the values at stake in the story.

From the moment of inspiration you reach into your fictional world in search of a design. You have to build a bridge of story from the opening to the ending, a progression of events that spans from Premise to Controlling Idea. These events echo the contradictory voices of one theme. Sequence by sequence, often scene by scene, the positive Idea and its negative Counter-Idea argue, so to speak, back and forth, creating a dramatized dialectical debate. At climax one of these two voices wins and becomes the story's Controlling Idea.

To illustrate with the familiar cadences of the *Crime Story*: A typical opening sequence expresses the negative *Counter-Idea*, "Crime pays because the criminals are brilliant and/or ruthless" as it dramatizes a crime so enigmatic (VERTIGO) or committed by such diabolical criminals (DIE HARD) that the audience is stunned: "They're going to get away with it!" But as a veteran detective discovers a clue left by the fleeing killer (THE BIG SLEEP), the next sequence contradicts this fear with the positive *Idea*, "Crime doesn't pay because the protagonist is even more brilliant and/or ruthless." Then perhaps the cop is misled into suspecting the wrong person (FAREWELL, MY LOVELY): "Crime pays." But soon the protagonist uncovers the real identity of the villain (THE FUGITIVE): "Crime doesn't pay." Next the criminal captures, may even seem to kill, the protagonist (ROBOCOP): "Crime pays." But the cop virtually resurrects from the dead (SUDDEN IMPACT) and goes back on the hunt: "Crime doesn't pay."

The positive and negative assertions of the same idea contest back and forth through the film, building in intensity, until at *Crisis* they collide head-on in a last impasse. Out of this rises the Story Climax, in which one or the other idea succeeds. This may be the positive Idea: "Justice triumphs because the protagonist is tenaciously resourceful and courageous" (BAD DAY AT BLACK ROCK, SPEED, THE SILENCE OF THE LAMBS), or the negative Counter-Idea: "Injustice prevails because the antagonist is overwhelmingly ruthless and powerful" (SEVEN, Q & A, CHINATOWN). Whichever of the two is dramatized in the final climatic action becomes the Controlling Idea of Value plus Cause, the purest statement of the story's conclusive and decisive meaning.

This rhythm of Idea versus Counter-Idea is fundamental and essential to our art. It pulses at the heart of all fine stories, no matter how internalized the action. What's more, this simple dynamic can become very complex, subtle, and ironic.

In SEA OF LOVE detective Keller (Al Pacino) falls in love with his chief suspect (Ellen Barkin). As a result, each scene that points toward her guilt turns with irony: positive on the value of justice, negative on the value of love. In the maturation plot SHINE, David's (Noah Taylor) musical victories (positive) provoke his father's (Armin Mueller-Stahl) envy and brutal repression (negative), driving the pianist into a pathological immaturity (doubly negative), which makes his final success a triumph of maturity in both art and spirit (doubly positive).

DIDACTICISM

A note of caution: In creating the dimensions of your story's "argument," take great care to build the power of both sides. Compose the scenes and sequences that contradict your final statement with as much truth and energy as those that reinforce it. If your film ends on the Counter-Idea, such as "Crime pays because . . . ," then amplify the sequences that lead the audience to feel justice will win out. If your film ends on the Idea, such as "Justice triumphs because . . . ," then enhance the sequences expressing "Crime pays and pays big." In other words, do not slant your "argument."

If, in a morality tale, you were to write your antagonist as an ignorant fool who more or less destroys himself, are we persuaded that good will prevail? But if, like an ancient myth-maker, you were to create an antagonist of virtual omnipotence who reaches the brink of success, you would force yourself to create a protagonist who will rise to the occasion and become even more powerful, more brilliant. In this balanced telling your victory of good over evil now rings with validity.

The danger is this: When your Premise is an idea you feel you must prove to the world, and you design your story as an undeniable certification of that idea, you set yourself on the road to didacticism. In your zeal to persuade, you will stifle the voice of the other side. Misusing and abusing art to preach, your screenplay will become a thesis film, a thinly disguised sermon as you strive in a single stroke to convert the world. Didacticism results from the naive enthusiasm that fiction can be used like a scalpel to cut out the cancers of society.

More often than not, such stories take the form of *Social Drama*, a lead-handed genre with two defining conventions: Identify a social ill; dramatize its remedy. The writer, for example, may decide that war is the scourge of humanity, and pacifism is the cure. In his zeal to convince us all his good people are very, very good people, and all his bad people are very, very bad people. All the dialogue is "on the nose" laments about the futility and insanity of war, heartfelt declarations that the cause of war is the "establishment." From outline to last draft, he fills the screen with stomach-turning images, making certain that each and every scene says loud and clear: "War is a scourge, but it can be cured by pacifism . . . war is a scourge cured by pacifism . . . war is a scourge cured by pacifism . . ." until you want to pick up a gun.

But the pacifist pleas of antiwar films (OH! WHAT A LOVELY WAR, APOCALYPSE NOW, GALLIPOLI, HAMBURGER HILL) rarely sensitize us to war. We're unconvinced because in the rush to prove he has the answer, the writer is blind to a truth we know too well—men love war.

This does not mean that starting with an idea is certain to produce didactic work . . . but that's the risk. As a story develops, you must willingly entertain opposite, even repugnant ideas. The finest writers have dialectical, flexible minds that easily shift points of view. They see the positive, the negative, and all shades of irony, seeking the truth of these views honestly and convincingly. This omniscience forces them to become even more creative, more imaginative, and more insightful. Ultimately, they express what they deeply believe, but not until they have allowed themselves to weigh each living issue and experience all its possibilities.

Make no mistake, no one can achieve excellence as a writer without being something of a philosopher and holding strong convictions. The trick is not to be a slave to your ideas, but to immerse yourself in life. For the proof of your vision is not how well you can assert your Controlling Idea, but its victory over the enormously powerful forces that you array against it.

Consider the superb balance of three antiwar films directed by Stanley Kubrick. Kubrick and his screenwriters researched and explored the Counter-Idea to look deep within the human psyche itself. Their stories reveal war to be the logical extension of an intrinsic dimension of human nature that loves to fight and kill, chilling us with the realization that what humanity loves to do, it will do—as it has for aeons, through the now and into all foreseeable futures.

In Kubrick's PATHS OF GLORY the fate of France hangs on winning the war against the Germans at any cost. So when the French army retreats from battle, an outraged general devises an innovative motivational strategy: He orders his artillery to bombard his own troops. In DR. STRANGELOVE the United States and Russia both realize that in nuclear war, not losing is more important than winning, so each concocts a scheme for not losing so effective it incinerates all life on Earth. In FULL METAL JACKET, the Marine Corps faces a tough task: how to persuade human beings to ignore the genetic prohibition against killing their own kind. The simple solution is to brainwash recruits into believing that the enemy is not human; killing a man then becomes easy, even if he's your drill instructor. Kubrick knew that if he gave the humanity enough ammunition, it would shoot itself.

A great work is a living metaphor that says, "Life is like *this*." The classics, down through the ages, give us not solutions but lucidity, not answers but poetic candor; they make inescapably clear the problems all generations must solve to be human.

IDEALIST, PESSIMIST, IRONIST

Writers and the stories they tell can be usefully divided into three grand categories, according to the emotional charge of their Controlling Idea.

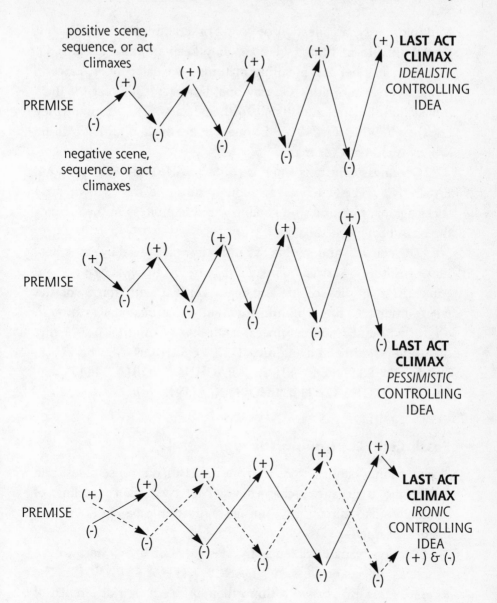

Idealistic Controlling Ideas

"Up-ending" stories expressing the optimism, hopes, and dreams of mankind, a positively charged vision of the human spirit; life as we wish it to be. Examples:

"Love fills our lives when we conquer intellectual illusions and follow our instincts": HANNAH AND HER SISTERS. In this

Multiplot story, a collection of New Yorkers are seeking love, but they're unable to find it because they keep thinking, analyzing, trying to decipher the meaning of things: sexual politics, careers, morality or immortality. One by one, however, they cast off their intellectual illusions and listen to their hearts. The moment they do, they all find love. This is one of the most optimistic films Woody Allen has ever made.

"Goodness triumphs when we outwit evil": THE WITCHES OF EASTWICK. The witches ingeniously turn the devil's own dirty tricks against him and find goodness and happiness in the form of three chubby-cheeked babies.

"The courage and genius of humanity will prevail over the hostility of Nature." *Survival Films*, a subgenre of *Action/Adventure*, are "up-ending" stories of life-and-death conflict with forces of the environment. At the brink of extinction, the protagonists, through dint of will and resourcefulness, battle the often cruel personality of Mother Nature and endure: THE POSEIDON ADVENTURE, JAWS, QUEST FOR FIRE, ARACHNOPHOBIA, FITZCAR-RALDO, FLIGHT OF THE PHOENIX, ALIVE.

Pessimistic Controlling Ideas

"Down-ending" stories expressing our cynicism, our sense of loss and misfortune, a negatively charged vision of civilization's decline, of humanity's dark dimensions; life as we dread it to be but know it so often is. Examples:

"Passion turns to violence and destroys our lives when we use people as objects of pleasure": DANCE WITH A STRANGER. The lovers in this British work think their problem is a difference of class, but class has been overcome by countless couples. The deep conflict is that their affair is poisoned by desires to possess each other as objects for neurotic gratification, until one seizes the ultimate possession—the life of her lover.

"Evil triumphs because it's part of human nature": CHINA-TOWN. On a superficial level, CHINATOWN suggests that the rich get away with murder. They do indeed. But more profoundly the film expresses the ubiquity of evil. In reality, because good and evil are equal parts of human nature, evil vanquishes good as often as good conquers evil. We're both angel and devil. If our natures leaned just slightly toward one or the other, all social dilemmas would have been solved centuries ago. But we're so divided, we never know from day to day which we'll be. One day we build the Cathedral of Notre Dame; the next, Auschwitz.

"The power of nature will have the final say over mankind's futile efforts." When the Counter-Idea of survival films becomes the Controlling Idea, we have that rare "down-ending" movie in which again human beings battle a manifestation of nature, but now nature prevails: SCOTT OF THE ANTARCTIC, THE ELE-PHANT MAN, EARTHQUAKE, and THE BIRDS, in which nature lets us off with a warning. These films are rare because the pessimistic vision is a hard truth that some people wish to avoid.

Ironic Controlling Ideas

"Up/down-ending" stories expressing our sense of the complex, dual nature of existence, a simultaneously charged positive and negative vision; life at its most complete and realistic.

Here optimism/idealism and pessimism/cynicism merge. Rather than voicing one extreme or the other, the story says both. The *Idealistic* "Love triumphs when we sacrifice our needs for others," as in KRAMER VS. KRAMER, melds with the *Pessimistic* "Love destroys when self-interest rules," as in THE WAR OF THE ROSES, and results in an ironic Controlling Idea: "Love is both pleasure and pain, a poignant anguish, a tender cruelty we pursue because without it life has no meaning," as in ANNIE HALL, MANHATTAN, ADDICTED TO LOVE.

What follows are two examples of Controlling Ideas whose ironies have helped define the ethics and attitudes of contemporary American society. First, the positive irony:

The compulsive pursuit of contemporary values—success, fortune, fame, sex, power—will destroy you, but if you

see this truth in time and throw away your obsession, you can redeem yourself.

Until the 1970s an "up-ending" could be loosely defined as "The protagonist gets what he wants." At climax the protagonist's object of desire became a trophy of sorts, depending on the value at stake—the lover of one's dreams (love), the dead body of the villain (justice), a badge of achievement (fortune, victory), public recognition (power, fame)—and he won it.

In the 1970s, however, Hollywood evolved a highly ironic version of the success story, *Redemption Plots,* in which protagonists pursue values that were once esteemed—money, reknown, career, love, winning, success—but with a compulsiveness, a blindness that carries them to the brink of self-destruction. They stand to lose, if not their lives, their humanity. They manage, however, to glimpse the ruinous nature of their obsession, stop before they go over the edge, then throw away what they once cherished. This pattern gives rise to an ending rich in irony: At climax the protagonist sacrifices his dream (positive), a value that has become a soul-corrupting fixation (negative), to gain an honest, sane, balanced life (positive).

THE PAPER CHASE, THE DEER HUNTER, KRAMER VS. KRAMER, AN UNMARRIED WOMAN, 10, AND JUSTICE FOR ALL, TERMS OF ENDEARMENT, THE ELECTRIC HORSEMAN, GOING IN STYLE, QUIZ SHOW, BULLETS OVER BROADWAY, THE FISHER KING, GRAND CANYON, RAIN MAN, HANNAH AND HER SISTERS, AN OFFICER AND A GENTLEMAN, TOOTSIE, REGARDING HENRY, ORDINARY PEOPLE, CLEAN AND SOBER, NORTH DALLAS FORTY, OUT OF AFRICA, BABY BOOM, THE DOCTOR, SCHINDLER'S LIST, and JERRY MAGUIRE all pivot around this irony, each expressing it in a unique and powerful way. As these titles indicate, this idea has been a magnet for Oscars.

In terms of technique, the execution of the climactic action in these films is fascinating. Historically, a positive ending is a scene in which the protagonist takes an action that gets him what he wants. Yet in all the works cited above, the protagonist either refuses to act on his obsession or throws away what he once desired. He or she wins by "losing." Like solving the Zen riddle of the sound of one hand clapping, the writer's problem in each case was how to make a nonaction or negative action feel positive.

At the climax of NORTH DALLAS FORTY All-Star wide receiver Phillip Elliot (Nick Nolte) opens his arms and lets the football bounce off his chest, announcing in his gesture that he won't play this childish game anymore.

THE ELECTRIC HORSEMAN ends as the former rodeo star Sonny Steele (Robert Redford), now reduced to peddling breakfast cereal, releases his sponsor's prize stallion into the wild, symbolically freeing himself from his need for fame.

OUT OF AFRICA is the story of a woman living the 1980s ethic of "I am what I own." Karen's (Meryl Streep) first words are: "I had a farm in Africa." She drags her furniture from Denmark to Kenya to build a home and plantation. She so defines herself by her possessions that she calls the laborers "her people" until her lover points out that she doesn't actually own these people. When her husband infects her with syphilis, she doesn't divorce him because her identity is "wife," defined by her possession of a husband. In time, however, she comes to realize you are not what you own; you are your values, talents, what you can do. When her lover is killed, she grieves but is not lost because she is not he. With a shrug, she lets husband, home, everything go, surrendering all she had, but gaining herself.

TERMS OF ENDEARMENT tells of a very different obsession. Aurora (Shirley MacLaine) lives the Epicurean philosophy that happiness means never suffering, that the secret of life is to avoid all negative emotion. She refuses two renowned sources of misery, career and lovers. She's so afraid of the pain of growing old, she dresses twenty years too young for herself. Her home has the un-lived-in look of a doll's house. The only life she leads is over the telephone vicariously through her daughter. But on her fifty-second birthday she begins to realize that the depth of joy you experience is in direct proportion to the pain you're willing to bear. In the last act she throws away the emptiness of a pain-free life to embrace children, lover, age, and all the pleasure and woe they bring.

Second, the negative irony:

If you cling to your obsession, your ruthless pursuit will achieve your desire, then destroy you.

WALL STREET; CASINO; THE WAR OF THE ROSES; STAR '80; NASHVILLE; NETWORK; THEY SHOOT HORSES, DON'T THEY?—these films are the *Punitive Plot* counterpart to the *Redemption Plots* above. In them the "down-ending" Counter-Idea becomes the Controlling Idea as protagonists remain steadfastly driven by their need to achieve fame or success, and never think to abandon it. At Story Climax the protagonists achieve their desire (positive), only to be destroyed by it (negative). In NIXON the president's (Anthony Hopkins) blind, corrupt trust in his political power destroys him and with him the nation's faith in government. In THE ROSE Rose (Bette Midler) is destroyed by her passion for drugs, sex, and rock 'n' roll. In ALL THAT JAZZ Joe Gideon (Roy Scheider) is brought down by his neurotic need for drugs, sex, and musical comedy.

On Irony

The effect of irony on an audience is that wonderful reaction, "Ah, life is just like that." We recognize that idealism and pessimism are at the extremes of experience, that life is rarely all sunshine and strawberries, nor is it all doom and drek; it is *both*. From the worst of experiences something positive can be gained; for the richest of experiences a great price must be paid. No matter how we try to plot a straight passage through life, we sail on the tides of irony. Reality is relentlessly ironic, and this is why stories that end in irony tend to last the longest through time, travel the widest in the world, and draw the greatest love and respect from audiences.

This is also why, of the three possible emotional charges at climax, irony is by far the most difficult to write. It demands the deepest wisdom and the highest craft for three reasons.

First, it's tough enough to come up with either a bright, idealistic ending or a sober, pessimistic climax that's satisfying and convincing. But an ironic climax is a single action that makes both a positive and a negative statement. How to do two in one?

Second, how to say both *clearly*? Irony doesn't mean ambiguity. Ambiguity is a blur; one thing cannot be distinguished from another. But there's nothing ambiguous about irony; it's a clear, double declaration of what's gained and what's lost, side by side. Nor does irony mean coincidence. A true irony is honestly motivated. Stories that end by random chance, doubly charged or not, are meaningless, not ironic.

Third, if at climax the life situation of the protagonist is both positive and negative, how to express it so that the two charges remain separated in the audience's experience and don't cancel each other out, and you end up saying nothing?

MEANING AND SOCIETY

Once you discover your Controlling Idea, respect it. Never allow yourself the luxury of thinking, "It's just entertainment." What, after all, is "entertainment"? Entertainment is the ritual of sitting in the dark, staring at a screen, investing tremendous concentration and energy into what one hopes will be a satisfying, meaningful emotional experience. Any film that hooks, holds, and pays off the story ritual is entertainment. Whether it be THE WIZARD OF OZ (USA/1939) or THE 400 BLOWS (France/1959), LA DOLCE VITA (Italy/1960) or SNOW WHITE AND THE THREE STOOGES (USA/1961), no story is innocent. All coherent tales express an idea veiled inside an emotional spell.

In 388 B.C. Plato urged the city fathers of Athens to exile all poets and storytellers. They are a threat to society, he argued. Writers deal with ideas, but not in the open, rational manner of philosophers. Instead, they conceal their ideas inside the seductive emotions of art. Yet felt ideas, as Plato pointed out, are ideas nonetheless. Every effective story sends a charged idea out to us, in effect compelling the idea into us, so that we must believe. In fact, the persuasive power of a story is so great that we may believe its meaning even if we find it morally repellent. Storytellers, Plato insisted, are dangerous people. He was right.

Consider DEATH WISH. Its Controlling Idea is "Justice triumphs when citizens take the law into their own hands and kill the people who need killing." Of all the vile ideas in human history, this is the vilest. Armed with it, the Nazis devastated Europe. Hitler believed he would turn Europe into a paradise once he killed the people who needed killing . . . and he had his list.

When DEATH WISH opened, newspaper reviewers across the country were morally outraged at the sight of Charles Bronson stalking Manhattan, gunning down people if they happened to look like muggers: "Hollywood thinks this passes for justice?" they ranted. "Whatever became of due process of law?" But in nearly every review I read, at some point the critic noted: ". . . and yet the audience seemed to enjoy it." A code for: ". . . and so did the critic." Critics never cite the pleasure of the audience unless they share it. In spite of their scandalized sensibilities, the film got to them too.

On the other hand, I wouldn't want to live in a country where DEATH WISH couldn't be made. I oppose all censorship. In pursuit of truth, we must willingly suffer the ugliest of lies. We must, as Justice Holmes argued, trust the marketplace of ideas. If everyone is given a voice, even the irrationally radical or cruelly reactionary, humanity will sort through all possibilities and make the right choice. No civilization, including Plato's, has ever been destroyed because its citizens learned too much truth.

Authoritative personalities, like Plato, fear the threat that comes not from idea, but from emotion. Those in power never want us to feel. Thought can be controlled and manipulated, but emotion is willful and unpredictable. Artists threaten authority by exposing lies and inspiring passion for change. This is why when tyrants seize power, their firing squads aim at the heart of the writer.

Lastly, given story's power to influence, we need to look at the issue of an artist's social responsibility. I believe we have no responsibility to cure social ills or renew faith in humanity, to uplift the spirits of society or even express our inner being. We have only one responsibility: *to tell the truth*. Therefore, study your Story

Climax and extract from it your Controlling Idea. But before you take another step, ask yourself this question: Is this the truth? Do I believe in the meaning of my story? If the answer is no, toss it and start again. If yes, do everything possible to get your work into the world. For although an artist may, in his private life, lie to others, even to himself, when he creates he tells the truth; and in a world of lies and liars, an honest work of art is always an act of social responsibility.

PART 3

THE PRINCIPLES OF STORY DESIGN

When forced to work within a strict framework the imagination is taxed to its utmost—and will produce its richest ideas. Given total freedom the work is likely to sprawl.

—T. S. ELIOT

7

THE SUBSTANCE OF STORY

From what material do we create the scenes that will one day walk and talk their way across the screen? What is the clay we twist and shape, keep or throw away? What is the "substance" of story?

In all other arts the answer is self-evident. The composer has his instrument and the notes it sounds. The dancer calls her body her instrument. Sculptors chisel stone. Painters stir paint. All artists can lay hands on the raw material of their art—except the writer. For at the nucleus of a story is a "substance," like the energy swirling in an atom, that's never *directly* seen, heard, or touched, yet we know it and feel it. The stuff of story is alive but intangible.

"Intangible?" I hear you thinking. "But I have my *words*. Dialogue, description. I can put hands on my pages. The writer's raw material is language." In fact, it's not, and the careers of many talented writers, especially those who come to screenwriting after a strong literary education, flounder because of the disastrous misunderstanding of this principle. For just as glass is a medium for light, air a medium for sound, language is only a medium, one of many, in fact, for storytelling. Something far more profound than mere words beats at the heart of a story.

And at the opposite end of story sits another equally profound phenomenon: the audience's reaction to this substance. When you think about it, going to the movies is bizarre. Hundreds of strangers sit in a blackened room, elbow to elbow, for two or more hours. They don't go to the toilet or get a smoke. Instead, they stare wide-eyed at a screen, investing more uninterrupted concentration than they give to work, paying money to suffer emotions they'd do anything to avoid in life. From this perspective, a second question arises: What is the source of story energy? How does it compel such intense mental and sentient attention from the audience? How do stories work?

The answers to these questions come when the artist explores the creative process *subjectively*. To understand the substance of story and how it performs, you need to view your work from the inside out, from the center of your character, looking *out* at the world through your character's eyes, experiencing the story as if you were the living character yourself. To slip into this subjective and highly imaginative point of view, you need to look closely at this creature you intend to inhabit, a *character*. Or more specifically, a *protagonist*. For although the protagonist is a character like any other, as the central and essential role, he embodies all aspects of character in absolute terms.

THE PROTAGONIST

Generally, the protagonist is a single character. A story, however, could be driven by a duo, such as THELMA & LOUISE; a trio, THE WITCHES OF EASTWICK; more, THE SEVEN SAMURAI or THE DIRTY DOZEN. In THE BATTLESHIP POTEMKIN an entire class of people, the proletariat, create a massive *Plural-Protagonist*.

For two or more characters to form a Plural-Protagonist, two conditions must be met: First, all individuals in the group share the same desire. Second, in the struggle to achieve this desire, they mutually suffer and benefit. If one has a success, all benefit. If one has a setback, all suffer. Within a Plural-Protagonist, motivation, action, and consequence are communal.

A story may, on the other hand, be *Multiprotagonist*. Here, unlike the Plural-Protagonist, characters pursue separate and individual desires, suffering and benefiting independently: PULP FICTION, HANNAH AND HER SISTERS, PARENTHOOD, DINER, DO THE RIGHT THING, THE BREAKFAST CLUB, EAT DRINK MAN WOMAN, PELLE THE CONQUEROR, HOPE AND GLORY,

HIGH HOPES. Robert Altman is the master of this design: A WEDDING, NASHVILLE, SHORT CUTS.

On screen the Multiprotagonist story is as old as GRAND HOTEL; in the novel older still, *War and Peace*; in the theatre older yet, *A Midsummer Night's Dream*. Multiprotagonist stories become Multiplot stories. Rather than driving the telling through the focused desire of a protagonist, either single or plural, these works weave a number of smaller stories, each with its own protagonist, to create a dynamic portrait of a specific society.

The protagonist need not be human. It may be an animal, BABE, or a cartoon, BUGS BUNNY, or even an inanimate object, such as the hero of the children's story *The Little Engine That Could*. Anything that can be given a free will and the capacity to desire, take action, and suffer the consequences can be a protagonist.

It's even possible, in rare cases, to switch protagonists halfway through a story. PSYCHO does this, making the shower murder both an emotional and a formal jolt. With the protagonist dead, the audience is momentarily confused; whom is this movie about? The answer is a Plural-Protagonist as the victim's sister, boyfriend, and a private detective take over the story. But no matter whether the story's protagonist is single, multi or plural, no matter how he is characterized, all protagonists have certain hallmark qualities, and the first is *willpower*.

A PROTAGONIST is a willful character.

Other characters may be dogged, even inflexible, but the protagonist in particular is a willful being. The exact quantity of this willpower, however, may not be measurable. A fine story is not necessarily the struggle of a gigantic will versus absolute forces of inevitability. Quality of will is as important as quantity. A protagonist's willpower may be less than that of the biblical Job, but powerful enough to sustain desire through conflict and ultimately take actions that create meaningful and irreversible change.

What's more, the true strength of the protagonist's will may hide behind a passive characterization. Consider Blanche DuBois, protagonist of A STREETCAR NAMED DESIRE. At first glance she seems weak, drifting and *will-less*, only wanting, she says, to live in reality. Yet beneath her frail characterization, Blanche's deep character owns a powerful will that drives her unconscious desire: What she really wants is *to escape from reality*. So Blanche does everything she can to buffer herself against the ugly world that engulfs her: She acts the grand dame, puts doilies on frayed furniture, lampshades on naked light bulbs, tries to make a Prince Charming out of a dullard. When none of this succeeds, she takes the final escape from reality—she goes insane.

On the other hand, while Blanche only seems passive, the truly passive protagonist is a regrettably common mistake. A story cannot be told about a protagonist who doesn't want anything, who cannot make decisions, whose actions effect no change at any level.

The PROTAGONIST has a conscious desire.

Rather, the protagonist's will impels a known desire. The protagonist has a need or goal, *an object of desire,* and knows it. If you could pull your protagonist aside, whisper in his ear, "What do you want?" he would have an answer: "I'd like X today, Y next week, but in the end I want Z." The protagonist's object of desire may be external: the destruction of the shark in JAWS, or internal: maturity in BIG. In either case, the protagonist knows what he wants, and for many characters a simple, clear, conscious desire is sufficient.

The PROTAGONIST may also have a self-contradictory unconscious desire.

However, the most memorable, fascinating characters tend to have not only a conscious but an unconscious desire. Although these complex protagonists are unaware of their subconscious need, the audience senses it, perceiving in them an inner contradiction. The conscious and unconscious desires of a multidimensional protagonist contradict each other. What he believes he wants is the antithesis of what he actually but unwittingly wants.

This is self-evident. What would be the point of giving a character a subconscious desire if it happens to be the very thing he knowingly seeks?

The PROTAGONIST has the capacities to pursue the Object of Desire convincingly.

The protagonist's characterization must be appropriate. He needs a believable combination of qualities in the right balance to pursue his desires. This doesn't mean he'll get what he wants. He may fail. But the character's desires must be realistic enough in relationship to his will and capacities for the audience to believe that he could be doing what they see him doing and that he has a chance for fulfillment.

The PROTAGONIST must have at least a chance to attain his desire.

An audience has no patience for a protagonist who lacks all possibility of realizing his desire. The reason is simple: No one believes this of his own life. No one believes he doesn't have even the smallest chance of fulfilling his wishes. But if we were to pull the camera back on life, the grand overview might lead us to conclude that, in the words of Henry David Thoreau, "The mass of men lead lives of quiet desperation," that most people waste their precious time and die with the feeling they've fallen short of their dreams. As honest as this painful insight may be, we cannot allow ourselves to believe it. Instead, we carry hope to the end.

Hope, after all, is not unreasonable. It's simply hypothetical. "If this . . . if that . . . if I learn more . . . if I love more . . . if I discipline myself . . . if I win the lottery . . . if things change, then I'll have a chance of getting from life what I want." We all carry hope in our hearts, no matter the odds against us. A protagonist, therefore, who's literally hopeless, who hasn't even the minimal capacity to achieve his desire, cannot interest us.

The PROTAGONIST has the will and capacity to pursue the object of his conscious and/or unconscious desire to the end of the line, to the human limit established by setting and genre.

The art of story is not about the middle ground, but about the pendulum of existence swinging to the limits, about life lived in its most intense states. We explore the middle ranges of experience, but only as a path to the end of the line. The audience senses that limit and wants it reached. For no matter how intimate or epic the setting, instinctively the audience draws a circle around the characters and their world, a circumference of experience that's defined by the nature of the fictional reality. This line may reach inward to the soul, outward into the universe, or in both directions at once. The audience, therefore, expects the storyteller to be an artist of vision who can take his story to those distant depths and ranges.

A STORY must build to a final action beyond which the audience cannot imagine another.

In other words, a film cannot send its audience to the street rewriting it: "Happy ending . . . but shouldn't she have settled things with her father? Shouldn't she have broken up with Ed before she moved in with Mac? Shouldn't she have . . ." Or: "Downer . . . the guy's dead, but why didn't he call the cops? And didn't he keep a gun under the dash, and shouldn't he have . . . ?" If people exit imagining scenes they thought they should have seen before or after the ending we give them, they will be less than happy moviegoers. We're supposed to be better writers than they. The audience wants to be taken to the limit, to where all questions are answered, all emotion satisfied—the end of the line.

The protagonist takes us to this limit. He must have it within himself to pursue his desire to the boundaries of human experience in depth, breadth, or both, to reach absolute and irreversible change. This, by the way, doesn't mean your film can't have a sequel; your protagonist may have more tales to tell. It means that each story must find closure for itself.

The PROTAGONIST must be empathetic; he may or may not be sympathetic.

Sympathetic means likable. Tom Hanks and Meg Ryan, for example, or Spencer Tracy and Katharine Hepburn in their typical roles: The moment they step onscreen, we like them. We'd want them as friends, family members, or lovers. They have an innate likability and evoke sympathy. Empathy, however, is a more profound response.

Empathetic means "like me." Deep within the protagonist the audience recognizes a certain shared humanity. Character and audience are not alike in every fashion, of course; they may share only a single quality. But there's something about the character that strikes a chord. In that moment of recognition, the audience suddenly and instinctively wants the protagonist to achieve whatever it is that he desires.

The unconscious logic of the audience runs like this: "This character is like me. Therefore, I want him to have whatever it is he wants, because if I were he in those circumstances, I'd want the same thing for myself." Hollywood has many synonymic expressions for this connection: "somebody to get behind," "someone to root for." All describe the empathetic connection that the audience strikes between itself and the protagonist. An audience may, if so moved, empathize with every character in your film, but it must empathize with your protagonist. If not, the audience/story bond is broken.

THE AUDIENCE BOND

The audience's emotional involvement is held by the glue of empathy. If the writer fails to fuse a bond between filmgoer and protagonist, we sit outside feeling nothing. Involvement has nothing to do with evoking altruism or compassion. We empathize for very personal, if not egocentric, reasons. When we identify with a protagonist and his desires in life, we are in fact rooting for our own desires in life. Through empathy, the vicarious linking of ourselves to a fictional human being, we test and stretch our humanity. The gift of story is the opportunity to live lives beyond our own, to desire and struggle in a myriad of worlds and times, at all the various depths of our being.

Empathy, therefore, is absolute, while sympathy is optional. We've all met likable people who don't draw our compassion. A protagonist, accordingly, may or may not be pleasant. Unaware of the difference between sympathy and empathy, some writers automatically devise nice-guy heroes, fearing that if the star role isn't nice, the audience won't relate. Uncountable commercial disasters, however, have starred charming protagonists. Likability is no guarantee of audience involvement; it's merely an aspect of characterization. The audience identifies with deep character, with innate qualities revealed through choice under pressure.

At first glance creating empathy does not seem difficult. The protagonist is a human being; the audience is full of human beings. As the filmgoer looks up on the screen, he recognizes the character's humanity, senses that he shares it, identifies with the protagonist, and dives into the story. Indeed, in the hands of the greatest writers, even the most unsympathetic character can be made empathetic.

Macbeth, for example, viewed objectively, is monstrous. He butchers a kindly old King while the man is sleeping, a King who had never done Macbeth any harm—in fact, that very day he'd given Macbeth a royal promotion. Macbeth then murders two servants of the King to blame the deed on them. He kills his best friend. Finally he orders the assassination of the wife and infant children of his enemy. He's a ruthless killer; yet, in Shakespeare's hands he becomes a tragic, empathetic hero.

The Bard accomplished this feat by giving Macbeth a conscience. As he wanders in soliloquy, wondering, agonizing, "Why am I doing this? What kind of a man am I?" the audience listens and thinks, "What kind? Guilt-ridden . . . just like me. I feel bad when I'm thinking about doing bad things. I feel awful when I do them and afterward there's no end to the guilt. Macbeth is a human being; he has a conscience just like mine." In fact, we're so drawn to Macbeth's writhing soul, we feel a tragic loss when at climax Macduff decapitates him. *Macbeth* is a breathtaking display of the godlike power of the writer to find an empathetic center in an otherwise contemptible character.

On the other hand, in recent years many films, despite otherwise splendid qualities, have crashed on these rocks because they failed to create an audience bond. Just one example of many: INTERVIEW WITH A VAMPIRE. The audience's reaction to Brad Pitt's Louis went like this: "If I were Louis, caught in his hell-after-death, I'd end it in a flash. Bad luck he's a vampire. Wouldn't wish that on anybody. But if he finds it revolting to suck the life out of innocent victims, if he hates himself for turning a child into a devil, if he's tired of rat blood, he should take this simple solution: Wait for sunrise, and poof, it's over." Although Anne Rice's novel steered us through Louis's thoughts and feelings until we fell into empathy with him, the dispassionate eye of the camera sees him for what he is, a whining fraud. Audiences always disassociate themselves from hypocrites.

THE FIRST STEP

When you sit down to write, the musing begins: "How to start? What would my character do?"

Your character, indeed all characters, in the pursuit of any desire, at any moment in story, will always take the minimum, conservative action *from his point of view.* All human beings always do. Humanity is fundamentally conservative, as indeed is all of nature. No organism ever expends more energy than necessary, risks anything it doesn't have to, or takes any action unless it must. Why should it? If a task can be done in an easy way without risk of loss or pain, or the expenditure of energy, why would any creature do the more difficult, dangerous, or enervating thing? It won't. Nature doesn't allow it . . . and human nature is just an aspect of universal nature.

In life we often see people, even animals, acting with extreme behavior that seems unnecessary, if not stupid. But this is our objective view of their situation. Subjectively, from within the experience of the creature, this apparently intemperate action was minimal, conservative, and necessary. What's thought "conservative," after all, is always relative to point of view.

For example: If a normal person wanted to get into a house, he'd take the minimum and conservative action. He'd knock on the door, thinking, "If I knock, the door'll be opened. I'll be invited in and that'll be a positive step toward my desire." A martial arts hero, however, as a conservative first step, might karate-chop the door to splinters, feeling that this is prudent and minimal.

What is necessary but minimal and conservative is relative to the point of view of each character at each precise moment. In life, for example, I say to myself: "If I cross the street now, that car's far enough away for the driver to see me in time, slow down if needed, and I'll get across." Or: "I can't find Dolores's phone number. But I know that my friend Jack has it in his Rolodex. If I call him in the midst of his busy day, because he's my friend, he'll interrupt what he's doing and give me the number."

In other words, in life we take an action consciously or unconsciously (and life is spontaneous most of the time as we open our mouths or take a step), thinking or sensing within to this effect: "If in these circumstances I take this minimum, conservative action, the world will react to me in a fashion that will be a positive step toward getting me what I want." And in life, 99 percent of the time we are right. The driver sees you in time, taps the brakes, and you reach the other side safely. You call Jack and apologize for interrupting him. He says, "No problem," and gives you the number. This is the great mass of experience, hour by hour, in life. BUT NEVER, EVER IN A STORY.

The grand difference between story and life is that in story we cast out the minutiae of daily existence in which human beings take actions expecting a certain enabling reaction from the world, and, more or less, get what they expect.

In story, we concentrate on that moment, and only that moment, in which a character takes an action expecting a useful reaction from his world, but instead the effect of his action is to provoke forces of antago-

nism. The world of the character reacts differently than expected, more powerfully than expected, or both.

I pick up the phone, call Jack, and say: "Sorry to bother you, but I can't find Dolores's phone number. Could you—" and he shouts: "Dolores? Dolores! How dare you ask me for her number?" and slams down the phone. Suddenly, life is interesting.

THE WORLD OF A CHARACTER

This chapter seeks the substance of story as seen from the perspective of a writer who in his imagination has placed himself at the very center of the character he's creating. The "center" of a human being, that irreducible particularity of the innermost self, is the awareness you carry with you twenty-four hours a day that watches you do everything you do, that chides you when you get things wrong, or compliments you on those rare occasions when you get things right. It's that deep observer that comes to you when you're going through the most agonizing experience of your life, collapsed on the floor, crying your heart out . . . that little voice that says, "Your mascara is running." This inner eye is you: your identity, your ego, the conscious focus of your being. Everything outside this subjective core is the objective world of a character.

A character's world can be imagined as a series of concentric circles surrounding a core of raw identity or awareness, circles that mark the levels of conflict in a character's life. The inner circle or level is his own self and conflicts arising from the elements of his nature: mind, body, emotion.

When, for example, a character takes an action, his mind may not react the way he anticipates. His thoughts may not be as quick, as insightful, as witty as he expected. His body may not react as he imagined. It may not be strong enough or deft enough for a particular task. And we all know how emotions betray us. So the closest circle of antagonism in the world of a character is his own being: feelings and emotions, mind and body, all or any of which may or may not react from one moment to the next the way he expects. As often as not, we are our own worst enemies.

THE THREE LEVELS OF CONFLICT

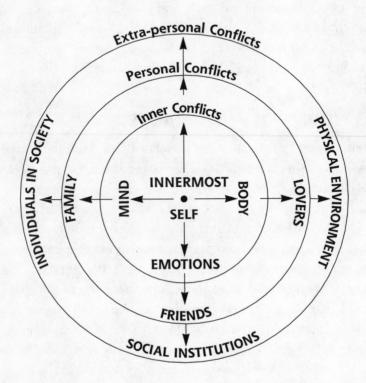

The second circle inscribes personal relationships, unions of intimacy deeper than the social role. Social convention assigns the outer roles we play. At the moment, for example, we're playing teacher/student. Someday, however, our paths may cross and we may decide to change our professional relationship to friendship. In the same manner, parent/child begins as social roles that may or may not go deeper than that. Many of us go through life in parent/child relationships that never deepen beyond social definitions of authority and rebellion. Not until we set the conventional role aside do we find the true intimacy of family, friends, and lovers—who then do not react the way we expect and become the second level of personal conflict.

The third circle marks the level of extra-personal conflict—

all the sources of antagonism outside the personal: conflict with social institutions and individuals—government/citizen, church/worshipper; corporation/client; conflict with individuals—cop/criminal/victim, boss/worker, customer/waiter, doctor/patient; and conflict with both man-made and natural environments—time, space, and every object in it.

THE GAP

STORY is born in that place where the subjective and objective realms touch.

The protagonist seeks an object of desire beyond his reach. Consciously or unconsciously he chooses to take a particular action, motivated by the thought or feeling that this act will cause the world to react in a way that will be a positive step toward achieving his desire. From his subjective point of view the action he has chosen seems minimal, conservative, yet sufficient to effect the reaction he wants. But the moment he takes this action, the objective realm of his inner life, personal relationships, or extra-personal world, or a combination of these, react in a way that's more powerful or different than he expected.

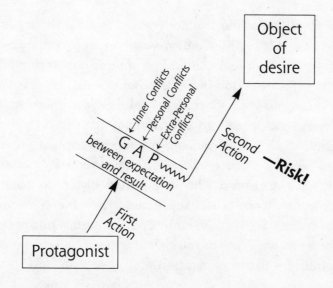

This reaction from his world blocks his desire, thwarting him and bending him further from his desire than he was before he took this action. Rather than evoking cooperation from his world, his action provokes forces of antagonism that open up the *gap* between his subjective expectation and the objective result, between what he thought would happen when he took his action and what in fact does happen between his sense of probability and true necessity.

Every human being acts, from one moment to the next, knowingly or unknowingly, on his sense of probability, on what he expects, in all likelihood, to happen when he takes an action. We all walk this earth thinking, or at least hoping, that we understand ourselves, our intimates, society, and the world. We behave according to what we believe to be the truth of ourselves, the people around us, and the environment. But this is a truth we cannot know absolutely. It's what we *believe* to be true.

We also believe we're free to make any decision whatsoever to take any action whatsoever. But every choice and action we make and take, spontaneous or deliberate, is rooted in the sum total of our experience, in what has happened to us in actuality, imagination, or dream to that moment. We then choose to act based on what this gathering of life tells us will be the probable reaction from our world. It's only then, when we take action, that we discover necessity.

Necessity is absolute truth. Necessity is what in fact happens when we act. This truth is known—*and can only be known*—when we take action into the depth and breadth of our world and brave its reaction. This reaction is the truth of our existence at that precise moment, no matter what we believed the moment before. Necessity is what must and does actually happen, as opposed to probability, which is what we hope or expect to happen.

As in life, so in fiction. When objective necessity contradicts a character's sense of probability, a gap suddenly cracks open in the fictional reality. This gap is the point where the subjective and objective realms collide, the difference between anticipation and result, between the world as the character perceived it before acting and the truth he discovers in action.

Once the gap in reality splits open, the character, being willful and having capacity, senses or realizes that he cannot get what he wants in a minimal, conservative way. He must gather himself and struggle through this gap to take a second action. This next action is something the character would not have wanted to do in the first case because it not only demands more willpower and forces him to dig more deeply into his human capacity, but most important, *the second action puts him at risk*. He now stands to lose in order to gain.

ON RISK

We'd all like to have our cake and eat it too. In a state of jeopardy, on the other hand, we must risk something that we want or have in order to gain something else that we want or to protect something we have—a dilemma we strive to avoid.

Here's a simple test to apply to any story. Ask: What is the risk? What does the protagonist stand to lose if he does not get what he wants? More specifically, what's the worst thing that will happen to the protagonist if he does not achieve his desire?

If this question cannot be answered in a compelling way, the story is misconceived at its core. For example, if the answer is: "Should the protagonist fail, life would go back to normal," this story is not worth telling. What the protagonist wants is of no real value, and a story of someone pursuing something of little or no value is the definition of boredom.

Life teaches that the measure of the value of any human desire is in direct proportion to the risk involved in its pursuit. The higher the value, the higher the risk. We give the ultimate values to those things that demand the ultimate risks—our freedom, our lives, our souls. This imperative of risk, however, is far more than an aesthetic principle, it's rooted in the deepest source of our art. For we not only create stories as metaphors for life, we create them as metaphors for meaningful life—and to live meaningfully is to be at perpetual risk.

Examine your own desires. What's true of you will be true of every character you write. You wish to write for the cinema, the foremost media of creative expression in the world today; you wish to give us works of beauty and meaning that help shape our vision of reality; in return you would like to be acknowledged. It's a noble ambition and a grand achievement to fulfill. And because you're a serious artist, you're willing to risk vital aspects of your life to live that dream.

You're willing to risk time. You know that even the most talented writers—Oliver Stone, Lawrence Kasdan, Ruth Prawer Jhabvala— didn't find success until they were in their thirties or forties, and just as it takes a decade or more to make a good doctor or teacher, it takes ten or more years of adult life to find something to say that tens of millions of people want to hear, and ten or more years and often as many screenplays written and unsold to master this demanding craft.

You're willing to risk money. You know that if you were to take the same hard work and creativity that goes into a decade of unsold screenplays and apply it to a normal profession, you could retire before you see your first script on the screen.

You're willing to risk people. Each morning you go to your desk and enter the imagined world of your characters. You dream and write until the sun's setting and your head's throbbing. So you turn off your word processor to be with the person you love. Except that, while you can turn off your machine, you can't turn off your imagi- nation. As you sit at dinner, your characters are still running through your head and you're wishing there was a notepad next to your plate. Sooner or later, the person you love will say: "You know . . . you're not really here." Which is true. Half the time you're somewhere else, and no one wants to live with somebody who isn't really there.

The writer places time, money, and people at risk because his ambition has life-defining force. What's true for the writer is true for every character he creates:

The measure of the value of a character's desire is in direct proportion to the risk he's willing to take to achieve it; the greater the value, the greater the risk.

THE GAP IN PROGRESSION

The protagonist's first action has aroused forces of antagonism that block his desire and spring open a gap between anticipation and result, disconfirming his notions of reality, putting him in greater conflict with his world, at even greater risk. But the resilient human mind quickly remakes reality into a larger pattern that incorporates this disconfirmation, this unexpected reaction. Now he takes a second, more difficult and risk-taking action, an action consistent with his revised vision of reality, an action based on his new expectations of the world. But again his action provokes forces

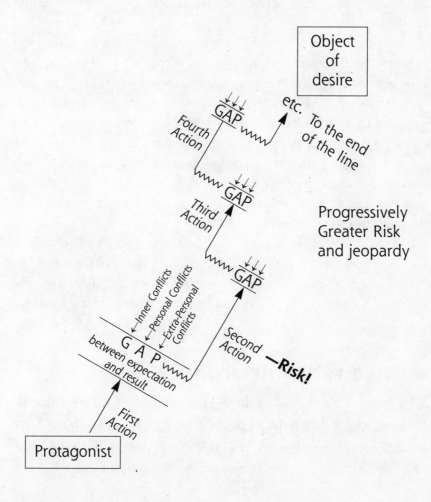

of antagonism, splitting open a gap in his reality. So he adjusts to the unexpected, ups the ante yet again and decides to take an action that he feels is consistent with his amended sense of things. He reaches even more deeply into his capacities and willpower, puts himself at greater risk, and takes a third action.

Perhaps this action achieves a positive result, and for the moment he takes a step toward his desire, but with his next action, the gap will again spring open. Now he must take an even more difficult action that demands even more willpower, more capacity, and more risk. Over and over again in a progression, rather than cooperation, his actions provoke forces of antagonism, opening gaps in his reality. This pattern repeats on various levels to the end of the line, to a final action beyond which the audience cannot imagine another.

These cracks in moment-to-moment reality mark the difference between the dramatic and the prosaic, between action and activity. True action is physical, vocal, or mental movement that opens gaps in expectation and creates significant change. Mere activity is behavior in which what is expected happens, generating either no change or trivial change.

But the gap between expectation and result is far more than a matter of cause and effect. In the most profound sense, the break between the cause as it seemed and the effect as it turns out marks the point where the human spirit and the world meet. On one side is the world as we believe it to be, on the other is reality as it actually is. In this gap is the nexus of story, the caldron that cooks our tellings. Here the writer finds the most powerful, life-bending moments. The only way we can reach this crucial junction is by working from the inside out.

WRITING FROM THE INSIDE OUT

Why must we do this? Why during the creation of a scene must we find our way to the center of each character and experience it from his point of view? What do we gain when we do? What do we sacrifice if we don't?

Like anthropologists, we could, for example, discover social and environmental truths through careful observations. Like note-taking psychologists, we could find behavioral truths. We could, by working from the outside in, render a surface of character that's genuine, even fascinating. But the one crucial dimension we would not create is *emotional truth*.

The only reliable source of emotional truth is yourself. If you stay outside your characters, you inevitably write emotional clichés. To create revealing human reactions, you must not only get inside your character, but get inside yourself. So, how to do this? How, as you sit at your desk, do you crawl inside the head of your character to feel your heart pounding, your palms sweating, a knot in your belly, tears in your eyes, laughter in your heart, sexual arousal, anger, outrage, compassion, sadness, joy, or any of the uncountable responses along the spectrum of human emotions?

You've determined that a certain event must take place in your story, a situation to be progressed and turned. How to write a scene of insightful emotions? You could ask: How *should* someone take this action? But that leads to clichés and moralizing. Or you could ask: How *might* someone do this? But that leads to writing "cute"—clever but dishonest. Or: "If my character were in these circumstances, what would he do?" But that puts you at a distance, picturing your character walking the stage of his life, guessing at his emotions, and guesses are invariably clichés. Or you could ask: "If I were in these circumstances, what would I do?" As this question plays on your imagination, it may start your heart pounding, but obviously you're not the character. Although it may be an honest emotion for you, your character might do the reverse. So what do you do?

You ask: "If I were this character in these circumstances, what would I do?" Using Stanislavski's "Magic if," you act the role. It is no accident that many of the greatest playwrights from Euripides to Shakespeare to Pinter, and screenwriters from D. W. Griffith to Ruth Gordon to John Sayles were also actors. Writers are improvisationalists who perform sitting at their word processors, pacing their rooms, acting all their characters: man, woman, child, monster. We act in our imaginations until honest, character-specific

emotions flow in our blood. When a scene is emotionally meaningful to us, we can trust that it'll be meaningful to the audience.
By creating work that moves us, we move them.

CHINATOWN

To illustrate writing from the inside out, I'll use one of the most
famous and brilliantly written scenes in film, the second act climax
of CHINATOWN by screenwriter Robert Towne. I'll work from the
scene as performed on screen, but it can also be found in the third
draft of Towne's screenplay, dated October 9, 1973.

Synopsis

Private detective J. J. Gittes is investigating the death of Hollis Mulwray, commissioner of the Los Angeles Department of Water and
Power. Mulwray has apparently drowned in a reservoir, and the
crime baffles Gittes's rival, Police Lieutenant Escobar. Near the end
of the Act Two, Gittes has narrowed suspects and motives to two:
either a conspiracy of millionaires led by the ruthless Noah Cross
killed Mulwray for political power and riches; or Evelyn Mulwray
killed her husband in a jealous rage after he was found with
another woman.

Gittes follows Evelyn to a house in Santa Monica. Peering
through a window, he sees the "other woman," seemingly drugged
and held prisoner. When Evelyn comes out to her car, he forces her
to talk and she claims that the woman is her sister. Gittes knows
she doesn't have a sister, but for the moment says nothing.

The next morning he discovers what appears to be the dead
man's eyeglasses in a salt water pond at the Mulwray home in the
hills above L.A. Now he knows how and where the man was killed.
With this evidence he goes back to Santa Monica to confront
Evelyn and turn her over to Escobar, who's threatening to pull
Gittes's private investigator's license.

CHARACTERS

J. J. GITTES, while working for the district attorney, fell in love with a woman in Chinatown and while trying to help her somehow caused her death. He resigned and became a PI, hoping to escape corrupt politics and his tragic past. But now he's drawn back into both. What's worse, he finds himself in this predicament because, days before the murder, he was duped into investigating Mulwray for adultery. Someone's made a fool of Gittes and he's a man of excessive pride. Behind his cool demeanor is an impulsive risk-taker; his sarcastic cynicism masks an idealist's hunger for justice. To further complicate matters, he's fallen in love with Evelyn Mulwray. Gittes's scene objective: *to find the truth.*

EVELYN MULWRAY is the victim's wife and daughter of Noah Cross. She's nervous and defensive when questioned about her husband; she stammers when her father is mentioned. She is, we sense, a woman with something to hide. She has hired Gittes to look into the murder of her husband, perhaps to conceal her own guilt. During the investigation, however, she seems drawn to him. After a close escape from some thugs, they make love. Evelyn's scene objective: *to hide her secret and escape with Katherine.*

KHAN is Evelyn's servant. Now that she's widowed, he also sees himself as her bodyguard. He prides himself on his dignified manner and ability to handle difficult situations. Khan's scene objective: *to protect evelyn.*

KATHERINE is a shy innocent who has lead a very protected life. Katherine's scene objective: *to obey evelyn.*

THE SCENE:

INT./ EXT. SANTA MONICA—BUICK—MOVING—DAY

Gittes drives through Los Angeles.

To work from the inside out, slip in Gittes' mind while he drives to Evelyn's hideaway. Imagine yourself in Gittes' pov. As the streets roll past, you ask:

"If I were Gittes at this moment, what would I do?"

Letting your imagination roam, the answer comes:

"Rehearse. I always rehearse in my head before taking on life's big confrontations."

Now work deeper into Gittes's emotions and psyche:

Hands white-knuckled on the steering wheel, thoughts racing: "She killed him, then used me. She lied to me, came on to me. Man, I fell for her. My guts are in a knot, but I'll be cool. I'll stroll to the door, step in and accuse her. She lies. I send for the cops. She plays innocent, a few tears. But I stay ice cold, show her Mulwray's glasses, then lay out how she did it, step by step, as if I was there. She confesses. I turn her over to Escobar; I'm off the hook."

EXT. BUNGALOW—SANTA MONICA

Gittes' car speeds into the driveway.

You continue working from inside Gittes' pov, thinking:

"I'll be cool, I'll be cool . . ." Suddenly, with the sight of her house, an image of Evelyn flashes in your imagination. A rush of anger. A gap cracks open between your cool resolve and your fury.

The Buick SCREECHES to a halt. Gittes jumps out.

"To hell with her!"

Gittes SLAMS the car door and bolts up the steps.

"Grab her now, before she runs."

He twists the door knob, find it locked, then BANGS on the door.

"Goddamn it."

INT. BUNGALOW

KHAN, Evelyn's Chinese servant, hears POUNDING and heads for the door.

As characters enter and exit, shift back and forth in your imagination, taking the pov of one, then the other. Moving to Khan's point of view, ask yourself:

"If I were Khan at this moment, what would I think, feel, do?"

As you settle into this character's psyche, your thoughts run to:

"Who the hell's that?" Paste on a butler's smile. "Ten to one it's that loud mouth detective again. I'll handle him."

Khan unlocks the door and finds Gittes on the step.

                    KHAN
          You wait.

Shifting back into Gittes' mind:

"That snotty butler again."

                    GITTES
          You wait. Chow hoy kye dye!
               (translation: Fuck
               off, punk)

Gittes shoves Khan aside and pushes into the house.

As you switch back to Khan, the sudden gap between expectation and result inverts your smile:

Confusion, anger. "He not only barges in but insults me in Cantonese! Throw him out!"

Gittes looks up as Evelyn appears on the stairs behind Khan, nervously adjusting her necklace as she descends.

As Khan:

"It's Mrs. Mulwray. Protect her!"

Evelyn has been calling Gittes all morning, hoping to get his help. After packing for hours, she's in a hell-bent rush to catch the 5:30 train to Mexico. You shift to her pov:

"If I were Evelyn in this situation, what would I do?"

Now find your way to the heart of this very complex woman:

"It's Jake. Thank God. I know he cares. He'll help me. How do I look?" Hands instinctively flutter to hair, face. "Khan looks worried."

Evelyn smiles reassuringly to Khan and gestures for him to leave.

                    EVELYN
          It's all right, Khan.

As Evelyn turning back to Gittes:

Feeling more confident. "Now I'm not alone."

> EVELYN
> How are you? I've been
> calling you.

INT. LIVING ROOM—SAME

Gittes turns away and steps into the living room.

> *As Gittes:*

**"She's so beautiful. Don't look at her. Stay tough, man. Be
ready. She'll tell lie on lie."**

> GITTES
> . . . Yeah?

Evelyn follows, searching his face.

> *As Evelyn:*

**"I can't get his eye. Something's bothering him. He looks
exhausted . . . "**

> EVELYN
> Did you get some sleep?

> GITTES
> Sure.

". . . and hungry, poor man."

> EVELYN
> Have you had lunch? Khan
> can fix you something.

As Gittes:

"What's this lunch bullshit? Do it now."

                    GITTES
            Where's the girl?

Back in Evelyn's thoughts as a gap in expectation flies open with a shock:

"Why's he asking that? What's gone wrong? Keep calm. Feign innocence."

                    EVELYN
            Upstairs, why?

As Gittes:

"The soft voice, the innocent 'why?' Keep cool."

                    GITTES
            I want to see her.

As Evelyn:

"What does he want with Katherine? No. I can't let him see her now. Lie. Find out first."

                    EVELYN
            . . . She's having a bath now.
            Why do you want to see her?

As Gittes:

Disgusted with her lies. "Don't let her get to ya."

Gittes looks around the room and sees half-packed suitcases.

"She's making a run for it. Good thing I got here. Keep sharp. She'll lie again."

GITTES
Going somewhere?

As Evelyn:

"Should have told him, but there wasn't time. Can't hide it. Tell the truth. He'll understand."

EVELYN
Yes, we have a 5:30 train to
catch.

As Gittes, a minor gap opens:

"What do ya know? Sounds honest. Doesn't matter. Put an end to her bullshit. Let her know you mean business. Where's the phone? There."

Gittes picks up the telephone.

As Evelyn:

Bewilderment, choking fear. "Who's he calling?"

EVELYN
Jake . . . ?

"He's dialing. God, help me . . . "

As Gittes, ear to the phone:

"Answer, damn it." Hearing the desk sergeant pick up.

                    GITTES
          J. J. Gittes for Lt. Escobar.

As Evelyn:

**"The police!" A rush of adrenaline hits. Panic. "No, no.
Keep calm. Keep calm. It must be about Hollis. But I can't
wait. We have to leave now."**

                    EVELYN
          Look, what's the matter?
          What's wrong? I told you
          we've got a 5:30 train—

As Gittes:

"Enough! Shut her up."

                    GITTES
          You're gonna miss your train.
                 (into phone)
          Lou, meet me at 1972 Canyon
          Drive . . . yeah, soon as you
          can.

As Evelyn:

**Anger rises. "The fool . . ." A shred of hope. "But maybe
he's calling the police to help me."**

                    EVELYN
          Why did you do that?

As Gittes:

Smug satisfaction. "She's trying to get tough, but I've got her now. Feels good. I'm right at home."

> GITTES
> (tossing his hat on
> the table)
> You know any good criminal
> lawyers?

As Evelyn, trying to close an ever-widening gap:

"Lawyers? What the hell does he mean?" A chilling fear of something terrible about to happen.

> EVELYN
> No.

As Gittes:

"Look at her, cool and collected, playing it innocent to the end."

> GITTES
> (taking out a silver
> cigarette case)
> Don't worry. I can recommend
> a couple. They're expensive,
> but you can afford it.

Gittes calmly takes a lighter from his pocket, sits down and lights a cigarette.

As Evelyn:

"My God, he's threatening me. I slept with him. Look at him swagger. Who does he think he is?" Throat tightens in anger. "Don't panic. Handle it. There must be a reason for this."

> EVELYN
> Will you please tell me what
> this is all about?

As Gittes:

"Pissed off, are ya? Good. Watch this."

Gittes slips the cigarette lighter back into his pocket and with the same motion brings out a wrapped handkerchief. He sets it on the table and carefully pulls back the four corners of the cloth to reveal the eyeglasses.

> GITTES
> I found these in your back-
> yard in the pond. They
> belonged to your husband,
> didn't they . . . didn't they?

As Evelyn:

The gap refuses to close. Dazed. Nothing makes sense. A rising dread. "Glasses? In Hollis' fish pond? What's he after?"

> EVELYN
> I don't know. Yes, probably.

As Gittes:

"An opening. Get her now. Make her confess."

> GITTES
> (jumping up)
> Yes, positively. That's where
> he was drowned.

As Evelyn:

Stunned. "At home?!"

> EVELYN
> What?!

As Gittes:

Fury. "Make her talk. Now!"

> GITTES
> There's no time to be shocked
> by the truth. The coroner's
> report proves that he had salt
> water in his lungs when he
> was killed. Just take my word
> for it, all right? Now I want to
> know how it happened, and I
> want to know why, and I
> want to know before Escobar
> gets here because I don't
> want to lose my license.

As Evelyn:

His sneering, livid face pushes into yours. Chaos, paralyzing fear, grasping for control.

> EVELYN
> I don't know what you are
> talking about. This is the
> craziest, the most insane
> thing . . .
> GITTES
> Stop it!

As Gittes:

Losing control, hands shoot out, grasp her, fingers digging in, making her wince. But then the look of shock and pain in her eyes brings a stab of compassion. A gap opens. Feelings for her struggle against the rage. Hands drop. "She's hurting. Come on, man, she didn't do it in cold blood. could happen to anybody. Give her a chance. Lay it out, point by point, but get the truth out of her!"

> GITTES
> I'm gonna make it easy for
> you. You were jealous, you
> had a fight, he fell, hit his
> head . . . it was an accident
> . . . but his girl's a witness. So
> you had to shut her up. You
> don't have the guts to harm
> her, but you've got the money
> to shut her mouth. Yes or no?

As Evelyn:

The gap crashes shut with a horrible meaning: "My God, he thinks I did it!"

<pre>   EVELYN
          No!
</pre>

As Gittes, hearing her emphatic answer:

"Good. Finally sounds like the truth." Cooling off. "But what the hell's going on?"

<pre>   GITTES
          Who is she? And don't give
          me that crap about a sister
          because you don't have a
          sister.
</pre>

As Evelyn:

The greatest shock of all splits you in two: "He wants to know who she is . . . God help me." Weak with years of carrying the secret. Back to wall. "If I don't tell him, he'll call the police, but if I do . . ." No place to turn . . . except to Gittes.

<pre>   EVELYN
          I'll tell you . . . I'll tell you the
          truth.
</pre>

As Gittes:

Confident. Focused. "At last."

> GITTES
> Good. What's her name?

As Evelyn:

"Her name. . . . Dear God, her name . . . "

> EVELYN
> . . . Katherine.

> GITTES
> Katherine who?

As Evelyn:

Bracing for the worst. "Tell it all. See if he can take it . . . if I can take it . . . "

> EVELYN
> She's my daughter.

Back in Gittes pov as the expectation of finally prying loose her confession explodes:

"Another goddamned lie!"

Gittes lashes out and slaps her flush across the face.

As Evelyn:

Searing pain. Numbness. The paralysis that comes from a life time of guilt.

> GITTES
> I said the truth.

She stands passively, offering herself to be hit again.

                    EVELYN
          She's my sister—

As Gittes:

slapping her again . . .

                    EVELYN
          —she's my daughter—

As Evelyn:

Feeling nothing but a letting go.

As Gittes:

. . . hitting her yet again, seeing her tears . . .

                    EVELYN
          —my sister—

. . . slapping her even harder . . .

                    EVELYN
          —my daughter, my sister—

. . . backhand, open fist, grasp her, hurl her into a sofa.

                    GITTES
          I said I want the truth.

As Evelyn:

At first his assault seems miles away, but slamming against the sofa jolts you back to the now, and you scream out words you've never said to anyone:

> EVELYN
> She's my sister and my
> daughter.

As Gittes:

A blinding gap! Dumbfounded. Fury ebbs away as the gap slowly closes and you absorb the terrible implications behind her words.

Suddenly, Khan POUNDS down the stairs.

As Khan:

Ready to fight to protect her.

As Evelyn, suddenly remembering:

"Katherine! Sweet Jesus, did she hear me?"

> EVELYN
> (quickly to Kahn)
> Khan, please, go back.
> For God's sake, keep her
> upstairs. Go back.

Khan gives Gittes a hard look, then retreats upstairs.

As Evelyn, turning to see the frozen expression on Gittes' face:

An odd sense of pity for him. "Poor man . . . still doesn't get it."

> EVELYN
> . . . my father and I . . .
> understand? Or is it too tough
> for you?

Evelyn drops her head to her knees and sobs.

As Gittes:

A wave of compassion. "Cross . . . that sick bastard . . . "

> GITTES
> (quietly)
> He raped you?

As Evelyn:

Images of you and your father, so many years ago. Crushing guilt. But no more lies:

Evelyn shakes her head "no."

This is the location of a critical rewrite. In the third draft Evelyn explains at great length that her mother died when she was fifteen and her father's grief was such that he had a "breakdown" and became " a little boy," unable to feed or dress himself. This led to incest between them. Unable to face what he had done, her father then turned his back on her. This exposition not only slowed the pace of the scene, but more importantly, it seriously weakened the power of the antagonist, giving him a sympathetic vul-nerability. It was cut and replaced by Gittes' "He raped you?" and Evelyn's denial—a brilliant stroke that main-

tains Cross's cruel core, and severely tests Gittes' love for Evelyn.

This opens at least two possible explanations for why Evelyn denies she was raped: Children often have a self-destructive need to protect their parents. It could well have been rape, but even now she cannot bring herself to accuse her father. Or was she complicit. Her mother was dead, making her the "woman of the house." In those circumstances, incest between father and daughter is not unknown. That, however, doesn't excuse Cross. The responsibility is his in either case, but Evelyn has punished herself with guilt. Her denial forces Gittes to face character defining choices: whether or not to continue loving this woman, whether or not to turn her over to the police for murder. Her denial contradicts his expectation and a void opens:

As Gittes:

"If she wasn't raped . . . ?" Confusion. "There must be more."

> GITTES
> Then what happened?

As Evelyn:

Flashing memories of the shock of being pregnant, your father's sneering face, fleeing to Mexico, the agony of giving birth, a foreign clinic, loneliness . . .

> EVELYN
> I ran away . . .

> GITTES
> . . . to Mexico.

As Evelyn:

Remembering when Hollis found you in Mexico, proudly showing him Katherine, grief as your child is taken from you, the faces of the nuns, the sound of Katherine crying . . .

> EVELYN
> (nodding "yes")
> Hollis came and took care of
> me. I couldn't see her . . . I
> was fifteen. I wanted to but I
> couldn't. Then . . .

Images of your joy at getting Katherine to Los Angeles to be with you, of keeping her safe from your father, but then sudden fear: "He must never find her. He's mad. I know what he wants. If he gets his hands on my child, he's going to do it again."

> EVELYN
> (a pleading look to
> Gittes)
> Now I want to be with her.
> I want to take care of her.

As Gittes:

"I've finally got the truth." Feeling the gap close, and with it, a growing love for her. Pity for all she's suffered, respect for her courage and devotion to the child. "Let her go. No, better yet, get her out of town yourself. She'll never make it on her own. And, man, you owe it to her."

> GITTES
> Where are you gonna take
> her now?

As Evelyn:

Rush of hope. "What does he mean? Will he help?"

> EVELYN
> Back to Mexico.

As Gittes:

Wheels turning. "How to get her past Escobar?"

> GITTES
> Well, you can't take the train.
> Escobar'll be looking for you
> everywhere.

As Evelyn:

Disbelief. Elation. "He is going to help me!"

> EVELYN
> How . . . how about a plane?

> GITTES
> No, that's worse. You better
> just get out of here, leave all
> this stuff here.
>   (beat)
> Where does Kahn live? Get
> the exact address.

> EVELYN
> All right . . .

Light glints off the glasses on the table, catching Evelyn's eye.

As Evelyn:

"Those glasses . . ." An image of Hollis reading . . . without glasses.

> EVELYN
> Those didn't belong to Hollis.

> GITTES
> How do you know?

> EVELYN
> He didn't wear bifocals.

She goes upstairs as Gittes stares down at the glasses.

As Gittes:

"If not Mulwray's glasses . . . ? A gap breaks open. One last piece of truth yet to find. Memory rewinds and flashes back to . . . lunch with Noah Cross, and him peering over bifocals, eyeing the head of a broiled fish. The gap snaps shut. "Cross killed Mulwray because his son-in-law wouldn't tell him where his daughter by his daughter was hiding. Cross wants the kid. But he won't get her because I've got the evidence to nail him . . . in my pocket."

Gittes carefully tucks the bifocals into his vest, then looks up to see Evelyn on the stairs with her arm around a shy teenager.

"Lovely. Like her mother. A little scared. Must have heard us."

> EVELYN
> Katherine, say hello to Mister
> Gittes.

You move into Katherine's pov:

If I were Katherine in this moment, what would I feel?

As Katherine:

Anxious. Flustered. "Mother's been crying. Did this man hurt her? She's smiling at him. I guess it's okay."

> KATHERINE
>
> Hello.

> GITTES
>
> Hello.

Evelyn gives her daughter a reassuring look and sends her back upstairs.

> EVELYN
> (to Gittes)
> He lives at 1712 Alameda. Do
> you know where that is?

> GITTES
>
> Sure . . .

As Gittes:

A last gap opens, flooded with images of a woman you once loved and her violent death on Alameda in Chinatown. Feelings of dread, of life coming full circle. The gap slowly closes with the thought, "This time I'll do it right."

•   •   •

CREATING WITHIN THE GAP

In writing out what actors call "inner monologues" I've put this well-paced scene into ultra-slow motion, and given words to what would be flights of feeling or flashes of insight. Nonetheless, that's how it is at the desk. It may take days, even weeks, to write what will be minutes, perhaps seconds, on screen. We put each and every moment under a microscope of thinking, rethinking, creating, recreating as we weave through our characters' moments, a maze of unspoken thoughts, images, sensations, and emotions.

Writing from the inside out, however, does not mean that we imagine a scene from one end to the other locked in a single character's point of view. Rather, as in the exercise above, the writer shifts points of view. He settles into the conscious center of a character and asks the question: "If I were this character in these circumstances, what would I do?" He feels within his own emotions a specific human reaction and imagines the character's next action.

Now the writer's problem is this: how to progress the scene? To build a next beat, the writer must move out of the character's subjective point of view and take an objective look at the action he just created. This action anticipates a certain reaction from the character's world. But that must not occur. Instead, the writer must pry open the gap. To do so, he asks the question writers have been asking themselves since time began: "*What is the opposite of that?*"

Writers are by instinct dialectical thinkers. As Jean Cocteau said, "The spirit of creation is the spirit of contradiction—the breakthrough of appearances toward an unknown reality." You must doubt appearances and seek the opposite of the obvious. Don't skim the surface, taking things at face value. Rather, peel back the skin of life to find the hidden, the unexpected, the seemingly inappropriate—in other words, the truth. And you will find your truth in the gap.

Remember, you are the God of your universe. You know your characters, their minds, bodies, emotions, relationships, world. Once you've created an honest moment from one point of view, you move around your universe, even into the inanimate, looking for another point of view so you can invade that, create an unexpected reaction, and splinter open the cleft between expectation and result.

Having done this, you then go back into the mind of the first character, and find your way to a new emotional truth by asking again: "If I were this character under these *new* circumstances, what would I do?" Finding your way to that reaction and action, you then step right out again, asking: "And what is the opposite of *that*?"

Fine writing emphasizes REACTIONS.

Many of the actions in any story are more or less expected. By genre convention, the lovers in a *Love Story* will meet, the detective in a *Thriller* will discover a crime, the protagonist's life in an *Education Plot* will bottom out. These and other such commonplace actions are universally known and anticipated by the audience. Consequently, fine writing puts less stress on *what* happens than on to *whom* it happens and *why* and *how* it happens. Indeed, the richest and most satisfying pleasures of all are found in stories that focus on the *reactions* that events cause and the *insight gained*.

Looking back at the CHINATOWN scene: Gittes knocks on the door expecting to be let in. What's the reaction he gets? Khan blocks his way, expecting Gittes to wait. Gittes's reaction? He shocks Khan by insulting him in Cantonese and barging in. Evelyn comes downstairs expecting Gittes's help. The reaction to that? Gittes calls the police, expecting to force her to confess the murder and tell the truth about the "other woman." Reaction? She reveals that the other woman is her daughter by incest, indicting her lunatic father for the murder. Beat after beat, even in the quietest, most internalized of scenes, a dynamic series of action/*reaction*/gap, renewed action/surprising *reaction*/gap builds the scene to and around its Turning Point as reactions amaze and fascinate.

If you write a beat in which a character steps up to a door, knocks, and waits, and in reaction the door is politely opened to invite him in, and the director is foolish enough to shoot this, in all probability it will never see the light of the screen. Any editor worthy of the title would instantly scrap it, explaining to the director: "Jack, these are eight dead seconds. He knocks on the door and it's actually opened for him? No, we'll cut to the sofa. That's the first real beat. Sorry you squandered fifty thousand dollars walking your star through a door, but it's a pace killer and pointless." A "pointless pace killer" is any scene in which reactions lack insight and imagination, forcing expectation to equal result.

Once you've imagined the scene, beat by beat, gap by gap, you write. What you write is a vivid description of what happens and the reactions it gets, what is seen, said, and done. You write so that when someone else reads your pages he will, beat by beat, gap by gap, live through the roller coaster of life that you lived through at your desk. The words on the page allow the reader to plunge into each gap, seeing what you dreamed, feeling what you felt, learning what you understood until, like you, the reader's pulse pounds, emotions flow, and meaning is made.

THE SUBSTANCE AND ENERGY OF STORY

The answers to the questions that began this chapter should now be clear. The stuff of a story is not its words. Your text must be lucid to express the desk-bound life of your imagination and feelings. But words are not an end, they are a means, a medium. The substance of story is the gap that splits open between what a human being expects to happen when he takes an action and what really does happen; the rift between expectation and result, probability and necessity. To build a scene, we constantly break open these breaches in reality.

As to the source of energy in story, the answer is the same: the gap. The audience empathizes with the character, vicariously seeking his desire. It more or less expects the world to react the way the character expects. When the gap opens up for character, it opens up for audience. This is the "Oh, my God!" moment, the "Oh, no!" or "Oh, yes!" you've experienced again and again in well-crafted stories.

The next time you go to the movies, sit in the front row at the wall, so you can watch an audience watch a film. It's very instructive: Eyebrows fly up, mouths drop open, bodies flinch and rock, laughter explodes, tears run down faces. Every time the gap splits open for character, it opens for audience. With each turn, the character must pour more energy and effort into his next action. The audience, in empathy with the character, feels the same surges of energy building beat by beat through the film.

As a charge of electricity leaps from pole to pole in a magnet, so the spark of life ignites across the gap between the self and reality. With this flash of energy we ignite the power of story and move the heart of the audience.

8

THE INCITING INCIDENT

A story is a design in five parts: The *Inciting Incident*, the first major event of the telling, is the primary cause for all that follows, putting into motion the other four elements—*Progressive Complications, Crisis, Climax, Resolution*. To understand how the Inciting Incident enters into and functions within the work, let's step back to take a more comprehensive look at *setting*, the physical and social world in which it occurs.

THE WORLD OF THE STORY

We've defined *setting* in terms of period, duration, location, and level of conflict. These four dimensions frame the story's world, but to inspire the multitude of creative choices you need to tell an original, cliché-free story, and you must fill that frame with a depth and breadth of detail. Below is a list of general questions we ask of all stories. Beyond these, each work inspires a unique list of its own, driven by the writer's thirst for insight.

How do my characters make a living? We spend a third or more of our lives at work, yet rarely see scenes of people doing their jobs. The reason is simple: Most work is boring. Perhaps not to the person doing the work, but boring to watch. As any lawyer, cop, or doctor knows, the vast majority of their time is spent in routine duties, reports, and meetings that change little or nothing—the epitome of expectation meeting result. That's why in the professional genres—*Courtroom, Crime, Medical*—we focus on only those moments when work causes more problems than it solves. Nonetheless, to get inside a character, we must question all aspects of their twenty-four-hour day. Not only work, but how do they play? Pray? Make love?

What are the politics of my world? Not necessarily politics in terms of right-wing/left-wing, Republican/Democrat, but in the true sense of the word: power. Politics is the name we give to the orchestration of power in any society. Whenever human beings gather to do anything, there's always an uneven distribution of power. In corporations, hospitals, religions, government agencies, and the like, someone at the top has great power, people at the bottom have little or none, those in between have some. How does a worker gain power or lose it? No matter how we try to level inequalities, applying egalitarian theories of all kinds, human societies are stubbornly and inherently pyramidal in their arrangement of power. In other words, politics.

Even when writing about a household, question its politics, for like any other social structure, a family is political. Is it a patriarchal home where Dad has the clout, but when he leaves the house, it transfers to Mom, then when she's out, to the oldest child? Or is it a matriarchal home, where Mom runs things? Or a contemporary family in which the kid is tyrannizing his parents?

Love relationships are political. An old Gypsy expression goes: "He who confesses first loses." The first person to say "I love you" has lost because the other, upon hearing it, immediately smiles a knowing smile, realizing that he's the one loved, so he now controls the relationship. If you're lucky, those three little words will be said in unison over candlelight. Or, if very, very lucky, they won't need to be said . . . they'll be *done*.

What are the rituals of my world? In all corners of the world life is bound up in ritual. This is a ritual, is it not? I've written a book and you're reading it. In another time and place we might sit under a tree or take a walk, like Socrates and his students. We create a ritual for every activity, not only for public ceremony but for our very private rites. Heaven help the person who rearranges my organization of toiletries around the bathroom basin.

How do your characters take meals? Eating is a different ritual everywhere in the world. Americans, for example, according to a recent survey, now eat 75 percent of all their meals in restaurants. If your characters eat at home, is it an old-fashioned family that dresses for dinner at a certain hour, or a contemporary one that feeds from an open refrigerator?

What are the values in my world? What do my characters consider good? Evil? What do they see as right? Wrong? What are my society's laws? Realize that good/evil, right/wrong, and legal/illegal don't necessarily have anything to do with one another. What do my characters believe is worth living for? Foolish to pursue? What would they give their lives for?

What is the genre or combination of genres? With what conventions? As with setting, genres surround the writer with creative limitations that must be kept or brilliantly altered.

What are the biographies of my characters? From the day they were born to the opening scene, how has life shaped them?

What is the Backstory? This is an oft-misunderstood term. It doesn't mean life history or biography. *Backstory* is the set of significant events that occurred in the characters' past that the writer can use to build his story's progressions. Exactly how we use Backstory to tell story will be discussed later, but for the moment note that we do not bring characters out of a void. We landscape character biographies, planting them with events that become a garden we'll harvest again and again.

What is my cast design? Nothing in a work of art is there by accident. Ideas may come spontaneously, but we must weave them consciously and creatively into the whole. We cannot allow any character who comes to mind to stumble into the story and play a part. Each role must fit a purpose, and the first principle of cast design is polarization. Between the various roles we devise a network of contrasting or contradictory attitudes.

If the ideal cast sat down for dinner and something happened, whether as trivial as spilled wine or as important as a divorce announcement, from each and every character would come a separate and distinctively different reaction. No two would react the same because no two share the same attitude toward anything. Each is an individual with a character-specific view of life, and the disparate reaction of each contrasts with all others.

If two characters in your cast share the same attitude and react in kind to whatever occurs, you must either collapse the two into one, or expel one from the story. When characters react the same, you minimize opportunities for conflict. Instead, the writer's strategy must be to maximize these opportunities.

Imagine this cast: father, mother, daughter, and a son named Jeffrey. This family lives in Iowa. As they sit down for dinner, Jeffrey turns to them and says: "Mom, Dad, Sis, I've come to a big decision. I have an airline ticket and tomorrow I'm leaving for Hollywood to pursue a career as an art director in the movies." And all three respond: "Oh, what a wonderful idea! Isn't that great? Jeff's going off to Hollywood!" And they toast him with their glasses of milk.

CUT TO: Jeff's room, where they help him pack while admiring his pictures on the wall, reflecting nostalgically on his days in art school, complimenting his talent, predicting success.

CUT TO: The airport as the family puts Jeff on the plane, tears in their eyes, embracing him: "Write when you get work, Jeff."

Suppose, instead, Jeffrey sits down for dinner, delivers his declaration, and suddenly Dad's fist POUNDS the table: "What the hell are you talking about, Jeff? You're not going off to Hollyweird to become some art director . . . whatever an art director is. No, you're staying right here in Davenport. Because, Jeff, as you know, I have never done anything for myself. Not in my entire life. It's all for you, Jeff, for you! Granted, I'm the king of plumbing supplies in Iowa . . . but someday, son, you'll be emperor of plumbing supplies all over the Midwest and I won't hear another word of this nonsense. End of discussion."

CUT TO: Jeff sulking in his room. His mother slips in whispering: "Don't you listen to him. Go off to Hollywood, become an art director . . . whatever that is. Do they win Oscars for that, Jeff?" "Yes, Mom, they do," Jeff says. "Good! Go off to Hollywood and win me an Oscar and prove that bastard wrong. And you can do it, Jeff. Because you've got talent. I know you've got talent. You got that from my side of the family. I used to have talent too, but I gave it all up when I married your father, and I've regretted it ever since. For God's sake, Jeff, don't sit here in Davenport. Hell, this town was named after a sofa. No, go off to Hollywood and make me proud."

CUT TO: Jeff packing. His sister comes in, shocked, "Jeff! What are you doing? Packing? Leaving me alone? With those two? You know how they are. They'll eat me alive. If you go off to Hollywood, I'll end up in the plumbing supply business!" Pulling his stuff out of the suitcase: "If you wanna be an artist, you can be an artist anywhere. A sunset's a sunset. A landscape's a landscape. What the hell difference does it make? And someday you'll have success. I know you will. I've seen paintings just like yours . . . in Sears. Don't leave, Jeff! I'll die!"

Whether or not Jeff goes off to Hollywood, the polarized cast gives the writer something we all desperately need: scenes.

AUTHORSHIP

When research of setting reaches the saturation point, something miraculous happens. Your story takes on a unique atmosphere, a personality that sets it apart from every other story ever told, no matter how many millions there have been through time. It's an amazing phenomenon: Human beings have told one another stories since they sat around the fire in caves, and every time the storyteller uses the art in its fullest, his story, like a portrait by a master painter, becomes one of a kind.

Like the stories you're striving to tell, you want to be one of a kind, recognized and respected as an original. In your quest, consider these three words: "author," "authority," "authenticity."

First, "author." "Author" is a title we easily give novelists and playwrights, rarely screenwriters. But in the strict sense of "originator," the screenwriter, as creator of setting, characters, and story, is an *author*. For the test of authorship is knowledge. A true author, no matter the medium, is an artist with godlike knowledge of his subject, and the proof of his authorship is that his pages smack of *authority.* What a rare pleasure it is to open a screenplay and immediately surrender to the work, giving over emotion and concentration because there is something ineffable between and under the lines that says: *"This writer knows.* I'm in the hands of an authority." And the effect of writing with authority is *authenticity.*

Two principles control the emotional involvement of an audience. First, empathy: identification with the protagonist that draws us into the story, vicariously rooting for our own desires in life. Second, authenticity: *We must believe,* or as Samuel Taylor Coleridge suggested, we must willingly suspend our disbelief. Once involved, the writer must keep us involved to FADE OUT. To do so, he must convince us that the world of his story is authentic. We know that storytelling is a ritual surrounding a metaphor for life. To enjoy this ceremony in the dark we react to stories as if they're real. We suspend our cynicism and believe in the tale as long as we find it authentic. The moment it lacks credibility, empathy dissolves and we feel nothing.

Authenticity, however, does not mean actuality. Giving a story a contemporary milieu is no guarantee of authenticity; authenticity means an internally consistent world, true to itself in scope, depth, and detail. As Aristotle tells us: "For the purposes of [story] a convincing impossibility is preferable to an unconvincing possibility." We can all list films that had us moaning: "I don't buy it. People aren't like that. Makes no sense. That's not how things happen."

Authenticity has nothing to do with so-called reality. A story set in a world that could never exist could be absolutely authentic. Story arts do not distinguish between reality and the various nonrealities of fantasy, dream, and ideality. The creative intelligence of the writer merges all these into a unique yet convincing fictional reality.

ALIEN: In the opening sequence the crew of an interstellar cargo ship awakes from its stasis chambers and gathers at the mess table. Dressed in work shirts and dungarees, they drink coffee and smoke cigarettes. On the table a toy bird bobs in a glass. Elsewhere, little collectibles of life clutter the living spaces. Plastic bugs hang from the ceiling, pinups and family photos are taped to the bulkhead. The crew talks—not about work or getting home—but about money. Is this unscheduled stop in their contract? Will the company pay bonuses for this extra duty?

Have you ever ridden in the cab of an eighteen-wheeler? How are they decorated? With the little collectibles of life: a plastic saint on the dashboard, blue ribbons won at a county fair, family photos, magazine clippings. Teamsters spend more time in their trucks than at home, so they take pieces of home on the road. And when they take a break, what's the first topic of talk? Money—golden time, overtime, is this in our contract? Understanding this psychology, screenwriter Dan O'Bannon recreated it in subtle details, so as that the scene played, the audience surrendered, thinking: "Wonderful! They're not spacemen like Buck Rogers or Flash Gordon. They're truck drivers."

In the next sequence, as Kane (John Hurt) investigates an alien growth, something springs out and smashes through the helmet of his space suit. Like a huge crab, the creature covers Kane's face, its legs locked around his head. What's worse, it's forced a tube down his throat and into his belly, putting him in a coma. Science Officer Ash (Ian Holm) realizes he can't pry the creature loose without ripping Kane's face apart, so he decides to release the creature's grip by severing its legs one at a time.

But as Ash applies a laser saw to the first leg, the flesh splits and out spits a viscous substance; a blistering "acid blood" that dissolves steel like sugar and eats a hole through the floor as big as a watermelon. The crew rushes to the deck below and looks up to see the acid eating through the ceiling, then burning a hole just as big through that floor. They rush down another deck and it's eating through that ceiling and floor until three decks down the acid finally peters out. At this point, one thought passed through the audience: "These people are in deep shit."

In other words, O'Bannon researched his alien. He asked himself, "What is the biology of my beast? How does it evolve? Feed? Grow? Reproduce? Does it have any weaknesses? What are its strengths?" Imagine the list of attributes O'Bannon must have concocted before seizing on "acid blood." Imagine the many sources he may have explored. Perhaps he did an intense study of earth-bound parasitical insects, or remembered the eighth-century Anglo-Saxon epic *Beowulf* in which the blood of Grendel the water monster burns through the hero's shield, or it came to him in a nightmare. Whether through investigation, imagination, or memory, O'Bannon's alien is a stunning creation.

All the artists making ALIEN—writer, director, designers, actors—worked to the limit of their talents to create an authentic world. They knew that believability is the key to terror. Indeed, if the audience is to feel *any* emotion, it must believe. For when a film's emotional load becomes too sad, too horrifying, even too funny, how do we try to escape? We say to ourselves: "It's only a movie." We deny its authenticity. But if the film's of quality, the second we glance back at the screen, we're grabbed by the throat and pulled right back into those emotions. We won't escape until the film lets us out, which is what we paid our money for in the first place.

Authenticity depends on the "telling detail." When we use a few selected details, the audience's imagination supplies the rest, completing a credible whole. On the other hand, if the writer and director try too hard to be "real"—especially with sex and violence—the audience reaction is: "That's not really real," or "My God, that's so real," or "They're not really fucking," or "My God, they're really fucking." In either case, credibility shatters as the audience is yanked out of the story to notice the filmmaker's technique. An audience believes as long as we don't give them reason to doubt.

Beyond physical and social detail, we must also create emotional authenticity. Authorial research must pay off in believable character behavior. Beyond behavioral credibility, the story itself must persuade. From event to event, cause and effect must be convincing, logical. The art of story design lies in the fine adjustment of things both usual and unusual to things universal and archetypal. The writer whose knowledge of subject has taught him exactly what to stress and expand versus what to lay down quietly and subtly will stand out from the thousands of others who always hit the same note.

Originality lies in the struggle for authenticity, not eccentricity. A personal style, in other words, cannot be achieved self-consciously.

Rather, when your authorial knowledge of setting and character meets your personality, the choices you make and the arrangements you create out of this mass of material are unique to you. Your work becomes what you are, an original.

Compare a Waldo Salt story (MIDNIGHT COWBOY, SERPICO) with an Alvin Sargent story (DOMINICK AND EUGENE, ORDINARY PEOPLE): one hard-edged, the other tender, one elliptical, the other linear, one ironic, the other compassionate. The unique story styles of each is the natural and spontaneous effect of an author mastering his subject in the never-ending battle against clichés.

THE INCITING INCIDENT

Starting from any Premise at any point in the story's chronology, our research feeds the invention of events, the events redirect research. We do not, in other words, necessarily design a story by beginning with its first major event. But at some point as you create your universe, you'll face these questions: How do I set my story into action? Where do I place this crucial event?

When an Inciting Incident occurs it must be a dynamic, fully developed event, not something static or vague. This, for example, is not an Inciting Incident: A college dropout lives off-campus near New York University. She wakes one morning and says: "I'm bored with my life. I think I'll move to Los Angeles." She packs her VW and motors west, but her change of address changes nothing of value in her life. She's merely exporting her apathy from New York to California.

If, on the other hand, we notice that she's created an ingenious kitchen wallpaper from hundreds of parking tickets, then a sudden POUNDING on the door brings the police, brandishing a felony warrant for ten thousand dollars in unpaid citations, and she flees down the fire escape, heading West—this could be an Inciting Incident. It has done what an Inciting Incident must do.

The INCITING INCIDENT radically upsets the balance of forces in the protagonist's life.

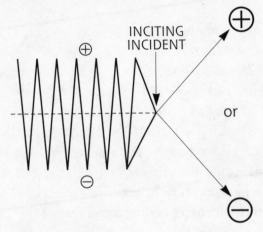

As a story begins, the protagonist is living a life that's more or less in balance. He has successes and failures, ups and downs. Who doesn't? But life is in relative control. Then, perhaps suddenly but in any case decisively, an event occurs that radically upsets its balance, swinging the value-charge of the protagonist's reality either to the negative or to the positive.

Negative: Our dropout reaches L.A., but she balks at taking a normal job when she's asked for her social security number. Fearful that in a computerized world the Manhattan police will track her down through the Internal Revenue Service, what does she do? Go underground? Sell drugs? Turn to prostitution?

Positive: Perhaps the knock at the door is an heir hunter with news of a million-dollar fortune left by an anonymous relative. Suddenly rich, she's under terrible pressure. With no more excuses for failure, she has a heart-thumping fear of screwing up this dream come true.

In most cases, the Inciting Incident is a single event that either happens directly to the protagonist or is caused by the protagonist. Consequently, he's immediately aware that life is out of balance for better or worse. When lovers first meet, this face-to-face event turns life, for the moment, to the positive. When Jeffrey abandons the security of his Davenport family for Hollywood, he knowingly puts himself at risk.

Occasionally, an Inciting Incident needs two events: a setup and a payoff. JAWS: Setup, a shark eats a swimmer and her body washes onto the beach. Payoff, the sheriff (Roy Scheider) discovers the corpse. If the logic of an Inciting Incident requires a setup, the writer cannot delay the payoff—at least not for very long—and keep the protagonist ignorant of the fact that his life is out of balance. Imagine JAWS with this design: Shark eats girl, followed by sheriff goes bowling, gives out parking tickets, makes love to his wife, goes to PTA meeting, visits his sick mother . . . while the corpse rots on the beach. A story is not a sandwich of episodic slices of life between two halves of an Inciting Incident.

Consider the unfortunate design of THE RIVER: The film opens with the first half of an Inciting Incident: a businessman, Joe Wade (Scott Glenn) decides to build a dam across a river, knowing he'll flood five farms in the process. One of these belongs to Tom and Mae Garvey (Mel Gibson and Sissy Spacek). No one, however, tells Tom or Mae. So for the next hundred minutes we watch: Tom plays baseball, Tom and Mae struggle to make the farm turn a profit, Tom goes to work in a factory caught up in a labor dispute, Mae breaks her arm in a tractor accident, Joe makes romantic passes at Mae, Mae goes to the factory to visit her husband who's now a scab locked in the factory, a stressed-out Tom fails to get it up, Mae whispers a gentle word, Tom gets it up, and so on.

Ten minutes from its end, the film delivers the second half of the Inciting Incident: Tom stumbles into Joe's office, sees a model of the dam, and says, in effect: "If you build that dam, Joe, you'll flood my farm." Joe shrugs. Then, deus ex machina, it starts to rain and the river rises. Tom and his buddies get their bulldozers to shore up the levee; Joe gets his bulldozer and goons to tear down the levee. Tom and Joe have a bulldozer-to-bulldozer Mexican standoff. At this point, Joe steps back and declares that he didn't want to build the dam in the first place. FADE OUT.

The protagonist must react to the Inciting Incident.

Given the infinitely variable nature of protagonists, however, any reaction is possible. For example, how many Westerns began like this? Bad guys shoot up the town and kill the old marshal. Townspeople gather and go down to the livery stable, run by Matt, a retired gunslinger who's sworn a sacred oath never to kill again. The mayor pleads: "Matt, you've got to pin on the badge and come to our aid. You're the only one that can do it." Matt replies: "No, no, I hung up my guns long ago." "But, Matt," begs the schoolmarm, "they killed your mother." Matt toes the dirt and says: "Well . . . she was old and I guess her time had come." He refuses to act, but that is a reaction.

The protagonist responds to the sudden negative or positive change in the balance of life in whatever way is appropriate to character and world. A refusal to act, however, cannot last for very long, even in the most passive protagonists of minimalist Nonplots. For we all wish some reasonable sovereignty over our existence, and if an event radically upsets our sense of equilibrium and control, what would we want? What does anyone, including our protagonist, want? To restore balance.

Therefore, the Inciting Incident first throws the protagonist's life out of balance, then arouses in him the desire to restore that balance. Out of this need—often quickly, occasionally with deliberation—the protagonist next conceives of an Object of Desire: something physical or situational or attitudinal that he feels he lacks or needs to put the ship of life on an even keel. Lastly, the Inciting Incident propels the protagonist into an active pursuit of this object or goal. And for many stories or genres this is sufficient: An event pitches the protagonist's life out of kilter, arousing a conscious desire for something he feels will set things right, and he goes after it.

But for those protagonists we tend to admire the most, the Inciting Incident arouses not only a conscious desire, but an unconscious one as well. These complex characters suffer intense inner battles because these two desires are in direct conflict with each other. No matter what the character consciously thinks he wants, the audience senses or realizes that deep inside he unconsciously wants the very opposite.

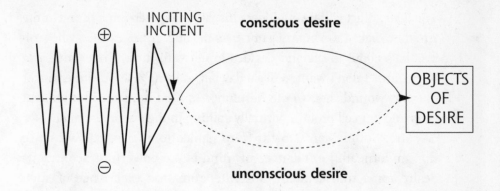

CARNAL KNOWLEDGE: If we were to pull the protagonist Jonathan (Jack Nicholson) aside and ask him "What do you want?" his conscious answer would be: "I'm a good-looking guy, lot of fun to be with, make a terrific living as a CPA. My life would be paradise if I could find the perfect woman to share it." The film takes Jonathan from his college years to middle age, a thirty-year search for his dream woman. Again and again he meets a beautiful, intelligent woman, but soon their candlelit romance turns to dark emotions, acts of physical violence, then breakup. Over and over he plays the great romantic until he has a woman head over heels in love with him, then he turns on her, humiliates her, and hurls her out of his life.

At Climax, he invites Sandy (Art Garfunkel), an old college buddy, for dinner. For amusement he screens 35mm slides of all the women from his life; a show he entitles "Ballbusters on Parade." As each woman appears, he trashes her to Sandy for "what was wrong with her." In the Resolution scene, he's with a prostitute (Rita Moreno) who has to read him an ode he's written in praise of his penis so he can get it up. He thinks he's hunting for the perfect woman, but we know that unconsciously he wants to degrade and destroy women and has done that throughout his life. Jules Feiffer's screenplay is a chilling delineation of a man that too many women know only too well.

MRS. SOFFEL: In 1901 a thief (Mel Gibson) who's committed murder awaits execution. The wife of the prison warden (Diane Keaton) decides to save his soul for God. She reads Bible quotations to him, hoping that when he's hanged he'll go to heaven and not hell.

They are attracted. She engineers his jailbreak, then joins him. On the run they make love, but only once. As the authorities close in, she realizes he's about to die and decides to die with him: "Shoot me," she begs him, "I don't want to live a day beyond you." He pulls the trigger but only wounds her. In the Resolution, she's imprisoned for life, but goes into her cell proudly, virtually spitting in the eye of her jailer.

Mrs. Soffel seems to flit from choice to choice, but we sense that underneath her changes of mind is the powerful unconscious desire for a transcendent, absolute, romantic experience of such intensity that if nothing ever happened to her again it wouldn't matter . . . because for one sublime moment she will have lived. Mrs. Soffel is the ultimate romantic.

THE CRYING GAME: Fergus (Stephen Rea), a member of the Irish Republican Army, is put in charge of a British corporal (Forest Whitaker) held prisoner by his IRA unit. He finds himself in sympathy with the man's plight. When the corporal is killed, Fergus goes AWOL to England, hiding out from both the British and the IRA. He looks up the corporal's lover, Dil (Jaye Davidson). He falls in love, only to discover that Dil's a transvestite. The IRA then tracks him down. Fergus volunteered for the IRA knowing it isn't a college fraternity, so when they order him to assassinate an English judge, he must finally come to terms with his politics. Is he or is he not an Irish patriot?

Beneath Fergus's conscious political struggle, the audience senses from his first moments with the prisoner to his last tender scenes with Dil that this film isn't about his commitment to the cause. Hidden behind his zigzag politics Fergus harbors the most human of needs: to love and be loved.

THE SPINE OF THE STORY

The energy of a protagonist's desire forms the critical element of design known as the *Spine* of the story (AKA *Through-line* or *Superobjective*). The Spine is the deep desire in and effort by the protagonist to restore the balance of life. It's the primary unifying force that holds all other story elements together. For no matter what happens on the surface of the story, each scene, image, and word is

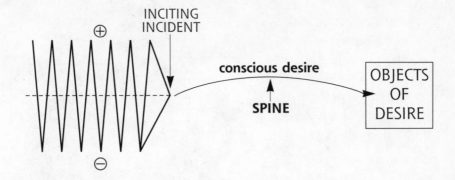

ultimately an aspect of the Spine, relating, causally or thematically, to this core of desire and action.

If the protagonist has no unconscious desire, then his conscious objective becomes the Spine. The Spine of any Bond film, for example, can be phrased as: *To defeat the arch-villain.* James has no unconscious desires; he wants and only wants to save the world. As the story's unifying force, Bond's pursuit of his conscious goal cannot change. If he were to declare, "To hell with Dr. No. I'm bored with the spy business. I'm going south to work on my backswing and lower my handicap," the film falls apart.

If, on the other hand, the protagonist has an unconscious desire, this becomes the Spine of the story. An unconscious desire is always more powerful and durable, with roots reaching to the protagonist's innermost self. When an unconscious desire drives the story, it allows the writer to create a far more complex character who may repeatedly change his conscious desire.

MOBY DICK: If Melville had made Ahab sole protagonist, his novel would be a simple but exciting work of *High Adventure*, driven by the captain's monomania to destroy the white whale. But by adding Ishmael as dual protagonist, Melville enriched his story into a complex classic of the *Education Plot*. For the telling is in fact driven by Ishmael's unconscious desire to battle inner demons, seeking in himself the destructive obsessions he sees in Ahab—a desire that not only contradicts his conscious hope to survive Ahab's mad voyage, but may destroy him as it does Ahab.

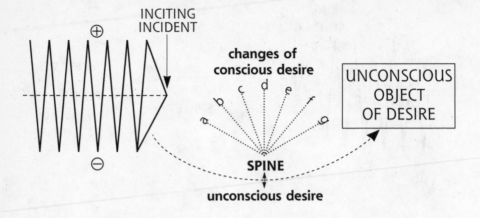

In THE CRYING GAME Fergus agonizes over politics while his unconscious need *to love and be loved* drives the telling. Jonathan searches for the "perfect woman" in CARNAL KNOWLEDGE, flitting from relationship to relationship, while his unconscious desire *to humiliate and destroy women* never varies. The leaps of desire in Mrs. Soffel's mind are enormous—from salvation to damnation—while unconsciously she seeks *to experience the transcendent romance.* The audience senses that the shifting urges of the complex protagonist are merely reflections of the one thing that never changes: the unconscious desire.

THE QUEST

From the point of view of the writer looking from the Inciting Incident "down the Spine" to the last act's Climax, in spite of all we've said about genres and the various shapes from Archplot to Antiplot, in truth there's only one story. In essence we have told one another the same tale, one way or another, since the dawn of humanity, and that story could be usefully called *the Quest.* All stories take the form of a Quest.

For better or worse, an event throws a character's life out of balance, arousing in him the conscious and/or unconscious desire for that which he feels will restore

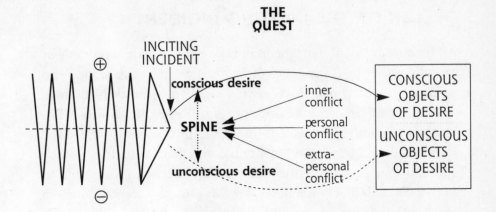

balance, launching him on a Quest for his Object of
Desire against forces of antagonism (inner, personal,
extra-personal). He may or may not achieve it. This is
story in a nutshell.

The essential form of story is simple. But that's like saying that
the essential form of music is simple. It is. It's twelve notes. But
these twelve notes conspire into everything and anything we have
ever called music. The essential elements of the Quest are the
twelve notes of our music, the melody we've listened to all our lives.
However, like the composer sitting down at the piano, when a writer
takes up this seemingly simple form, he discovers how incredibly
complex it is, how inordinately difficult to do.

To understand the Quest form of your story you need only
identify your protagonist's Object of Desire. Penetrate his psychology and find an honest answer to the question: "What does he
want?" It may be the desire for something he can take into his
arms: *someone to love* in MOONSTRUCK. It may be the need for
inner growth: *maturity* in BIG. But whether a profound change in
the real world—*security from a marauding shark* in JAWS—or a
profound change in the spiritual realm—*a meaningful life* in
TENDER MERCIES—by looking into the heart of the protagonist
and discovering his desire, you begin to see the arc of your story,
the Quest on which the Inciting Incident sends him.

DESIGN OF THE INCITING INCIDENT

An Inciting Incident happens in only one of two ways: randomly or causally, either by coincidence or by decision. If by decision, it can be made by the protagonist—Ben's decision to drink himself to death in LEAVING LAS VEGAS, or, as in KRAMER vs. KRAMER, by someone with the power to upset the protagonist's life—Mrs. Kramer's decision to leave Mr. Kramer and their child. If by coincidence, it may be tragic—the accident that kills Alice's husband in ALICE DOESN'T LIVE HERE ANYMORE, or serendipitous—a sports promoter meets beautiful and gifted athlete in PAT AND MIKE. By choice or accident; there are no other means.

The Inciting Incident of the Central Plot must happen onscreen—not in the Backstory, not between scenes offscreen. Each subplot has its own Inciting Incident, which may or may not be onscreen, but the presence of the audience at the Central Plot's Inciting Incident is crucial to story design for two reasons.

First, when the audience experiences an Inciting Incident, the film's Major Dramatic Question, a variation on "How will this turn out?" is provoked to mind. JAWS: Will the sheriff kill the shark, or the shark the sheriff? LA NOTTE: After Lidia (Jeanne Moreau) tells her husband (Marcello Mastroianni) that he disgusts her and she's leaving, will she go or stay? JALSAGHER (THE MUSIC ROOM): Biswas (Huzur Roy), an aristocrat with a life-consuming love of music, decides to sell his wife's jewels, then his palace to finance his passion for beauty. Will extravagance destroy or redeem this connoisseur?

In Hollywood jargon, the Central Plot's Inciting Incident is the "big hook." It must occur onscreen because this is the event that incites and captures the audience's curiosity. Hunger for the answer to the Major Dramatic Question grips the audience's interest, holding it to the last act's climax.

Second, witnessing the Inciting Incident projects an image of the Obligatory Scene into the audience's imagination. The Obligatory Scene (AKA Crisis) is an event the audience knows it must see before the story can end. This scene will bring the protagonist into a confrontation with the most powerful forces of antagonism in his quest, forces stirred to life by the Inciting Incident that will gather focus and strength through the course of the story. The scene is called "obligatory" because having teased the audience into anticipating this moment, the writer is obligated to keep his promise and show it to them.

JAWS: When the shark attacks a vacationer and the sheriff discovers her remains, an vivid image comes to mind: The shark and the sheriff do battle face-to-face. We don't know how we'll get there, or how it'll turn out. But we do know the film can't be over until the shark has the sheriff virtually in its jaws. Screenwriter Peter Benchley could not have played this critical event from the point of view of townspeople peering out to sea with binoculars, wondering: "Is that the sheriff? Is that the shark?" BOOM! Then have sheriff and marine biologist (Richard Dreyfuss) swim ashore, shouting, "Oh, what a fight. Let us tell you about it." Having projected the image in our mind, Benchley was obligated to put us with the sheriff when it happens.

Unlike action genres that bring the Obligatory Scene immediately and vividly to mind, other more interior genres hint at this scene in the Inciting Incident, then like a photo negative in acid solution, slowly bring it into focus. In TENDER MERCIES Mac Sledge is drowning in booze and an utterly meaningless life. His ascent from rock bottom begins when he meets a lonely woman with a son who needs a father. He's inspired to write some new songs, then accepts baptism and tries to make peace with his estranged daughter. Gradually he pieces together a meaningful life.

The audience, however, senses that because the dragon of meaninglessness drove Sledge to rock bottom, it must once again rear its gruesome head, that the story can't end until he is slapped in the face with the cruel absurdity of life—this time in all its soul-destroying force. The Obligatory Scene comes in the form of a hideous accident that kills his only child. If a drunk needed an excuse to pick up a bottle again, this would do. Indeed, his daughter's death plunges his ex-wife into a drugged stupor, but Sledge finds strength to go on.

The death of Sledge's daughter was "obligatory" in this sense: Suppose Horton Foote had written this scenario: The friendless alcoholic Sledge wakes up one morning with nothing to live for. He meets a woman, falls in love, likes her kid and wants to raise him, finds religion, and writes a new tune. FADE OUT. This isn't story; it's daydream. If the quest for meaning has brought about a profound inner change in Sledge, how is Foote to express this? Not through declarations of a change of heart. Self-explanatory dialogue convinces no one. It must be tested by an ultimate event, by pressure-filled character choice and action—the Obligatory (Crisis) Scene and Climax of the last act.

When I say that the audience "knows" an Obligatory Scene awaits, it doesn't know in an objective, checklist sense. If this event is mishandled, the audience won't exit thinking, "Lousy flick. No Obligatory Scene." Rather, the audience knows intuitively when something is missing. A lifetime of story ritual has taught the audience to anticipate that the forces of antagonism provoked at the Inciting Incident will build to the limit of human experience, and that the telling cannot end until the protagonist is in some sense face to face with these forces at their most powerful. Linking a story's Inciting Incident to its Crisis is an aspect of *Foreshadowing*, the arrangement of early events to prepare for later events. In fact, every choice you make—genre, setting, character, mood—foreshadows. With each line of dialogue or image of action you guide the audience to anticipate certain possibilities, so that when events arrive, they somehow satisfy the expectations you've created. The primary component of foreshadowing, however, is the projection of the Obligatory Scene (Crisis) into the audience's imaginaton by the Inciting Incident.

LOCATING THE INCITING INCIDENT

Where to place the Inciting Incident in the overall story design? As a rule of thumb, the first major event of the Central Plot occurs within the first 25 percent of the telling. This is a useful guide, no matter what the medium. How long would you make a theatre audience sit in the dark before engaging the story in a play? Would you make a reader plow through the first hundred pages of a four-hundred-page novel before finding the Central Plot? How long before irredeemable boredom sets in? The standard for a two-hour feature film is to locate the Central Plot's Inciting Incident somewhere within the first half-hour.

It could be the very first thing that happens. In the first thirty seconds of SULLIVAN'S TRAVELS Sullivan (Joel McCrea), a director of vapid but profitable films, defies studio bosses and sets out to make a film with social significance. Within the first two minutes of ON THE WATERFRONT Terry (Marlon Brando) unwittingly helps gangsters murder a friend.

Or much later. Twenty-seven minutes into TAXI DRIVER a teenage prostitute, Iris (Jodie Foster), jumps into Travis Bickle's (Robert De Niro) taxi. Her abusive pimp, Matthew (Harvey Keitel) yanks her back to the street, igniting Travis's desire to rescue her. A half-hour into ROCKY an obscure club fighter, Rocky Balboa (Sylvester Stallone), agrees to fight Apollo Creed (Carl Weathers) for the heavyweight championship of the world. When Sam plays "As Time Goes By" thirty-two minutes into CASABLANCA, Ilsa suddenly reappears in Rick's life, launching one of the screen's great love stories.

Or anywhere in between. However, if the Central Plot's Inciting Incident arrives much later than fifteen minutes into the film, boredom becomes a risk. Therefore, while the audience waits for the main plot, a subplot may be needed to engage their interest.

In TAXI DRIVER, the subplot of Travis's lunatic attempt at political assassination grips us. In ROCKY we're held by the ghetto love story of the painfully shy Adrian (Talia Shire) and the equally troubled Rocky. In CHINATOWN Gittes is duped into investigating Hollis Mulwray for adultery, and this subplot fascinates us as he struggles to untangle himself from the ruse. CASABLANCA's Act One hooks us with the Inciting Incidents of no fewer than five well-paced subplots.

But why make an audience sit through a subplot, waiting half an hour for the main plot to begin? ROCKY, for example, is in the *Sports Genre*. Why not start with two quick scenes: The heavyweight champion gives an obscure club fighter a shot at the title (setup), followed by Rocky choosing to take the fight (payoff). Why not open the film with its Central Plot?

Because if ROCKY's Inciting Incident were the first event we saw, our reaction would have been a shrug and "So what?" Therefore, Stallone uses the first half-hour to delineate Rocky's world and character with craft and economy, so that when Rocky agrees to the fight, the audience's reaction is strong and complete: "Him? That loser?!" They sit in shock, dreading the blood-soaked, bone-crushing defeat that lies ahead.

Bring in the Central Plot's Inciting Incident as soon as possible . . . but not until the moment is ripe.

An Inciting Incident must "hook" the audience, a deep and complete response. Their response must not only be emotional, but rational. This event must not only pull at audience's feelings, but cause them to ask the Major Dramatic Question and imagine the Obligatory Scene. Therefore, the location of the Central Plot's Inciting Incident is found in the answer to this question: How much does the audience need to know about the protagonist and his world to have a full response?

In some stories, nothing. If an Inciting Incident is archetypal in nature, it requires no setup and must occur immediately. The first sentence of Kafka's *Metamorphosis* reads: "One day Gregor Samsa awoke to discover he had been changed into a large cockroach." KRAMER VS. KRAMER: A wife walks out on her husband and leaves her child with him in the film's first two minutes. It needs no preparation, for we immediately understand the terrible impact that would have on anybody's life. JAWS: Shark eats swimmer, sheriff discovers body. These two scenes strike within the first seconds as we instantly grasp the horror.

Suppose Peter Benchley had opened JAWS with scenes of the sheriff quitting his job with the New York City police and moving out to Amity Island, looking forward to a peaceful life as a law officer in this resort town. We meet his family. We meet the town council and mayor. Early summer brings the tourists. Happy times. Then a shark eats somebody. And suppose Spielberg had been foolish enough to shoot all of this exposition, would we have seen it? No. Editor Verna Fields would have dumped it on the cutting room floor, explaining that all the audience needs to know about the sheriff, his family, the mayor, city council, and tourists will be nicely dramatized in the town's *reaction* to the attack . . . but JAWS starts with the shark.

As soon as possible, but not until the moment is ripe . . . Every story world and cast are different, therefore, every Inciting Incident is a different event located at a different point. If it arrives too soon, the audience may be confused. If it arrives too late, the audience may be bored. The instant the audience has a sufficient understanding of character and world to react fully, execute your Inciting Incident. Not a scene earlier, or a scene later. The exact moment is found as much by feeling as by analysis.

If we writers have a common fault in design and placement of the Inciting Incident, it's that we habitually delay the Central Plot while we pack our opening sequences with exposition. We consistently underestimate knowledge and life experience of the audience, laying out our characters and world with tedious details the filmgoer has already filled in with common sense.

Ingmar Bergman is one of the cinema's best directors because he is, in my opinion, the cinema's finest screenwriter. And the one quality that stands above all the others in Bergman's writing is his extreme economy—how little he tells us about anything. In his THROUGH A GLASS DARKLY, for example, all we ever learn about his four characters is that the father is a widowed, best-selling novelist, his son-in-law a doctor, his son a student, and his daughter a schizophrenic, suffering from the same illness that killed her mother. She's been released from a mental hospital to join her family for a few days by the sea, and that act alone upsets the balance of forces in all their lives, propelling a powerful drama from the first moments.

No book-signing scenes to help us understand that the father is a commercial but not critical success. No scenes in an operating room to demonstrate the doctor's profession. No boarding school scenes to explain how much the son needs his father. No electric shock treatment sessions to explain the daughter's anguish. Bergman knows that his urbane audience quickly grasps the implications behind best-seller, doctor, boarding school, and mental hospital . . . and that less is always more.

THE QUALITY OF THE INCITING INCIDENT

A favorite joke among film distributors goes like this: A typical European film opens with golden, sunlit clouds. Cut to even more splendid, bouffant clouds. Cut again to yet more magnificent, rubescent clouds. A Hollywood film opens with golden, billowing clouds. In the second shot a 747 jumbo jet comes out of the clouds. In the third, it explodes.

What quality of event need an Inciting Incident be?

ORDINARY PEOPLE carries a Central Plot and subplot that are often mistaken for each other because of their unconventional design. Conrad (Timothy Hutton) is the protagonist of the film's subplot with an Inciting Incident that takes the life of his older brother during a storm at sea. Conrad survives but is guilt-ridden and suicidal. The brother's death is in the Backstory and is dramatized in flashback at the Crisis/Climax of the subplot when Conrad relives the boating accident and chooses to live.

The Central Plot is driven by Conrad's father, Calvin (Donald Sutherland). Although seemingly passive, he is by definition the protagonist: the empathetic character with the will and capacity to pursue desire to the end of the line. Throughout the film, Calvin is on a quest for the cruel secret that haunts his family and makes reconciliation between his son and wife impossible. After a painful struggle, he finds it: His wife hates Conrad, not since the death of her older son, but since Conrad's birth.

At the Crisis Calvin confronts his wife, Beth (Mary Tyler Moore) with the truth: She's an obsessively orderly woman who wanted only one child. When her second son came along, she resented his craving for love when she could love only her first-born. She's always hated Conrad, and he's always felt it. This is why he's been suicidal over his brother's death. Calvin then forces the Climax: She must learn to love Conrad or leave. Beth goes to a closet, packs a suitcase, and heads out the door. She cannot face her inability to love her son.

This Climax answers the Major Dramatic Question: Will the family solve its problems within itself or be torn apart? Working backward from it, we seek the Inciting Incident, the event that has upset the balance of Calvin's life and sent him on his quest.

The film opens with Conrad coming home from a psychiatric hospital, presumably cured of his suicidal neurosis. Calvin feels that the family has survived its loss and balance has been restored. The next morning Conrad, in a grim mood, sits opposite his father at the breakfast table. Beth puts a plate of French toast under her son's face. He refuses to eat. She snatches the plate away, marches to the sink, and scrapes his breakfast down a garbage disposal, muttering: "You can't keep French toast."

Director Robert Redford's camera cuts to the father as the man's life crashes. Calvin instantly senses that the hatred is back with a vengeance. Behind it hides something fearful. This chilling event grips the audience with dread as it reacts, thinking: "Look what she did to her child! He's just home from the hospital and she's doing this number on him."

Novelist Judith Guest and screenwriter Alvin Sargent gave Calvin a quiet characterization, a man who won't leap up from the table and try to bully wife and son into reconciliation. His first thought is to give them time and loving encouragements, such as the family photo scene. When he learns of Conrad's troubles at school, he hires a psychiatrist for him. He talks gently with his wife, hoping to understand.

Because Calvin is a hesitant, compassionate man, Sargent had to build the dynamic of the film's progressions around the subplot. Conrad's struggle with suicide is far more active than Calvin's subtle quest. So Sargent foregrounded the boy's subplot, giving it inordinate emphasis and screentime, while carefully increasing the momentum of the Central Plot in the background. By the time the subplot ends in the psychiatrist's office, Calvin is ready to bring the Central Plot to its devastating end. The point, however, is that the Inciting Incident of ORDINARY PEOPLE is triggered by a woman scraping French toast down a garbage disposal.

Henry James wrote brilliantly about story art in the prefaces to his novels, and once asked: "What, after all, is an event?" An event, he said, could be as little as a woman putting her hand on the table and looking at you "that certain way." In the right context, just a gesture and a look could mean, "I'll never see you again," or "I'll love you forever"—a life broken or made.

The quality of the Inciting Incident (for that matter, any event) must be germane to the world, characters, and genre surrounding it. Once it is conceived, the writer must concentrate on its function. Does the Inciting Incident radically upset the balance of forces in the protagonist's life? Does it arouse in the protagonist the desire to restore balance? Does it inspire in him the conscious desire for that object, material or immaterial, he feels would restore the balance? In a complex protagonist, does it also bring to life an unconscious desire that contradicts his conscious need? Does it launch the protagonist on a quest for his desire? Does it raise the Major Dramatic Question in the mind of the audience? Does it project an image of the Obligatory Scene? If it does all this, then it can be as little as a woman putting her hand on the table, looking at you "that certain way."

CREATING THE INCITING INCIDENT

The Climax of the last act is far and away the most difficult scene to create: It's the soul of the telling. If it doesn't work, the story doesn't work. But the second most difficult scene to write is the Central Plot's Inciting Incident. We rewrite this scene more than any other. So here are some questions to ask that should help bring it to mind.

What is the worst possible thing that could happen to my protagonist? How could that turn out to be the best possible thing that could happen to him?

KRAMER VS. KRAMER. The worst: Disaster strikes the workaholic Kramer (Dustin Hoffman) when his wife walks out on him and her child. The best: This turns out to be the shock he needed to fulfill his unconscious desire to be a loving human being.

AN UNMARRIED WOMAN. The worst: When her husband says he's leaving her for another woman, Erica (Jill Clayburgh) retches. The best: His exit turns out to be the freeing experience that allows this male-dependent woman to fulfill her unconscious desire for independence and self-possession.

Or: What's the best possible thing that could happen to my protagonist? How could it become the worst possible thing?

DEATH IN VENICE. Von Aschenbach (Dirk Bogarde) has lost his wife and children to a plague. Since then he's buried himself in his work to the point of physical and mental collapse. His doctor sends him to the Venice spa to recuperate. The best: There he falls madly, helplessly in love . . . but with a boy. His passion for the impossibly beautiful youth, and the impossibility of it, leads to despair. The worst: When a new plague invades Venice and the child's mother hurries her son away, Von Aschenbach lingers to wait for death and escape from his misery.

THE GODFATHER, PART II. The best: After Michael (Al Pacino) is made Don of the Corleone crime family, he decides to take his family into the legitimate world. The worst: His ruthless enforcement of the mafia code of loyalty ends in the assassination of his closest associates, estrangement from his wife and children, and the murder of his brother, leaving him a hollowed-out, desolate man.

A story may turn more than one cycle of this pattern. What is the best? How could that become the worst? How could that reverse yet again into the protagonist's salvation? Or: What is the worst? How could that become the best? How could that lead the protagonist to damnation? We stretch toward the "bests" and "worsts" because story—when it is art—is not about the middle ground of human experience.

The impact of the Inciting Incident creates our opportunity to reach the limits of life. It's a kind of explosion. In *Action* genres it may be in fact an explosion; in other films, as muted as a smile. No matter how subtle or direct, it must upset the status quo of the protagonist and jolt his life from its existing pattern, so that chaos invades the character's universe. Out of this upheaval, you must find, at Climax, a resolution, for better or worse, that rearranges this universe into a new order.

9

ACT DESIGN

PROGRESSIVE COMPLICATIONS

The second element of the five-part design is *Progressive Complications*: that great sweeping body of story that spans from Inciting Incident to Crisis/Climax of the final act. To complicate means to make life difficult for characters. To complicate progressively means to generate more and more conflict as they face greater and greater forces of antagonism, creating a succession of events that passes points of no return.

Points of No Return

The Inciting Incident launches the protagonist on a quest for a conscious or unconscious Object of Desire to restore life's balance. To begin the pursuit of his desire, he takes a minimum, conservative action to provoke a positive response from his reality. But the effect of his action is to arouse forces of antagonism from inner, personal, or social/environmental Levels of Conflict that block his desire, cracking open the Gap between expectation and result.

When the Gap opens, the audience realizes that this is a point of no return. Minimal efforts won't work. The character can't restore the balance of life by taking lesser actions. Henceforth, all action like the character's first effort, actions of minor quality and magnitude, must be eliminated from the story.

Realizing he's at risk, the protagonist draws upon greater willpower and capacity to struggle through this gap and take a second, more difficult action. But again the effect is to provoke forces of antagonism, opening a second gap between expectation and result.

The audience now senses that this too is a point of no return. Moderate actions like the second won't succeed. Therefore, all actions of this magnitude and quality must be eliminated.

At greater risk, the character must adjust to his changed circumstances and take an action that demands even more willpower and personal capacity, expecting or at least hoping for a helpful or manageable reaction from his world. But once more the gap flies open as even more powerful forces of antagonism react to his third action.

Again, the audience recognizes that this is yet another point of no return. The more extreme actions won't get the character what he wants, so these too are canceled out of consideration.

Progressions build by drawing upon greater and greater capacities from characters, demanding greater and greater willpower from them, putting them at greater and greater risk, constantly passing points of no return in terms of the magnitude or quality of action.

A story must not retreat to actions of lesser quality or magnitude, but move progressively forward to a final action beyond which the audience cannot imagine another.

How many times have you had this experience? A film begins well, hooking you into the lives of the characters. It builds with strong interest over the first half-hour to a major Turning Point. But then forty or fifty minutes into the film, it starts to drag. Your eyes wander from the screen; you glance at your watch; you wish you'd bought more popcorn; you start paying attention to the anatomy of the person you came with. Perhaps the film gains pace again and finishes well, but for twenty or thirty flabby minutes in the middle you lost interest.

If you look closely at the soft bellies that hang out over the belt of so many films, you'll discover that this is where the writer's insight and imagination went limp. He couldn't build progressions, so in effect he put the story in retrograde. In the middle of Act Two he's given his characters lesser actions of the kind they've already done in Act One—not identical actions but actions of a similar size or kind: minimal, conservative, and by now trivial. As we watch, our instincts tell us that these actions didn't get the character what he wanted in Act One, therefore they're not going to get him what he wants in Act Two. The writer is recycling story and we're treading water.

The only way to keep a film's current flowing and rising is research—imagination, memory, fact. Generally, a feature-length Archplot is designed around forty to sixty scenes that conspire into twelve to eighteen sequences that build into three or more acts that top one another continuously to the end of the line. To create forty to sixty scenes and *not repeat yourself*, you need to invent hundreds. After sketching this mountain of material, tunnel to find those few gems that will build sequences and acts into memorable and moving points of no return. For if you devise only the forty to sixty scenes needed to fill the 120 pages of a screenplay, your work is almost certain to be antiprogressive and repetitious.

The Law of Conflict

When the protagonist steps out of the Inciting Incident, he enters a world governed by the Law of Conflict. To wit: *Nothing moves forward in a story except through conflict.*

Put another way, conflict is to storytelling what sound is to music. Both story and music are temporal arts, and the single most difficult task of the temporal artist is to hook our interest, hold our uninterrupted concentration, then *carry us through time without an awareness of the passage of time.*

In music, this effect is accomplished through sound. Instruments or voices capture us and move us along, making time vanish. Suppose we were listening to a symphony and the orchestra suddenly fell silent. What would be the effect? First, confusion as we wonder why they've stopped, then very quickly we would hear in our imaginations the sound of a ticking clock. We would become acutely aware of the passage of time, and because time is so subjective, if the orchestra were silent for just three minutes, it would seem like thirty.

The music of story is conflict. As long as conflict engages our thoughts and emotions we travel through the hours unaware of the voyage. Then suddenly the film's over. We glance at our watches, amazed. But when conflict disappears, so do we. The pictorial interest of eye-pleasing photography or the aural pleasures of a beautiful score may hold us briefly, but if conflict is kept on hold for too long, our eyes leave the screen. And when our eyes leave the screen they take thought and emotion with them.

The Law of Conflict is more than an aesthetic principle; it is the soul of story. Story is metaphor for life, and to be alive is to be in seemingly perpetual conflict. As Jean-Paul Sartre expressed it, the essence of reality is scarcity, a universal and eternal lacking. There isn't enough of anything in this world to go around. Not enough food, not enough love, not enough justice, and never enough time. Time, as Heidegger observed, is the basic category of existence. We live in its ever-shrinking shadow, and if we are to achieve anything in our brief being that lets us die without feeling we've wasted our time, we will have to go into heady conflict with the forces of scarcity that deny our desires.

Writers who cannot grasp the truth of our transitory existence, who have been mislead by the counterfeit comforts of the modern world, who believe that life is easy once you know how to play the game, give conflict a false inflection. Their scripts fail for one of two reasons: either a glut of meaningless and absurdly violent conflict, or a vacancy of meaningful and honestly expressed conflict.

The former are exercises in turbo special effects, written by those who follow textbook imperatives to create conflict, but, because they're disinterested in or insensitive to the honest struggles of life, devise phony, overwrought excuses for mayhem.

The latter are tedious portraits written in reaction against conflict itself. These writers take the Pollyanna view that life would really be nice . . . if it weren't for conflict. Therefore, their films avoid it in favor of low-key depictions to suggest that if we learned to communicate a little better, be a little more charitable, respect the environment, humanity could return to paradise. But if history has taught us anything, it's that when toxic nightmare is finally cleaned up, the homeless provided shelter, and the world converted to solar energy, each of us will still be up to our eyebrows in mulch.

Writers at these extremes fail to realize that while the *quality* of conflict changes as it shifts from level to level, *the quantity of conflict in life is constant.* Something is always lacking. Like squeezing a balloon, the volume of conflict never changes, it just bulges in another direction. When we remove conflict from one level of life, it amplifies ten times over on another level.

If, for example, we manage to satisfy our external desires and find harmony with the world, in short order serenity turns to boredom. Now Sartre's "scarcity" is the absence of conflict itself. Boredom is the inner conflict we suffer when we lose desire, when we lack a lacking. What's worse, if we were to put on screen the conflictless existence of a character who, day-in, day-out, lives in placid contentment, the boredom in the audience would be palpably painful.

By and large, the struggle for physical survival has been eliminated for the educated classes of the industrialized nations. This security from the outside world gives us time to reflect on the world inside. Once housed, dressed, fed, and medicated, we take a breath and realize how incomplete we are as human beings. We want more than physical comfort, we want, of all things, happiness, and so begin the wars of the inner life.

If, as a writer, however, you find that the conflicts of mind, body, emotions, and soul do not interest you, then look into the Third World and see how the rest of humanity lives. The majority suffer short, painful existences, ridden with disease and hunger, terrorized by tyranny and lawless violence, without hope that life will ever be any different for their children.

If the depth and breadth of conflict in the inner life and the greater world do not move you, let this: death. Death is like a freight train in the future, heading toward us, closing the hours, second by second, between now and then. If we're to live with any sense of satisfaction, we must engage life's forces of antagonism before the train arrives.

An artist intent on creating works of lasting quality comes to realize that life isn't about subtle adjustments to stress, or hyper-

conflicts of master criminals with stolen nuclear devices holding cities for ransom. Life is about the ultimate questions of finding love and self-worth, of bringing serenity to inner chaos, of the titanic social inequities everywhere around us, of time running out. Life is conflict. That is its nature. The writer must decide where and how to orchestrate this struggle.

Complication Versus Complexity

To complicate a story the writer builds conflict progressively to the end of the line. Difficult enough. But the task increases geometrically when we take story from mere complication to full complexity.

Conflict may come, as we've seen, from any one, two, or all three of the levels of antagonism. To simply complicate a story means to place all conflict on only one of these three levels.

From the *Horror Film* to *Action/Adventure* to *Farce*, action heroes face conflict only on the extra-personal level. James Bond, for example, has no inner conflicts, nor would we mistake his encounters with women as personal—they're recreational.

<u>COMPLICATION:</u>
<u>CONFLICT AT ONLY ONE LEVEL</u>

INNER CONFLICT — Stream of Consciousness

PERSONAL CONFLICT — Soap Opera

EXTRA-PERSONAL CONFLICT — Action/Adventure, Farce

Complicated films share two hallmarks. The first is a large cast. If the writer restricts the protagonist to social conflict, he'll need, as the advertising declares, "a cast of thousands." James Bond faces arch-villains along with their minions, assassins, femmes fatale, and armies, plus helper characters and civilians needing rescue—

more and more characters to build more and more powerful conflicts between Bond and society.

Second, a complicated film needs multiple sets and locations. If the writer progresses via physical conflict, he must keep changing the environment. A Bond film might start in a Viennese opera house, then go to the Himalayas, across the Sahara Desert, under the polar ice cap, up to the moon, and down to Broadway, giving Bond more and more opportunities for fascinating feats of derring-do.

Stories that are complicated only on the level of personal conflict are known as *Soap Opera*, an open-ended combination of *Domestic Drama* and *Love Story* in which every character in the story has an intimate relationship with every other character in the story—a multitude of family, friends, and lovers, all needing sets to house them: living rooms, bedrooms, offices, nightclubs, hospitals. *Soap Opera* characters have no inner or extra-personal conflicts. They suffer when they don't get what they want, but because they're either good people or bad, they rarely face true inner dilemmas. Society never intervenes in their air-conditioned worlds. If, for example, a murder should bring a detective, a representative of society, into the story, you can be certain that within a week this cop will have an intimate and personal relationship with every other character in the *Soap*.

Stories that are complicated only on the level of inner conflict are not films, plays, or conventional novels. They're prose works in the *Stream of Consciousness* genre, a verbalization of the inscape of thought and feeling. Again, a large cast. Even though we're placed inside a single character, that character's mind is populated with the memories and imaginings of everyone he has ever met or could hope to meet. What's more, the density of imagery in the *Stream of Consciousness* work, such as NAKED LUNCH, is so intense that locations change, as it were, three or four times in a single sentence. A barrage of places and faces pours through the reader's imagination, but these works are all on one, albeit richly subjective, level and, therefore, merely complicated.

COMPLEXITY:
CONFLICT AT ALL THREE LEVELS

INNER CONFLICT
PERSONAL CONFLICT
EXTRA-PERSONAL CONFLICT

To achieve complexity the writer brings his characters into conflict on all three levels of life, often simultaneously. For example, the deceptively simple but complex writing of one of the most memorable events in any film for the last two decades: the French toast scene from KRAMER VS. KRAMER. This famous scene turns on a complex of three values: self-confidence, a child's trust and esteem for his father, and domestic survival. As the scene begins, all three are at the positive charge.

In the film's first moments Kramer discovers his wife has left him and his son. He's torn with an inner conflict that takes the form of doubts and fears that he's in over his head versus a male arrogance telling him whatever women do is easy. As he opens the scene, however, he's confident.

Kramer has personal conflict. His son is hysterical, afraid he'll starve without his mother to feed him. Kramer tries to calm his son, telling him not to worry, Mom will be back, but meantime it'll be fun, like camping out. The child dries his eyes, trusting his father's promises.

Finally, Kramer has extra-personal conflict. The kitchen is an alien world, but he strolls into it as if he were a French chef.

Perching his son on a stool, Kramer asks what he wants for breakfast and the kid says, "French toast." Kramer takes a breath, pulls out a frying pan, pours in some grease, puts the pan on the stove, and turns the flame to high while he looks for ingredients. He knows French toast involves eggs, so he searches the refrigerator and finds some, but doesn't know into what to break them. He rummages in the cupboard and comes down with a coffee mug that reads "Teddy."

The son sees the handwriting on the wall and warns Kramer that he's seen his mother do this and she doesn't use a mug. Kramer tells him it'll work. He cracks the eggs. Some actually gets into the mug, the rest makes a gooey mess . . . and the child starts to cry.

The grease starts to spatter in the frying pan and Kramer panics. It doesn't occur to him to turn off the gas; instead, he engages in a race against time. He bangs more eggs into the mug, rushes back to the refrigerator, grabs a quart of milk, and slops it up and over the brim of the mug. He finds a butter knife to break up the yolks, making an even gooier mess. The child can see he is not going to eat this morning and cries his eyes out. The grease is now smoking in the pan.

Kramer, desperate, angry, losing the fight to control his fears, grabs a slice of Wonder Bread, stares at it, and realizes it won't fit in the mug. He folds it in half and stuffs it in, coming up with a dripping handful of soggy bread, yolk, and milk that he flings at the griddle, spattering and burning him and the child. He snatches the pan from the stove, scalding his hand, clutches his son's arm, and pushes him through the door, saying, "We'll go to a restaurant."

Kramer's male arrogance is overwhelmed by his fears, his self-confidence turning positive to negative. He's humiliated in front of his frightened child, whose trust and esteem turn positive to negative. He's defeated by a seemingly animated kitchen, as blow by blow, eggs, grease, bread, milk, and pan send him stumbling out the door, turning domestic survival from positive to negative. With very little dialogue and the simple activity of a man trying to make breakfast for his son, the scene becomes one of the most memorable in film—a three-minute drama of a man in simultaneous conflict with the complexities of life.

Unless it's your ambition to write in the *Action* genres, *Soap Opera,* or *Stream of Consciousness* prose, my advice to most writers is to design relatively simple but complex stories. "Relatively simple" doesn't mean simplistic. It means beautifully turned and told stories restrained by these two principles: Do not proliferate characters; do not multiply locations. Rather than hopscotching through time, space, and people, discipline yourself to a reasonably contained cast and world, while you concentrate on creating a rich complexity.

Act Design

As a symphony unfolds in three, four, or more movements, so story is told in movements called *acts*—the macro-structure of story.

Beats, changing patterns of human behavior, build scenes. Ideally, every scene becomes a Turning Point in which the values at stake swing from the positive to the negative or the negative to the positive, creating significant but *minor* change in their lives. A series of scenes build a sequence that culminates in a scene that has a *moderate* impact on the characters, turning or changing values for better or worse to a greater degree than any scene. A series of sequences builds an act that climaxes in a scene that creates a *major* reversal in the characters' lives, greater than any sequence accomplished.

In the *Poetics,* Aristotle deduces that there is a relationship between the size of the story—how long it takes to read or perform—and the number of major Turning Points necessary to tell it: the longer the work, the more major reversals. In other words, in his polite way, Aristotle is pleading, "Please don't bore us. Don't make us sit for hours on those hard marble seats listening to choral chants and laments while nothing actually happens."

Following Aristotle's principle: A story can be told in one act—a series of scenes that shape a few sequences that build up to one major reversal, ending the story. But if so, it must be brief. This is the prose short story, the one-act play, or the student or experimental film of perhaps five to twenty minutes.

A story can be told in two acts: two major reversals and it's over. But again it must be relatively brief: the sitcom, the novella, or hour-length plays such as Anthony Shaffer's *Black Comedy* and August Strindberg's *Miss Julie.*

But when a story reaches a certain magnitude—the feature film, an hour-long TV episode, the full-length play, the novel—three acts is the minimum. Not because of an artificial convention, but to serve a profound purpose.

As audience we embrace the story artist and say: "I'd like a poetic experience in breadth and depth to the limits of life. But I'm a reasonable person. If I give you only a few minutes to read or witness your work, it would be unfair of me to demand that you to take me to the limit. Instead I'd like a moment of pleasure, an insight or two, no more than that. But if I give you important hours of my life, I expect you to be an artist of power who can reach the boundaries of experience."

In our effort to satisfy the audience's need, to tell stories that touch the innermost and outermost sources of life, two major reversals are never enough. No matter the setting or scope of the telling, no matter how international and epic or intimate and interior, *three* major reversals are the necessary minimum for a full-length work of narrative art to reach the end of the line.

Consider these rhythms: Things were bad, then they were good—end of story. Or things were good, then they were bad—end of story. Or things were bad, then they were very bad—end of story. Or things were good, then they were very good—end of story. In all four cases we feel something's lacking. We know that the second event, whether positively or negatively charged, is neither the end nor the limit. Even if the second event kills the cast: Things were good (or bad), then everyone died—end of story—it's not enough. "Okay, they're all dead. Now what?" we're wondering. The third turn is missing and we know we haven't touched the limit until at least one more major reversal occurs. Therefore, the three-act story rhythm was the foundation of story art for centuries before Aristotle noted it.

But it's only a foundation, not a formula, so I'll begin with it, then delineate some of its infinite variations. The proportions I'll use are the rhythms of the feature film, but in principle they apply equally to the play and novel. Again, I caution that these are approximations, not formulas.

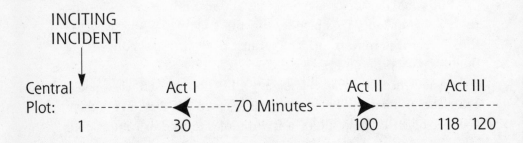

The first act, the opening movement, typically consumes about 25 percent of the telling, the Act One Climax occurring between twenty and thirty minutes into a 120-minute film. The last act wants to be the shortest of all. In the ideal last act we want to give the audience a sense of acceleration, a swiftly rising action to Climax. If the writer tries to stretch out the last act, the pace of acceleration is almost certain to slow in mid-movement. So last acts are generally brief, twenty minutes or less.

Let's say a 120-minute film places its Central Plot's Inciting Incident in the first minute, the Act One Climax at the thirty-minute point, has an eighteen-minute Act Three, and a two-minute Resolution to FADE OUT. This rhythm creates an Act Two that's seventy minutes long. If an otherwise well-told story bogs down, that's where it'll happen—as the writer sloshes through the swamps of the long second act. There are two possible solutions: Add subplots or more acts.

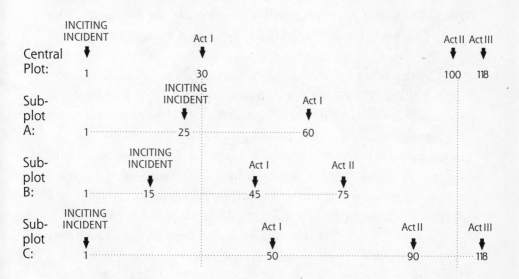

Subplots have their own act structure, although usually brief. Between the central plot's three-act design above, let's weave three subplots: a one-act Subplot A with an Inciting Incident twenty-five minutes into the film, climaxing and ending at sixty minutes; a two-act Subplot B with an Inciting Incident at the fifteen-minute point, an Act One Climax at forty-five minutes, ending with an Act Two Climax at seventy-five minutes; a three-act Subplot C is with its Inciting Incident happening inside the Inciting Incident of the Central Plot (lovers meet, for example, and start a subplot in the same scene cops discover the crime that launches the central plot), an Act One Climax at fifty minutes, an Act Two Climax at ninety minutes, and a third act climaxing inside the Central Plot's last Climax (the lovers decide to marry in the same scene that they apprehend the criminal).

Although the Central Plot and three subplots may have up to four different protagonists, an audience could empathize with all of them, and each subplot raises its own Major Dramatic Question. So the interest and emotions of the audience are hooked, held, and amplified by four stories. What's more, the three subplots have five major reversals that fall between the Central Plot's Act One and Act Two climaxes—more than enough storytelling to keep the overall film progressing, deepen the involvement of the audience, and tighten the soft belly of the Central Plot's second act.

On the other hand, not every film needs or wants a subplot: THE FUGITIVE. How then does the writer solve the problem of the long second act? By creating more acts. *The three-act design is the minimum.* If the writer builds progressions to a major reversal at the halfway point, he breaks the story into four movements with no act more than thirty or forty minutes long. David's collapse after performing Rachmaninoff's Piano Concerto No. 3 in SHINE is a superb example. In Hollywood this technique is known as the *Mid-Act Climax*, a term that sounds like sexual dysfunction, but means a major reversal in the middle of Act Two, expanding the design from three acts to an Ibsen-like rhythm of four acts, accelerating the mid-film pace.

A film could have a Shakespearean rhythm of five acts: FOUR WEDDINGS AND A FUNERAL. Or more. RAIDERS OF THE LOST ARK is in seven acts; THE COOK, THE THIEF, HIS WIFE & HER LOVER in eight. These films turn a major reversal every fifteen or twenty minutes, decisively solving the long second act problem. But the five- to eight-act design is the exception, for the cure of one problem is the cause of others.

SHINE:

	INCITING INCIDENT	(MID-ACT CLIMAX)			
	↓	↓			
	Act I	Act II	Act III	Act IV	

Central plot:

| 1 | 30 | 60 | 100 | 118 | 120 |

Subplot ➡

FOUR WEDDINGS AND A FUNERAL:

INCITING
INCIDENT
↓

	Act I	Act II	Act III	Act IV	Act V	

Central plot:

| 1 | 25 | 50 | 75 | 100 | 118 | 120 |

THE COOK, THE THIEF, HIS WIFE & HER LOVER:

INCITING
INCIDENT
↓

	Act I	Act II	Act III	Act IV	Act V	Act VI	Act VII	Act VIII

Central plot:

| 1 | 15 | 30 | 45 | 60 | 75 | 90 | 105 | 120 |

First, the multiplication of act climaxes invites clichés.

Generally, a three-act story requires four memorable scenes: the Inciting Incident that opens the telling, and an Act One, Act Two, and Act Three Climax. In the Inciting Incident of KRAMER VS. KRAMER Mrs. Kramer walks out on her husband and her son. Act One Climax: She returns, demanding custody of the child. Act Two Climax: The court awards custody of the son to his mother. Act Three Climax: Like her ex-husband, she realizes that they must act selflessly for the best interest of the child they love and returns the boy to Kramer. Four powerful turning points spanned with excellent scenes and sequences.

When the writer multiplies acts, he's forcing the invention of five, perhaps six, seven, eight, nine, or more brilliant scenes. This becomes a creative task beyond his reach, so he resorts to the clichés that infest so many action films.

Second, the multiplication of acts reduces the impact of climaxes and results in repetitiousness.

Even if the writer feels he's up to creating a major reversal every fifteen minutes, turning act climaxes on scenes of life and death, life and death, life and death, life and death, life and death, seven or eight times over, boredom sets in. Before too long the audience is yawning: "That's not a major turn. That's his day. Every fifteen minutes somebody tries to kill the guy."

What is major is relative to what is moderate and minor. If every scene screams to be heard, we go deaf. When too many scenes strive to be powerhouse climaxes, what should be major becomes minor, repetitious, running downhill to a halt. This is why a three-act Central Plot with subplots has become a kind of standard. It fits the creative powers of most writers, provides complexity, and avoids repetition.

Design Variations

First, stories vary according to the number of major reversals in the telling: from the one- or two-act design of Miniplots, LEAVING LAS VEGAS, through the three- or four-acts plus subplots of most Archplots, THE VERDICT, to the seven or eight acts of many action genres, SPEED, to the helter-skelter patterns of Antiplots, THE DISCREET CHARM OF THE BOURGEOISIE, and beyond to Multiplot films that have no Central Plot, THE JOY LUCK CLUB, but may contain a dozen or more major Turning Points over their various story lines.

Second, the shapes of stories vary according to the placement of the Inciting Incident. Conventionally, the Inciting Incident occurs very early in the telling and progressions build to a major reversal at the Act One Climax twenty or thirty minutes later. This pattern requires the writer to place two major scenes in the first quarter of the film. However, the Inciting Incident may enter as late as twenty, thirty, or more minutes into the telling. ROCKY, for example, has a very late-arriving Central Plot Inciting Incident. The effect of this is that the Inciting Incident becomes, in effect, the first act Climax and serves two purposes.

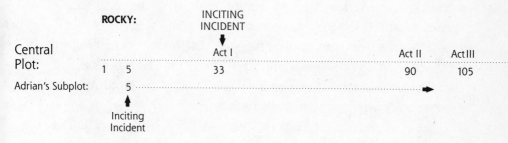

This, however, cannot be done for the convenience of the writer. The only reason to delay the entrance of the Central Plot is the audience's need to know the protagonist at length so it can fully react to the Inciting Incident. If this is necessary, then a setup subplot must open the telling. ROCKY has one, the Adrian/Rocky *Love Story*; CASABLANCA uses five with Laszlo, Ugarte, Yvonne, and the Bulgarian wife as single protagonists and refugees as the plural protagonist. Story must be told to hold the audience while it waits for a late-arriving Central Plot to ripen.

Suppose, however, the ripe moment is reached somewhere between the first and thirtieth minute. Does a film then need a setup subplot to carry the opening? Maybe . . . maybe not. The Inciting Incident of THE WIZARD OF OZ occurs at the fifteen-minute mark when a cyclone carries Dorothy (Judy Garland) to Munchkinland. There's no subplot to set this up, rather we're held by dramatized exposition of her longing to go "somewhere over the rainbow." In ADAM'S RIB the Inciting Incident also arrives fifteen minutes into the film, as district attorney Adam Bonner (Spencer Tracy) and his defense attorney wife Amanda (Katharine Hepburn) discover themselves on opposing sides of a trial. In this case, the film opens with a setup subplot as defendant (Judy Holliday) discovers her husband's philandering and shoots him. This hooks and carries us to the Central Plot's Inciting Incident.

With an Inciting Incident at the fifteen-minute point, does the writer need a major reversal at the thirty-minute point? Maybe . . . maybe not. In THE WIZARD OF OZ Dorothy is threatened by the Wicked Witch of the West, given the red slippers, and sent on her quest along the yellow brick road fifteen minutes after the Inciting Incident. In ADAM'S RIB the next major reversal of the Central Plot happens forty minutes after the Inciting Incident when Amanda wins a key point in court. However, a relationship subplot complicates this stretch as a composer (David Wayne), to Adam's great annoyance, flirts openly with Amanda.

The rhythm of act movements is established by the location of the Central Plot's Inciting Incident. Act structure, therefore, varies enormously. The number and placement of the major reversals for both main plot and subplots are choices made in the creative play between artist and material, depending on quality and number of protagonists, sources of antagonism, genre, and, ultimately, the personality and worldview of the writer.

False Ending

Occasionally, especially in *Action* genres, at the Penultimate Act Climax or within the last act's movement, the writer creates a *False Ending*: a scene so seemingly complete we think for a moment the story is over. E.T. is dead—end of movie, we think. In ALIEN Ripley blows up her spaceship and escapes, we think. In ALIENS she blows up an entire planet and escapes, we hope. In BRAZIL Jonathan (Sam Lowry) rescues Kim (Jill Layton) from a tyrannical regime, the lovers embrace, happy ending . . . or is it?

TERMINATOR devised a double False Ending: Reese (Michael Biehn) and Sarah (Linda Hamilton) blow up the Terminator (Arnold Schwarzenegger) with a tankard of gasoline, its flesh burning away. The lovers celebrate. But then the chrome inner version of this half-man/half-robot rises out of the flames. Reese sacrifices his life to put a pipe bomb in the belly of the Terminator and blow it in half. But then the creature's torso revives and crawls claw over claw toward the wounded heroine until Sarah finally destroys him.

False Endings may even find their way into *Art Films*. Near the climax of JESUS OF MONTREAL Daniel (Lothaire Bluteau), an actor playing Christ in a Passion Play, is bludgeoned by his falling crucifix. Other actors rush him unconscious to the emergency room, but he awakes, resurrected, we pray.

Hitchcock loved False Endings, placing them unconventionally early for shock effect. The "suicide" of Madeleine (Kim Novak) is the Mid-Act Climax of VERTIGO before she reappears as Judy. The shower murder of Marion (Janet Leigh) marks the Act One Climax of PSYCHO, suddenly shifting genres from *Caper* to *Psycho-Thriller* and switching protagonists from Marion to a plural protagonist of the dead woman's sister, lover, and a private eye.

For most films, however, the False Ending is inappropriate. Instead, the Penultimate Act Climax should intensify the Major Dramatic Question: "*Now* what's going to happen?"

Act Rhythm

Repetitiousness is the enemy of rhythm. The dynamics of story depend on the alternation of its value-charges. For example, the two most powerful scenes in a story are the last two act climaxes. Onscreen they're often only ten or fifteen minutes apart. Therefore, they cannot repeat the same charge. If the protagonist achieves his Object of Desire, making the last act's Story Climax positive, then the Penultimate Act Climax must be negative. You cannot set up an up-ending with an up-ending: "Things were wonderful . . . then they got even better!" Conversely, if the protagonist fails to achieve his desire, the Climax of the Penultimate Act cannot be negative. You cannot set up a down-ending with a down-ending: "Things were terrible . . . then they got even worse." When emotional experience repeats, the power of the second event is cut in half. And if the power of the Story Climax is halved, the power of the film is halved.

On the other hand, a story may climax in irony, an ending that's both positive and negative. What then must be the emotional charge of the Penultimate Climax? The answer's found in close study of the Story Climax, for although irony is somewhat positive, somewhat negative, it should never be balanced. If it is, the positive and negative values cancel each other out and the story ends in a bland neutrality.

For example, Othello finally achieves his desire: a wife who loves him and has never betrayed him with another man—positive. However, when he discovers this, it's too late because he's just murdered her—an overall negative irony. Mrs. Soffel goes to prison for the rest of her life—negative. But she goes into jail with her head up because she's achieved her desire, the transcendent romantic experience—an overall positive irony. With careful thought and feeling the writer studies his irony to make certain it leans one way or the other, and then designs a Penultimate Climax to contradict its overall emotional charge.

Working back from the Penultimate Climax to the opening scene, previous act climaxes are further apart, often with subplot and sequence climaxes coming into emotional play between them, creating a unique rhythm of positive and negative turnings. Consequently, although we know that the Ultimate and Penultimate Climaxes must contradict each other, from story to story there is no way to predict the charges of the other act climaxes. Each film finds its own rhythm and all variations are possible.

Subplots and Multiple Plots

A subplot receives less emphasis and screentime than a Central Plot, but often it's the invention of a subplot that lifts a troubled screenplay to a film worth making. WITNESS, for example, without its *Love Story* subplot of big-city cop and Amish widow would be a less than compelling *Thriller*. Multiplot films, on the other hand, never develop a Central Plot; rather they weave together a number of stories of subplot size. Between the Central Plot and its subplots or between the various plot lines of a Multi-plot, four possible relationships come into play.

A subplot may be used to contradict the Controlling Idea of the Central Plot and thus enrich the film with irony.

Suppose you were writing a happy-ending *Love Story* with the Controlling Idea "Love triumphs because the lovers sacrifice their needs for each other." You believe in your characters, their passion and self-sacrifice, yet you feel the story's becoming too sweet, too pat. To balance the telling, you might then create a subplot of two other characters whose love ends tragically because they betray each other out of emotional greed. This down-ending subplot contradicts the up-ending Central Plot, making the film's overall meaning more complex and ironic: "Love cuts two ways: we possess it when we give it freedom, but destroy it with possessiveness."

Subplots may be used to resonate the Controlling Idea of the Central Plot and enrich the film with variations on a theme.

If a subplot expresses the same Controlling Idea as the main plot, but in a different, perhaps unusual way, it creates a variation that strengthens and reinforces the theme. All the many love stories in A MIDSUMMER NIGHT'S DREAM, for example, end happily—but some sweetly, some farcically, some sublimely.

The principle of thematic contradiction and variation is the genesis of Multiplot films. A Multiplot has no Central Plot Spine to structurally unify the telling. Instead, a number of plot lines either cross-cut, as in SHORT CUTS, or connect via a motif such as the twenty-dollar bill that passes from story to story in TWENTY BUCKS or the series of swimming pools that link the tales in THE SWIMMER—a collection of "ribs" but no individual plot line strong enough to carry from first scene to last. What then holds the film together? An idea.

PARENTHOOD plays variations on the notion that in the game of parenthood you cannot win. Steve Martin plays the world's most attentive father whose child still ends up in therapy. Jason Robards plays the world's most neglectful father whose kid comes back late in life needing him, then betraying him. Dianne Wiest portrays a mother who tries to make all the safe life decisions for her child, but the child knows better than she does. All parents can do is love their children, support them, pick them up when they fall. But there's no such thing as winning this game.

DINER resonates with the idea that men cannot communicate with women. Fenwick (Kevin Bacon) cannot bring himself to speak to a woman. Boogie (Mickey Rourke) talks nonstop to women, but only to get them into bed. Eddie (Steve Guttenberg) won't marry his fiancée until she can pass a test in football trivia. When Billy (Timothy Daly) faces his emotional issues with the woman he loves, he lets his guard down and talks honestly with her. Once able to communicate with a woman, he leaves his friends—a resolution that contradicts all others to add a layer of irony.

The Multiplot frames an image of a particular society, but, unlike the static Nonplot, it weaves small stories around an idea, so that these group photos vibrate with energy. DO THE RIGHT THING depicts the universality of big-city racism; SHORT CUTS landscapes the soullessness of the American middle class; EAT DRINK MAN WOMAN paints a triptych of the father/daughter relationship. Multiplot gives the writer the best of both worlds: a portrait that captures the essence of a culture or community along with ample narrative drive to compel interest.

When the Central Plot's Inciting Incident must be delayed, a setup subplot may be needed to open the storytelling.

A late-arriving Central Plot—ROCKY, CHINATOWN, CASA-BLANCA—leaves a story vacuum for the first thirty minutes that must be filled by subplots to engage the audience's interest and acquaint it with the protagonist and his world in order to evoke a full reaction to its Inciting Incident. A setup subplot dramatizes the Central Plot's exposition so that it's absorbed in a fluid, indirect manner.

A subplot may be used to complicate the Central Plot.

This fourth relationship is the most important: use of the subplot as an additional source of antagonism. For example, the *Love Story* typically found inside *Crime Stories*: In SEA OF LOVE Frank Keller (Al Pacino) falls in love with Helen (Ellen Barkin). While hunting down her psychotic ex-husband, he risks his life to protect the woman he loves. In BLACK WIDOW a federal agent (Debra Winger) becomes infatuated with the killer herself (Theresa Russell). In THE VER-DICT, a *Courtroom Drama*, Frank (Paul Newman) falls in love with Laura (Charlotte Rampling), a spy from the opposing law firm. These subplots add dimension to characters, create comic or romantic relief from the tensions or violence of the Central Plot, but their primary purpose is to make life more difficult for the protagonist.

The balance of emphasis between the Central Plot and subplot has to be carefully controlled, or the writer risks losing focus on the primary story. A setup subplot is particularly dangerous in that it may mislead the audience as to genre. The opening *Love Story* of ROCKY, for example, was carefully handled so that we knew we were heading for the *Sports Genre*.

Additionally, if the protagonists of the Central Plot and subplot are not the same character, care must be taken not to draw too much empathy to the subplot's protagonist. CASABLANCA, for example, has a *Political Drama* subplot involving the fate of Victor Laszlo (Paul Heinreid) and a *Thriller* subplot centered on Ugarte (Peter Lorre), but both were deemphasized to keep the emotional spotlight on the Central Plot's *Love Story* of Rick (Humphrey Bogart) and Ilsa (Ingrid Bergman). To deemphasize a subplot, some of its elements—Inciting Incident, act climaxes, Crisis, Climax, or Resolution—may be kept offscreen.

If, on the other hand, as you develop your screenplay, your subplot seems to demand greater focus and empathy, then reconsider the overall design and turn your subplot into the Central Plot.

If a subplot doesn't thematically contradict or resonate the Controlling Idea of the main plot, if it doesn't set up the introduction of the main plot's Inciting Incident, or complicate the action on the main plot, if it merely runs alongside, it will split the story down the middle and destroy its effect. The audience understands the principle of aesthetic unity. It knows that every story element is there because of the relationship it strikes to every other element. This relationship, structural or thematic, holds the work together. If the audience can't find it, it'll disengage from the story and consciously try to force a unity. When this fails, it sits in confusion.

In the screen adaptation of the best-selling *Psycho-Thriller* THE FIRST DEADLY SIN, the Central Plot takes a police lieutenant (Frank Sinatra) on the hunt for a serial killer. In a subplot, his wife (Faye Dunaway) is in intensive care with only weeks to live. The detective hunts for the killer, then commiserates with his dying wife; he hunts the killer, then reads to his wife; he hunts for the killer some more, then visits her in the hospital again. Before long this alternating story design ignited a burning curiosity in the audience: When will the *killer* come to the hospital? But he never does. Instead, the wife dies, the cop catches the killer, plot and subplot never connect, and the audience is left in disgruntled confusion.

In Lawrence Sanders' novel, however, this design succeeds with powerful effect because on the page main plot and subplot complicate each other *in the mind of the protagonist*: the cop's fierce preoccupation with a psychotic killer conflicts with a desperate desire to give his wife the comfort she needs, while at the same time his dread of losing her and the pain of watching the woman he loves suffer contradicts his need for clear, rational deduction in pursuit of a ruthless but brilliant lunatic. A novelist can enter a character's mind and in first- or third-person delineate inner conflict directly in prose description. The screenwriter cannot.

The screenwriting is the art of making the mental *physical*. We create visual correlatives for inner conflict—not dialogue or narration to describe ideas and emotions, but images of character choice and action to indirectly and ineffably express the thoughts and feelings within. Therefore, the interior life a novel must be reinvented for the screen.

In adapting Manuel Puig's novel KISS OF THE SPIDER WOMAN, screenwriter Leonard Schrader was faced with a similar structural problem. Once again, main plot and subplot complicate one another only within the mind of the protagonist. The subplot, in fact, is Luis' (William Hurt) fantasies of the Spider Woman (Sonia Braga), a character he idolizes, drawn from films he vaguely remembers and greatly embellishes. Schrader visualizes Luis' dreams and desires by turning his fantasy into a film-within-the-film.

Still, these two plots cannot causally interact because they're on different planes of reality. They are connected, however, by making the subplot's story mirror the Central Plot. This gives Luis the chance to act out his fantasy in reality. At that moment the two plots collide in Luis' psyche and the audience imagines the emotional battle raging within: Will Luis do in life what the Spider Woman did in his dreams? Will he too betray the man he loves? What's more, the two plotlines ironize the Controlling Idea of *Love Through Self-sacrifice* and give the film an added thematic unity.

There's yet another revealing exception in the design of KISS OF THE SPIDER WOMAN. In principle, the Central Plot's Inciting Incident must be onscreen. But here the Inciting Incident is not revealed until the Mid-Act Climax. In the Backstory Luis, a homosexual convict imprisoned in a fascist dictatorship, is called into the warden's office and made this offer: A leftist revolutionary, Valentin (Raul Julia), will be put in his cell. If Luis spies on him and gets valuable information, the warden will give Luis his freedom. The audience, unaware of this deal, waits through the first hour of the film to finally discover this Central Plot when Luis visits the warden asking for medicine and camomile tea for the ailing Valentin.

For many this film began so tediously they nearly walked out. So why not open conventionally with the Inciting Incident, as does the novel, and start the story with a strong hook? Because, if

Schrader had placed the scene in which Luis agrees to spy on a freedom fighter at the opening of the film, the audience would have instantly hated the protagonist. With a choice of a fast opening versus empathy for the protagonist, the screenwriter violated the design of the novel. While the novelist used inner narration to gain empathy, the screenwriter knew that he would first have to convince the audience that Luis loved Valentin before revealing Luis' pact with the fascists. The right choice. Without empathy the film would be a hollow exercise in exotic photography.

Faced with irreconcilable choices, such as pace versus empathy, the wise writer redesigns the story to preserve what's vital. You're free to break or bend convention, but for one reason only: *to put something more important in its place.*

10

SCENE DESIGN

This chapter focuses on the components of scene design: *Turning Points, Setups/Payoffs, Emotional Dynamics,* and *Choice*. Chapter 11 will analyze two scenes to demonstrate how Beats, changing character behaviors, shape a scene's inner life.

TURNING POINTS

A scene is a story in miniature—an action through conflict in a unity or continuity of time and space that turns the value-charged condition of a character's life. In theory there's virtually no limit to a scene's length or locations. A scene may be infinitesimal. In the right context a scene consisting of a single shot in which a hand turns over a playing card could express great change. Conversely, ten minutes of action spread over a dozen sites on a battlefield may accomplish much less. No matter locations or length, a scene is unified around desire, action, conflict, and change.

In each scene a character pursues a desire related to his immediate time and place. But this *Scene-Objective* must be an aspect of his *Super-Objective* or Spine, the story-long quest that spans from Inciting Incident to Story Climax. Within the scene, the character acts on his Scene-Objective by choosing under pressure to take one action or another. However, from any or all levels of conflict comes a reaction he didn't anticipate. The effect is to crack open the gap between expectation and result, turning his outer fortunes, inner life, or both from the positive to the negative or the negative to the positive in terms of values the audience understands are at risk.

A scene causes change in a minor, albeit significant way. A *Sequence Climax* is a scene that causes a moderate reversal—change with more impact than a scene. An *Act Climax* is a scene that causes a major reversal—change with greater impact than Sequence Climax. Accordingly, we never write a scene that's merely a flat, static display of exposition; rather we strive for this ideal: to create a story design in which every scene is a minor, moderate, or major *Turning Point*.

TRADING PLACES: The value at stake is wealth. Inspired by *Porgy and Bess*, Billy Ray Valentine (Eddie Murphy) begs on the streets, pretending to be a paraplegic on a skateboard. A gap opens when police try to bust him, then widens enormously when two elderly businessmen, the Duke brothers (Ralph Bellamy and Don Ameche), suddenly intervene with the cops to save him. Billy's begging has caused his world to react differently and more powerfully than he expected. He doesn't resist, but wisely chooses to surrender to the gap. CUT TO: A walnut-paneled office where the Duke brothers have dressed him in a three-piece suit and made him a commodities broker. Billy's financial life goes from beggar to broker around this delightful Turning Point.

WALL STREET: The values at stake are wealth and honesty. A young stockbroker, Bud Fox (Charlie Sheen), secures a meeting with billionaire Gordon Gekko (Michael Douglas). Bud lives from paycheck to paycheck, but his integrity is intact. When he proposes legitimate business ideas, his sales pitch provokes forces of antagonism he couldn't anticipate as Gekko retorts: "Tell me something I don't know." Suddenly Bud realizes Gekko doesn't want to do honest business. He pauses, then reveals a corporate secret that his own father had told him. Bud chooses to join Gekko in an unlawful conspiracy, reversing his inner nature from honest to criminal and his fortunes from poor to rich around this powerful and ironic Turning Point.

The effects of Turning Points are fourfold: *surprise, increased curiosity, insight,* and *new direction.*

When a gap opens between expectation and result, it jolts the audience with surprise. The world has reacted in a way neither character nor audience had foreseen. This moment of shock instantly provokes curiosity as the audience wonders "Why?" TRADING PLACES: Why are these two old men saving this beggar from the police? WALL STREET: Why is Gekko saying: "Tell me something I don't know." In an effort to satisfy its curiosity, the audience rushes back through what story it's seen so far, seeking answers. In a beautifully designed story, these answers have been quietly but carefully layered in.

TRADING PLACES: Our thoughts flit back to previous scenes with the Duke brothers and we realize that these old men are so bored with life they'll use their wealth to play sadistic games. Further, they must have seen a spark of genius in this beggar or they wouldn't have picked him to be their pawn.

WALL STREET: The "why?" provoked by Gekko's "Tell me something I don't know" is instantly answered by this insight: Of course Gekko's a billionaire, he's a crook. Almost no one becomes immensely rich honestly. He too likes games ... of a criminal kind. When Bud joins him, our memory dashes back to previous scenes at his office, and we realize that Bud was too ambitious and greedy—ripe for a fall.

The nimble and perceptive mind of the audience finds these answers in a flash of understanding. The question "Why?" propels it back through the story, and what it's seen so far instantly clicks into a new configuration; it experiences a rush of insight into character and world, a satisfying layer of hidden truth.

Insight adds to curiosity. This new understanding amplifies the questions "What's going to happen next?" and "How will this turn out?" This effect, true in all genres, is vividly clear in *Crime Stories*. Someone goes to a closet for a clean shirt and a dead body falls out. This huge gap triggers a fusillade of questions: "Who committed this murder? How? When? Why? Will the killer be caught?" The writer must now satisfy the curiosity he's created. From each point of changed value, he must move his story in a new direction to create Turning Points yet to come.

KRAMER VS. KRAMER: The moment we see that a thirty-two-year-old man can't make breakfast the scene turns. The question "Why?" sends us back through the few minutes of film that precede the gap. Armed with our life experience and common sense, we seek answers.

First, Kramer's a workaholic, but many workaholics make excellent breakfasts at five A.M. before anyone else is up. More, he's never contributed to his family's domestic life, but many men don't and their wives remain loyal, respecting their husbands' efforts to provide income. Our deeper insight is this: Kramer is a child. He's a spoiled-rotten brat whose mother always made breakfast for him. Later her role was filled by girlfriends and waitresses. Now he's turned his wife into a waitress/mother. Women have spoiled Kramer all his life and he's been only too happy to let them. Joanna Kramer was, in essence, raising two children, and overwhelmed by the impossibility of a mature relationship, she abandoned the marriage. What's more, we feel she was right to do it. New direction: Kramer's growth into manhood.

The Climax of THE EMPIRE STRIKES BACK propels the longest rush for insight I know. As Darth Vader (David Prowse/James Earl Jones) and Luke Skywalker (Mark Hamill) fight to the death with light sabers, Vader steps back and says: "You can't kill me, Luke, I'm your father." The word "father" explodes one of the most famous gaps in film history and hurls the audience back through two whole films separated by three years. Instantly we grasp why Ben Obi-Wan Kenobi (Alec Guinness) was so worried about what would happen if Darth and Luke ever met face to face. We know why Yoda (voice of Frank Oz) was so desperate to teach Luke command of the Force. We realize why Luke's had so many close escapes: His father has been secretly protecting him. Two films that made perfect sense to this moment now have a new, deeper layer of meaning. New direction: RETURN OF THE JEDI.

CHINATOWN: Before the Act Two Climax we believe that Mulwray was murdered either for financial gain or in a jealous rage. But when Evelyn says: "She's my sister and my daughter . . ." the gap splits with a shock. To understand her words, we race back through the film and gain a powerful set of insights: incest between father and daughter, the real motivation for the murder, and the identity of the killer. New direction: the corkscrew twists of Act Three.

The Question of Self-Expression

A storyteller puts a friendly arm around the audience, saying: "Let me show you something." He takes us to a scene, such as the one in CHINATOWN, and says: "Watch Gittes drive to Santa Monica, intent on arresting Evelyn. When he knocks on her door, do you think he'll be invited in? Watch this. Now the beautiful Evelyn comes downstairs, happy to see him. Think he'll soften and let her off the hook? Watch this. Next she fights to protect her secret. Think she'll keep it? Watch this. As he listens to her confession, will he help her or arrest her? Watch this."

The storyteller leads us into expectation, makes us think we understand, then cracks open reality, creating surprise and curiosity, sending us back through his story again and again. On each trip back, we gain deeper and deeper insight into the natures of his characters and their world—a sudden awareness of the ineffable truths that lie hidden beneath the film's images. He then takes his story in a new direction in an ever-escalating progression of such moments.

To tell story is to make a promise: If you give me your concentration, I'll give you surprise followed by the pleasure of discovering life, its pains and joys, at levels and in directions you have never imagined. And most important, this must be done with such seeming ease and naturalness that we lead the audience to these discoveries as if spontaneously. The effect of a beautifully turned moment is that filmgoers experience a rush of knowledge *as if they did it for themselves*. In a sense they did. Insight is the audience's reward for paying attention, and a beautifully designed story delivers this pleasure scene after scene after scene.

Yet, if we were to ask writers how they express themselves, more often than not they'll reply: "With my words. My descriptions of the world and the dialogue I create for my characters. I'm a writer. I express myself in language." But language is merely our text. First, last, and always, self-expression occurs in the flood of insight that pours out of a Turning Point. Here the writer opens his arms to the world, saying: "This is my vision of life, of the nature of the human beings that inhabit my world. This is what I think happens to people in these circumstances for these reasons. My ideas, my emotions. Me." Our most powerful means of self-expression is the unique way we turn the story.

Then come words. We apply our literary talent with vividness and skill, so that when a beautifully written scene is acted, the audience is carried willingly and pleasurably through our Turning Points. As important as language is, however, it's only the surface by which we capture the reader to lead him to the inner life of the story. Language is a tool for self-expression and must never become a decorative end of its own.

Imagine now the difficulties of designing a story so that thirty, forty, fifty times over, scenes turn in minor, moderate, or major ways, each expressing an aspect of our vision. This is why weak storytelling resorts to substituting information for insight. Why many writers choose to explain their meanings out of the mouths of their characters, or worse, in voice-over narration. Such writing is always inadequate. It forces characters to a phony, self-conscious knowledge rarely found in actuality. More important, even exquisite, perceptive prose cannot substitute for the global insight that floods the mind when we match our life experiences against an artist's well-placed setup.

SETUPS/PAYOFFS

To express our vision scene by scene we crack open the surface of our fictional reality and send the audience back to gain insight. These insights, therefore, must be shaped into *Setups* and *Payoffs*. To set up means to layer in knowledge; to pay off means to close the gap by delivering that knowledge to the audience. When the gap between expectation and result propels the audience back through the story seeking answers, it can only find them if the writer has prepared or planted these insights in the work.

CHINATOWN: When Evelyn Mulwray says: "She's my sister and my daughter," we instantly remember a scene between her father and Gittes in which the detective asks Noah Cross what he and his son-in-law were arguing about the day before Mulwray was murdered. Cross replies, "My daughter." The first time we hear this, we think he means Evelyn. In a flash, we now realize he meant Katherine, his daughter by his daughter. Cross said it knowing that Gittes would draw the wrong conclusion, and, by implication, would suspect Evelyn of the murder he committed.

THE EMPIRE STRIKES BACK: When Darth Vader reveals that he's Luke's father, we rush back to the scenes in which Ben Kenobi and Yoda are greatly troubled over Luke's command of the Force, fearing, we presume, for the young man's safety. We now realize that Luke's mentors were actually concerned for his soul, dreading that his father would seduce him to the "dark side."

SULLIVAN'S TRAVELS: John L. Sullivan is a film director with a string of hits such as *So Long, Sarong* and *Ants in Your Pants of 1939*. Conscience-stricken by the appalling condition of the world, Sullivan determines that his next film must have "social significance." Angry studio bosses point out that he's from Hollywood and therefore doesn't know anything about "social significance."

So Sullivan decides to do research. He trudges off into America, followed by an air-conditioned travel van, equipped with his butler, cook, secretary, girlfriend, and a press agent intent on turning Sullivan's lunatic adventure into a publicity stunt. Then, in a case of mistaken identity, Sullivan's thrown on a chain gang in the swamps of Louisiana. Suddenly he's up to his nostrils in "social significance" without a dime to call his agent.

One evening Sullivan hears uproarious laughter coming from a building in the prison compound and discovers a makeshift movie theatre filled with his fellow prisoners laughing themselves help-less at a Mickey Mouse cartoon. His face drops as he realizes that these men do not need "social significance" from him. They have more than enough in their lives already. What they need is what he does best—good light entertainment.

With this brilliant reversal, we're swept back through the film coming to Sullivan's insight . . . and much more. As we gather in all the scenes that satirize Hollywood aristocracy, we realize that commercial films that presume to instruct society on how to solve its shortcomings are certain to be false. For, with few exceptions, most filmmakers, like Sullivan, are not interested in the suffering poor as much as the picturesque poor.

Setups must be handled with great care. They must be planted in such a way that when the audience first sees them, they have one meaning, but with a rush of insight, they take on a second, more important meaning. It's possible, in fact, that a single setup may have meanings hidden to a third or fourth level.

CHINATOWN: When we meet Noah Cross, he's a murder suspect, but he's also a father worried about his daughter. When Evelyn reveals their incest, we then realize Cross's true concern is Katherine. In Act Three, when Cross uses his wealth to block Gittes and capture Katherine, we realize that under Cross's previous scenes lurked a third level, a madness driven by the virtually omnipotent power to escape justice while committing murder. In the final scene, when Cross draws Katherine into the shadows of Chinatown, we realize that festering under all this grotesque corruption has been Cross's lust to have incest with the offspring of his own incest.

Setups must be planted firmly enough so that when the audience's mind hurls back, they're remembered. If setups are too subtle, the audience will miss the point. If too heavy-handed, the audience will see the Turning Point coming a mile away. Turning Points fail when we overprepare the obvious and underprepare the unusual.

Additionally, the firmness of the setup must be adjusted to the target audience. We set up more prominently for youth audiences, because they're not as story literate as middle-aged filmgoers. Bergman, for example, is difficult for the young—not because they couldn't grasp his ideas if they were explained, but because Bergman never explains. He dramatizes his ideas subtly, using setups intended for the well-educated, socially experienced, and psychologically sophisticated.

Once the setup closes the gap, that payoff will, in all probability, become yet another setup for payoffs ahead.

CHINATOWN: When Evelyn reveals her child by incest, she repeatedly warns Gittes that her father is dangerous, that Gittes doesn't know what he's dealing with. We then realize that Cross killed Mulwray in a fight for possession of the child. This Act Two payoff sets up an Act Three Climax in which Gittes fails to apprehend Cross, Evelyn is killed, and the father/grandfather pulls the terrified Katherine into the darkness.

THE EMPIRE STRIKES BACK: When Darth Vader reveals himself to Luke, this pays off multiple setups strung back through two films. In an instant, however, this also becomes the setup for Luke's next action. What will the young hero do? He chooses to try to kill his father, but Darth Vader cuts off his son's hand—a payoff to set up the next action. Now defeated, what will Luke do? He hurls himself out of the sky city, trying to commit an honorable suicide—a payoff to set up the next action. Will he die? No, he's rescued virtually in mid-air by his friends. This stroke of luck pays off the suicide and becomes the setup for a third film to resolve the conflict between father and son.

SULLIVAN'S TRAVELS: When Sullivan realizes what a pretentious fool he's been, this pays off all the arrogant folly underlying the previous acts. It in turn sets up his next action. How will he escape the chain gang? His discovery of who he really is puts his head back in the Hollywood groove. He realizes, like any Hollywood pro, that the way out of prison, indeed out of any trouble, is publicity. Sullivan confesses to a murder he didn't commit to get back into court and the limelight of the press so the studio bosses and their powerhouse attorneys can rescue him. This payoff sets up the Resolution scene where we see Sullivan back in the Hollywood harness, making the fluffy entertainment films he has always made—but now he knows why.

The juggling act of setting up, paying off, setting up again and paying off again often sparks our most creative flashes.

Suppose you were developing a story about orphaned brothers, Mark and Michael, who are raised from infancy in a brutal institution. The brothers are inseparable, protecting and supporting each other through the years. Then they escape the orphanage. Now on the streets they struggle to survive while always defending each other. Mark and Michael love each other, and you love them. But you have a problem: no story. This is a portrait entitled: "Two brothers against the world." The only variation in the repetitious demonstration of their fraternal loyalty is its location. Nothing essential changes.

But, as you stare at your open-ended chain-link of episodes, you have a crazy idea: "What if Mark stabbed Michael in the back? Ripped him off, took his money, his girl . . ." Now you're pacing, arguing: "That's stupid! They love each other. Fought the world together. Makes no sense! Still, it'd be great. Forget it. But it'd be a hell of a scene. Cut it out. It's not logical!"

Then the light goes on: "I could make it logical. I could go back through everything and layer that in. Two brothers against the world? What about Cain and Abel? Sibling rivalry? I could rewrite from the opening and under every scene slip a bitter taste of envy in Mark, superiority and arrogance in Michael. All quietly there behind the sweet loyalty. If I do it well, when Mark betrays Mike, the audience will glimpse that repressed jealousy in Mark and it'll all make sense."

Now your characters aren't repeating but growing. Perhaps you realize you're finally expressing what you really feel toward your own brother and couldn't admit. Still, it's not over. Suddenly, out of the blue, a second thought: "If Mark betrays Mike, that could be the Penultimate Climax. And that Climax could set up a last act Story Climax in which Mike takes his revenge and . . ." You've found your story because you've allowed yourself to think the unthinkable. In storytelling, logic is retroactive.

In story, unlike life, you can always go back and fix it. You can set up what may seem absurd and make it rational. Reasoning is secondary and postcreativity. Primary and preconditional to everything else is imagination—the willingness to think any crazy idea, to let images that may or may not make sense find their way to you.

Nine out of ten will be useless. Yet one illogical idea may put butterflies in your belly, a flutter that's telling you something wonderful is hidden in this mad notion. In an intuitive flash you see the connection and realize you can go back and make it make sense. Logic is child's play. Imagination takes you to the screen.

EMOTIONAL TRANSITIONS

We do not move the emotions of an audience by putting glistening tears in a character's eyes, by writing exuberant dialogue so an actor can recite his joy, by describing an erotic embrace, or by calling for angry music. Rather, we render the precise experience necessary to *cause* an emotion, then take the audience through that experience. For Turning Points not only deliver insight, they create the dynamics of emotion.

The understanding of how we create the audience's emotional experience begins with the realization that there are only two emotions—pleasure and pain. Each has its variations: joy, love, happiness, rapture, fun, ecstasy, thrill, bliss, and many others on one hand, and anguish, dread, anxiety, terror, grief, humiliation, malaise, misery, stress, remorse, and many others on the other hand. But at heart life gives us only one or the other.

As audience, we experience an emotion when the telling takes us through a transition of values. First, we must empathize with the character. Second, we must know what the character wants and want the character to have it. Third, we must understand the values at stake in the character's life. Within these conditions, a change in values moves our emotions.

Suppose a comedy were to begin with a poverty-stricken protagonist at the negative in terms of the value of wealth. Then over scene, sequence, or act, his life undergoes change to the positive, a transition from poor to rich. As the audience watches this character move toward his desire, the transition from less to more will lift it into a positive emotional experience.

As soon as this plateau is reached, however, emotion quickly dissipates. An emotion is a relatively short-term, energetic experience that peaks and burns and is over. Now the audience is thinking: "Terrific. He's rich. What happens next?"

Next, the story must turn in a new direction to shape a transition from positive to negative that's deeper than his previous penniless state. Perhaps the protagonist falls from riches into debt to the mafia, far worse than poverty. As this transition moves from more to less than nothing, the audience will have a negative emotional response. However, once the protagonist owes all to a loan shark, the audience's emotion wanes as it thinks: "Bad move. He blew the money and owes the mob. What's going to happen next?"

Now the story must turn in yet another new direction. Perhaps he escapes his debt by impersonating the Don and taking over the mob. As the telling makes the transition from the doubly negative to the ironically positive, the audience has an even stronger positive emotion. Story must create these dynamic alternations between positive and negative emotion in order to obey the *Law of Diminishing Returns*.

The Law of Diminishing Returns, true in life as well as in story, is this: *The more often we experience something, the less effect it has.* Emotional experience, in other words, cannot be repeated back-to-back with effect. The first ice cream cone tastes great; the second isn't bad; the third makes you sick. The first time we experience an emotion or sensation it has its full effect. If we try to repeat this experience immediately, it has half or less than half of its full effect. If we go straight to the same emotion for the third time, it not only doesn't have the original effect, it delivers the opposite effect.

Suppose a story contains three tragic scenes contiguously. What would be the effect? In the first, we shed tears; in the second, we sniffle; in the third, we laugh . . . loudly. Not because the third scene isn't sad—it may be the saddest of the three—but because the previous two have drained us of grief and we find it insensitive, if not ludicrous, of the storyteller to expect us to cry yet again. The repetition of "serious" emotion is, in fact, a favorite comic device.

Although comedy may seem the exception to this principle in that we often seem to laugh repeatedly, it's not. Laughter is not an emotion. Joy is an emotion. Laughter is a criticism we hurl at something we find ridiculous or outrageous. It may occur inside any emotion, from terror to love. Nor do we laugh without relief. A joke has two parts: setup and punch. The setup raises the tension in the audience, if only for a moment, through danger, sex, the scatological—a host of taboos—then the punch explodes laughter. This is the secret to comic timing: When is the setup ripe to hit the punchline or gag? The comic senses this intuitively, but one thing he learns objectively is that he can't deliver punch, punch, punch without wearing out his welcome.

There is, however, one exception: a story can go from positive to positive or negative to negative, *if* the contrast between these events is so great, in retrospect the first takes on shades of its opposite. Consider these two events: Lovers argue and break up. Negative. Next, one kills the other. The second turn is so powerfully negative that the argument begins to seem positive. In the light of the murder, the audience will look back at the breakup and think: "At least they were talking then."

If the contrast between emotional charges is great, events can move from positive to positive without sentimentality, or from negative to negative without forced seriousness. However, if the progression changes only by degree, as it normally would, then a repeated emotion has half its expected effect, and if repeated yet again, the charge unfortunately reverses itself.

The Law of Diminishing Returns is true of everything in life, except sex, which seems endlessly repeatable with effect.

Once a transition of value creates an emotion, feeling comes into play. Although they're often mistaken for each other, feeling is not emotion. Emotion is a short-term experience that peaks and burns rapidly. Feeling is a long-term, pervasive, sentient background that colors whole days, weeks, even years of our lives. Indeed, a specific feeling often dominates a personality. Each of the core emotions in life—pleasure and pain—has many variations. So which particular negative or positive emotion will we experience? The answer is found in the feeling that surrounds it. For, like adding pigment to a pencil sketch or an orchestra to a melody, feeling makes emotion specific.

Suppose a man is feeling good about life, his relationships and career both going well. Then he receives a message that his lover has died. He'll grieve but in time recover and go on with life. On the other hand, suppose his days are dark, stressed, and depressed by everything he tries. Then suddenly he receives a message that his lover has died. Well . . . he might join her.

In film, feeling is known as mood. Mood is created in the film's text: the quality of light and color, tempo of action and editing, casting, style of dialogue, production design, and musical score. The sum of all these textural qualities creates a particular mood. In general, mood, like setups, is a form of foreshadowing, a way of preparing or shaping the audience's anticipations. Moment by moment, however, while the dynamic of the scene determines whether the emotion it causes is positive or negative, the mood makes this emotion specific.

This sketch, for example, is designed to create a positive emotion: Estranged lovers haven't spoken to each other for over a year. Without her, his life's taken a dangerous turn. Desperate and broke, he comes to her, hoping to borrow money. The scene begins at the negative in two values: his survival and their love.

He knocks on her door. She sees him on the step and refuses to let him in. He makes a noise loud enough to disturb the neighbors, hoping to embarrass her into letting him in. She picks up a phone and threatens to call the police. He calls her bluff, shouting through the door that he is in such deep trouble prison may be the only safe place for him. She shouts back that that's fine with her.

Frightened and angry, he smashes through the door. But from the look on her face, he realizes this is no way to borrow money from anybody. He frantically explains that loan sharks are threatening to break his arms and his legs. Rather than sympathizing, she laughs and tells him she hopes they break his head as well. He bursts into tears and crawls to her, begging. The mad look on his face frightens her and she takes a gun out of a drawer to scare him off. He laughs, saying he remembers giving her the gun a year ago and the firing pin was broken. She laughs, saying she had it fixed and blows up the lamp next to him to prove it.

He grabs her wrist and they fall to floor wrestling for the gun, rolling over each other, until suddenly an emotion they haven't felt for over a year ignites and they start to make love on the floor next to the smashed lamp and shattered door. A little voice in his head says, "This could work," but then a gap opens between him . . . and his body. That, she thinks, smiling, is his real problem. Moved to pity and affection, she decides to take him back into her life. The scene ends on the positive: He has her help to survive, their love is restored.

If the audience empathizes with these characters, the movement from the negative to the positive will create a positive emotion. But *which*? There are many.

Suppose the writer calls for a summer's day, brightly colored flowers in window boxes, blossoms on the trees. The producer casts Jim Carrey and Mira Sorvino. The director composes them in head-to-foot shots. Together they've created a comic mood. Comedy likes bright light and color. Comics need full shots because they act with their whole bodies. Carrey and Sorvino are brilliant zanies. The audience will feel tingling fear spiced with laughter as Carrey bangs through the door, as Sorvino pulls a gun, as these two try to make love. Then a burst of joy when she takes him back.

But suppose the scene were set in the dead of night, the house spackled with shadows of trees blowing in the wind, moonlight, street light. The director shoots tight, canted angles and orders the lab to mute the colors. The producer casts Michael Madsen and Linda Fiorentino. Without changing a beat, the scene is now drenched in a *Thriller* mood. Our hearts will be in our throats as we fear that one of these two isn't getting out of this alive. Imagine Madsen bulling his way in, Fiorentino grabbing a gun, those two fighting for it. When they're finally in each other's arms, we'll breathe a sigh of relief.

The arc of the scene, sequence, or act determines the basic emotion. Mood makes it specific. *But mood will not substitute for emotion.* When we want mood experiences, we go to concerts or museums. When we want meaningful emotional experience, we go to the storyteller. It does the writer no good to write an exposition-filled scene in which nothing changes, then set it in a garden at sundown, thinking that a golden mood will carry the day. All the writer has done is dump weak writing on the shoulders of the director and cast. Undramatized exposition is boring in any light. Film is not about decorative photography.

THE NATURE OF CHOICE

A Turning Point is centered in the choice a character makes under pressure to take one action or another in the pursuit of desire. Human nature dictates that each of us will always choose the "good" or the "right" *as we perceive the "good" or the "right."* It is impossible to do otherwise. Therefore, if a character is put into a situation where he must choose between a clear good versus a clear evil, or right versus wrong, the audience, understanding the character's point of view, will know in advance how the character will choose.

The choice between good and evil or between right and wrong is no choice at all.

Imagine Attila, King of the Huns poised on the borders of fifth-century Europe, surveying his hordes and asking himself: "Should I invade, murder, rape, plunder, burn, and lay waste . . . or should I go home?" For Attila this is no choice at all. He must invade, slay, plunder, and lay waste. He didn't lead tens of thousands of warriors across two continents to turn around when he finally came within sight of the prize. In the eyes of his victims, however, his is an evil decision. But that's their point of view. For Attila his choice is not only the right thing to do, but probably the moral thing to do. No doubt, like many of history's great tyrants, he felt he was on a holy mission.

Or, closer to home: A thief bludgeons a victim on the street for the five dollars in her purse. He may know this isn't the moral thing to do, but moral/immoral, right/wrong, legal/illegal often have little to do with one another. He may instantly regret what he's done. But at the moment of murder, *from the thief's point of view,* his arm won't move until he's convinced himself that this is the right choice.

If we do not understand that much about human nature—that a human being is only capable of acting toward the right or the good as he has come to believe it or rationalize it—then we understand very little. Good/evil, right/wrong choices are dramatically obvious and trivial.

True choice is dilemma. It occurs in two situations. First, *a choice between irreconcilable goods:* From the character's view two things are desirable, he wants both, but circumstances are forcing him to choose only one. Second, *a choice between the lesser of two evils:* From the character's view two things are undesirable, he wants neither, but circumstances are forcing him to choose one. How a character chooses in a true dilemma is a powerful expression of his humanity and of the world in which he lives.

Writers since Homer have understood the principle of dilemma, and realized that the story of a two-sided relationship cannot be sustained, that the simple conflict between Character A and Character B cannot be told to satisfaction.

Positive / Neutral / Negative

(A) ———————▶   ◀——————— (B)

+ / −

A two-sided conflict is not dilemma but vacillation between the positive and the negative. "She loves me/she loves me not, she loves me/she loves not," for example, swings back and forth between good and bad, and presents insoluble story problems. It isn't only tediously repetitious, but it has no ending.

If we try to climax this pattern on the positive with the protagonist believing "She loves me," the audience leaves thinking, "Wait till tomorrow when she'll love you not again." Or if on the negative "She loves me not," the audience exits thinking, "She'll come back. She always did." Even if we kill the loved one, it's not a true ending because the protagonist is left wondering, "She loved me? She loved me not?" and the audience exits groping for a point that was never made.

For example, here are two stories: one that wavers back and forth between inward states of pleasure and pain and one of inner dilemma. Compare BETTY BLUE with THE RED DESERT. In the former, Betty (Beatrice Dalle) slides from obsession to madness to catatonia. She has impulses but never makes a true decision. In the later Giuliana (Monica Vitti) faces profound dilemmas: retreat into comforting fantasies versus making meaning out of a harsh reality, madness versus pain. BETTY BLUE'S "mock-minimalism" is an over two-hour long snapshot of a helpless victim of schizophrenia that mistakes suffering for drama. IL DESERTO ROSSO is a minimalist masterpiece that delineates a human being grappling with the terrifying contradictions within her nature.

To construct and create genuine choice, we must frame a three-sided situation. As in life, meaningful decisions are triangular.

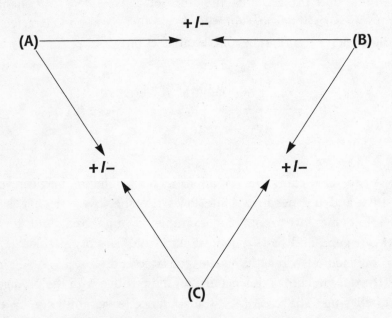

The moment we add C we generate ample material to avoid repetition. First, to the three possible relationships between A and B: positive/negative/neutral, love/hate/indifference, for example, we add the same three between A and C and between B and C. This gives us nine possibilities. Then we may join A and B against C; A and C against B; B and C against A. Or put them all in love or all in hate or all indifferent. By adding a third corner, the triangle breeds over twenty variations, more than enough material to progress without repetition. A fourth element would produce compound interlocking triangles, a virtual infinitude of changing relationships.

What's more, triangular design brings closure. If a telling is two-sided so that A vacillates between B and no-B, the ending is open. But if choice is three-sided so that A is caught between B and C, A's choice of one or the other closes the ending with satisfaction. Whether B and C represent the lesser of two evils or irreconcilable goods, the protagonist can't have both. A price must be paid. One must be risked or lost to gain the other. If, for example, A relinquishes C to have B, the audience feels a true choice has been taken. C has been sacrificed, and this irreversible change ends the story.

The most compelling dilemmas often combine the choice of irreconcilable goods with the lesser of two evils. In the *Supernatural Romance* DONA FLOR AND HER TWO HUSBANDS, for example, Dona (Sonia Braga) faces a choice between a new husband who's warm, secure, faithful, but dull versus an ex-husband who's sexy, exciting, but dead, yet his ghost appears to her in private as flesh and blood and sexually insatiable as ever. Is she hallucinating or not? What's the widow to do? She's caught in the dilemma between a boringly pleasant life of normality versus a bizarre, perhaps mad, life of emotional fulfillment. She makes the wise decision: She takes both.

An original work poses choices between unique but irreconcilable desires: It may be between two persons, a person and a lifestyle, two lifestyles, two ideals, two aspects of the innermost self—between any conflicting desires at any level of conflict, real or imagined, the writer may devise. But the principle is universal: Choice must not be doubt but dilemma, not between right/wrong or good/evil, but between either positive desires or negative desires of equal weight and value.

11

SCENE ANALYSIS

TEXT AND SUBTEXT

Just as a personality structure can be disclosed through psychoanalysis, the shape of a scene's inner life can be uncovered through
a similar inquiry. If we ask the right questions, a scene that speeds
past in the reading and hides its flaws brakes into ultra-slow
motion, opens up, and reveals its secrets.

If you feel a scene plays, don't fix what works. But often a first
draft falls flat or seems forced. Our tendency then is to rewrite dialogue over and over, hoping that by paraphrasing speeches we can
bring it to life . . . until we hit a dead end. For the problem won't
be in the scene's activity but in its action; not in how characters
are talking or behaving on the surface, but in what they're *doing*
behind their masks. Beats build scenes, and the flaws of an ill-
designed scene are in these exchanges of behavior. To find out
why a scene fails, the whole must be broken into its parts. An
analysis begins, therefore, by separating the scene's text from its
subtext.

Text means the sensory surface of a work of art. In film it's the
images onscreen and the soundtrack of dialogue, music, and sound
effects. What we see. What we hear. What people say. What people
do. Subtext is the life under that surface—thoughts and feelings
both known and unknown, hidden by behavior.

Nothing is what it seems. This principle calls for the screenwriter's constant awareness of the duplicity of life, his recognition

that everything exists on at least two levels, and that, therefore, he must write a simultaneous duality: First, he must create a verbal description of the sensory surface of life, sight and sound, activity and talk. Second, he must create the inner world of conscious and unconscious desire, action and reaction, impulse and id, genetic and experiential imperatives. As in reality, so in fiction: He must veil the truth with a living mask, the actual thoughts and feelings of characters behind their saying and doing.

An old Hollywood expression goes: "If the scene is about what the scene is about, you're in deep shit." It means writing "on the nose," writing dialogue and activity in which a character's deepest thoughts and feelings are expressed by what the character says and does—writing the subtext directly into the text.

Writing this, for example: Two attractive people sit opposite each other at a candlelit table, the light glinting off the crystal wine-glasses and the dewy eyes of the lovers. Soft breezes billow the curtains. A Chopin nocturne plays in the background. The lovers reach across the table, touch hands, look longingly in each others' eyes, say, "I love you, I love you" . . . *and actually mean it*. This is an unactable scene and will die like a rat in the road.

Actors are not marionettes to mime gestures and mouth words. They're artists who create with material from the subtext, not the text. An actor brings a character to life from the inside out, from unspoken, even unconscious thoughts and feelings out to a surface of behavior. The actors will say and do whatever the scene requires, but they find their sources for creation in the inner life. The scene above is unactable because it has no inner life, no subtext. It's unactable because there's nothing to act.

When we reflect on our filmgoing, we realize we've witnessed the phenomenon of subtext all our lives. The screen isn't opaque but transparent. When we look up at the screen, don't we have the impression that we're reading minds and feelings? We constantly say to ourselves, "I know what that character's *really* thinking and feeling. I know what's going on inside her better than she does, and I know it better than the guy she's talking to because he's busy with his own agenda."

In life our eyes tend to stop at the surface. We're so consumed by our own needs, conflicts, and daydreams that we rarely manage to take a step back and coolly observe what's going on inside other human beings. Occasionally we put a frame around a couple in the corner of a coffee shop and create a movie moment as we look through their smiles to the boredom beneath or through the pain in their eyes to the hope they have for each other. But rarely and only for a moment. In the ritual of story, however, we continuously see through the faces and activities of characters to depths of the unspoken, the unaware.

This is why we go to the storyteller, the guide who takes us beyond what seems to what *is* . . . at all levels and not for a mere moment but to the end of the line. The storyteller gives us the pleasure that life denies, the pleasure of sitting in the dark ritual of story, looking through the face of life to the heart of what is felt and thought beneath what's said and done.

How then might we write a love scene? Let two people change the tire on a car. Let the scene be a virtual textbook on how to fix a flat. Let all dialogue and action be about jack, wrench, hubcap, and lug nuts: "Hand me that, would ya?" "Watch out." "Don't get dirty." "Let me . . . whoops." The actors will interpret the real action of the scene, so leave room for them to bring romance to life wholly from the inside. As their eyes meet and sparks fly, we'll know what's happening because it's in the unspoken thoughts and emotions of the actors. As we see through the surface, we'll lean back with a knowing smile: "Look what happened. They're not just changing the tire on a car. He thinks she's hot and she knows it. Boy has met girl."

In other words, write as these things happen in life. For if we give that candlelit scene to fine actors, they'll smell the lie, refuse to act it, and walk off until the scene is cut or rewritten with an actable subtext. If the cast lacks the clout to demand a rewrite, then they'll do this: They will put a subtext in the scene whether or not it has anything to do with the story. Good actors will not step in front of a camera without their subtext.

For example, an actor forced to do the candlelit scene might attack it like this: "Why have these people gone out of their way to create this movie scene? What's with the candlelight, soft music, billowing curtains? Why don't they just take their pasta to the TV set like normal people? What's *wrong* with this relationship?" Because isn't that life? When do the candles come out? When everything's fine? No. When everything's fine we take our pasta to the TV set like normal people. So from that insight the actor will create a subtext. Now as we watch, we think: "He says he loves her and maybe he does, but look, he's scared he's losing her. He's desperate." Or from another subtext: "He says he loves her, but look, he's setting her up for bad news. He's getting ready to walk out."

The scene is not about what the scene seems to be about. It's about something else. And it's that something else—trying to regain her affection or softening her up for the breakup—that will make the scene work. There's always a subtext, an inner life that contrasts with or contradicts the text. Given this, the actor will create a multilayered work that allows us to see through the text to the truth that vibrates behind the eyes, voice, and gestures of life.

This principle does not mean that people are insincere. It's a commonsense recognition that we all wear a public mask. We say and do what we feel we should, while we think and feel something else altogether. As we must. We realize we can't go around saying and doing what we're actually thinking and feeling. If we all did that, life would be a lunatic asylum. Indeed, that's how you know you're talking to a lunatic. Lunatics are those poor souls who have lost their inner communication and so they allow themselves to say and do exactly what they are thinking and feeling and that's why they're mad.

In truth, it's virtually impossible for anyone, even the insane, to fully express what's going on inside. No matter how much we wish to manifest our deepest feelings, they elude us. We never fully express the truth, for in fact we rarely know it. Consider the situation in which we are desperate to express our truest thoughts and feelings—psychoanalysis: A patient lies on a couch, pouring his heart out. Wanting to be understood. No holds barred. No intimacy too private to reveal. And as he rips terrible thoughts and desires to the surface, what does the analyst do? Quietly nods and takes notes. And what's in those notes? What is not *being said*, the secret, unconscious truths that lie behind the patient's gut-wrenching confession. Nothing is what is seems. No text without a subtext.

Nor does this mean that we can't write powerful dialogue in which desperate people try to tell the truth. It simply means that the most passionate moments must conceal an even deeper level.

CHINATOWN: Evelyn Mulwray cries out: "She's my sister and my daughter. My father and I . . ." But what she doesn't say is: "Please help me." Her anguished confession is in fact a plea for help. Subtext: "I didn't kill my husband; my father did . . . to possess my child. If you arrest me, he'll take her. Please help me." In the next beat Gittes says, "We'll have to get you out of town." An illogical reply that makes perfect sense. Subtext: "I've understood everything you've told me. I now know your father did it. I love you and I'm going to risk my life to save you and your child. Then I'm going after the bastard." All this is underneath the scene, giving us truthful behavior without phony "on the nose" dialogue, and what's more, without robbing the audience of the pleasure of insight.

STAR WARS: When Darth Vader offers Luke the chance to join him in running the universe, bringing "order to things," Luke's reaction is to attempt suicide. Again not a logical reaction, but one that makes perfect sense, for both Luke and the audience read Darth Vader's subtext: Behind "bring order to things" is the unspoken implication ". . . and enslave billions." When Luke attempts to kill himself, we read a heroic subtext: "I'll die before I'd join your evil enterprise."

Characters may say and do anything you can imagine. But because it's impossible for any human being to tell or act the complete truth, because at the very least there's always an unconscious dimension, the writer must layer in a subtext. And when the audience senses that subtext, the scene plays.

This principle also extends to the first-person novel, theatrical soliloquy, and direct-to-camera or voice-over narration. For if characters talk privately to us, that doesn't mean for a moment that they know the truth or are capable of telling it.

ANNIE HALL: When Alvy Singer (Woody Allen) speaks directly to the audience "confessing" his fears and inadequacies, he also lies, dissembles, cajoles, exaggerates, and rationalizes, all in a self-deceived effort to win us over and convince himself his heart's in the right place.

Subtext is present even when a character is alone. For if no one else is watching us, we are. We wear masks to hide our true selves from ourselves.

Not only do individuals wear masks, but institutions do as well and hire public relations experts to keep them in place. Paddy Chayefsky's satire HOSPITAL cuts to the core of that truth. Hospital staffs all wear white and act as if professional, caring, and scientific. But if you've ever worked inside a medical institution, you know that greed and ego and a touch of madness are invisibly there. If you want to die, go to a hospital.

The constant duality of life is true even for the inanimate. In Robert Rossen's adaptation of Melville's BILLY BUDD a man-o-war rests in tropical waters at night. Uncountable stars gleam above, all magnificently reflected in a black, calm sea. A low, full moon trails its light from the horizon to the ship's prow. The limp sails tremble in the warm breezes. The cruel master-at-arms, Claggart (Robert Ryan) is holding watch. Billy (Terence Stamp) can't sleep, so he comes out on deck, stands at the gunnels with Claggart, and remarks on what a beautiful evening it is. Claggart answers, "Yes, Billy, yes, but remember, beneath that glittering surface is a universe of gliding monsters." Even Mother Nature wears her masks.

THE TECHNIQUE OF SCENE ANALYSIS

To analyze a scene you must slice into its pattern of behaviors at the levels of both text and subtext. Once properly examined, its flaws become vividly clear. Below is a five-step process designed to make a scene give up its secrets.

Step One: Define Conflict

First ask, who drives the scene, motivates it, and makes it happen? Any character or force might drive a scene, even an inanimate object or act of nature. Then look into both the text and subtext of this character or force, and ask: What does he (or it) want? Desire is always the key. Phrase this desire (or in the actor's idiom: scene objective) as an infinitive: such as, "to do this . . ." or "to get that . . . "

Next, look across the scene and ask: What forces of antagonism block this desire? Again, these forces may come from any level or combination. After identifying the source of antagonism, ask: What do the forces of antagonism want? This too is best expressed as an infinitive: "Not to do that . . ." or "To get this instead . . ." If the scene is well written, when you compare the set of phrases expressing the desires from each side, you'll see that they're in direct conflict—not tangential.

Step Two: Note Opening Value

Identify the value at stake in the scene and note its charge, positive or negative, at the opening of the scene. Such as: "Freedom. The protagonist is at the negative, a prisoner of his own obsessive ambition." Or: "Faith. The protagonist is at the positive, he trusts in God to get him out of this situation."

Step Three: Break the Scene into Beats

A beat is an exchange of action/reaction in character behavior. Look carefully at the scene's first action on two levels: outwardly, in terms of what the character seems to be doing, and, more important, look beneath the surface to what he is actually doing. Name this *subtextural action* with an active gerund phrase, such as "Begging." Try to find phrases that not only indicate action but touch the feelings of the character. "Pleading" for example, suggests a character acting with a sense of formality, whereas "Groveling at her feet" conveys a desperate servility.

The phrases that express the action in the subtext do not describe character activity in literal terms; they go deeper to name the character's essential action with emotive connotations.

Now look across the scene to see what reaction that action brought, and describe that reaction with an active gerund phrase. For example, "Ignoring the plea."

This exchange of action and reaction is a beat. As long as it continues, Character A is "Groveling at her feet" but Character B is "Ignoring the plea," it's one beat. Even if their exchange repeats a number of times, it's still one and the same beat. A new beat doesn't occur until behavior clearly changes.

If, for example, Character A's groveling changed to "Threatening to leave her" and in reaction Character B's ignoring changed to "Laughing at the threat," then the scene's second beat is "Threatening/Laughing" until A and B's behavior changes for a third time. The analysis then continues through the scene, parsing it into its beats.

Step Four: Note Closing Value and Compare with Opening Value

At the end of the scene, examine the value-charged condition of the character's situation and describe it in positive/negative terms. Compare this note to the one made in Step Two. If the two notations are the same, the activity between them is a nonevent. Nothing has changed, therefore nothing has happened. Exposition may have been passed to the audience, but the scene is flat. If, on the other hand, the value has undergone change, then the scene has turned.

Step Five: Survey Beats and Locate Turning Point

Start from the opening beat and review the gerund phrases describing the actions of the characters. As you trace action/reaction to the end of the scene, a shape or pattern should emerge. In a well-designed scene, even behaviors that seem helter-skelter will have an arc and a purpose. In fact, in such scenes, it's their careful design that makes the beats feel random. Within the arc locate the moment when the major gap opens between expectation and result, turning the scene to its changed end values. This precise moment is the Turning Point.

An analysis of the design of the following two scenes illustrates this technique.

CASABLANCA

Casablanca's Mid-Act Climax is played within a unity of time and place that puts emphasis on personal conflict and expresses its primary action verbally.

SYNOPSIS

Rick Blaine, an antifascist freedom fighter, and Ilsa Lund, a Norwegian expatriate, meet in Paris in 1940. They fall in love and begin an affair. He asks her to marry him, but she avoids an answer. Rick is on the Gestapo arrest list. On the eve of the Nazi invasion the lovers agree to meet at the train station and escape the city together. But Ilsa doesn't show. Instead, she sends a note saying she loves Rick but will never see him again.

A year later, Rick runs a cafe in Casablanca. He's become an isolate, determinedly neutral, uninvolved in all matters personal and political. As he says, "I stick my neck out for no man." He drinks too much and feels as if he has killed his former self. Then Ilsa walks in on the arm of Victor Laszlo, a renowned resistance leader. The lovers meet again. Behind their cocktail chat their passion is palpable. Ilsa leaves with Laszlo, but Rick sits in the dark cafe drinking through the night, waiting.

Hours after midnight she reappears. By now Rick is very maudlin and equally drunk. Ilsa tells him guardedly that she admires but doesn't love Laszlo. Then, before she can tell him that she loves him, Rick, in drunken bitterness, belittles her story by comparing it to one told in a brothel. Staring at her with a twisted smile he adds insult to injury: "Tell me. Who'd you leave me for? Was it Laszlo? Or were there others in between? Or aren't you the kind that tells?" This slur, implying she's a whore, sends her out the door as he collapses in drunken tears.

THE MID-ACT CLIMAX

The next day Ilsa and Laszlo go in search of black market exit visas. While he tries to make a deal in a cafe, she waits at a linen stall on the street. Seeing her alone, Rick approaches.

Step One: Define Conflict

Rick initiates and drives the scene. Despite inner conflict over the pain he has suffered since she abandoned him in Paris, and the anger he suppresses at seeing her with another man, Rick's desire is clear: "To win Ilsa back." His source of antagonism is equally clear: Ilsa. Her feelings are very complex and clouded by mixed emotions of guilt, regret, and duty. She loves Rick passionately and would go back to him if she could; but for reasons only she knows, she can't. Caught between irreconcilable needs, Ilsa's desire can be phrased as "To keep her affair with Rick in the past and move on with her life." Although entangled with inner conflicts, their desires are in direct opposition.

Step Two: Note Opening Value

Love governs the scene. Rick's insulting behavior in their last scene turned the value toward the negative, yet it leans to the positive because the audience and Rick see a ray of hope. In previous scenes Ilsa has been addressed as "Miss Ilsa Lund," a single woman traveling with Laszlo. Rick wants to change that.

Step Three: Break the Scene into Beats

BEAT #1

EXT. BAZAAR—LINEN STALL

The sign over the Arab Vendor's stall reads LINGERIE. He shows Ilsa a lace bed sheet.

Vendor's action: SELLING.

> ARAB
> You'll not find a treasure
> like this in all Morocco,
> Mademoiselle.

Just then, Rick walks up behind her.

Rick's action: APPROACHING HER.

Without looking Ilsa senses his prescence. She feigns interest in the lace.

Ilsa's reaction: IGNORING HIM.

The Vendor holds up a sign reading 700 FRANCS.

> ARAB
> Only seven hundred francs.

BEAT #2

> RICK
> You're being cheated.

Rick's action: PROTECTING HER.

Ilsa takes a second to compose herself. She glances at Rick, then with polite formality turns to the Vendor.

> ILSA
> It doesn't matter, thank you.

Ilsa's reaction: REJECTING RICK'S ADVANCE.

*To win Ilsa away from Lazlo, Rick's first task is to break
the ice—no easy task given the recriminations and angry
emotions of their last scene. His warning seems to insult
the Arab Vendor, who takes no offense, but in the subtext
it hints at more: her relationship with Lazlo.*

BEAT #3

> ### ARAB
> Ah . . . the lady is a friend of
> Rick's? For friends of Rick we
> have a small discount. Seven
> hundred francs, did I say?
> > (holding up a new
> > sign)
> You can have it for two hun-
> dred.

> ### RICK
> I'm sorry I was in no condi-
> tion to receive visitors when
> you called on me last night.

Rick's action: APOLOGIZING.

> ### ILSA
> It doesn't matter.

Ilsa's reaction: REJECTING HIM AGAIN.

> ### ARAB
> Ah! For special friends of
> Rick's we have a special
> discount.

He replaces the second sign with a third, reading 100 FRANCS.

*Rick's protective action of the first beat comes naturally;
the apology in the second beat is more difficult and rare.
He masks his embarassment by using an excessive formality to make light of it. Ilsa is unmoved.*

BEAT #4

> RICK
> Your story left me a little
> confused. Or maybe it was
> the bourbon.

Rick's action: EXCUSE MAKING.

> ARAB
> I have some tablecloths, some
> napkins . . .

> ILSA
> Thank you, I'm really not
> interested.

**Ilsa's reaction: REJECTING RICK FOR THE FOURTH
TIME.**

> ARAB
> (exiting hurriedly)
> Only one moment . . .please . . .

*The Arab vendor enriches the scene in a number of ways.
He opens it in a comic tone to counterpoint a dark ending; he
sells lace which adds connotations of weddings and the sexu-
ality of lingerie; most importantly, however, he tries to sell
Rick to Ilsa. The vendor's first line declares Rick a treasure.
To demonstrate the power of Rick, the vendor drops his*

price for "friends of Rick's." Then, hearing something about last night, the vendor cuts it even more for "special friends of Rick's."

This is followed by Rick's second reference to his drinking, as he tries to make this take the blame for his insulting behavior. Ilsa will hear none of it, and yet she stands and waits and it's safe to assume she isn't waiting to buy lace.

BEAT #5

A small silence as she pretends to examine the lace goods.

>   RICK
> Why'd you come back? To
> tell me why you ran out on
> me at the railway station?

Rick's action: GETTING HIS FOOT IN THE DOOR.

>   ILSA
>   (quietly)
> Yes.

Ilsa's reaction: OPENING THE DOOR A CRACK.

After hearing no four times in a row, Rick wants her to say yes to anything. So he asks a question that supplies its own answer. Her quiet yes opens the door—keeping the chain on, perhaps, but indicating she's willing to talk.

BEAT #6

>   RICK
> Well, you can tell me now. I'm
> reasonably sober.

Rick's action: GETTING DOWN ON HIS KNEES.

> ILSA
> I don't think I will, Rick.

Ilsa's reaction: ASKING FOR MORE.

The taciturn Rick insults himself over his drinking for the third time. In his tough guy manner, this is begging, and it works. Ilsa demurs, opposing him in a mild, polite way, yet continuing her lace-buying guise. To paraphrase her subtext: "That begging was nice for a change. Could I hear a little more, please?"

BEAT #7

> RICK
> Why not? After all, I was
> stuck with the railroad ticket.
> I think I'm entitled to know.

Rick's action: GUILT-TRIPPING HER.

> ILSA
> Last night I saw what has
> happened to you. The Rick I
> knew in Paris, I could tell
> him. He'd understand—but
> the Rick who looked at me
> with such hatred . . .

Ilsa's reaction: GUILT-TRIPPING HIM BACK.

These two people have a relationship. Each feels like the injured party, and each knows the sensitivity of the other so well that they hurt each other with ease.

BEAT #8

> ILSA
> (turning to look at
> Rick)
> I'll be leaving Casablanca
> soon. We'll never see each
> other again. We knew very
> little about each other when
> we were in love in Paris. If we
> leave it that way, maybe we'll
> remember those days—not
> Casablanca—not last night—

Ilsa's action: SAYING GOODBYE.

Rick simply stares at her.

Rick's reaction: REFUSING TO REACT.

In the subtext, Ilsa's kind, forgiving prose is a clear goodbye. No matter how well-mannered, no matter how much her language implies her love for Rick, this is the kiss-off: "Let's be friends, let's remember the good times, and forget the bad."

Rick will have none of this. He reacts by refusing to react; for ignoring someone's action is, of course, a reaction. Instead he starts the next beat.

BEAT #9

> RICK
> (voice low and
> intense)
> Did you run out on me
> because you couldn't take it?

> Because you knew what it
> would be like, hiding from the
> police, running away all the
> time?

Rick's action: CALLING HER A COWARD.

> ILSA
> You can believe that if you
> want to.

Ilsa's reaction: CALLING HIM A FOOL.

Rick's had a year to figure out why she left him, and his best guess is that she was a coward. She, however, dares death with Laszlo every day, and so she insults him in return with a cool sarcasm that implies: "I don't care what you think; fools believe such nonsense; if you want to join them, believe it too."

BEAT #10

> RICK
> Well, I'm not running away
> anymore. I'm settled now—
> above a saloon, it's true—but
> walk up a flight. I'll be
> expecting you.

Rick's action: SEXUALLY PROPOSITIONING HER.

Ilsa drops her eyes and turns away from Rick, her face shaded by the wide brim of her hat.

Ilsa's reaction: HIDING HER REACTION.

Despite her denials, he senses that her feelings lean the other way. He well remembers their sex life in Paris, and has seen the cold, aloof Laszlo. So he takes a chance and propositions her on the street. Again, it works. Ilsa too remembers, and hides her blush under her hat brim. For a moment Rick feels she's within reach, but he can't resist sticking his foot in his mouth.

BEAT #11

> RICK
> All the same, some day you'll
> lie to Laszlo—you'll be there.

Rick's action: CALLING HER A WHORE.

> ILSA
> No, Rick. You see, Victor
> Laszlo is my husband.
> And was . . .
> > (pause, coolly)
> . . . even when I knew you in
> Paris.

Ilsa's reaction: CRUSHING HIM WITH THE NEWS.

With dignity and poise, Ilsa walks away, leaving the stunned Rick to stare after her.

Rick can't contain the pain caused by Ilsa's abandonment. As in the climax of their previous scene, he strikes out with a sexual slur, implying that she'll betray Laszlo to come back to his bed. Called a slut for a second time, Ilsa reaches back for the hardest thing she has, and strikes Rick with it as hard as she can. Notice, however, that this is a half-truth; she doesn't add that she thought her husband was

dead. Instead, she leaves a terrible implication in her wake:
She was a married woman who used Rick in Paris, then
walked out on him when her husband came back. There-
fore, her love was never real. We know from the subtext
that the opposite is the truth, but Rick is devastated.

Step Four: Note Closing Value and Compare with Opening Value

The Central Plot turns sharply from a hopeful positive to a negative
at a darker depth than Rick could have imagined. For not only does
Ilsa make it clear she doesn't love him now; she implies she never
did. Her secret marriage turns their Paris romance into a sham and
Rick into a cuckold.

Step Five: Survey the Beats and Locate the Turning Point

1. Approaching Her/Ignoring Him
2. Protecting Her/Rejecting Him (and Arab)
3. Apologizing/Rejecting Him
4. Excuse Making/Rejecting Him (and Arab)
5. Getting His Foot in the Door/Opening the Door
6. Getting Down on His Knees/Asking for More
7. Guilt-Tripping Her/Guilt-Tripping Him
8. Saying Goodbye/Refusing to React
9. Calling Her a Coward/Calling Him a Fool
10. Sexually Propositioning Her/Hiding Her Reaction
11. Calling Her a Slut/Destroying His Hope

The action/reaction pattern builds a rapid progression of beats.
Each exchange tops the previous beat, placing their love in greater
and greater risk, demanding more and more willpower and
capacity to take painful, even cruel actions, but at the same time
remain in cool control.

The gap opens in the middle of the eleventh beat, on the revelation that Ilsa was married to Laszlo while having an affair with Rick. Until this moment, Rick has hopes of winning her over, but with this Turning Point his hope is shattered.

THROUGH A GLASS DARKLY

In contrast to the stationary dialogue duet in CASABLANCA, the Climax of the Karin/God plot in THROUGH A GLASS DARKLY shifts from place to place with slight ellipses of time, involves four characters, anchors itself at the level of inner conflict, and conveys its primary action physically.

SYNOPSIS

For this film Bergman designed a Multiplot of six interconnected stories. The most powerful is the conflict between Karin and her "God." She suffers from delusional schizophrenia. During a period of lucidity, she's released from a hospital to join her family for a brief holiday at their cottage on an island in the Baltic. While she struggles to hold on to her sanity, she's surrounded by weak, troubled men who turn to her for support.

David, Karin's father, is outwardly kind but emotionally repressed. He's a popular novelist but hounded by his lack of critical recognition. He prefers to observe life at a safe distance before cannibalizing it for his art. Karin wants her father to be happy and prays for his artistic success.

Karin's husband, Martin, is an MD. She craves his understanding and approval; instead, he patronizes her like one of his patients and pesters her for sex.

Karin's brother, Minus, is her only true intimate. She confides in him, telling him the secrets of her terrifying delusions, but he's so troubled with adolescent sexuality and estrangement from his father that he gives her little consolation. Instead, Karin, sensing his fears, offers Minus comfort.

Soon Karin's acute sensitivity (perhaps even psychic awareness) gives way to hallucination. She hears voices from behind an attic wall, telling her that God will appear. Scared, she turns to Martin, but he humiliates her over the lack of sex in their marriage. When she seeks out her father, he gently dismisses her like a child. Alone, Karin sneaks a look at her father's diary and discovers that his only interest in her is as a character study for his next novel. She tries to tell her brother about the coming miracle of God's visitation, but Minus is so confused and tormented by his cravings that he doesn't understand. Suddenly, Karin's madness takes a sexual turn. With feral intensity, she drags her brother down into incest.

When David discovers what has happened, he's moved more by self-pity than by concern for his children. Amazingly, Karin sympathizes with him, and knowing that he's only interested in her as story material, gives her father insights into her illness. Martin interrupts, declaring that he must take Karin back to the mental hospital. He calls for an ambulance and starts to pack.

Step One: Define Conflict

Karin drives the scene. She believes in her voices and desperately hopes to see God, not only for her own needs but for her men. She wants to give them her epiphany, perhaps to win acceptance, but more importantly to help their troubled lives. Her sources of antagonism are two: first, her husband. Martin is drawn to her sexually and pities her, but he can no longer cope with her madness, so he wants to take her away from her "God" and put her safely back in the hospital. The second, and more powerful, is herself. While she hopes to have a glimpse of heaven, her subconscious waits to give her a vision of hell.

Step Two: Note Opening Value

Hope, in a strange way, fills the opening of the scene. Karin is the most empathetic character in the film. We want her desire to see God to be fulfilled. Even if it's a mad fantasy, it would give joy to a tormented woman. Furthermore, her many psychic experiences earlier in the film have led us to suspect that she may not be hallucinating. We hold out hope for a supernatural event; Karin's triumph over the self-centered men around her.

Step Three: Break the Scene into Beats

BEAT #1

INT. COTTAGE BEDROOM—DAY

Karin and Martin pack for the ambulance. Martin rummages through a chest of drawers, searching for a shirt. Karin's thoughts seem far away as she struggles with an overstuffed suitcase.

> KARIN
> Your shirts are washed but
> not ironed.

Karin's action: PLANNING HER ESCAPE.

> MARTIN
> I've got shirts in town
> anyway.

Martin's reaction: CONCEALING HIS GUILT.

> KARIN
> Help me shut the case, please.

Martin wrestles with the lid, but a pair of shoes keeps the latch from catching. He takes them out and looks at them.

> MARTIN
> It's my shoes. I can leave
> them here.

> KARIN

Why not wear these and leave
those?

> MARTIN
> (indicating the pair
> he is wearing)

These have to be mended.

He drops the shoes on the floor and hurriedly puts on his
jacket. Karin slowly closes the suitcase lid.

> *This beat is almost comic. Karin's dressed and packed, but
> Martin, like a boy needing a mother, fumbles around.
> She's a psychiatric patient returning to electric shock
> treatments, yet remains practical and composed; he's a
> doctor flustered over which shoes to wear. On the text
> Karin seems to be packing, but in the subtext she's plan-
> ning her next move. He's so distracted by his guilty con-
> science, he doesn't see that her outward calm conceals a
> mind scheming to pursue her "miracle" in the attic.*

BEAT #2

Karin fingers the suitcase, quietly and thoughtfully. Then:

> KARIN

Have you a headache pill?

Karin's action: ESCAPING TO HER "GOD."

> MARTIN
> (looking around the
> room)

Where's the brown case?

Martin's reaction: HELPING HER.

> KARIN
>
> In the kitchen.

> MARTIN
> (remembering)
> Yes, so it is.

Martin rushes into the

INT. KITCHEN—SAME

and finds his medical case on the table. He takes out some pills, fills a glass with water, then pads through the

INT. MAIN HALL—SAME

back to the

INT. BEDROOM—SAME

As he enters, a quick glance tells him that Karin's gone. Martin puts down the water and pills and rushes back into the

INT. MAIN HALL—SAME

looking for her.

Karin is more perceptive than Martin, but it's a measure of his self-absorption that she gives him the slip so easily. He knows schizophrenics can't be left alone, but his guilt over taking her back to the hospital has him doing everything possible to please her. His caring attitude isn't about her suffering but his.

BEAT #3

He glances outside, then runs to

INT. DAVID'S BEDROOM—SAME

and opens the door, surprising David at the window.

> MARTIN
> Seen Karin?

Martin's action: SEARCHING FOR KARIN.

> DAVID
> No.

David's reaction: HELPING HIM SEARCH.

As Martin leaves in a panic, David follows out into the

INT. MAIN HALL—SAME

where he and Martin exchange uncertain glances.

BEAT #4

Then suddenly they hear Karin's voice in WHISPERS . . .
upstairs.

Karin's action: PRAYING.

Martin prepares a sedative while David climbs the stairs.

David's reaction: RUSHING TO HER.

Martin's reaction: PREPARING TO RECAPTURE HER.

UPPER HALL

Karin's WHISPERS grow louder.

> KARIN
> (repeating the
> phrase)
> Yes, I see, I see . . .

Karin's hallucination gives these men what they want. For Martin, the chance to play doctor; for David, the chance to observe his daughter's illness at its most dramatic.

BEAT #5

David quietly steps to an unused

INT. ATTIC ROOM—SAME

and opens the door a few inches to peer inside.

DAVID'S POV

through the half-opened door of Karin standing in the middle of the room, staring at a wall with a closed closet door. Her voice is formal and prayerlike as she nearly chants the words.

> KARIN
> (talking to the wall)
> Yes, I quite see.

Karin's action: PREPARING FOR HER EPIPHANY.

ON DAVID

staring at his daughter, transfixed by the scene she's creating.

> KARIN (OFFSCREEN)
> I know it won't be long now.

David's reaction: OBSERVING KARIN'S MADNESS.

Martin, carrying his medical bag, joins David at the door. He glares at the sight of Karin talking to her imaginary listener.

> KARIN (OS)
> It's good to know that. But
> we've been happy to wait.

Martin's reaction: FIGHTING HIS EMOTIONS.

Karin supplicates before the voices behind the cracked wallpaper, but she's been well aware of the efforts to find her and of the now watchful eyes of her father, the suppressed anger of her husband.

BEAT #6

Martin hurries into the room and over to Karin, who anxiously twists the beads around her neck and stares fixedly, reverently, at the wall and closet door.

Martin's action: STOPPING HER HALLUCINATION.

> KARIN
> (to Martin)
> Walk quietly! They say he'll
> be here very soon. We must
> be ready.

Karin's reaction: PROTECTING HER VISION.

BEAT #7

> MARTIN
> Karin, we're going to town.

Martin's action: PULLING HER AWAY.

> KARIN
> I can't leave now.

Karin's reaction: STANDING HER GROUND.

BEAT #8

> MARTIN
> You're wrong, Karin.
> (looking at the
> closed door)
> Nothing is happening in there.
> (taking her
> shoulders)
> No God will come through the
> door.

Martin's action: DENYING THE EXISTENCE OF HER GOD.

> KARIN
> He'll come at any moment.
> And I must be here.

Karin's reaction: DEFENDING HER FAITH.

> MARTIN
> Karin, it's not so.

BEAT #9

> KARIN
>
> Not so loud! If you can't be
> quiet, go.

Karin's action: ORDERING MARTIN AWAY.

> MARTIN
>
> Come with me.

> KARIN
>
> Must you spoil it? Leave me
> alone.

As David watches from the door, Karin pulls away from Martin, who withdraws to a chair, sits down, and cleans his glasses.

Martin's reaction: RETREATING.

Karin is simply stronger than Martin. Unable to match her powerful will, he gives up and withdraws.

BEAT #10

Karin kneels to face the wall and clasps her hands in prayer.

> KARIN
>
> Martin, dearest, forgive me
> for being so cross. But can't
> you kneel down beside me?
> You look so funny sitting
> there. I know you don't
> believe, but for my sake.

Karin's action: DRAWING MARTIN INTO HER RITUAL.

Tears well up in Martin's eyes, as in helpless anguish, he comes back to her and kneels.

Martin's reaction: SURRENDERING TO HER.

All the while David watches from the doorway.

Karin wants everything to be perfect for the arrival of her God, so she brings the unbelieving Martin into her strange ritual.

BEAT #11

Martin takes Karin by the shoulders and buries himself in the crook of her neck, rubbing his tearful face against her skin.

> MARTIN
> Karin, dearest, dearest,
> dearest.

Martin's action: CARESSING HER.

Karin is repulsed. She pries his hand off and yanks away.

Karin's reaction: FIGHTING HIM OFF.

Helpless in the face of her madness, Martin instinctively tries to seduce her out of her mania, but his caresses fail miserably.

BEAT #12

Karin folds her hands in front of her in prayer.

Karin's action: **PRAYING WITH ALL HER POWER.**

Suddenly an ear-splitting ROAR fills the room. Karin's eyes shift along the wall to the closet.

"God's" reaction: **ANNOUNCING "GOD'S" ARRIVAL.**

BEAT #13

The closet door swings open, seemingly of its own accord.

"God's" action: **APPEARING TO KARIN.**

Karin stands respectfully and smiles at something that seems to be emerging from the empty closet.

Karin's reaction: **RECEIVING HER "GOD."**

Outside the window, an ambulance helicopter descends from the sky.

In the background, David eyes the scene intently.

How and why does the door open by itself? Vibrations from the helicopter perhaps, but that's not a satisfactory explanation. By pure coincidence, just as Karin prays for a miracle, door and helicopter join forces to give it to her. Yet, amazingly, the action doesn't seem contrived. For Bergman's created, in Jungian terms, an event of Synchronicity: the fusion of meaningful coincidence around a center of tremendous emotion. By allowing us to hear Karin's voices, by showing us her acute sensitivity to nature, and by dramatizing her burning need for a miracle, we come to expect the supernatural. Karin's religious passion is at such a fever pitch that it creates a synchronous event that gives us a glimpse of something beyond the real.

BEAT #14

Karin stares into the closet; her face freezes as she sees something startling.

Karin's "God's" action: ATTACKING HER.

Suddenly, she screams in terror, and as if being pursued, runs across the room, jamming herself into a corner, bringing her legs and arms up to protect herself.

Karin's reaction: FIGHTING OFF HER "GOD."

BEAT #15

Martin grabs her.

Martin's action: RESTRAINING HER.

She pushes him off and flees to another corner.

Karin's reaction: ESCAPING MARTIN.

BEAT #16

As if something were crawling up her body, she presses her fists into her groin, then flails wildly at an unseen assailant.

"God's" action: TRYING TO RAPE KARIN.

Karin's reaction: BATTLING "GOD'S" RAPE.

Now David joins Martin and tries to hold her.

David's reaction: HELPING HOLD HER.

BEAT #17

But she breaks away and rushes out of the door into the

INT. UPSTAIRS HALL—SAME

and down the stairs.

Karin's action: FLEEING.

INT. ON THE STAIRS—SAME

Suddenly, Minus appears at the bottom.

Minus blocks her way. Karin stops and stares at her brother.

Minus's reaction: TRAPPING HER.

BEAT #18

David grabs her and pulls her down onto the stairs. Martin
arrives with a syringe. Karin fights like a trapped animal.

Martin's and David's action: SEDATING HER.

> MARTIN
>
> Hold her legs.

She thrashes in their arms as Martin struggles to give her an
injection.

Karin's reaction: WILDLY RESISTING THE NEEDLE.

BEAT #19

She leans against her father and looks steadily into the anxious face of her brother.

The sedative's action: CALMING HER.

Karen's reaction: SURRENDERING TO THE DRUG.

David's and Martin's reaction: CALMING THEMSELVES.

Minus's reaction: TRYING TO UNDERSTAND.

BEAT #20

> KARIN
> I was suddenly afraid.

Karin's action: WARNING MINUS.

All three men's reaction: LISTENING QUIETLY.

> KARIN
> (slowly explaining
> to her brother)
> The door opened. But the god
> that came out was a spider.
> He came towards me and I
> saw his face. It was a hor-
> rible, stony face. He crawled
> up me and tried to force him-
> self into me. But I defended
> myself. The whole time I saw
> his eyes. They were calm and
> cold. As he couldn't force his
> way into me, he climbed up
> onto my breast, onto my face
> and went up the wall.
> (a long look into
> Minus's eyes)
> I have seen God.

286 ◆ ROBERT MCKEE

Although the spider-god rape is a delusion thrown up from her subconscious, once back in reality she treats the hallucination with ironic respect. She offers her terrifying discovery to all three men, but primarily to Minus as a cautionary tale, warning her brother that prayers will not be answered.

Step Four: Note Closing Value and Compare with Opening Value

Karin's encounter with the spider-god turns the scene from hope to hopelessness. She prays for an epiphany and gives this "miracle" to her father, knowing that because of his own incapacity for authentic emotion, he's hungry for the life experiences of others to fill the pages of his novels. She offers faith to her husband, but his responses are limited to sexual gestures and medical posturing. Her "miracle" then explodes into a nightmare and her trust in God is shattered.

In the final beat, Karin gives her grotesque vision to her brother as a warning, but this last gesture is slight, compared to the scene's dramatization of overwhelming despair. We're left with the feeling that intellectualizing love, as the novelist and doctor do throughout the film, is pitifully weak in the face of the incomprehensible forces that inhabit our natures.

Step Five: Survey the Beats and Locate the Turning Point

1. Planning Her Escape/Concealing His Guilt
2. Escaping Her "God"/Helping Her
3. Searching for Karin/Helping Him Search
4. Praying/Rushing to Her and Preparing to Recapture Her
5. Preparing for Her Epiphany/Observing Her Madness and Fighting His Emotions.
6. Stopping Her Hallucination/Protecting Her Dream
7. Pulling Her Away/Standing Her Ground

8. Denying the Existence of God/Defending Her Faith
9. Ordering Martin Away/Retreating
10. Drawing Martin to Her Ritual/Surrendering to Her
11. Caressing Her/Fighting Him Off
12. Praying with All Her Power/Announcing "God's" Arrival
13. Appearing to Karin/Receiving Her "God"
14. Attacking Karin/Fighting Off Her "God"
15. Restraining Her/Escaping Martin
16. Trying to Rape Karin/Battling "God"
17. Fleeing/Trapping Her
18. Sedating Her/Resisting the Needle
19. Calming Her/Calming Themselves and Trying to Understand
20. Warning Minus/Listening Quietly

Beats begin lightly, almost comically, then progress rapidly. Each action/reaction tops the previous exchange, demanding more from all the characters, and, in particular, demanding more and more willpower from Karin to survive her horrifying visions. The gap opens between Beats #13 and #14 when Karin's expectation of God results in a sexual attack by a hallucinatory spider. Unlike the revelation that turns the scene from CASABLANCA, the Turning Point of this Climax pivots on action—in this case, an action of appalling power taken by the protagonist's subconscious mind.

These superb scenes have been used to demonstrate the technique of analysis. Although they differ in levels of conflict and quality of actions, they share the same essential form. What is virtually perfect in them would be flawed in others of lesser worth. Ill-written scenes may lack conflict because desires are not opposed, may be antiprogressive because they're repetitious or circular, lopsided because their Turning Points come too early or too late, or lacking credibility because dialogue and action are "on the nose." But an analysis of a problematic scene that tests beats against scene objectives, altering behavior to fit desire or desire to fit behavior, will lead to a rewrite that brings the scene to life.

12

COMPOSITION

Composition means the ordering and linking of scenes. Like a composer choosing notes and chords, we shape progressions by selecting what to include, to exclude, to put before and after what. The task can be harrowing, for as we come to know our subject, every story possibility seems alive and squirming in a different direction. The disastrous temptation is to somehow include them all. Fortunately, to guide our efforts the art has evolved canons of composition: *Unity and Variety, Pacing, Rhythm and Tempo, Social and Personal Progression, Symbolic and Ironic Ascension,* and the *Principle of Transition.*

UNITY AND VARIETY

A story, even when expressing chaos, must be unified. This sentence, drawn from any plot, should be logical: "Because of the Inciting Incident, the Climax *had to happen.*" JAWS: "Because the shark killed a swimmer, the sheriff had to destroy the shark." KRAMER VS. KRAMER: "Because Kramer's wife left him and her child, only husband and wife could finally settle custody." We should sense a causal lock between Inciting Incident and Story Climax. The Inciting Incident is the story's most profound cause, and, therefore, the final effect, the Story Climax, should seem inevitable. The cement that binds them is the Spine, the protagonist's deep desire to restore the balance of life.

Unity is critical, but not sufficient. Within this unity, we must induce as much variety as possible. CASABLANCA, for example, is not only one of the most loved films of all time, it's also one of the most various. It's a brilliant *Love Story*, but more than half the film is *Political Drama*. Its excellent action sequences are counter-pointed by urbane comedy. And it's the next thing to a *Musical*. Over a dozen tunes, strategically placed throughout, comment on or set up event, meaning, emotion.

Most of us are not capable of this much variety, nor would our stories warrant it, but we don't want to hit the same note over and over, so that every scene sounds like every other. Instead, we seek the tragic in the comic, the political in the personal, the personal driving the political, the extraordinary behind the usual, the trivial in the exalted. The key to varying a repetitious cadence is research. Superficial knowledge leads to a bland, monotonous telling. With authorial knowledge we can prepare a feast of pleasures. Or at the very least, add humor.

PACING

If we slowly turn the screw, increasing tension a little more, a little more, a little more, scene by scene by scene by scene, we wear the audience out long before the ending. It goes limp and has no energy to invest in the Story Climax. Because a story is a metaphor for life, we expect it to feel like life, to have the rhythm of life. This rhythm beats between two contradictory desires: On one hand, we desire serenity, harmony, peace, and relaxation, but too much of this day after day and we become bored to the point of ennui and need therapy. As a result, we also desire challenge, tension, danger, even fear. But too much of this day after day and again we end up in the rubber room. So the rhythm of life swings between these poles.

The rhythm of a typical day, for example: You wake up full of energy, meet your gaze in the morning mirror, and say: "Today I'm going to get something done. No, I mean it for a change. Today I'm definitely getting something done." Off you go to "get something done" through a minefield of missed appointments, unreturned calls, pointless errands, and unrelenting hassle until you take a welcome midday lunch with friends to chat, sip wine, relocate your sanity, relax and gather your energies so you can go off to do battle with the demons of the afternoon, hoping to get done all the things you didn't get done in the morning—more missed calls, more useless tasks, and never, never enough time.

Finally you hit the highway home, a road packed with cars with only one person in each. Do you car pool? No. After a hard day on the job, the last thing you want is to jump into a car with three other jerks from work. You escape into your car, snap on the radio, and get in the proper lane according to the music. If classical, you hug the right; if pop, down the middle of the road; if rock, head left. We moan about traffic but never do anything about it because, in truth, we secretly enjoy rush hour; drive-time is the only time most of us are ever alone. You relax, scratch what needs scratching, and add a primal scream to the music.

Home for a quick shower, then off into the night looking for fun. What's fun? Amusement park rides that scare the life out of you, a film that makes you suffer emotions you'd never want in life, a singles bar and the humiliation of rejection. Weary, you fall into the rack and next dawn start this rhythm all over again.

This alternation between tension and relaxation is the pulse of living, the rhythm of days, even years. In some films it's salient, in others subtle. TENDER MERCIES eases dramatic pressure gently up, then gently down, each cycle slowly increasing the overall tension to Climax; THE FUGITIVE sculpts tension to sharp peaks, then ebbs briefly before accelerating higher still. Each film speaks in its natural accent, but never in flat, repetitious, passive nonevents, or in unrelenting, bludgeoning action. Whether Archplot, Miniplot, or Antiplot, all fine stories flux with the rhythm of life.

We use our act structure to start at a base of tension, then rise scene by sequence to the Climax of Act One. As we enter Act Two, we compose scenes that reduce this tension, switching to comedy, romance, a counterpointing mood that lowers the Act One intensity so that the audience can catch its breath and reach for more energy. We coach the audience to move like a long-distance runner who, rather than loping at a constant pace, speeds, slows, then speeds again, creating cycles that allow him to reach the limit of his reserves.

After retarding pace, we build the progressions of the following act until we top the previous Climax in intensity and meaning. Act by act, we tighten and release tension until the final Climax empties out the audience, leaving it emotionally exhausted but fulfilled. Then a brief Resolution scene to recuperate before going home.

It's just like sex. Masters of the bedroom arts pace their love-making. They begin by taking each other to a state of delicious tension short of—and we use the same word in both cases—climax, then tell a joke and shift positions before building each other to an even higher tension short of climax; then have a sandwich, watch TV, and gather energy to then reach greater and greater intensity, making love in cycles of rising tension until they finally climax simultaneously and the earth moves and they see colors. The gracious storyteller makes love to us. He knows we're capable of a tremendous release . . . if he paces us to it.

RHYTHM AND TEMPO

Rhythm is set by the length of scenes. How long are we in the same time and place? A typical two-hour feature plays forty to sixty scenes. This means, on average, a scene lasts two and a half minutes. But not every scene. Rather, for every one-minute scene there's a four-minute scene. For every thirty-second scene, a six-minute scene. In a properly formatted screenplay a page equals a minute of screen time. Therefore, if as you turn through your script, you discover a two-page scene followed by an eight-page scene, a seven-page scene, three-page scene, four-page, six-page, five-page, one-page, nine-page—in other words, if the average length of scene in your script is five pages, your story will have the pace of a postal worker on Valium.

Most directors' cameras drink up whatever is visually expressive in one location within two or three minutes. If a scene goes on longer, shots become redundant. The editor keeps coming back to the same establishing shot, same two-shot, close-up. When shots repeat, expressivity drains away; the film becomes visually dull and the eye loses interest and wanders from the screen. Do this enough and you'll lose the audience for good. The average scene length of two to three minutes is a reaction to the nature of cinema and the audience's hunger for a stream of expressive moments.

When we study the many exceptions to this principle, they only prove the point. TWELVE ANGRY MEN takes place over two days in a jury room. In essence, it consists of two fifty-minute scenes in one location, with a brief break for a night's sleep. But because it's based on a play, director Sidney Lumet could take advantage of its *French Scenes*.

In the Neoclassical period (1750–1850) the French theatre strictly obeyed the *Unities*: A set of conventions that restricted a play's performance to one basic action or plot, taking place in one location within the time it takes to perform. But the French realized that within this unity of time and space the entrance or exit of principal characters radically changes the dynamics of relationships and in effect creates a new scene. For example, in a garden setting young lovers play a scene together, then her mother discovers them. Her entrance so alters character relationships that it effects a new scene. This trio has a scene, then the young man exits. His exit so rearranges the relationship between mother and daughter that masks fall and a new scene begins.

Understanding the principle of *French scenes,* Lumet broke the jury room into sets within the set—the drinking fountain, cloakroom, window, one end of the table versus the other. Within these sublocations, he staged *French Scenes:* First jury members #1 and #2, then #2 exits while #5 and #7 enter, CUT TO #6 alone, CUT TO all twelve, CUT TO five of them off in a corner, and so on. The over eighty *French Scenes* in TWELVE ANGRY MEN build an exciting *rhythm*.

MY DINNER WITH ANDRE is even more contained: a two-hour film about a two-hour dinner with two characters and therefore no *French Scenes*. Yet the film pulses with *rhythm* because it's paced with scenes created, as in literature, by painting word pictures on the imagination of the listener: the adventure in the Polish forest, Andre's friends burying him alive in a bizarre ritual, the synchronistic phenomenon he encounters in his office. These erudite recountings wrap an *Education Plot* around an *Education Plot*. As Andre (Andre Gregory) relates his quixotic adventure toward spiritual development, he so cants his friend's view of life that Wally (Wallace Shawn) leaves the restaurant a changed man.

Tempo is the level of activity within a scene via dialogue, action, or a combination. For example, lovers talking quietly from pillow to pillow may have low tempo; an argument in a courtroom, high tempo. A character staring out a window coming to a vital life decision may have low tempo; a riot, high tempo.

In a well-told story, the progression of scenes and sequences accelerates pace. As we head toward act climaxes, we take advantage of *rhythm* and *tempo* to progressively shorten scenes while the activity in them becomes more and more brisk. Like music and dance, story is kinetic. We want to use cinema's sensory power to hurl the audience toward act climaxes because scenes of major reversal are, in fact, generally long, slow, and tense. "Climactic" doesn't mean short and explosive; it means *profound change*. Such scenes are not to be skimmed over. So we open them and let them breathe; we retard pace while the audience holds its breath, wondering what's going to happen next.

Again, the Law of Diminishing Returns applies: The more often we pause, the less effective a pause is. If the scenes before a major Climax are long and slow, the big scene in which we want the tension to hold falls flat. Because we've dragged the energies of the audience through sluggish scenes of minor importance, events of great moment are greeted with a shrug. Instead, we must "earn the pause" by telescoping *rhythm* while spiraling *tempo,* so that when the Climax arrives, we can put the brakes on, stretch the playing time, and the tension holds.

The problem with this design, of course, is that it's a cliché. D. W. Griffith mastered it. Filmmakers of the Silent Era knew that something as trivial as another chase to collar the bad guys can feel tremendous if pace is excited by making scenes ever shorter and *tempo* ever hasty. But techniques don't become clichés unless they have something important going for them in the first place. We, therefore, cannot, out of ignorance or arrogance, ignore the principle. If we lengthen and slow scenes prior to a major reversal, we cripple our Climax.

Pace begins in the screenplay. Cliché or not, we must control *rhythm* and *tempo*. It needn't be a symmetrical swelling of activity and shaving of scene lengths, but progressions must be shaped. For if we don't, the film editor will. And if to trim our sloppy work he cuts some of our favorite moments, we have no one to blame but ourselves. We're screenwriters, not refugees from the novel. Cinema is a unique art form. The screenwriter must master the aesthetics of motion pictures and create a screenplay that prepares the way for the artists who follow.

EXPRESSING PROGRESSION

When a story genuinely progresses it calls upon greater and greater human capacity, demands greater and greater willpower, generates greater and greater change in characters' lives, and places them at greater and greater jeopardy. How are we to express this? How will the audience sense the progressions? There are four primary techniques.

SOCIAL PROGRESSION

Widen the impact of character actions into society.

Let your story begin intimately, involving only a few principal characters. But as the telling moves forward, allow their actions to ramify outward into the world around them, touching and changing the lives of more and more people. Not all at once. Rather, spread the effect gradually through the progressions.

LONE STAR: Two men searching for spent shells on a deserted rifle range in Texas uncover the skeletal remains of a sheriff who vanished decades before. Evidence at the scene leads the current sheriff to suspect that his own father may have committed the murder. As he investigates, the story spreads outward into society and back through time, tracing a pattern of corruption and injustice that has touched and changed the lives of three generations of Texan-, Mexican- and African Americans—virtually every citizen in Rio County.

MEN IN BLACK: A chance encounter between a farmer and a fugitive alien searching for a rare gem slowly ramifies outward to jeopardize all of creation.

This principle of starting with intimate problems that ramify outward into the world to build powerful progressions explains why certain professions are overrepresented in the roles of protagonists. This is why we tend to tell stories about lawyers, doctors, warriors, politicians, scientists—people so positioned in society by profession that if something goes haywire in their private lives, the writer can expand the action into society.

Imagine a story that begins like this: The President of the United States gets up one morning to shave and as he stares in the mirror, he hallucinates about imaginary enemies around the globe. He tells no one, but soon his wife realizes he's gone mad. His close associates too. They gather and decide that since he has only six months left in office, why spoil things now? They'll cover up for him. But we know he has "his finger on the button" and a madman in this position could turn our troubled world into universal hell.

PERSONAL PROGRESSION

Drive actions deeply into the intimate relationships and inner lives of the characters.

If the logic of your setting doesn't allow you to go wide, then you must go deep. Start with a personal or inner conflict that demands balancing, yet seems relatively solvable. Then, as the work progresses, hammer the story downward—emotionally, psychologically, physically, morally—to the dark secrets, the unspoken truths that hide behind a public mask.

ORDINARY PEOPLE is confined to the family, a friend, and a doctor. From a tension between mother and son that seems solvable with communication and love, it descends to grievous pain. As the father slowly comes to realize he must choose between the sanity of his son and the unity of his family, the story drives the child to the brink of suicide, the mother to reveal her hatred of her own child, and the husband to lose a wife he deeply loves.

CHINATOWN is an elegant design that combines both techniques, reaching simultaneously wide and deep. A private eye is hired to investigate a man for adultery. Then, like an oil slick, the story moves outward in an ever-widening circle that engulfs city hall, millionaire conspirators, farmers of the San Fernando Valley, until it contaminates all the citizens of Los Angeles. At the same time it plunges inward. Gittes is under constant assault: kicks to the groin, blows to the head, his nose split open. Mulwray is killed, incest exposed between father and daughter until the protagonist's tragic past repeats to trigger the death of Evelyn Mulwray and throw an innocent child into the hands of an insane father/grandfather.

SYMBOLIC ASCENSION

Build the symbolic charge of the story's imagery from the particular to the universal, the specific to the archetypal.

A good story well told fosters a good film. But a good story well told with the added power of subliminal symbolism lifts the telling to the next level of expressivity, and the payoff may be a *great* film. Symbolism is very compelling. Like images in our dreams, it invades the unconscious mind and touches us deeply—as long as we're unaware of its presence. If, in a heavy-handed way, we label images as "symbolic," their effect is destroyed. But if they are slipped quietly, gradually, and unassumingly into the telling, they move us profoundly.

Symbolic progression works in this way: start with actions, locations, and roles that represent only themselves. But as the story progresses, chose images that gather greater and greater meaning, until by the end of the telling characters, settings, and events stand for universal ideas.

THE DEER HUNTER introduces steel workers in Pennsylvania who like to hunt, drink beer, and carouse. They're as ordinary as the town they live in. But as events progress, sets, roles, and actions become more and more symbolically charged, building from the tiger cages in Vietnam to the highly symbolic scenes in a Saigon casino where men play Russian Roulette for money, culminating in a Crisis at the top of a mountain. The protagonist, Michael (Robert De Niro) progresses from factory worker to warrior to "The Hunter," the man who kills.

The film's Controlling Idea is: *We save our own humanity when we stop killing other living beings.* If the hunter spills enough blood, sooner or later he runs out of targets and turns the gun on himself. He either literally kills himself, as does Nick (Christopher Walken), or more likely, he kills himself in the sense that he stops feeling anything and falls dead inside. The Crisis sends Michael in his hunter's garb, armed with a weapon, to a mountaintop. There, on a precipice, the prey, a magnificent elk, comes out of the mist. An archetypal image: *hunter and prey at the top of a mountain.* Why the top of a mountain? Because tops of mountains are places where "great things happen." Moses is given the Ten Commandments, not in his kitchen, but *at the top of a mountain.*

THE TERMINATOR takes symbolic progression in a different direction, not up the mountain but into the maze. Opening with step-down imagery of commonplace people in commonplace settings, it tells the story of Sarah Connor, a fast-food waitress in Los Angeles. Suddenly, the Terminator and Reese explode into the present from the year 2029, and pursue Sarah through the streets of L.A., one trying to kill her, the other to save her.

We learn that in the future robots become self-aware and try to stamp out the human race that created them. They nearly succeed when the remnants of humanity are led in a revolt by the charismatic John Connor. He turns the tide against the robots and all but stamps them out, when the robots invent a time machine and send into the past an assassin to kill Connor's mother before he's born, thus eliminating Connor from existence and winning the war for the robots. Connor captures the time machine, discovers the plan, and sends back his lieutenant, Reese, to kill this monster before it kills his mother.

The streets of Los Angeles conspire into the ancient archetype of the labyrinth. Freeways, alleyways, cul-de-sacs, and corridors of buildings twist and turn the characters until they work their way down to its tangled heart. There Sarah, like Theseus at the center of the Minoan maze battling the half-man/half-bull Minotaur, confronts the half-man/half-robot Terminator. If she vanquishes the demon, she will, like the Virgin Mary, give birth to the savior of humanity, John Connor (JC), and raise him to lead humanity to deliverance in the coming holocaust. Sarah progresses from waitress to goddess, and the film's symbolic progression lifts it above almost all others in its genre.

IRONIC ASCENSION

Turn progression on irony.

Irony is the subtlest manifestation of story pleasure, that delicious sense of "Ah, life is just like that." It sees life in duality; it plays with our paradoxical existence, aware of the bottomless chasm between what seems and what is. Verbal irony is found in the discrepancy between words and their meanings—a primary source of jokes. But in story, irony plays between actions and results—the primary source of story energy, between appearance and reality—the primary source of truth and emotion.

An ironic sensibility is a precious asset, a razor to cut to the truth, but it can't be used directly. It does us no good to have a character wander the story saying, "How ironic!" Like symbolism, to point at irony destroys it. Irony must be coolly, casually released with a seemingly innocent unawareness of the effect it's creating and a faith that the audience will get it. Because irony is by nature slippery, it defies a hard and fast definition, and is best explained by example. Below are six ironic story patterns with an example for each.

1. **He gets at last what he's always wanted . . . but too late to have it.**
   OTHELLO: The Moor finally gets what he always wanted,

a wife who is true to him and who never betrayed him with another man . . . but when he finds that out, it's too late, because he just killed her.

2. **He's pushed further and further from his goal . . . only to discover that in fact he's been led right to it.**

RUTHLESS PEOPLE: The greedy businessman, Sam (Danny Devito), steals an idea from Sandy (Helen Slater) and makes a fortune without paying her a cent of royalties. Sandy's husband, Ken (Judge Reinhold), decides to kidnap Sam's wife, Barbara (Bette Midler), and ransom her for the two million dollars he feels his wife is owed. But when Ken abducts Barbara, he doesn't know that Sam is coming home to murder his shrewish and overweight wife. Ken calls Sam demanding millions, but the gleeful Sam puts him off. Ken keeps lowering the price until at ten thousand dollars Sam says, "Oh, why don't you just kill her and get it over with."

Meanwhile, Barbara, held captive in the Kessler basement, has turned her prison into a spa. She's following all the exercise programs on TV, Sandy's an excellent natural foods cook, and as a result, Barbara loses more weight than she ever did at the best fat farms in America. Consequently, she loves her kidnappers. And when they tell her they'll have to let her go because her husband won't pay the ransom, she turns to them and says, "I'll get the money for ya." That was Act One.

3. **He throws away what he later finds is indispensable to his happiness.**

MOULIN ROUGE: The crippled artist Toulouse-Lautrec (Jose Ferrer) falls in love with the beautiful Suzanne (Myriamme Hayem) but can't bring himself to tell her this. She accompanies him as a friend around Paris. Lautrec becomes convinced that the only reason she spends time with him is that it gives her the opportunity to meet handsome men. In a drunken rage he accuses her of using him and storms out of her life.

Some time later he receives a letter from Suzanne: "Dear Toulouse, I always hoped that some day you might love me. Now I realize that you never will. So I have taken the offer of another man. I don't love him, but he's kind and as you know my situation is desperate. Adieu." Lautrec frantically searches for her, but indeed she's left to marry another. So he drinks himself to death.

4. **To reach a goal he unwittingly takes the precise steps necessary to lead him away.**

   TOOTSIE: Michael (Dustin Hoffman), an out-of-work actor whose perfectionism has alienated every producer in New York, impersonates a woman and is cast in a soap opera. On the set he meets and falls in love with Julie (Jessica Lange). But he's such a brilliant actor, her father (Charles Durning) wants to marry him while Julie suspects he's a lesbian.

5. **The action he takes to destroy something becomes exactly what are needed to be destroyed by it.**

   RAIN: The religious bigot Reverend Davidson (Walter Huston) battles to save the soul of the prostitute Sadie Thompson (Joan Crawford), but falls into lust for her, rapes her, then kills himself in shame.

6. **He comes into possession of something he's certain will make him miserable, does everything possible to get rid of it . . . only to discover it's the gift of happiness.**

   BRINGING UP BABY: When the madcap socialite Susan (Katharine Hepburn) inadvertently steals the car of the naive and repressed paleontologist Dr. David Huxley (Cary Grant), she likes what she sees and sticks to him like glue. He tries everything possible to get rid of her, but she foils his lunatic evasions, chiefly by stealing his bone, the "intercostal clavicle" of a brontosaurus. (If there were such a thing as an "intercostal clavicle," it would belong to a creature with its head attached well below its shoulders.)

Susan's persistence pays off as she transforms David from fossilized child to life-embracing adult.

The key to ironic progression is certainty and precision. Like CHINATOWN, SULLIVAN'S TRAVELS, and many other superb films, these are stories of protagonists who feel they know for certain what they must do and have a precise plan how to do it. They think life is A, B, C, D, E. That's just when life likes to turn you around, kick you in the butt, and grin: "Not today, my friend. Today it's E, D, C, B, A. Sorry."

PRINCIPLE OF TRANSITION

A story without a sense of progression tends to stumble from one scene to the next. It has little continuity because nothing links its events. As we design cycles of rising action, we must at the same time transition the audience smoothly through them. Between two scenes, therefore, we need a third element, the link that joins the tail of Scene A with the head of Scene B. Generally, we find this third element in one of two places: what the scenes have in common or what they have in opposition.

> **The third element is the hinge for a transition; something held in common by two scenes or counterpointed between them.**

Examples:

1. *A characterization trait.* In common: cut from a bratty child to a childish adult. In opposition: cut from awkward protagonist to elegant antagonist.
2. *An action.* In common: From the foreplay of lovemaking to savoring the afterglow. In opposition: From chatter to cold silence.
3. *An object.* In common: From greenhouse interior to woodland exterior. In opposition: From the Congo to Antarctica.

4. *A word.* In common: A phrase repeated from scene to scene. In opposition: From compliment to curse.

5. *A quality of light.* In common: From shadows at dawn to shade at sunset. In opposition: From blue to red.

6. *A sound.* In common: From waves lapping a shore to the rise and fall of a sleeper's breath. In opposition: From silk caressing skin to the grinding of gears.

7. *An idea.* In common: From a child's birth to an overture. In opposition: From a painter's empty canvas to an old man dying.

After a century of filmmaking, transition clichés abound. Yet we can't put down the task. An imaginative study of almost any two scenes will find a link.

13

CRISIS, CLIMAX, RESOLUTION

CRISIS

Crisis is the third of the five-part form. It means decision. Characters make spontaneous decisions each time they open this mouths to say "this" not "that." In each scene they make a decision to take one action rather than another. But Crisis with a capital C is the ultimate decision. The Chinese ideogram for Crisis is two terms: Danger/Opportunity—"danger" in that the wrong decision at this moment will lose forever what we want; "opportunity" in that the right choice will achieve our desire.

The protagonist's quest has carried him through the Progressive Complications until he's exhausted all actions to achieve his desire, save one. He now finds himself at the end of the line. His next action is his last. No tomorrow. No second chance. This moment of dangerous opportunity is the point of greatest tension in the story as both protagonist and audience sense that the question "How will this turn out?" will be answered out of the next action.

The Crisis is the story's Obligatory Scene. From the Inciting Incident on, the audience has been anticipating with growing vividness the scene in which the protagonist will be face to face with the most focused, powerful forces of antagonism in his existence. This is the dragon, so to speak, that guards the Object of Desire: be it the literal dragon of JAWS or the metaphorical dragon of meaninglessness in TENDER MERCIES. The audience leans into the Crisis filled with expectation mingled with uncertainty.

The Crisis must be true dilemma—a choice between irreconcilable goods, the lesser of two evils, or the two at once that places the protagonist under the maximum pressure of his life.

This dilemma confronts the protagonist who, when face-to-face with the most powerful and focused forces of antagonism in his life, must make a decision to take one action or another in a last effort to achieve his Object of Desire.

How the protagonist chooses here gives us the most penetrating view of his deep character, the ultimate expression of his humanity.

This scene reveals the story's most important value. If there's been any doubt about which value is central, as the protagonist makes the Crisis Decision, the primary value comes to the fore.

At Crisis the protagonist's willpower is most severely tested. As we know from life, decisions are far more difficult to make than actions are to take. We often put off doing something for as long as possible, then as we finally make the decision and step into the action, we're surprised by its relative ease. We're left to wonder why we dreaded doing it until we realize that most of life's actions are within our reach, but decisions take willpower.

CRISIS WITHIN THE CLIMAX

The action the protagonist chooses to take becomes the story's consummate event, causing a positive, negative, or ironically positive/negative Story Climax. If, however, as the protagonist takes the climactic action, we once more pry apart the gap between expectation and result, if we can split probability from necessity just one more time, we may create a majestic ending the audience will treasure for a lifetime. For a Climax built around a Turning Point is the most satisfying of all.

We've taken the protagonist through progressions that exhaust one action after another until he reaches the limit and thinks he finally understands his world and knows what he must do in a last effort. He draws on the dregs of his willpower, chooses an action he believes will achieve his desire, but, as always, his world won't cooperate. Reality splits and he must improvise. The protagonist may or may not get what he wants, but it won't be the way he expects.

Compare STAR WARS with THE EMPIRE STRIKES BACK: At the Crisis of STAR WARS Luke Skywalker attacks the "Death Star," a manmade fortress as huge as a planet. But it's not fully constructed. A vulnerable slot lies open on one side of the sphere. Luke must not only attack into the slot, but hit a vulnerable spot within it. He's an expert fighter pilot but tries without success to hit the spot. As he maneuvers his craft by computer, he hears the voice of Obi-Wan Kenobi: "Go with the Force, go with the Force."

A sudden dilemma of irreconcilable goods: the computer versus the mysterious "Force." He wrestles with the anguish of choice, then pushes his computer aside, flies by instinct into the slot, and fires a torpedo that hits the spot. The destruction of the Death Star climaxes the film, a straight action out of the Crisis.

THE EMPIRE STRIKES BACK, by contrast, corkscrews its Climax: Face to face with Darth Vader, Luke is met by a Crisis of courage. Irreconcilable goods: He could attack and kill Vader, or he could flee and save his life. The lesser of two evils: He could attack Vader and be killed, or he could flee, making him a coward and betraying his friends. Luke musters his courage and chooses to fight. However, when Vader suddenly steps back and says: "You can't kill me, Luke . . . I'm your father," Luke's reality splinters. In a flash he realizes the truth and now must make yet another Crisis Decision: whether to kill his father.

Luke confronts the agony of this decision and chooses to fight. But Vader cuts off his hand and Luke drops to the deck. Still, it's not over. Vader announces that he wants Luke to join his campaign to bring "order to things" in the universe. A second Gap opens as Luke realizes that his father doesn't want him dead, he's offering him a job. He must make a third Crisis Decision, a lesser-of-two-evils dilemma: to join the "dark side" or take his own life? He makes the heroic choice, and as these Gaps explode, the Climax delivers deep rushes of insight uniting two films.

Placement of the Crisis

The location of the Crisis is determined by the length of the climactic action.

Generally, Crisis and Climax happen in the last minutes and in the same scene.

THELMA & LOUISE: At Crisis the women brave the lesser of two evils: imprisonment versus death. They look at each other and make their *Crisis Decision* to "go for it," a courageous choice to take their own lives. They immediately drive their car into the Grand Canyon—an unusually brief Climax elongated by filming it in slow-motion and freeze-framing on the car suspended over the abyss.

However, in other stories the Climax becomes an expansive action with its own progressions. As a result, it's possible to use the Crisis Decision to turn the Penultimate Act Climax, filling all of the final act with climactic action.

CASABLANCA: Rick pursues Ilsa until she surrenders to him in the Act Two Climax, saying that he must make the decisions for everyone. In the next scene, Laszlo urges Rick to rejoin the antifascist cause. This irreconcilable-goods dilemma turns the act on Rick's selfless Crisis Decision to return Ilsa to Laszlo and put wife and husband on the plane to America, a character-defining choice that reverses his conscious desire for Ilsa. The third act of CASABLANCA is fifteen minutes of climactic action that unravels Rick's surprise-filled scheme to help the couple escape.

In rarer examples the Crisis Decision immediately follows the Inciting Incident and the entire film becomes climactic action.

JAMES BOND: Inciting Incident: Bond is offered the task of hunting down an arch-villain. Crisis Decision: Bond takes the assignment—a right/wrong choice and not a true dilemma, for it would never occur to him to choose otherwise. From this point on, all Bond films are an elaborate progression of a single action: the pursuit of the villain. Bond never makes another decision of substance, simply choices of which ploys to use in the pursuit.

LEAVING LAS VEGAS has the identical form. Inciting Incident: the protagonist is fired and given a sizable severance check. He immediately makes his Crisis Decision to go to Las Vegas and drink himself to death. From this point on the film becomes a sad progression toward death as he follows his desire.

IN THE REALM OF THE SENSES: Inciting Incident: Lovers meet within the first ten minutes and decide to abandon society and normalcy for a life of sexual obsession. The remaining hundred minutes are devoted to sexual experimentations that eventually lead to death.

The great risk of placing the Crisis on the heels of the Inciting Incident is repetitiousness. Whether it's high-budget action repeating patterns of chase/fight, chase/fight, or low-budget repetitions of drinking/drinking/drinking or lovemaking/lovemaking/lovemaking, the problems of variety and progression are staggering. Yet mastery of this task may produce brilliance, as it did in the examples above.

Design of the Crisis

Although the Crisis Decision and climactic action usually take place in continuous time within the same location at the very end of the telling, it's not uncommon for the Crisis decision to occur in one location, the Story Climax later in another setting.

The value of love in KRAMER VS. KRAMER turns negative at the Act Two Climax as a judge awards custody to Kramer's ex-wife. As Act Three opens Kramer's lawyer lays out the situation: Kramer has lost, but he could win on appeal. To do so, however, he'll have to put his son on the witness stand and make the child choose with whom he wants to live. The boy will probably choose his father, and Kramer will win. But to put a child at this tender age in public and force him to choose between his mother and his father will psychologically scar him for life. A double dilemma of the needs of self versus the needs of another, the suffering of the self versus the suffering of another. Kramer looked up and said, "No, I can't do that." Cut to the Climax: a walk in Central Park and a river of tears as the father explains to his son how their life will be now that they'll live apart.

If the Crisis takes place in one location and the Climax later in another, we must splice them together on a cut, fusing them in filmic time and space. If we do not, if we cut from the Crisis to other material—a subplot, for example—we drain the pent-up energy of the audience into an anticlimax.

The Crisis decision must be a deliberately static moment.

This is the Obligatory Scene. *Do not put it offscreen, or skim over it.* The audience wants to suffer with the protagonist through the pain of this dilemma. We freeze this moment because the rhythm of the last movement depends on it. An emotional momentum has built to this point, but the Crisis dams its flow. As the protagonist goes through this decision, the audience leans in, wondering: "What's he going to do? What's he going to do?" Tension builds and builds, then as the protagonist makes a choice of action, that compressed energy explodes into the Climax.

THELMA & LOUISE: This Crisis is masterfully delayed as the women stutter over the word "go." "I say, let's go." "Go? What do you mean 'go'?" "Well . . . just go." "You mean . . . go?" They hesitate and hesitate as tension builds and the audience prays they won't kill themselves but at the same time is thrilled by their courage. As they put the car in gear, the dynamite of compacted anxiety blasts into the Climax.

THE DEER HUNTER: Michael stalks to the top of a mountain. But with his prey in his sights, he pauses. Tension builds and tightens as the moment extends and the audience dreads the killing of this beautiful elk. At this Crisis point the protagonist makes a decision that takes him through a profound change of character. He lowers his weapon and transforms within from a man who takes life to a man who saves life. This stunning reversal turns the Penultimate Act Climax. The pent-up compassion in the audience pours into the story's last movement as Michael now rushes back to Vietnam to save his friend's life, filling the final act with rising climactic action.

CLIMAX

Story Climax is the fourth of the five-part structure. This crowning Major Reversal is not necessarily full of noise and violence. Rather, it must be full of meaning. If I could send a telegram to the film producers of the world, it would be these three words: *"Meaning Produces Emotion."* Not money; not sex; not special effects; not movie stars; not lush photography.

> **MEANING: A revolution in values from positive to negative or negative to positive with or without irony—a value swing at maximum charge that's absolute and irreversible. The meaning of that change moves the heart of the audience.**

The action that creates this change must be "pure," clear, and self-evident, requiring no explanation. Dialogue or narration to spell out it out is boring and redundant.

This action must be appropriate to the needs of the story. It may be catastrophic: The sublime battle sequence that climaxes GLORY, or outwardly trivial: A woman rises from a quiet talk with her husband, packs a suitcase, and goes out the door. That action, in the context of ORDINARY PEOPLE, is overwhelming. At Crisis, the values of family love and unity tip toward the positive as the husband desperately exposes his family's bitter secret. But at Climax, the moment his wife walks out, they swing to an absolute, irreversible negative. If, on the other hand, she were to stay, her hatred of her son might finally drive the boy to suicide. So her leaving is then toned with a positive counterpoint that ends the film on a painful, but overall negative, irony.

The Climax of the last act is your great imaginative leap. Without it, you have no story. Until you have it, your characters wait like suffering patients praying for a cure.

Once the Climax is in hand, stories are in a significant way rewritten backward, not forward. The flow of life moves from cause to effect, but the flow of creativity often flows from effect to cause. An idea for the Climax pops unsupported into the imagination. Now we must work backward to support it in the fictional reality, supplying the hows and whys. We work back from the ending to make certain that by Idea and Counter-Idea every image, beat, action, or line of dialogue somehow relates to or sets up this grand payoff. All scenes must be thematically or structurally justified in the light of the Climax. If they can be cut without disturbing the impact of the ending, they must be cut.

If logic allows, climax subplots within the Central Plot's Climax. This is a wonderful effect; one final action by the protagonist settles everything. When Rick puts Laszlo and Ilsa on the plane in CASABLANCA, he settles the *Love Story* main plot and the *Political Drama* subplot, converts Captain Renault to patriotism, kills Major Strasser, and, we feel, is the key to winning World War II . . . now that Rick is back in the fight.

If this multiplying effect is impossible, the least important subplots are best climaxed earliest, followed by the next most important, building overall to Climax of the Central Plot.

William Goldman argues that *the key to all story endings is to give the audience what it wants, but not the way it expects*. A very provocative principle: First of all, what does the audience want? Many producers state without blinking that the audience wants a happy ending. They say this because up-ending films tend to make more money than down-ending films.

The reason for this is that a small percentage of the audience won't go to any film that might give it an unpleasant experience. Generally their excuse is that they have enough tragedy in their lives. But if we were to look closely, we'd discover that they not only avoid negative emotions in movies, they avoid them in life. Such people think that happiness means never suffering, so they never feel anything deeply. The depth of our joy is in direct proportion to what we've suffered. Holocaust survivors, for example, don't avoid dark films. They go because such stories resonate with their past and are deeply cathartic.

In fact, down-ending films are often huge commercial successes: DANGEROUS LIAISONS, eighty million dollars; THE WAR OF THE ROSES, one hundred fifty million; THE ENGLISH PATIENT, two hundred twenty-five million. No one can count THE GODFATHER, PART II's money. For the vast majority doesn't care if a film ends up or down. *What the audience wants is emotional satisfaction*—a *Climax* that fulfills anticipation. How should THE GODFATHER, PART II end? Michael forgives Fredo, quits the mob, and moves to Boston with his family to sell insurance? The Climax of this magnificent film is truthful, beautiful, and very satisfying.

Who determines which particular emotion will satisfy an audience at the end of a film? The writer. From the way he tells his story from the beginning, he whispers to the audience: "Expect an up-ending" or "Expect a down-ending" or "Expect irony." Having pledged a certain emotion, it'd be ruinous not to deliver. So we give the audience the experience we've promised, but not in the way it expects. This is what separates artist from amateur.

In Aristotle's words, an ending must be both "inevitable and unexpected." Inevitable in the sense that as the Inciting Incident occurs, everything and anything seems possible, but at Climax, as the audience looks back through the telling, it should seem that the path the telling took was the *only* path. Given the characters and their world as we've come to understand it, the Climax was inevitable and satisfying. But at the same time it must be unexpected, happening *in a way* the audience could not have anticipated.

Anyone can deliver a happy ending—just give the characters everything they want. Or a downer—just kill everybody. An artist gives us the emotion he's promised . . . but with a rush of unexpected insight that he's withheld to a Turning Point within the Climax itself. So that as the protagonist improvises his final effort, he may or may not achieve his desire, but the flood of insight that pours from the gap delivers the hoped-for emotion but in a way we could never have foreseen.

The Turning Point within the Climax of LOVE SERENADE is a recent and perfect example. This brilliant Gap hurls the audience back through the entire film to glimpse with shock and delight the maniacal truth that has been lurking beneath every scene.

The key to a great film ending, as François Truffaut put it, is to create a combination of "Spectacle and Truth." When Truffaut says "Spectacle," he doesn't mean explosive effects. He means a Climax written, not for the ear, but the eye. By "Truth" he means Controlling Idea. In other words, Truffaut is asking us to create the *Key Image* of the film—a single image that sums up and concentrates all meaning and emotion. Like the coda of a symphony, the Key Image within the climactic action echoes and resonates all that has gone before. It is an image that is so tuned to the telling that when it's remembered the whole film comes back with a jolt.

GREED: McTeague collapsing into the desert, chained to the corpse he just killed. THE TREASURE OF THE SIERRA MADRE: Fred C. Dobbs (Humphrey Bogart) dying as the wind blows his gold dust back into the mountains. LA DOLCE VITA: Rubini (Marcello Mastroianni) smiling good-bye to his ideal woman—an ideal, he realizes, that doesn't exist. THE CONVERSATION: The paranoid Harry Caul (Gene Hackman) gutting his apartment in search of a hidden microphone. THE SEVENTH SEAL: The Knight (Max von Sydow) leading his family into oblivion. THE KID: The Little Chap (Charlie Chaplin) taking the Kid (Jackie Coogan) by the hand to lead him to a happy future. SLING BLADE: Karl Childers (Billy Bob Thornton) staring in blood-chilling silence out of the window of the lunatic asylum. Key Images of this quality are rarely achieved.

RESOLUTION

The *Resolution,* the fifth of the five-part structure, is any material left after Climax and has three possible uses.

First, the logic of the telling may not provide an opportunity to climax a subplot before or during the Climax of the Central Plot, so it'll need a scene of its own at the very end. This, however, can be awkward. The story's emotional heart is in the main plot. Moreover, the audience will be leaning toward the exits, yet forced to sit through a scene of secondary interest.

The problem can be solved, however.

THE IN-LAWS: The daughter of Dr. Sheldon Kornpett (Alan Arkin) is engaged to be married to the son of Vince Ricardo (Peter Falk). Vince is a crazed CIA agent who virtually kidnaps Sheldon out of his dental office and carries him off on a mission to stop a lunatic dictator from destroying the international monetary system with counterfeit twenty-dollar bills. The Central Plot climaxes with Vince and Sheldon fending off a firing squad, bringing down the dictator, then secretly pocketing five million dollars each.

But the marriage subplot has been left open. So writer Andrew Bergman cut from the firing squad to a Resolution scene outside the wedding. As the party waits impatiently, the fathers arrive by parachute, wearing tuxedos. Each gives his respective son and daughter a cash gift of $1 million. Suddenly a car screeches up and an angry CIA agent gets out. Tension tightens. It looks as if the main plot is back and the fathers will be busted for stealing the ten million. The stern-faced CIA agent stalks up and is indeed angry. Why? Because he wasn't invited to the wedding. What's more, he took up a collection at the office and has a fifty-dollar U.S. Savings Bond for bride and groom. The fathers accept his lavish gift and welcome him to the festivities. FADE OUT.

Bergman tweaked the main plot in the Resolution. Imagine if it had ended in front of the firing squad, then cut to a garden wedding with happy families reunited. The scene would have dragged on as the audience squirmed in its seats. But by bringing the Central Plot back to life for just a moment, the screenwriter gave it a comic false twist, yoked his Resolution back to the body of the film, and held tension to the end.

A second use of a Resolution is to show the spread of climactic effects. If a film expresses progressions by widening into society, its Climax may be restricted to the principal characters. The audience, however, has come to know many supporting roles whose lives will be changed by the climactic action. This motivates a social event that satisfies our curiosity by bringing the entire cast to one location where the camera can track around to show us how these lives have been changed: the birthday party, the picnic at the beach, an Easter Egg hunt in STEEL MAGNOLIAS, a satiric title roll in ANIMAL HOUSE.

Even if the first two uses don't apply, all films need a Resolution as a courtesy to the audience. For if the Climax has moved the film-goers, if they're laughing helplessly, riveted with terror, flushed with social outrage, wiping away tears, it's rude suddenly to go black and roll the titles. This is the cue to leave, and they will attempt to do so jangling with emotion, stumbling over one another in the dark, dropping their car keys on the Pepsi-sticky floor. A film needs what the theatre calls a "slow curtain." A line of description at the bottom of the last page that sends the camera slowly back or tracking along images for a few seconds, so the audience can catch its breath, gather its thoughts, and leave the cinema with dignity.

PART 4

THE
WRITER
AT WORK

The first draft of anything is shit.
—ERNEST HEMINGWAY

14

THE PRINCIPLE
OF ANTAGONISM

In my experience, the principle of antagonism is the most important and least understood precept in story design. Neglect of this fundamental concept is the primary reason screenplays and the films made from them fail.

> **THE PRINCIPLE OF ANTAGONISM: A protagonist and his story can only be as intellectually fascinating and emotionally compelling as the forces of antagonism make them.**

Human nature is fundamentally conservative. We never do more than we have to, expend any energy we don't have to, take any risks we don't have to, change *if we don't have to*. Why should we? Why do anything the hard way if we can get what we want the ease way? (The "easy way" is, of course, idiosyncratic and subjective.) Therefore, what will cause a protagonist to become a fully realized, multidimensional, and deeply empathetic character? What will bring a dead screenplay to life? The answer to both questions lies on the negative side of the story.

The more powerful and complex the forces of antagonism opposing the character, the more completely realized character and story *must* become. "Forces of antagonism" doesn't necessarily refer to a specific antagonist or villain. In appropriate genres arch-villains, like the Terminator, are a delight, but by "forces of antagonism" we mean the sum total of all forces that oppose the character's will and desire.

If we study a protagonist at the moment of the Inciting Incident and weigh the sum of his willpower along with his intellectual, emotional, social, and physical capacities against the total forces of antagonism from within his humanity, plus his personal conflicts, antagonistic institutions, and environment, we should see clearly that he's an underdog. He has a chance to achieve what he wants—but only a chance. Although conflict from one aspect of his life may seem solvable, the totality of all levels should seem overwhelming as he begins his quest.

We pour energy into the negative side of a story not only to bring the protagonist and other characters to full realization—roles to challenge and attract the world's finest actors—but to take the story itself to the end of the line, to a brilliant and satisfying climax.

Following this principle, imagine writing for a super-hero. How to turn Superman into an underdog? Kryptonite is a step in the right direction, but not nearly enough. Look at the ingenious design Mario Puzo created for the first SUPERMAN feature.

Puzo pits Superman (Christopher Reeve) against Lex Luthor (Gene Hackman), who engineers a diabolical plot to launch two nuclear rockets simultaneously in opposite directions, one aimed at New Jersey, the other at California. Superman can't be in two places at once, so he'll have to make the lesser-of-two-evils choice: Which to save? New Jersey or California? He chooses New Jersey.

The second rocket hits the San Andreas Fault and starts an earthquake that threatens to heave California into the ocean. Superman dives into the fault and fuses California back to the continent through the friction of his own body. But . . . the earthquake kills Lois Lane (Margot Kidder).

Superman kneels in tears. Suddenly, the visage of Jor-El (Marlon Brando) appears and says: "Thou shalt not interfere with human destiny." A dilemma of irreconcilable goods: his father's sacred rule versus the life of the woman he loves. He violates his father's law, flies around the Earth, reverses the spin of the planet, turns back time, and resurrects Lois Lane—a happily-ever-after fantasy, taking Superman from underdog to a virtual god.

TAKING STORY AND CHARACTER TO THE END OF THE LINE

Does your story contain negative forces of such power that the positive side *must* gain surpassing quality? Below is a technique to guide your self-critique and answer that critical question.

Begin by identifying the primary value at stake in your story. For example, Justice. Generally, the protagonist will represent the positive charge of this value; the forces of antagonism, the negative. Life, however, is subtle and complex, rarely a case of yes/no, good/evil, right/wrong. There are degrees of negativity.

First, the *Contradictory* value, the direct opposite of the positive. In this case, Injustice. Laws have been broken.

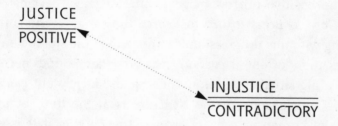

Between the Positive value and its Contradictory, however, is the *Contrary*: a situation that's somewhat negative but not fully the opposite. The Contrary of justice is unfairness, a situation that's negative but not necessarily illegal: nepotism, racism, bureaucratic delay, bias, inequities of all kinds. Perpetrators of unfairness may not break the law, but they're neither just nor fair.

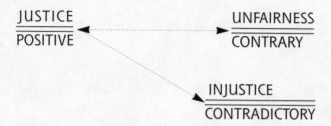

The Contradictory, however, is not the limit of human experience. At the end of the line waits the *Negation of the Negation*, a force of antagonism that's doubly negative.

Our subject is life, not arithmetic. In life two negatives don't make a positive. In English double negatives are ungrammatical, but Italian uses double and even triple negatives so that a statement *feels* like its meaning. In anguish an Italian might say, *"Non ho niente mia!"* (I don't have nothing never!). Italians know life. Double negatives turn positive only in math and formal logic. In life things just get worse and worse and worse.

A story that progresses to the limit of human experience in depth and breadth of conflict must move through a pattern that includes the Contrary, the Contradictory, and the Negation of the Negation.

(The positive mirror image of this negative declension runs from *Good* to *Better* to *Best* to *Perfect*. But for mysterious reasons, working with this progression is of no help to the storyteller.)

Negation of the Negation means a compound negative in which a life situation turns not just quantitatively but *qualitatively* worse. The Negation of the Negation is at the limit of the dark powers of human nature. In terms of justice, this state is *tyranny*. Or, in a phrase that applies to personal as well as social politics: "Might Makes Right."

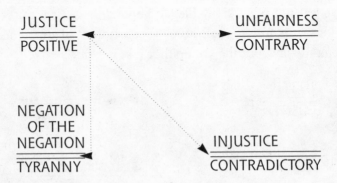

Consider TV detective series: Do they go to the limit? The protagonists of *Spenser: For Hire, Quincy, Columbo,* and *Murder, She Wrote* represent justice and struggle to preserve this ideal. First, they face unfairness: Bureaucrats won't let Quincy do the autopsy, a politician pulls strings to get Columbo off the case, Spenser's client lies to him. After struggling through gaps of expectation powered by forces of unfairness, the cop discovers true injustice: A crime has been committed. He defeats these forces and restores society to justice. The forces of antagonism in most crime dramas rarely reach beyond the Contradictory.

Compare this pattern to MISSING, a fact-based film about American Ed Horman (Jack Lemmon), who searched Chile for a son who disappeared during a coup d'etat. In Act One he meets unfairness: The U.S. ambassador (Richard Venture) feeds him half-truths, hoping to dissuade his search. But Horman perseveres. At the *Act Two Climax* he uncovers a grievous injustice: The junta murdered his son . . . with the complicity of the U.S. State Department and the CIA. Horman then tries to right this wrong, but in Act Three he reaches *the end of the line*—persecution without hope of retribution.

Chile is in the grip of tyranny. The generals can make illegal on Tuesday what you did legally on Monday, arrest you for it on Wednesday, execute you on Thursday, and make it legal again Friday morning. Justice does not exist; the tyrant makes it up at his whim. MISSING is a searing revelation of the final limits of injustice . . . with irony: Although Horman couldn't indict the tyrants in Chile, he exposed them onscreen in front of the world—which may be a sweeter kind of justice.

The *Black Comedy* . . . AND JUSTICE FOR ALL goes one step further. It pursues justice full cycle back to the Positive. In Act One attorney Arthur Kirkland (Al Pacino) struggles against unfairness: the Baltimore Bar Association pressures him to inform against other lawyers while a cruel judge (John Forsythe) uses red tape to block the retrial of Kirkland's innocent client. In Act Two he confronts injustice: The same judge is charged with brutally beating and raping a woman.

But the judge has a scheme: It's well known that the judge and attorney hate each other. Indeed, the lawyer recently punched the judge in public. So the judge will force this lawyer to represent him in court. When Kirkland appears to defend him, press and jury will perceive the judge as innocent, believing that no lawyer who hates a man would defend him unless he knew for certain that the accused was innocent, and is there on principle. The lawyer tries to escape this jam but hits the Negation of the Negation, a "legal" tyranny of high-court judges who blackmail him to represent their friend. If he doesn't, they'll expose a past indiscretion of his and have him disbarred.

The lawyer, however, battles through unfairness, injustice, and tyranny by breaking the law: He steps in front of the jury and announces that his client "did it." He knows that his client is the rapist, he says, because his client told him. He destroys the judge in public and wins justice for the victim. And although this stunt ends the lawyer's career, justice now shines like a diamond, for it isn't the momentary justice that comes when criminals are put behind bars, but the grand justice that brings down tyrants.

The difference between the Contradictory and the Negation of the Negation of justice is the difference between the relatively limited and temporary power of those who break the law versus the unlimited and enduring power of those who make the law. It's the difference between a world where law exists and a world where might makes right. The absolute depth of injustice is not criminality, but "legal" crimes committed by governments against their own citizens.

Below are more examples to demonstrate how this declension works in other stories and genres. First, love:

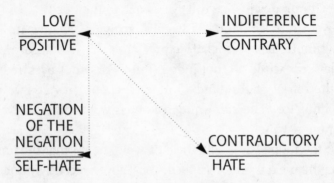

To hate other people is bad enough, but even a misanthrope loves one person. When self-love vanishes and a character loathes his own being, he reaches the Negation of the Negation and existence becomes a living hell: Raskolnikov in CRIME AND PUNISHMENT.

A second variation:

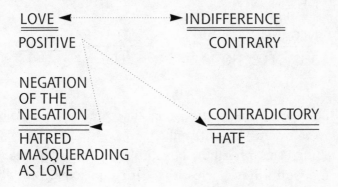

With whom would you rather have a relationship? With someone who hates you and honestly admits it, or with someone you know hates you but pretends to love you? This is what lifts ORDINARY PEOPLE and SHINE to the heights of *Domestic Drama*. Many parents hate their children, many children hate their parents, and they fight and scream and say it. In these fine films, although a parent bitterly resents and secretly hates his or her child, they pretend to love him. When the antagonist adds that lie, the story moves to the Negation of the Negation. How can a child defend himself against that?

When the primary value is truth:

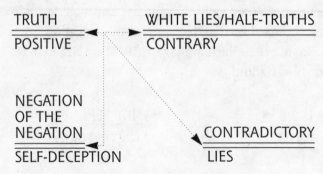

White lies are the Contrary because they're often told to do good: lovers waking up with pillow creases branded across their faces, telling each other how beautiful they look. The blatant liar knows the truth, then buries it to gain advantage. But when we lie to ourselves and believe it, truth vanishes and we're at the Negation of the Negation: Blanche in A STREETCAR NAMED DESIRE.

If the positive were Consciousness, being fully alive and aware:

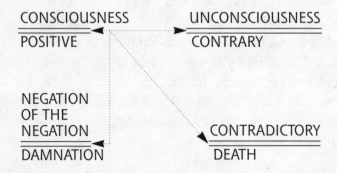

This is the declension of *Horror* films in which the antagonist is supernatural: DRACULA, ROSEMARY'S BABY. But we don't have to be religious to grasp the meaning of *damnation*. Whether or not hell exists, this world provides its own Infernos, plights in which death would be a mercy and we'd beg for it.

Consider THE MANCHURIAN CANDIDATE. Raymond Shaw (Laurence Harvey) seems fully alive and aware. Then we learn that he's been brainwashed by posthypnotic suggestion, a form of unconsciousness. Under this power he commits a string of murders, including that of his own wife, but does so with a degree of innocence, for he's a pawn in a vicious conspiracy. But when he recovers his mind and realizes what he's done and what's been done to him, he's taken down to hell.

He learns he was brainwashed on the order of his incestuous, power-mad mother, who's using him in a plot to seize control of the White House. Raymond could risk his life to expose his traitorous mother or kill her. He chooses to kill, not only his mother but his stepfather and himself as well, damning the three at once in a shocking climax at the Negation of the Negation.

If the positive were wealth:

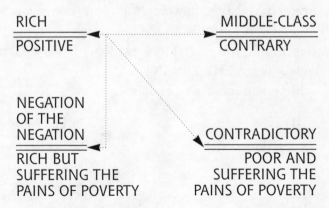

In WALL STREET Gekko feels impoverished because no amount of money is enough. A billionaire, he acts as if he were a starving thief, grasping for money at any illegal opportunity.

If the positive were open communication between people:

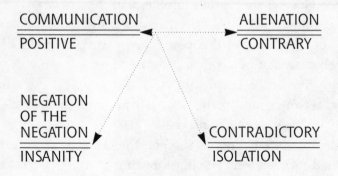

The Contrary has many varieties—silence, misunderstanding, emotional blocks. The all-inclusive term "alienation" means a situation of being with people, but feeling cut off and unable to fully communicate. In isolation, however, there's no one to talk to except yourself. When you lose this and suffer a loss of communication within your mind, you're at the Negation of the Negation and insane: Trelkovsky in THE TENANT.

Full achievement of ideals or goals:

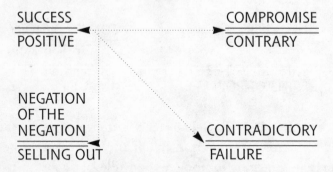

Compromise means "settling for less," the willingness to fall short of your ideal but not surrender it completely. The Negation of the Negation, however, is something people in show business have to guard against. Thoughts such as: "I can't make the fine films I'd like to make . . . but there's money in pornography": THE SWEET SMELL OF SUCCESS and MEPHISTO.

Intelligence:

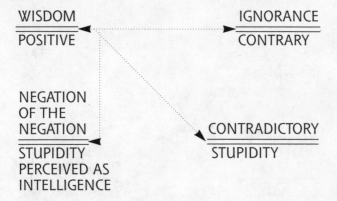

Ignorance is temporary stupidity due to a lack of information, but stupidity is resolute, no matter how much information is given. The Negation of the Negation cuts both ways: inwardly, when a stupid person believes he's intelligent, a conceit of numerous comic characters, or outwardly, when society thinks a stupid person is intelligent: BEING THERE.

Liberty:

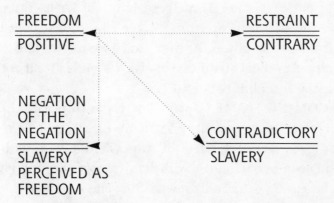

Restraint has many shades. Laws bind us but make civilization possible, while imprisonment is fully negative, although society finds it useful. The Negation of the Negation works two ways. Inwardly: *Self-enslavement* is qualitatively worse than slavery. A slave has his free will and would do all he could to escape. But to corrode your willpower with drugs or alcohol and turn yourself into a slave is far worse. Outwardly: *Slavery perceived as freedom* impels the novel and films 1984.

Courage:

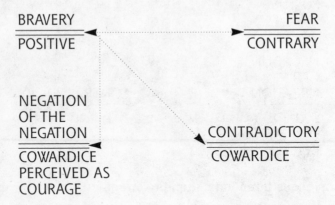

A courageous person can be temporarily stifled when fear strikes, but eventually he acts. The coward does not. *The end of the line* is reached, however, when a coward takes an action that outwardly appears courageous: A battle rages around a foxhole. In it a wounded officer turns to a coward and says: "Jack, your buddies are running out of ammo. Take these boxes of shells through the minefield or they'll be overrun." So the coward takes out his gun . . . and shoots the officer. At first glance we might think it would take courage to shoot an officer, but we'd soon realize that this was an act at the sheer limit of cowardice.

In COMING HOME Captain Boy Hyde (Bruce Dern) shoots himself in the leg to get out of Vietnam. Later, at the Crisis of his subplot Hyde faces the lesser of two evils: life with its humiliation and pain versus death with its dread of the unknown. He takes the easier path and drowns himself. Although some suicides are courageous, such as those of political prisoners on a hunger strike, in most cases the suicide reaches *the end of the line* and takes an action that may appear brave but lacks the courage to live.

Loyalty:

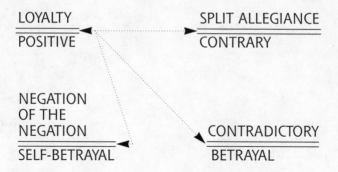

LOYALTY · · · · · · · · · · · · ▶ SPLIT ALLEGIANCE
POSITIVE ◀ CONTRARY

NEGATION
OF THE
NEGATION · · · · · · · · · · · · CONTRADICTORY
SELF-BETRAYAL ◀ BETRAYAL

Contrary: A married woman falls in love with another man, but doesn't act on it. Secretly, she feels loyalty to both men, but when her husband learns of it, he sees her split allegiance as a betrayal. She defends herself, arguing that she didn't sleep with the other man, so she was never disloyal. The difference between feeling and action is often subjective.

In the mid-nineteenth century the Ottoman Empire was losing its grip on Cyprus and the island was soon to fall to British rule. In PASCALI'S ISLAND, Pascali (Ben Kingsley) spies for the Turkish government, but he's a frightened man whose bland reports go unread. This lonely soul is befriended by a British couple (Charles Dance and Helen Mirren) who offer him a happier life in England. They're the only people who have ever taken Pascali seriously, and he's drawn to them. Although they claim to be archaeologists, in time he suspects they're British spies (split allegiance) and betrays them. Only when they're killed does he discover they were antiquity thieves after an ancient statue. His betrayal tragically betrays his own hopes and dreams.

Maturity:

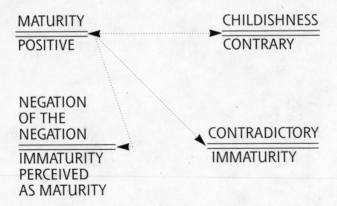

At the Inciting Incident of BIG the adolescent Josh Baskin (David Moscow) is transformed into what appears to be a thirty-two-year-old man (Tom Hanks). The film jumps immediately to the Negation of the Negation, then explores the grays and blacks of negativity. When Josh and his boss (Robert Loggia) tap dance on a toy piano at F.A.O. Schwartz, this is childish, but more positive than negative. When Josh and his coworker (John Heard) play "keep away" on the handball court, this is perfectly childish. In fact, we come to realize that the whole adult world is a playground full of children playing corporate "keep away."

At the Crisis Josh faces irreconcilable goods: an adult life with a fulfilling career and the woman he loves versus a return to adolescence. He makes the mature choice to have his childhood, expressing with a fine irony that he has at last become "big." For he and we sense that the key to maturity is to have had a complete childhood. But because life has short-changed so many of us in youth, we live, to one degree or another, at the Negation of the Negation of maturity. BIG is a very wise film.

Lastly, consider a story in which the positive value is sanctioned natural sex. *Sanctioned* meaning condoned by society; *natural* meaning sex for procreation, attendant pleasure, and an expression of love.

Under the Contrary falls acts of extramarital and premarital sex that, although natural, are frowned on. Society often does more

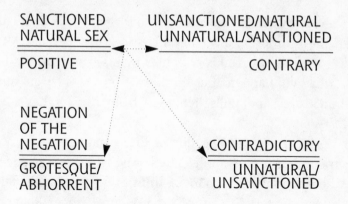

SANCTIONED
NATURAL SEX
——————————
POSITIVE

UNSANCTIONED/NATURAL
UNNATURAL/SANCTIONED
——————————————
CONTRARY

NEGATION
OF THE
NEGATION
——————————
GROTESQUE/
ABHORRENT

CONTRADICTORY
——————————
UNNATURAL/
UNSANCTIONED

than frown on prostitution, but it's arguably natural. Bigamy, polygamy, polyandry, and interracial and common-law marriage are condoned in some societies, unsanctioned in others. Chastity is arguably unnatural, but no one's going to stop you from being celibate, while sex with someone who has taken a vow of celibacy, such as a priest or a nun, is frowned on by the Church.

Under the Contradictory, humanity seems to know no limit of invention: voyeurism, pornography, satyriasis, nymphomania, fetishism, exhibitionism, frottage, transvestism, incest, rape, pedophilia, and sadomasochism, to name only a few acts that are unsanctioned and unnatural.

Homosexuality and bisexuality are difficult to place. In some societies they're thought natural, in others, unnatural. In many Western countries homosexuality is sanctioned; in some Third World countries it's still a hanging offense. Many of these designations may seem arbitrary, for sex is relative to social and personal perception.

But common perversions are not the end of the line. They're singular and committed, even with violence, with another human being. When, however, the sexual object is from another species—bestiality—or dead—necrophilia—or when compounds of perversities pile up, the mind revolts.

CHINATOWN: The end of the line of sanctioned natural sex is not incest. It's only a Contradictory. In this film the Negation of the Negation is incest with the offspring of your own incest. This is why Evelyn Mulwray risks her life to keep her child from her father. She knows he's mad and will do it again. This is the motivation for the murder. Cross killed his son-in-law because Mulwray wouldn't tell him where his daughter by his daughter was hiding. This is what will happen after the Climax as Cross covers the terrified child's eyes and pulls her away from her mother's horrific death.

The principle of the Negation of the Negation applies not only to the tragic but to the comic. The comic world is a chaotic, wild place where actions must go to the limit. If not, the laughs falls flat. Even the light entertainment of Fred Astaire/Ginger Rogers films touched the end of the line. They turned on the value of truth as Fred Astaire traditionally played a character suffering from self-deception, telling himself he was in love with the glitzy girl when we knew that his heart really belonged to Ginger.

Fine writers have always understood that opposite values are not the limit of human experience. If a story stops at the Contradictory value, or worse, the Contrary, it echoes the hundreds of mediocrities we suffer every year. For a story that is simply about love/hate, truth/lie, freedom/slavery, courage/cowardice, and the like is almost certain to be trivial. If a story does not reach the Negation of the Negation, it may strike the audience as satisfying—but never brilliant, never sublime.

All other factors of talent, craft, and knowledge being equal, greatness is found in the writer's treatment of the negative side.

If your story seems unsatisfying and lacking in some way, tools are needed to penetrate its confusions and perceive its flaws. When a story is weak, the inevitable cause is that forces of antagonism are weak. Rather than spending your creativity trying to invent likable, attractive aspects of protagonist and world, build the negative side to create a chain reaction that pays off naturally and honestly on the positive dimensions.

The first step is to question the values at stake and their progression. What are the positive values? Which is preeminent and turns the Story Climax? Do the forces of antagonism explore all shades of negativity? Do they reach the power of the Negation of the Negation at some point?

Generally, progressions run from the Positive to the Contrary in Act One, to the Contradictory in later acts, and finally to the Negation of the Negation in the last act, either ending tragically or going back to the Positive with a profound difference. BIG, on the other hand, leaps to the Negation of the Negation, then illuminates all degrees of immaturity. CASABLANCA is even more radical. It opens at the Negation of the Negation with Rick living in fascist tyranny, suffering self-hatred and self-deception, then works to a positive climax for all three values. Anything is possible, but *the end of the line* must be reached.

15

EXPOSITION

SHOW, DON'T TELL

Exposition means facts—the information about setting, biography, and characterization that the audience needs to know to follow and comprehend the events of the story.

Within the first pages of a screenplay a reader can judge the relative skill of the writer simply by noting how he handles exposition. Well-done exposition doesn't guarantee a superb story, but it does tell us that the writer knows the craft. Skill in exposition means making it *invisible*. As the story progresses, the audience absorbs all it needs to know effortlessly, even unconsciously.

The famous axiom "Show, don't tell" is the key. Never force words into a character's mouth to *tell* the audience about world, history, or person. Rather, *show* us honest, natural scenes in which human beings talk and behave in honest, natural ways . . . yet at the same time indirectly pass along the necessary facts. In other words, *dramatize exposition.*

Dramatized exposition serves two ends: Its primary purpose is to further the immediate conflict. Its secondary purpose is to convey information. The anxious novice reverses that order, putting expositional duty ahead of dramatic necessity.

For example: Jack says, "Harry, how the hell long have we known one another? What? About twenty years, huh? Ever since we were at college together. That's a long time, isn't it, Harry? Well, how the hell are ya this morning?" Those lines have no purpose except to tell the eavesdropping audience that Jack and Harry are friends, went to school together twenty years ago, and they haven't had lunch yet—a deadly beat of unnatural behavior. No one ever tells someone something they both already know unless saying the obvious fills another and compelling need. Therefore, if this information is needed, the writer must create a motivation for the dialogue that's greater than the facts.

To dramatize exposition apply this mnemonic principle: *Convert exposition to ammunition.* Your characters know their world, their history, each other, and themselves. Let them use what they know as ammunition in their struggle to get what they want. Converting the above to ammunition: Jack, reacting to Harry's stifled yawn and bloodshot eyes, says, "Harry, look at you. The same hippie haircut, still stoned by noon, the same juvenile stunts that got you kicked out of school twenty years ago. Are you ever gonna wake up and smell the coffee?" The audience's eye jumps across the screen to see Harry's reaction and indirectly hears "twenty years" and "school."

"Show, don't tell," by the way, doesn't mean that it's all right to pan the camera down a mantelpiece on a series of photographs that take Harry and Jack from their university days to boot camp to the double wedding to opening their dry cleaning business. That's telling, not showing. Asking the camera to do it turns a feature film into a home movie. "Show, don't tell" means that characters *and camera* behave truthfully.

Dealing with the knotty problems of exposition so intimidates some writers that they try to get it all out of the way as soon as possible, so the studio script analyst can concentrate on their stories. But when forced to wade through an Act One stuffed with exposition, the reader realizes that this is an amateur who can't handle the basic craft, and skims to the last scenes.

Confident writers parse out exposition, bit by bit, through the entire story, often revealing exposition well into the Climax of the last act. They follow these two principles: Never include anything the audience can reasonably and easily assume has happened. Never pass on exposition unless the missing fact would cause confusion. You do not keep the audience's interest by giving it information, but by *withholding* information, except that which is absolutely necessary for comprehension.

Pace the exposition. Like all else, exposition must have a progressive pattern: Therefore, the least important facts come in early, the next most important later, the critical facts last. And what are the critical pieces of exposition? Secrets. The painful truths characters do not want known.

In other words, don't write "California scenes." "California scenes" are scenes in which two characters who hardly know each other sit down over coffee and immediately begin an intimate discussion of the deep, dark secrets of their lives: "Oh, I had a rotten childhood. To punish me my mother used to flush my head in the toilet." "Huh! You think you had a bad childhood. To punish me my father put dog shit in my shoes and made me to go to school like that."

Unguardedly honest and painful confessions between people who have just met are forced and false. When this is pointed out to writers, they will argue that it actually happens, that people share very personal things with total strangers. And I agree. But only in California. Not in Arizona, New York, London, Paris, or anywhere else in the world.

A certain breed of West Coaster carries around prepared deep dark secrets to share with one another at cocktail parties to validate themselves one to the other as authentic Californians—"centered" and "in touch with their inner beings." When I'm standing over the tortilla dip at such parties and somebody tells me about dog shit in his Keds as a child, my thought is: "Wow! If that's the prepared deep dark secret he tells people over the guacamole, what's the real stuff?" For there's always something else. Whatever is said hides what cannot be said.

Evelyn Mulwray's confession, "She's my sister and my daughter" is nothing she would share over cocktails. She tells Gittes this to keep her child out of her father's hands. "You can't kill me, Luke, I'm your father" is a truth Darth Vader never wanted to tell his son, but if he doesn't, he'll have to kill or be killed by his child.

These are honest and powerful moments because the pressure of life is squeezing these characters between the lesser of two evils. And where in a well-crafted story is pressure the greatest? At *the end of the line*. The wise writer, therefore, obeys the first principle of temporal art: *Save the best for last*. For if we reveal too much too soon, the audience will see the climaxes coming long before they arrive.

Reveal only that exposition the audience absolutely needs and wants to know and no more.

On the other hand, since the writer controls the telling, he controls the need and desire to know. If at a certain point in the telling, a piece of exposition must be known or the audience wouldn't be able to follow, create the desire to know by arousing curiosity. Put the question "Why?" in the filmgoer's mind. "Why is this character behaving this way? Why doesn't this or that happen? Why?" With a hunger for information, even the most complicated set of dramatized facts will pass smoothly into understanding.

One way to cope with biographical exposition is to start the telling in the protagonist's childhood and then work through all the decades of his life. THE LAST EMPEROR, for example, covers over sixty years in the life of Pu Yi (John Lone). The story strings together scenes from his infancy when he's made Emperor of China, his teenage years and youthful marriage, his Western education, his fall into decadence, his years as a Japanese stooge, life under the Communists, and his last days as a laborer in Peking's Botanical Gardens. LITTLE BIG MAN spans a century. CARNAL KNOWLEDGE, FAREWELL, MY CONCUBINE, and SHINE all start in youth and leapfrog through the key events of the protagonists' lives into middle age or beyond.

However, as convenient as that design may be in terms of exposition, the vast majority of protagonists cannot be followed from birth to death for this reason: Their story would have no Spine. To tell a story that spans a lifetime a Spine of enormous power and persistence must be created. But for most characters, what single, deep desire, aroused out of an Inciting Incident in childhood, would go unquenched for decades? This is why nearly all tellings pursue the protagonist's Spine over months, weeks, even hours.

If, however, an elastic, endurable *Spine* can be created, then a story can be told over decades without being episodic. Episodic does not mean "covering long stretches of time" but rather "sporadic, irregular intervals." A story told over twenty-four hours could well be episodic if everything that happens in that day is unconnected to everything else that happens. On the other hand, LITTLE BIG MAN is unified around a man's quest to prevent the genocide of Native Americans by the whites—an atrocity that spanned generations, therefore a century of storytelling. CARNAL KNOWLEDGE is driven by a man's blind need to humiliate and destroy women, a soul-poisoning desire he never fathoms.

In THE LAST EMPEROR a man spends his life trying to answer the question: Who am I? At age three Pu Yi is made Emperor but has no idea what that means. To him a palace is a playground. He clings to his childhood identity until as a teenager he's still nursing from the breast. The Imperial officials insist he act like an emperor, but he then discovers there is no empire. Burdened with a false identity, he tries on one personality after another but none fit: first English scholar and gentleman; then sex athlete and hedonist; later international bon vivant doing Sinatra imitations at posh parties; next a statesman, only to end up a puppet to the Japanese. Finally, the Communists give him his last identity—gardener.

FAREWELL, MY CONCUBINE tells of Dieyi's (Leslie Cheung) fifty-year quest to live in the truth. When he is a child, the masters of the Peking Opera ruthlessly beat, brainwash, and force him to confess that he has a female nature—when he does not. If he did, torture wouldn't be necessary. He's effeminate, but like many effeminate men he is at heart male. So, forced to live a lie, he hates all lies, personal and political. From that point on all the conflicts in the story stem from his desire to speak the truth. But in China only liars survive. Finally realizing that truth is an impossibility, he takes his own life.

Because lifelong Spines are rare, we take Aristotle's advice to begin stories *in medias res*, "in the midst of things." After locating the date of the climactic event of the protagonist's life, we begin as close in time to it as possible. This design compresses the telling's duration, and lengthens the character's biography before the Inciting Incident. For example, if the Climax occurs on the day a character turns thirty-five, instead of starting the film when he's a teenager, we open the film perhaps a month before his birthday. This gives the protagonist thirty-five years of living to build the maximum value into his existence. As a result, when his life goes out of balance, he is now at risk and the story is filled with conflict.

Consider, for example, the difficulties of writing a story about a homeless alcoholic. What has he to lose? Virtually nothing. To a soul enduring the unspeakable stress of the streets, death may be a mercy, and a change in the weather might give him that. Lives with little or no value beyond their existence are pathetic to witness, but with so little at stake, the writer is reduced to painting a static portrait of suffering.

Rather, we tell stories about people who have something to lose—family, careers, ideals, opportunities, reputations, realistic hopes and dreams. When such lives go out of balance, the characters are placed at jeopardy. They stand to lose what they have in their struggle to achieve a rebalancing of existence. Their battle, risking hard-won values against the forces of antagonism, generates conflict. And when story is thick with conflict, the characters need all the ammunition they can get. As a result, the writer has little trouble dramatizing exposition and facts flow naturally and invisibly into the action. But when stories lack conflict, the writer is forced into "table dusting."

Here, for example, is how many playwrights of the nineteenth century handled exposition: The curtain comes up on a living room set. Enter two domestics: One who's worked there for the last thirty years, the other the young maid just hired that morning. The older maid turns to the newcomer and says, "Oh, you don't know about Dr. Johnson and his family, do you? Well, let me tell you . . ." And as they dust the furniture the older maid lays out the entire life history, world, and characterizations of the Johnson family. That's "table dusting," unmotivated exposition.

And we still see it today.

OUTBREAK: In the opening sequence, Colonel Daniels (Dustin Hoffman) flies to West Africa to halt an outbreak of the Ebola virus. On board is a young medical assistant. Daniels turns to him and says, in effect, "You don't know about Ebola, do you?" and lays out the pathology of the virus. If the young assistant is untrained to fight a disease that threatens all human life on the planet, what's he doing on this mission? Any time you find yourself writing a line of dialogue in which one character is telling another something that they both already know or should know, ask yourself, is it dramatized? Is it exposition as ammunition? If not, cut it.

If you can thoroughly dramatize exposition and make it invisible, if you can control its disclosure, parsing it out only when and if the audience needs and wants to know it, saving the best for last, you're learning your craft. But what's a problem for beginning writers becomes an invaluable asset to those who know the craft. Rather than avoiding exposition by giving their characters an anonymous past, they go out of their way to salt their biographies with significant events. Because what is the challenge that the storyteller faces dozens of times over in the telling? How to turn the scene. How to create Turning Points.

THE USE OF BACKSTORY

We can turn scenes only one of two ways: on action or on revelation. There are no other means. If, for example, we have a couple in a positive relationship, in love and together, and want to turn it to the negative, in hate and apart, we could do it on action: She slaps him across the face and says, "I'm not taking this anymore. It's over." Or on revelation: He looks at her and says, "I've been having an affair with your sister for the last three years. What are you going to do about it?"

Powerful revelations come from the BACKSTORY—previous significant events in the lives of the characters

that the writer can reveal at critical moments to create Turning Points.

CHINATOWN: "She's my sister and my daughter" is exposition, saved to create a stunning revelation that turns the second act Climax and sets up a spiraling Act Three. THE EMPIRE STRIKES BACK: "You can't kill me, Luke, I'm your father" is exposition from the Backstory of STAR WARS saved to create the greatest possible effect, to turn the Climax and set up an entire new film, RETURN OF THE JEDI.

Robert Towne could have exposed the Cross family incest early in CHINATOWN by having Gittes unearth this fact from a disloyal servant. George Lucas could have exposed Luke's paternity by having C3PO warn R2D2, "Don't tell Luke, he'd really be upset to hear this, but Darth's his dad." Rather, they used Backstory exposition to create explosive Turning Points that open the gap between expectation and result, and deliver a rush of insight. With few exceptions, scenes cannot be turned on nothing but action, action, action. Inevitably we need a mix of action and revelation. Revelations, in fact, tend to have more impact, and so we often reserve them for the major Turning Points, act climaxes.

FLASHBACKS

The *flashback* is simply another form of exposition. Like all else, it's done either well or ill. In other words, rather than boring the audience with long, unmotivated, exposition-filled dialogue passages, we could bore it with unwanted, dull, fact-filled flashbacks. Or we do it well. A flashback can work wonders if we follow the fine principles of conventional exposition.

First, dramatize flashbacks.

Rather than flashing back to flat scenes in the past, interpolate a minidrama into the story with its own Inciting Incident, progressions, and Turning Point. Although producers often claim that flashbacks slow a film's pace, and indeed badly done they do, a well-done flashback actually accelerates pace.

CASABLANCA: The Paris Flashback comes at the opening of Act Two. Rick is crying in his whiskey, drunk and depressed, the film's rhythm deliberately retarding to relieve the tension of the Act One Climax. But as Rick remembers his affair with Ilsa, the flashback to the tale of their love affair while the Nazis invade Paris sweeps the film into an ever swifter pace that peaks around a sequence Climax as Ilsa runs out on Rick.

RESERVOIR DOGS: The Inciting Incident of a *Murder Mystery* combines two events: A murder is committed; the protagonist discovers the crime. Agatha Christie, however, opens her stories with only the second half—a closet door opens and a body falls out. By starting with the discovery of the crime, she arouses curiosity in two directions: Into the past, how and why was the murder committed? Into the future, which of the many suspects did it?

Tarantino's design simply reworks Agatha Christie. After introducing his characters, Tarantino launched the film by skipping over the first half of the Inciting Incident—the botched heist—and cut immediately to the second half—the getaway. With one of the thieves wounded in the backseat of the getaway car we instantly realize the robbery has gone bad and our curiosity runs into the past and future. What went wrong? How will it turn out? Having created the need and desire to know both answers, whenever pace in the warehouse scenes flagged, Tarantino flashed back to the high-speed action of the heist. A simple idea, but no one had ever done it with such daring, and what could have been a less than energetic film had solid pace.

Second, do not bring in a flashback until you have created in the audience the need and desire to know.

CASABLANCA: The Act One Climax is also the Central Plot's Inciting Incident as Ilsa suddenly reappears in Rick's life and they share a powerful exchange of looks over Sam's piano. There follows a scene of cocktail chat, double entendres, and subtext that hint at a past relationship and a passion still very much alive. As Act Two opens, the audience is burning with curiosity, wondering what went on between these two in Paris. Then and only then, when the audience needs and wants to know, do the writers flash back.

We must realize that a screenplay is not a novel. Novelists can directly invade the thoughts and feelings of characters. We cannot. Novelists, therefore, can indulge the luxury of free association. We cannot. The prose writer can, if he wishes, walk a character past a shop window, have him look inside and remember his entire childhood: "He was walking through his hometown that afternoon when he glanced over at the barbershop and remembered the days when his father would take him there as a boy and he'd sit among the old-timers as they smoked cigars and talked about baseball. It was there that he first heard the word 'sex' and ever since he's unable to sleep with a woman without thinking he was hitting a home run."

Exposition in prose is relatively easy, but the camera is an X-ray machine for all things false. If we try to force exposition into a film through novel-like free associative editing or semisubliminal flutter cuts that "glimpse" a character's thoughts, it strikes us as contrived.

DREAM SEQUENCES

The *Dream Sequence* is exposition in a ball gown. Everything said above applies doubly to these usually feeble efforts to disguise information in Freudian clichés. One of the few effective uses of a dream opens Ingmar Bergman's WILD STRAWBERRIES.

MONTAGE

In the American use of this term, a montage is a series of rapidly cut images that radically condenses or expands time and often employs optical effects such as wipes, irises, split screens, dissolves, or other multiple images. The high energy of such sequences is used to mask their purpose: the rather mundane task of conveying information. Like the Dream Sequence, the montage is an effort to make undramatized exposition less boring by keeping the audience's eye busy. With few exceptions, montages are a lazy attempt to substitute decorative photography and editing for dramatization and are, therefore, to be avoided.

VOICE-OVER NARRATION

Voice-over narration is yet another way to divulge exposition. Like the Flashback, it's done well or ill. The test of narration is this: Ask yourself, "If I were to strip the voice-over out of my screenplay, would the story still be well told?" If the answer is yes . . . keep it in. Generally, the principle "Less is more" applies: the more economical the technique, the more impact it has. Therefore, anything that can be cut should be cut. There are, however, exceptions. If narration can be removed and the story still stands on its feet well told, then you've probably used narration for the only good reason—as counterpoint.

Counterpoint narration is Woody Allen's great gift. If we were to cut the voice-over from HANNAH AND HER SISTERS or HUS-BANDS AND WIVES his stories would still be lucid and effective. But why would we? His narration offers wit, ironies, and insights that can't be done any other way. Voice-over to add nonnarrative counterpoint can be delightful.

Occasionally, brief telling narration, especially at the opening or during transitions between acts, such as in BARRY LYNDON, is inoffensive, *but the trend toward using telling narration throughout a film threatens the future of our art.* More and more films by some of the finest directors from Hollywood and Europe indulge in this indolent practice. They saturate the screen with lush photography and lavish production values, then tie images together with a voice droning on the soundtrack, turning the cinema into what was once known as *Classic Comic Books.*

Many of us were first exposed to the works of major writers by reading *Classic Comics,* novels in cartoon images with captions that told the story. That's fine for children, but it's not cinema. The art of cinema connects Image A via editing, camera, or lens movement with Image B, and the effect is meanings C, D, and E, *expressed without explanation.* Recently, film after film slides a steady-cam through rooms and corridors, up and down streets, panning sets and cast while a narrator talks, talks, talks voice-over, telling us about a character's upbringing, or his dreams and fears, or explaining the politics of the story's society—until the film becomes little more than multimillion-dollar books-on-tape, illustrated.

It takes little talent and less effort to fill a soundtrack with explanation. "Show, don't tell" is a call for artistry and discipline, a warning to us not to give in to laziness but to set *creative limitations* that demand the fullest use of imagination and sweat. Dramatizing every turn into a natural, seamless flow of scenes is hard work, but when we allow ourselves the comfort of "on the nose" narration we gut our creativity, eliminate the audience's curiosity, and destroy narrative drive.

More importantly, "Show, don't tell" means respect the intelligence and sensitivity of your audience. Invite them to bring their best selves to the ritual, to watch, think, feel, and draw their own conclusions. Do not put them on your knee as if they were children and "explain" life, for the misuse and overuse of narration is not only slack, it's patronizing. And if the trend toward it continues, cinema will degrade into adulterated novels and our art will shrivel.

To study the skillful design of exposition, I suggest a close analysis of JFK. Obtain Oliver Stone's screenplay and/or the video and break the film down, scene by scene, listing all the facts, indisputable or alleged, it contains. Then note how Stone splintered this Mount Everest of information into its vital pieces, dramatized each bit, pacing the progression of revelations. It is a masterpiece of craftsmanship.

16

PROBLEMS
AND SOLUTIONS

This chapter examines eight enduring problems, from how to hold interest, to how to adapt from other media, to how to cope with holes in logic. For each problem the craft provides solutions.

THE PROBLEM OF INTEREST

Marketing may entice an audience into the theatre, but once the ritual begins, it needs compelling reasons to stay involved. A story must capture interest, hold it unswervingly through time, then reward it at Climax. This task is next to impossible unless the design attracts both sides of human nature—intellect and emotion.

Curiosity is the intellectual need to answer questions and close open patterns. Story plays to this universal desire by doing the opposite, posing questions and opening situations. Each Turning Point hooks curiosity. As the protagonist is put at increasingly greater risk, the audience wonders, "What's going to happen next? And after that?" And above all, "How will it turn out?" The answer to this will not arrive until the last act Climax, and so the audience, held by curiosity, stays put. Think of all the bad films you've sat through for no other reason than to get the answer to that nagging question. We may make the audience cry or laugh, but above all, as Charles Reade noted, we make it wait.

Concern, on the other hand, is the emotional need for the positive values of life: justice, strength, survival, love, truth, courage.

Human nature is instinctively repelled by what it perceives as negative, while drawn powerfully toward positive.

As a story opens, the audience, consciously or instinctively, inspects the value-charged landscape of world and characters, trying to separate good from evil, right from wrong, things of value from things of no value. It seeks the *Center of Good*. Once finding this core, emotions flow to it.

The reason we search for the Center of Good is that each of us believes that we are good or right and want to identify with the positive. Deep inside we know we're flawed, perhaps seriously so, even criminal, but somehow we feel that despite that, our heart is in the right place. The worst of people believe themselves good. Hitler thought he was the savior of Europe.

I once joined a gym in Manhattan not knowing it was a mafia hangout and met an amusing, likable guy whose nickname was Mr. Coney Island, a title he'd won as a bodybuilder in his teens. Now, however, he was a "button man." "To button up" means to shut up. A button man "puts the button on" or shuts people up . . . forever. One day in the steam room he sat down and said, "Hey, Bob, tell me something. Are you one of the 'good' people?" In other words, did I belong to the mob?

Mafia logic runs like this: "People want prostitution, narcotics, and illicit gambling. When they're in trouble, they want to bribe police and judges. They want to taste the fruits of crime, but they're lying hypocrites and won't admit it. We provide these services but we're not hypocrites. We deal in realities. We are the 'good' people." Mr. Coney Island was a conscienceless assassin, but inside he was convinced he was good.

No matter who's in the audience, each seeks the Center of Good, the positive focus for empathy and emotional interest.

At the very least the Center of Good must be located in the protagonist. Others may share it, for we can empathize with any number of characters, but we *must* empathize with the protagonist. On the other hand, the Center of Good doesn't imply "niceness." "Good" is defined as much by what it's not as by what it is. From the audience's point of view, "good" is a judgment made in relationship to or against a background of negativity, a universe that's thought or felt to be "not good."

THE GODFATHER: Not only is the Corleone family corrupt, but so too are the other mafia families, even the police and judges. Everyone in this film is a criminal or related to one. But the Corleones have one positive quality—loyalty. In other mob clans gangsters stab one another in the back. That makes them the bad bad guys. The loyalty of the Godfather's family makes them the *good* bad guys. When we spot this positive quality, our emotions move toward it and we find ourselves in empathy with gangsters.

How far can we take the Center of Good? With what kind of monsters will an audience empathize?

WHITE HEAT: Cody Jarrett (James Cagney), the film's Center of Good, is a psychopathic killer. But the writers design a masterful balancing act of negative/positive energies by first giving Jarrett attractive qualities, then landscaping around him a grim, fatalistic world: His is a gang of weak-willed yes-men, but he has leadership capacities. He's pursued by an FBI squad of lackluster dullards, whereas he's witty and imaginative. His "best friend" is an FBI informant, while Cody's friendship is genuine. No one shows affection for anyone in this film, except Cody, who adores his mother. This moral management draws the audience into empathy, feeling, "If I had to lead a life of crime, I'd want to be like Cody Jarrett."

THE NIGHT PORTER: In a Backstory of dramatized flashbacks, protagonists and lovers (Dirk Bogarde and Charlotte Rampling) met in this fashion: He was the sadistic commandant of a Nazi death camp, she a teenage prisoner of masochistic nature. Their passionate affair lasted for years inside the death camp. With the war's end, they went their separate ways. The film opens in 1957 as they eye each other in the lobby of a Viennese hotel. He's now a hotel porter, she a guest traveling with her concert pianist husband. Once up in their room she tells her husband she's ill, sends him on ahead to his concert, then stays behind to resume her affair with her former lover. This couple is the Center of Good.

Writer/director Liliana Cavani manages this feat by encircling the lovers with a depraved society of malevolent SS officers in hiding. Then she lights one little candle to blaze at the heart of this cold, dark world: Despite how the lovers met and the nature of their passion, in the deepest and truest sense, their love is real. What's more, it's tested to the limit. When SS officers tell their friend he must kill the woman because she may expose them, he replies, "No, she's my baby, she's my baby." He'd sacrifice his life for his lover and she for him. We feel a tragic loss when at Climax they choose to die together.

SILENCE OF THE LAMBS: The writers of novel and screen-play place Clarice (Jodie Foster) at the positive focal point, but also shape a second Center of Good around Hannibal Lecter (Anthony Hopkins) and draw empathy to both. First, they assign Dr. Lecter admirable and desirable qualities: massive intelligence, a sharp wit and sense of irony, gentlemanly charm, and most importantly, calmness. How, we wondered, could someone who lives in such a hellish world remain so poised and polite?

Next, to counterpoint these qualities the writers surround Lecter with a brutish, cynical society. His prison psychiatrist is a sadist and publicity hound. His guards are dimwits. Even the FBI, which wants Lecter's help on a baffling case, lies to him, trying to manipulate him with false promises of an open-air prison on a Carolina island. Soon we're rationalizing: "So he eats people. There are worse things. Off-hand I can't think what, but. . . ." We fall into empathy, musing, "If I were a cannibalistic psychopath, I'd want to be just like Lecter."

Mystery, Suspense, Dramatic Irony

Curiosity and *Concern* create three possible ways to connect the audience to the story: *Mystery, Suspense,* and *Dramatic Irony.* These terms are not to be mistaken for genres; they name story/audience relationships that vary according to how we hold interest.

In Mystery the audience knows less than the characters.

Mystery means gaining interest through curiosity alone. We create but then conceal expositional facts, particularly facts in the

Backstory. We arouse the audience's curiosity about these past events, tease it with hints of the truth, then deliberately keep it in the dark by misleading it with "red herrings," so that it believes or suspects false facts while we hide the real facts.

"Red herrings" has an amusing etymology: As peasant poachers of deer and grouse made off with their booty through medieval forests, they would drag a fish, a red herring, across the trail to confuse the lord of the manor's bloodhounds.

This technique of compelling interest by devising a guessing game of red herrings and suspects, of confusion and curiosity, pleases the audience of one and only one genre, the *Murder Mystery*, which has two subgenres, the *Closed Mystery* and the *Open Mystery*.

The *Closed Mystery* is the Agatha Christie form in which a murder is committed unseen in the Backstory. The primary convention of the "Who done it?" is multiple suspects. The writer must develop at least three possible killers to constantly mislead the audience to suspect the wrong person, the red herring, while withholding the identity of the real killer to Climax.

The *Open Mystery* is the *Columbo* form in which the audience sees the murder committed and therefore knows who did it. The story becomes a "How will he catch him?" as the writer substitutes multiple clues for multiple suspects. The murder must be an elaborate and seemingly perfect crime, a complex scheme involving a number of steps and technical elements. But the audience knows by convention that one of these elements is a fatal flaw of logic. When the detective arrives on the scene he instinctively knows who did it, sifts through the many clues searching for the telltale flaw, discovers it, and confronts the arrogant perfect-crime-committer, who then spontaneously confesses.

In the Mystery form the killer and detective know the facts long before Climax but keep it to themselves. The audience runs from behind trying to figure out what the key characters already know. Of course, if we could win the race, we'd feel like losers. We try hard to guess the who or how, but we want the writer's master detective to be just that.

These two pure designs may be mixed or satirized. CHINA-TOWN starts *Closed* but then turns *Open* at the Act Two Climax. THE USUAL SUSPECTS parodies the *Closed Mystery*. It starts as a "Who done it?" but becomes a "Nobody done it" . . . whatever "it" may be.

In Suspense the audience and characters know the same information.

Suspense combines both Curiosity and Concern. Ninety percent of all films, comedy and drama, compel interest in this mode. In Suspense, however, curiosity is not about fact but outcome. The outcome of a *Murder Mystery* is always certain. Although we don't know who or how, the detective will catch the killer and the story will end "up." But the Suspense story could end "up" or "down" or in irony.

Characters and audience move shoulder to shoulder through the telling, sharing the same knowledge. As the characters discover expositional fact, the audience discovers it. But what no one knows is "How will this turn out?" In this relationship we feel empathy and identify with the protagonist, whereas in pure Mystery our involvement is limited to sympathy. Master detectives are charming and likable, but we never identify with them because they're too perfect and never in real jeopardy. *Murder Mysteries* are like board games, cool entertainments for the mind.

In Dramatic Irony the audience knows more than the characters.

Dramatic Irony creates interest primarily through concern alone, eliminating curiosity about fact and consequence. Such stories often open with the ending, deliberately giving away the outcome. When the audience is given the godlike superiority of knowing events before they happen, its emotional experience switches. What in Suspense would be anxiety about outcome and fear for the protagonist's well-being, in Dramatic Irony becomes dread of the moment the character discovers what we already know and compassion for someone we see heading for disaster.

SUNSET BOULEVARD: In the first sequence the body of Joe Gillis (William Holden) floats facedown in Norma Desmond's (Gloria Swanson) swimming pool. The camera goes to the bottom of the pool, looks up at the corpse, and in voice-over Gillis muses that we're probably wondering how he ended up dead in a swimming pool, so he'll tell us. The film becomes a feature-length flashback, dramatizing a screenwriter's struggle for success. We're moved to compassion and dread as we watch this poor man heading toward a fate we already know. We realize that all of Gillis's efforts to escape the clutches of a wealthy harridan and write an honest screenplay will come to nothing and he'll end up a corpse in her swimming pool.

BETRAYAL: The Antiplot device of telling a story in reverse order from end to beginning was invented in 1934 by Phillip Kaufman and Moss Hart for their play *Merrily We Roll Along*. Forty years later Harold Pinter used this idea to exploit the ultimate use of Dramatic Irony. BETRAYAL is a *Love Story* that opens with former lovers, Jerry and Emma (Jeremy Irons and Patricia Hodge) meeting privately for the first time in the years since their breakup. In a tense moment she confesses that her husband "knows," her husband being Jerry's best friend. As the film proceeds it flashes back to scenes of the breakup, then follows with the events that brought about the breakup, back farther to cover the golden days of the romance, then ends on boy-meets-girl. As the eyes of the young lovers glitter with anticipation, we're filled with mixed emotions: We want them to have their affair, for it was sweet, but we also know all the bitterness and pain they'll suffer.

Placing the audience in the position of Dramatic Irony does not eliminate all curiosity. The result of showing the audience what will happen is to cause them to ask, "How and why did these characters do what I already know they did? Dramatic Irony encourages the audience to look more deeply into the motivations and causal forces at work in the characters' lives. This is why we often enjoy a fine film more, or at least differently, on second viewing. We not only flex the often underused emotions of compassion and dread, but freed from curiosity about facts and outcome, we now concentrate on inner lives, unconscious energies, and the subtle workings of society.

However, the majority of genres do not lend themselves to either pure Mystery or pure Dramatic Irony. Instead, within the Suspense relationship writers enrich the telling by mixing the other two. In an overall Suspense design, some sequences may employ Mystery to increase curiosity about certain facts, others may switch to Dramatic Irony to touch the audience's heart.

CASABLANCA: At the end of Act One we learn that Rick and Ilsa had an affair in Paris that ended in breakup. Act Two opens with a flashback to Paris. From the vantage of Dramatic Irony, we watch the young lovers head for tragedy and feel a special tenderness for their romantic innocence. We look deeply into their moments together, wondering why their love ended in heartbreak and how they'll react when they discover what we already know.

Later, at the climax of Act Two, Ilsa is back in Rick's arms, ready to leave her husband for him. Act Three switches to Mystery by showing Rick make his Crisis decision but not letting us in on what he's chosen to do. Because Rick knows more than we, curiosity is piqued: Will he run off with Ilsa? When the answer arrives, it hits us with a jolt.

Suppose you were working on a *Thriller* about a psychopathic axe murderer and a female detective, and you're ready to write the Story Climax. You've set it in the dimly lit corridor of an old mansion. She knows the killer is near and clicks the safety off her gun as she moves slowly past doors left and right extending into the dark distance. Which of the three strategies to use?

Mystery: Hide a fact known to the antagonist from the audience.

Close all the doors so that as she moves down the hall the audience's eyes search the screen, wondering, Where is he? Behind the first door? The next door? The next? Then he attacks by crashing through . . . the ceiling!

Suspense: Give the audience and characters the same information.

At the end of the hall a door is ajar with a light behind it casting a shadow on the wall of a man holding an axe. She sees the shadow and stops. The shadow retreats from the wall. CUT TO: Behind the door a man, axe in hand, waits: He knows that she's there and he knows that she knows that he's there because he heard her foot-steps stop. CUT TO: The hallway where she hesitates: She knows that he's there and she knows that he knows that she knows that he's there because she saw his shadow move. We know that she knows that he knows, but what no one knows is how will this turn out? Will she kill him? Or will he kill her?

Dramatic Irony: Employ Hitchcock's favorite device and hide from the protagonist a fact known to the audience.

She slowly edges toward a closed door at the end of the hall.

CUT TO: Behind the door a man waits, axe in hand. CUT TO: The hallway as she moves closer and closer to the closed door. The audience, knowing what she doesn't know, switches its emotions from anxiety to dread: "Don't go near that door! For God's sake, don't open that door! He's behind the door! Look out!"

She opens the door and . . . mayhem.

On the other hand, if she were to open the door and embrace the man. . . .

> MAN WITH AXE
> (rubbing sore
> muscles)
> Honey, I've been chopping
> wood all afternoon.
> Is dinner ready?

. . . this would not be Dramatic Irony, but *False Mystery* and its dim-witted cousin, *Cheap Surprise*.

A certain amount of audience curiosity is essential. Without it, Narrative Drive grinds to a halt. The craft gives you the power to conceal fact or outcome in order to keep the audience looking ahead and asking questions. It gives you the power to mystify the audience, if that's appropriate. But you must not abuse this power. If so, the audience, in frustration, will tune out. Instead, reward the filmgoer for his concentration with honest, insightful answers to his questions. No dirty tricks, no Cheap Surprise, no False Mystery.

False Mystery is a counterfeit curiosity caused by the artificial concealment of fact. Exposition that could and should have been given to the audience is withheld in hope of holding interest over long, undramatized passages.

FADE IN: The pilot of a crowded airliner battles an electrical storm. Lightning strikes the wing and the plane plunges toward a mountainside. CUT TO: Six months earlier, and a thirty-minute flash-back that tediously details the lives of the passengers and crew leading up to the fatal flight. This tease or *cliff-hanger* is a lame promise made by the writer: "Don't worry, folks, if you stick with me through this boring stretch, I'll eventually get back to the exciting stuff."

THE PROBLEM OF SURPRISE

We go to the storyteller with a prayer: "Please, let it be good. Let it give me an experience I've never had, insights into a fresh truth. Let me laugh at something I've never thought funny. Let me be moved by something that's never touched me before. Let me see the world in a new way. Amen." In other words, the audience prays for surprise, the reversal of expectation.

As characters arrive onscreen, the audience surrounds them with expectations, feeling "this" will happen, "that" will change, Miss A will get the money, Mr. B will get the girl, Mrs. C will suffer. If what the audience expects to happen happens, or worse, if it happens the *way* the audience expects it to happen, this will be a very unhappy audience. We must surprise them.

There are two kinds of surprise: cheap and true. True surprise springs from the sudden revelation of the Gap between expectation and result. This surprise is "true" because it's followed by a rush of insight, the revelation of a truth hidden beneath the surface of the fictional world.

Cheap Surprise takes advantage of the audience's vulnerability. As it sits in the dark, the audience places its emotions in the story-teller's hands. We can always shock filmgoers by smash cutting to something it doesn't expect to see or away from something it expects to continue. By suddenly and inexplicably breaking the narrative flow we can always jolt people. But as Aristotle complained, "To be about to act and not to act is the worst. It is shocking without being tragic."

In certain genres—*Horror, Fantasy, Thriller*—cheap surprise is a convention and part of the fun: The hero walks down a dark alley. A hand shoots in from the edge of the screen and grabs his shoulder, the hero spins around—and it's his best friend. Outside these genres, however, cheap surprise is a shoddy device.

MY FAVORITE SEASON: A woman (Catherine Deneuve) is married but not happily. Her possessive brother agitates his sister's marriage, until finally convinced she cannot be happy with her husband, she leaves and moves in with her brother. Brother and sister share a top-floor apartment. He comes home one day feeling uncertain qualms. As he enters, he sees a window open, curtains billowing. He rushes to look down. In his POV we see his sister smashed on the cobbles far below, dead, surrounded by a pool of blood. CUT TO: The bedroom and his sister waking up from a nap.

Why, in a serious *Domestic Drama*, would a director resort to horrific shock images from the brother's nervous imagination? Perhaps because the previous thirty minutes were so unbearably boring, he thought it was time to kick us in the shins with a trick he learned in film school.

THE PROBLEM OF COINCIDENCE

Story creates meaning. Coincidence, then, would seem our enemy, for it is the random, absurd collisions of things in the universe and is, by definition, meaningless. And yet coincidence is a part of life, often a powerful part, rocking existence, then vanishing as absurdly as it arrived. The solution, therefore, is not to avoid coincidence, but to dramatize how it may enter life meaninglessly, but in time gain meaning, how the antilogic of randomness becomes the logic of life-as-lived.

First, bring coincidence in early to allow time to build meaning out of it.

The Inciting Incident of JAWS: a shark, by random chance, eats a swimmer. But once in the story the shark doesn't leave. It stays and gathers meaning as it continuously menaces the innocent until we get the feeling that the beast is doing it on purpose and, what's more, enjoying it. Which is the definition of evil: Doing harm to others and taking pleasure in it. We all hurt people inadvertently but instantly regret it. But when someone purposely seeks to cause pain in others and takes pleasure from it, that's evil. The shark then becomes a powerful icon for the dark side of nature that would love to swallow us whole and laugh while doing it.

Coincidence, therefore, must not pop into a story, turn a scene, then pop out. Example: Eric desperately seeks his estranged lover, Laura, but she's moved. After searching in vain, he stops for a beer. On the stool next to him sits the real estate agent who sold Laura her new house. He gives Eric her exact address. Eric leaves with thanks and never sees the salesman again. Not that this coincidence couldn't happen, but it's pointless.

On the other hand, suppose that the salesman can't remember the address, but does recall that Laura bought a red Italian sports car at the same time. The two men leave together and spot her Maserati on the street. Now they both go up to her door. Still angry with Eric, Laura invites them in and flirts with the salesman to annoy her ex-lover. What was meaningless good luck now becomes a force of antagonism to Eric's desire. This triangle could build meaningfully through the rest of the story.

As a rule of thumb do not use coincidence beyond the midpoint of the telling. Rather, put the story more and more into the hands of the characters.

Second, never use coincidence to turn an ending. This is deus ex machina, the writer's greatest sin.

Deus ex machina is a Latin phrase taken from the classical theatres of Greece and Rome, meaning "god from machine." From 500 B.C. to A.D. 500 theatre flourished throughout the Mediterranean. Over those centuries hundreds of playwrights wrote for these stages but only seven have been remembered, the rest mercifully forgotten, due primarily to their propensity to use deus ex machina to get out of story problems. Aristotle complained about this practice, sounding much like a Hollywood producer: "Why can't these writers come up with endings that work?"

In these superb, acoustically perfect amphitheatres, some seating up to ten thousand people, at the far end of a horseshoe-shaped stage was a high wall. At the bottom were doors or arches for entrances and exits. But actors who portrayed gods would be lowered down to the stage from the top of the wall standing on a platform attached to ropes and pulley. This "god from machine" device was the visual analogy of the deities coming down from Mount Olympus and going back up to Mount Olympus.

Story climaxes were as difficult twenty-five hundred years ago as now. But ancient playwrights had a way out. They would cook a story, twist Turning Points until they had the audience on the edge of their marble seats, then if the playwright's creativity dried up and he was lost for a true Climax, convention allowed him to dodge the problem by cranking a god to the stage and letting an Apollo or Athena settle everything. Who lives, who dies, who marries who, who is damned for eternity. And they did this over and over.

Nothing has changed in twenty-five hundred years. Writers today still cook up stories they can't end. But instead of dropping a god in to get an ending, they use "acts of god"—the hurricane that saves the lovers in HURRICANE, the elephant stampede that resolves the love triangle in ELEPHANT WALK, the traffic accidents that end THE POSTMAN ALWAYS RINGS TWICE and THE UNBEARABLE LIGHTNESS OF BEING, the T-Rex that hops in just in time to devour the velociraptors in JURASSIC PARK.

Deus ex machina not only erases all meaning and emotion, it's an insult to the audience. Each of us knows we must choose and act, for better or worse, to determine the meaning of our lives. No one and nothing coincidental will come along to take that responsibility from us, regardless of the injustices and chaos around us. You could be locked in a cell for the rest of your life for a crime you did not commit. But every morning you would still have to get up and make meaning. Do I bludgeon my brains against this wall or do I find some way to get through my days with value? Our lives are ultimately in our own hands. Deus ex machina is an insult because it is a lie.

The one exception is Antistructure films that substitute coincidence for causality: WEEKEND, CHOOSE ME, STRANGERS IN PARADISE, and AFTER HOURS begin by coincidence, progress by coincidence, end on coincidence. When coincidence rules story, it creates a new and rather significant meaning: Life is absurd.

THE PROBLEM OF COMEDY

Comedy writers often feel that in their wild world the principles that guide the dramatist don't apply. But whether coolly satiric or madly farcical, comedy is simply another form of storytelling. There are, however, important exceptions that begin in the deep division between the comic and tragic visions of life.

The dramatist admires humanity and creates works that say, in essence: Under the worst of circumstances the human spirit is magnificent. Comedy points out that in the best of circumstances human beings find some way to screw up.

When we peek behind the grinning mask of comic cynicism, we find a frustrated idealist. The comic sensibility wants the world to be perfect, but when it looks around, it finds greed, corruption, lunacy. The result is an angry and depressed artist. If you doubt that, ask one over for dinner. Every host in Hollywood has made that mistake: "Let's invite some comedy writers to the party! That'll brighten things up." Sure . . . till the paramedics arrive.

These angry idealists, however, know that if they lecture the world about what a rotten place it is, no one will listen. But if they trivialize the exalted, pull the trousers down on snobbery, if they expose society for its tyranny, folly, and greed, and get people to laugh, then maybe things will change. Or balance. So God bless comedy writers. What would life be like without them?

Comedy is pure: If the audience laughs, it works; if it doesn't laugh, it doesn't work. End of discussion. That's why critics hate comedy; there's nothing to say. If I were to argue that CITIZEN KANE is a bloated exercise in razzle-dazzle spectacle, populated by stereotypical characters, twisted with manipulative storytelling, stuffed full of self-contradictory Freudian and Pirandellian clichés, made by a heavy-handed showoff out to impress the world, we might bicker forever because the CITIZEN KANE audience is silent. But if I were to say A FISH CALLED WANDA is not funny, you'll pity me and walk away. In comedy laughter settles all arguments.

The dramatist is fascinated by the inner life, the passions and sins, madness and dreams of the human heart. But not the comedy writer. He fixes on the social life—the idiocy, arrogance, and brutality in society. The comedy writer singles out a particular institution that he feels has become encrusted with hypocrisy and folly, then goes on the attack. Often we can spot the social institution under assault by noting the film's title.

THE RULING CLASS attacks the rich; so too TRADING PLACES, A NIGHT AT THE OPERA, MY MAN GODFREY. M*A*S*H assaults the military, as do PRIVATE BENJAMIN and STRIPES. *Romantic Comedies*—HIS GIRL FRIDAY, THE LADY EVE, WHEN HARRY MET SALLY—satirize the institution of courtship. NETWORK, POLICE ACADEMY, ANIMAL HOUSE, THIS IS SPINAL TAP, PRIZZI'S HONOR, THE PRODUCERS, DR. STRANGELOVE, NASTY HABITS, and CAMP NOWHERE strike at television, school, fraternities, rock 'n' roll, the mafia, the theatre, Cold War politics, the Catholic Church, and summer camp, respectively. If a film genre grows thick with self-importance, it too is ripe for mockery: AIRPLANE, YOUNG FRANKENSTEIN, NAKED GUN. What was known as *Comedy of Manners* has become the sitcom—a satire of middle-class behavior.

When a society cannot ridicule and criticize its institutions, it cannot laugh. The shortest book ever written would be the history of German humor, a culture that has suffered spells of paralyzing fear of authority. Comedy is at heart an angry, antisocial art. To solve the problem of weak comedy, therefore, the writer first asks: What am I angry about? He finds that aspect of society that heats his blood and goes on an assault.

Comic Design

In drama the audience continuously grabs handfuls of the future, pulling themselves through, wanting to know the outcome. But *Comedy* allows the writer to halt *Narrative Drive*, the forward projecting mind of the audience, and interpolate into the telling a scene with no story purpose. It's there just for the yucks.

LITTLE SHOP OF HORRORS: Masochistic patient (Bill Murray) visits sadistic dentist (Steve Martin), and as he cuddles up in the chair, says: "I want a long, slow root canal." It's drop-dead funny but has nothing to do with the story. If cut, no one would notice. But should it be cut? Hell no, it's hysterical. How little story can be told and how much pure comedy worked into a film? Watch the Marx Brothers. A sharp story, complete with Inciting Incident, first, second, and third act climaxes, always holds a Marx Brothers film together . . . for a total screentime of about ten minutes. The other eighty minutes are surrendered to the dizzying genius of Marx Brothers shtick.

Comedy tolerates more coincidence than drama, and may even allow a *deus ex machina* ending . . . if two things are done: First, the audience is made to feel that the comic protagonist has suffered enormously. Second, that he never despairs, never loses hope. Under these conditions the audience may think: "Oh, hell, give it to him."

THE GOLD RUSH: At Climax the Little Chap (Charlie Chaplin) is nearly frozen to death when a blizzard rips his cabin off the ground, blows it and Chaplin across Alaska, then drops him smack on a gold mine. CUT TO: He's rich, dressed to the nines, smoking a cigar, heading back to the States. A comic coincidence that leaves the audience thinking, "This guy ate his shoes, was almost cannibalized by other miners, devoured by a grizzly bear, rejected by the dance hall girls—he walked all the way to Alaska. Give 'im a break."

The incisive difference between comedy and drama is this: Both turn scenes with surprise and insight, but in comedy, when the Gap cracks open, the surprise explodes the great belly laughs of the night.

A FISH CALLED WANDA: Archie takes Wanda to a borrowed love nest. Panting with anticipation, she watches from the sleeping loft as Archie pirouettes around the room, stripping buck naked,

intoning Russian poetry that makes her writhe. He puts his under-
wear on his head and declares himself free of the fear of embarrassment . . . the door opens and in walks an entire family. A killer
Gap between expectation and result.

Simply put, a *Comedy* is a funny story, an elaborate rolling joke.
While wit lightens a telling, it doesn't alone make it a true *Comedy*.
Rather, wit often creates hybrids such as the *Dramedy* (ANNIE
HALL), or the *Crimedy* (LETHAL WEAPON). You know you've
written a true comedy when you sit an innocent victim down and
pitch your story. Just tell him what happens, without quoting witty
dialogue or sight gags, and he laughs. Every time you turn the
scene, he laughs; turn it again and he laughs again; turn, laugh,
until by the end of the pitch you have him collapsed on the floor.
That's a *Comedy*. If you pitch your story and people don't laugh,
you've not written a *Comedy*. You've written . . . something else.

The solution, however, is not found in trying to devise clever
lines or pie in the face. Gags come naturally when the comic structure calls for them. Instead, concentrate on Turning Points. For
each action first ask, "What's the opposite of that?" then take it a
step farther to "What's off-the-wall from that?" Spring gaps of
comic surprise—write a funny *story*.

THE PROBLEM OF POINT OF VIEW

For the screenwriter *Point of View* has two meanings. First, we
occasionally call for POV shots. For example:

INT. DINING ROOM—DAY

Jack sips coffee, when suddenly he hears a SCREECH OF BRAKES
and a CRASH that shakes the house. He rushes to the window.

JACK's POV

out the window: Tony's car crumpled against the garage door
and his son staggering across the lawn, giggling drunk.

ON JACK

throwing open the window in a rage.

The second meaning, however, applies to the writer's vision. From what Point of View is each scene written? From what Point of View is the story as a whole told?

POV WITHIN A SCENE

Each story is set in a specific time and place, yet scene by scene, as we imagine events, where do we locate ourselves *in space* to view the action? This is Point of View—the physical angle we take in order to describe the behavior of our characters, their interaction with one another and the environment. How we make our choices of Point of View has enormous influence on how the reader reacts to the scene and how the director will later stage and shoot it.

We can imagine ourselves anywhere 360 degrees around an action or at the center of the action looking out in 360 different degrees—high above the action, below it, anywhere globally. Each choice of POV has a different effect on empathy and emotion.

For example, continuing the father/son scene above, Jack calls Tony to the window and they argue. The father demands to know why a son in medical school is drunk and learns that the university has expelled him. Tony wanders off, distraught. Jack races through the house to the street and consoles his son.

There are four distinctively different POV choices in this scene: One, put Jack exclusively at the center of your imagination. Follow him from table to window, seeing what he sees and his reactions to it. Then move with him through the house to the street as he chases after Tony to embrace him. Two, do the same with Tony. Stay with him exclusively as he weaves his car up the street, across the lawn, and into the garage door. Show his reactions when he stumbles out of the wreck to confront his father at the window. Take him down the street, then suddenly turn him as his father runs up to hug him. Three, alternate between Jack's POV and Tony's POV. Four, take a neutral POV. Imagine them, as a comedy writer might, at a distance and in profile.

This first encourages us to empathize with Jack, the second asks empathy for Tony, the third draws us close to both, the fourth with neither and prompts us to laugh at them.

POV WITHIN THE STORY

If in the two hours of a feature film you can bring audience members to a complex and deeply satisfying relationship with just one character, an understanding and involvement they will carry for a lifetime, you have done far more than most films. Generally, therefore, it enhances the telling to style the whole story from the protagonist's Point of View—to discipline yourself to the protagonist, make him the center of your imaginative universe, and bring the whole story, event by event, to the protagonist. The audience witnesses events only as the protagonist encounters them. This, clearly, is the far more difficult way to tell story.

The easy way is to hopscotch through time and space, picking up bits and pieces to facilitate exposition, but this makes story sprawl and lose tension. Like limited setting, genre convention, and Controlling Idea, shaping a story from the exclusive Point of View of the protagonist is a creative discipline. It taxes the imagination and demands your very best work. The result is a tight, smooth, memorable character and story.

The more time spent with a character, the more opportunity to witness his choices. The result is more empathy and emotional involvement between audience and character.

THE PROBLEM OF ADAPTATION

The conceit of adaptation is that the hard work of story can be avoided by optioning a literary work and simply shifting it into a screenplay. That is almost never the case. To grasp the difficulties of adaptation we look again at story complexity.

In the twentieth century we now have three media for telling story: prose (novel, novella, short story), theatre (legit, musical, opera, mime, ballet), and screen (film and television). Each medium tells complex stories by bringing characters into simultaneous conflict on all three levels of life; however, each has a distinctive power and innate beauty at *one* of these levels.

The unique strength and wonder of the novel is the dramatization of inner conflict. This is what prose does best, far better than play or film. Whether in first- or third-person, the novelist slips inside thought and feeling with subtlety, density, and poetic imagery to project onto the reader's imagination the turmoil and passions of inner conflict. In the novel extra-personal conflict is delineated through description, word pictures of characters struggling with society or environment, while personal conflict is shaped through dialogue.

The unique command and grace of the theatre is the dramatization of personal conflict. This is what the theatre does best, far better than novel or film. A great play is almost pure dialogue, perhaps 80 percent is for the ear, only 20 percent for the eye. Nonverbal communication—gestures, looks, lovemaking, fighting—is important, but, by and large, personal conflicts evolve for better or worse through talk. What's more, the playwright has a license screenwriters do not—he may write dialogue in a way no human being has ever spoken. He may write, not just poetic dialogue, but, like Shakespeare, T. S. Eliot, and Christopher Frye, use poetry itself as dialogue, lifting the expressivity of personal conflict to incredible heights. In addition, he has the live voice of the actor to add nuances of shading and pause that take it even higher.

In the theatre inner conflict is dramatized through subtext. As the actor brings the character to life from the inside, the audience sees through the sayings and doings to the thoughts and feelings underneath. Like a first-person novel, the theatre can send a character to the apron in soliloquy to speak intimately with the audience. In direct address, however, the character isn't necessarily telling the truth, or if sincere, isn't able to understand his inner life and tell the whole truth. The theatre's power to dramatize inner conflict through unspoken subtext is ample but, compared to the novel, limited. The stage can also dramatize extra-personal conflicts, but how much of society can it hold? How much environment of sets and props?

The unique power and splendor of the cinema is the dramatization of extra-personal conflict, huge and vivid images of human beings wrapped inside their society and environment, striving with life. This is what film does best, better than play or novel. If we were to take a single frame from BLADE RUNNER and ask the world's finest prose stylist to create the verbal equivalent of that composition, he would fill page after page with words and never capture its essence. And that is only one of thousands of complex images flowing through the experience of an audience.

Critics often complain about chase sequences, as if they were a new phenomenon. The first great discovery of the Silent Era was the chase, enlivening Charlie Chaplin and the Keystone Cops, thousands of Westerns, most of D. W. Griffith's films, BEN HUR, THE BATTLESHIP POTEMKIN, STORM OVER ASIA, and the beautiful SUNRISE. The chase is a human being pursued by society, struggling through the physical world to escape and survive. It's pure extra-personal conflict, pure cinema, the most natural thing to want to do with a camera and editing machine.

To express personal conflict the screenwriter must use plainspoken dialogue. When we use theatrical language on screen the audience's rightful reaction is: "People don't talk like that." Other than the special case of filmed Shakespeare, screenwriting demands naturalistic talk. Film, however, gains great power in nonverbal communication. With close-up, lighting, and nuances of angle, gestures and facial expressions become very eloquent. Nonetheless, the screenwriter cannot dramatize personal conflict to the poetic fullness of the theatre.

The dramatization of inner conflict on screen is exclusively in the subtext as the camera looks through the face of the actor to thoughts and feelings within. Even the personal direct-to-camera narration in ANNIE HALL or Salieri's confession in AMADEUS is layered with subtext. The inner life can be expressed impressively in film, but it cannot reach the density or complexity of a novel.

That is the lay of the land. Now imagine the problems of adaptation. Over the decades hundreds of millions of dollars have been spent to option the film rights to literary works that are then tossed into the laps of screenwriters who read them and go running, screaming into the night, "Nothing's happens! The whole book is in the character's head!"

Therefore, the first principle of adaptation: **The purer the novel, the purer the play, the worse the film.**

"Literary purity" does not mean literary achievement. Purity of novel means a telling located exclusively at the level of inner conflict, employing linguistic complexities to incite, advance, and climax story with relative independence of personal, social, and environmental forces: Joyce's *Ulysses*. Purity of theatre means a telling located exclusively at the level of personal conflict, employing the spoken word in poetic excess to incite, advance, and climax story with relative independence of inner, social, and environmental forces: Eliot's *The Cocktail Party*.

Attempts to adapt "pure" literature fail for two reasons: One is aesthetic impossibility. Image is prelinguistic; no cinematic equivalences or even approximations exist for conflicts buried in the extravagant language of master novelists and playwrights. Two, when a lesser talent attempts to adapt genius, which is more likely? Will a lesser talent rise to the level of genius, or will genius be dragged down to the level of the adaptor?

The world's screens are frequently stained by pretentious filmmakers who wish to be regarded as another Fellini or Bergman, but unlike Fellini and Bergman cannot create original works, so they go to equally pretentious funding agencies with a copy of Proust or Woolf in hand, promising to bring art to the masses. The bureaucrats grant the money, politicians congratulate themselves to their constituents for bringing art to the masses, the director gets a paycheck, the film vanishes over a weekend.

If you must adapt, come down a rung or two from "pure" literature and look for stories in which conflict is distributed on all three levels . . . with an emphasis at the extra-personal. Pierre Boulle's *The Bridge on the River Kwai* won't be taught alongside Thomas Mann and Franz Kafka in postgraduate seminars, but it's an excellent work, populated with complex characters driven by inner and personal conflicts and dramatized primarily at extrapersonal level. Consequently, Carl Foreman's adaptation became, in my judgment, David Lean's finest film.

To adapt, first read the work over and over without taking notes until you feel infused with its spirit. Do not make choices or plan moves until you've rubbed shoulders with its society, read their faces, smelled their cologne. As with a story you're creating from scratch, you must achieve a godlike knowledge and never assume that the original writer has done his homework. That done, reduce each event to a one- or two-sentence statement of what happens and no more. No psychology, no sociology. For example: "He walks into the house expecting a confrontation with his wife, but discovers a note telling him she's left him for another man."

That done, read through the events and ask yourself, "Is this story well told?" Then brace yourself, for nine times out of ten you'll discover it's not. Just because a writer got a play to the stage or a novel into print doesn't mean that he has mastered the craft. Story is the hardest thing we all do. Many novelists are weak storytellers, playwrights even weaker. Or you'll discover that it's beautifully told, a clockwork of perfection . . . but four hundred pages long, three times as much material as you can use for a film, and if a single cog is taken out, the clock stops telling time. In either case, your task will not be one of adaptation but of reinvention.

The second principle of adaptation: **Be willing to reinvent.**

Tell the story in filmic rhythms while keeping the spirit of the original. To reinvent: No matter in what order the novel's events were told, reorder them in time from first to last, as if they were biographies. From these create a step-outline, using, where valuable, designs from the original work, but feeling free to cut scenes and, if necessary, to create new ones. Most testing of all, turn what is mental into the physical. Don't fill characters' mouths with self-explanatory dialogue but find visual expression for their inner conflicts. This is where you'll succeed or fail. Seek a design that expresses the spirit of the original yet stays within the rhythms of a film, ignoring the risk that critics may say, "But the film's not like the novel."

The aesthetics of the screen often demand reinvention of story, even when the original is superbly told and of feature-film size. As Milos Foreman told Peter Shaffer while adapting AMADEUS from stage to screen, "You're going to have to give birth to your child a second time." The result is that the world now has two excellent versions of the same story, each true to its medium. While struggling with an adaptation bear this in mind: If reinvention deviates radically from the original—PELLE THE CONQUEROR, DANGEROUS LIAISONS—but the film is excellent, critics fall silent. But if you butcher the original—THE SCARLET LETTER, THE BONFIRE OF THE VANITIES—and do not put a work as good or better in its place, duck.

To learn adaptation study the work of Ruth Prawer Jhabvala. She is, in my view, the finest adapter of novel to screen in film history. She's a Pole born in Germany who writes in English. Having reinvented her nationality, she's become the master reinventer for film. Like a chameleon or trance-medium, she inhabits the colors and spirit of other writers. Read *Quartet, A Room with a View, The Bostonians*, pull a step-outline from each novel, then scene by scene compare your work to Jhabvala. You'll learn a lot. Notice that she and director James Ivory restrict themselves to the social novelists—Jean Rhys, E. M. Forster, Henry James—knowing that the primary conflicts will be extra-personal and camera attractive. No Proust, no Joyce, no Kafka.

Although the natural expressivity of cinema is extra-personal, it shouldn't inhibit us. Rather, the challenge that great filmmakers have always accepted is to start with images of social/environmental conflict and lead us into the complexities of personal relationships, to begin on the surface of what's said and done and guide us to a perception of the inner life, the unspoken, the unconscious—to swim upstream and achieve on film what the playwright and novelist do most easily.

By the same token, playwright and novelist have always understood that their challenge is to do on stage or page what film does best. Flaubert's famous cinematic style was developed long before there was cinema. Eisenstein said he learned to cut film by reading Charles Dickens. Shakespeare's stunning fluidity through time and space suggests an imagination hungry for a camera. Great story-tellers have always known that "Show, don't tell" is the ultimate creative task: to write in a purely dramatic and visual way, to show a natural world of natural human being behavior, to express the complexity of life *without telling*.

THE PROBLEM OF MELODRAMA

To avoid the accusation "This script is melodramatic," many avoid writing "big scenes," passionate, powerful events. Instead, they write minimalist sketches in which little if anything happens, thinking they're subtle. This is folly. Nothing human beings do in and of itself is melodramatic, and human beings are capable of anything. Daily newspapers record acts of enormous self-sacrifice and cruelty, of daring and cowardliness, of saints and tyrants from Mother Teresa to Saddam Hussein. Anything you can imagine human beings doing, they have already done and in ways you cannot imagine. None of it is melodrama; it's simply human.

Melodrama is not the result of overexpression, but of under motivation; not writing too big, but writing with too little desire. The power of an event can only be as great as the sum total of its causes. We feel a scene is melodramatic if we cannot believe that motivation matches action. Writers from Homer to Shakespeare to Bergman have created explosive scenes no one would call melo-drama because they knew how to motivate characters. If you can imagine high drama or comedy, write it, but lift the forces that drive your characters to equal or surpass the extremities of their actions and we'll embrace you for taking us to the end of the line.

THE PROBLEM OF HOLES

A "hole" is another way to lose credibility. Rather than a lack of motivation, now the story lacks logic, a missing link in the chain of cause and effect. But like coincidence, holes are a part of life. Things often happen for reasons that cannot be explained. So if you're writing about life, a hole or two may find its way into your telling. The problem is how to handle it.

If you can forge a link between illogical events and close the hole, do so. This remedy, however, often requires the creation of a new scene that has no purpose other than making what's around it logical, causing an awkwardness as annoying as the hole.

In which case ask: Will they notice? You know it's a jump in logic because the story sits still on your desk with its hole glaring up at you. But onscreen the story flows in time. As the hole arrives, the audience may not have sufficient information at that point to realize that what just happened isn't logical or it may happen so quickly, it passes unnoticed.

CHINATOWN: Ida Sessions (Diane Ladd) impersonates Evelyn Mulwray and hires J. J. Gittes to investigate Hollis Mulwray for adultery. After Gittes discovers what appears to be an affair, the real wife shows up with her lawyer and a lawsuit. Gittes realizes that someone is out to get Mulwray, but before he can help the man is murdered. Early in Act Two Gittes gets a phone call from Ida Sessions telling him that she had no idea that things would lead to murder and wants him to know she's innocent. In this call she also gives Gittes a vital clue to the motivation for the killing. Her words, however, are so cryptic he's only more confused. Later, however, he pieces her clue to other evidence he unearths and thinks he knows who did it and why.

Early in Act Three he finds Ida Sessions dead and in her wallet discovers a Screen Actors Guild card. In other words, Ida Sessions couldn't possibly have known what she said over the phone. Her clue is a crucial detail of a citywide corruption run by millionaire businessmen and high government officials, something they would never have told the actress they hired to impersonate the victim's wife. But when she tells Gittes, we have no idea who Ida Sessions is and what she could or could not know. When she's found dead an hour and a half later, we don't see the hole because by then we've forgotten what she said.

So maybe the audience won't notice. But maybe it will. Then what? Cowardly writers try to kick sand over such holes and hope the audience doesn't notice. Other writers face this problem manfully. They expose the hole to the audience, then deny that it is a hole.

CASABLANCA: Ferrari (Sidney Greenstreet) is the ultimate capitalist and crook who never does anything except for money. Yet at one point Ferrari helps Victor Laszlo (Paul Henreid) find the precious letters of transit and wants nothing in return. That's out of character, illogical. Knowing this, the writers gave Ferrari the line: "Why I'm doing this I don't know because it can't possibly profit me . . ." Rather than hiding the hole, the writers admitted it with the bold lie that Ferrari might be impulsively generous. The audience knows we often do things for reasons we can't explain. Complimented, it nods, thinking, "Even Ferrari doesn't get it. Fine. On with the film."

THE TERMINATOR doesn't have a hole—it's built over an abyss: In 2029 robots have all but exterminated the human race, when the remnants of humanity, lead by John Connor, turn the tide of the war. To eliminate their enemy, the robots invent a time machine and send the Terminator back to 1984 to kill the mother of John Connor before he's born. Connor captures their device and sends a young officer, Reese, back to try to destroy the Terminator first. He does this knowing that indeed Reese will not only save his mother but get her pregnant, and therefore his lieutenant is his father. What?

But James Cameron and Gail Anne Hurd understand Narrative Drive. They knew that if they exploded two warriors from the future into the streets of Los Angeles and sent them roaring in pursuit of this poor woman, the audience wouldn't be asking analytical questions, and bit by bit they could parse out their setup. But respecting the intelligence of the audience, they also knew that after the film over coffee the audience might think: "Wait a minute . . . if Connor knew Reese would . . . ," and so on, and the holes would swallow up the audience's pleasure. So they wrote this resolution scene.

The pregnant Sarah Connor heads for the safety of remote mountains in Mexico, there to give birth and raise her son for his future mission. At a gas station she dictates memoirs to her unborn hero into a tape recorder and she says in effect: "You know, my son, I don't get it. If you know that Reese will be your father . . . then why . . . ? How? And does that mean that this is going to happen again . . . and again . . . ?" Then she pauses and says, "You know, you could go crazy thinking about this." And all over the world audiences thought: "Hell, she's right. It's not important." With that they happily threw logic into the trash.

17

CHARACTER

THE MIND WORM

As I traced the evolution of story through the twenty-eight centuries since Homer, I thought I'd save a thousand years and skip from the fourth century to the Renaissance because, according to my undergrad history text, during the Dark Ages all thinking stopped while monks dithered over such questions as "How many angels dance on the head of a pin?" Skeptical, I looked a little deeper and found that in fact intellectual life in the medieval epoch went on vigorously . . . but in poetic code. When the metaphor was deciphered, researchers discovered that "How many angels dance on the head of pin?" isn't metaphysics, it's physics. The topic under discussion is atomic structure: "How small is small?"

To discuss psychology, medieval scholarship devised another ingenious conceit: the *Mind Worm*. Suppose a creature had the power to burrow into the brain and come to know an individual completely—dreams, fears, strength, weakness. Suppose that this Mind Worm also had the power to cause events in the world. It could then create a specific happening geared to the unique nature of that person that would trigger a one-of-a-kind adventure, a quest that would force him to use himself to the limit, to live to his deepest and fullest. Whether a tragedy or fulfillment, this quest would reveal his humanity absolutely.

Reading that I had to smile, for the writer is a Mind Worm. We too burrow into a character to discover his aspects, his potential, then create an event geared to his unique nature—the Inciting Incident. For each protagonist it's different—for one perhaps finding a fortune, for another losing a fortune—but we design the event to fit the character, the precise happening needed to send him on a quest that reaches the limits of his being. Like the Mind Worm, we explore the inscape of human nature, expressed in poetic code. For as centuries pass, nothing changes within us. As William Faulkner observed, human nature is the only subject that doesn't date.

Characters Are Not Human Beings

A character is no more a human being than the Venus de Milo is a real woman. A character is a work of art, a metaphor for human nature. We relate to characters as if they were real, but they're superior to reality. Their aspects are designed to be clear and knowable; whereas our fellow humans are difficult to understand, if not enigmatic. We know characters better than we know our friends because a character is eternal and unchanging, while people shift—just when we think we understand them, we don't. In fact, I know Rick Blaine in CASABLANCA better than I know myself. Rick is always Rick. I'm a bit iffy.

Character design begins with an arrangement of the two primary aspects: *Characterization* and *True Character*. To repeat: Characterization is the sum of all the observable qualities, a combination that makes the character unique: physical appearance coupled with mannerisms, style of speech and gesture, sexuality, age, IQ, occupation, personality, attitudes, values, where he lives, how he lives. True Character waits behind this mask. Despite his characterization, at heart who is this person? Loyal or disloyal? Honest or a liar? Loving or cruel? Courageous or cowardly? Generous or selfish? Willful or weak?

> **TRUE CHARACTER can only be expressed through choice in dilemma. How the person chooses to act under pressure is who he is—the greater the pressure, the truer and deeper the choice to character.**

The key to True Character is desire. In life, if we feel stifled, the fastest way to get unstuck is to ask, "What do I want?," listen to the honest answer, then find the will to pursue that desire. Problems still remain, but now we're in motion with the chance of solving them. What's true of life is true of fiction. A character comes to life the moment we glimpse a clear understanding of his desire—not only the conscious, but in a complex role, the unconscious desire as well.

Ask: What does this character want? Now? Soon? Overall? Knowingly? Unknowingly? With clear, true answers comes your command of the role.

Behind desire is motivation. Why does your character want what he wants? You have your ideas about motive, but don't be surprised if others see it differently. A friend may feel that parental upbringing shaped your character's desires; someone else may think it's our materialist culture; another may blame the school system; yet another may claim it's in the genes; still another thinks he's possessed by the devil. Contemporary attitudes tend to favor mono-explanations for behavior, rather than the complexity of forces that's more likely the case.

Do not reduce characters to case studies (an episode of child abuse is the cliché in vogue at the moment), for in truth there are no definitive explanations for anyone's behavior. *Generally, the more the writer nails motivation to specific causes, the more he diminishes the character in the audience's mind.* Rather, think through to a solid understanding of motive, but at the same time leave some mystery around the whys, a touch of the irrational perhaps, room for the audience to use its own life experience to enhance your character in its imagination.

In *King Lear*, for example, Shakespeare cast one of his most complex villains, Edmund. After a scene in which astrological influences, yet another mono-explanation of behavior, are blamed for someone's misfortune, Edmund turns in soliloquy and laughs, "I should have been what I am had the maidenliest star in the firmament twinkled on my bastardy." Edmund does evil for the pure pleasure of it. Beyond that, what matters? As Aristotle observed, why a man does a thing is of little interest once we see the thing he does. A character is the choices he makes to take the actions he takes. Once the deed is done his reasons why begin to dissolve into irrelevancy.

The audience comes to understand your character in a variety of ways: The physical image and setting say a lot, but the audience knows that appearance is not reality, characterization is not true character. Nonetheless, a character's mask is an important clue to what may be revealed.

What other characters say about a character is a hint. We know that what one person says of another may or may not be true, given the axes people have to grind, but that it's said and by whom is worth knowing. What a character says about himself may or may not be true. We listen, but then put it in our pockets.

In fact, characters with lucid self-knowledge, those reciting self-explanatory dialogue meant to convince us that they are who they say they are, are not only boring but phony. The audience knows that people rarely, if ever, understand themselves, and if they do, they're incapable of complete and honest self-explanation. There's always a subtext. If, by chance, what a character says about himself is actually true, we don't *know* it's true until we witness his choices made under pressure. Self-explanation must be validated or contradicted in action. In CASABLANCA when Rick says, "I stick my neck out for no man," we think, "Well, not yet, Rick, not yet." We know Rick better than he knows himself, for indeed he's wrong; he'll stick his neck out many times.

Character Dimension

"Dimension" is the least understood concept in character. When I was an actor, directors would insist on "round, three-dimensional characters," and I was all for that, but when I asked them what exactly is a dimension and how do I create one, let alone three, they'd waffle, mumble something about rehearsal, then stroll away.

Some years ago a producer pitched me what he believed to be a "three-dimensional" protagonist in these terms: "Jessie just got out of prison, but while he was in the slammer he boned up on finance and investment, so he's an expert on stocks, bonds, and securities. He can also break dance. He's got a black belt in karate and plays a mean jazz saxophone." His "Jessie" was as flat as a desktop—a cluster of traits stuck on a name. Decorating a protagonist with quirks does not open his character and draw empathy. Rather, eccentricities may close him off and keep us at a distance.

A favorite academic tenet argues that, instead, fine characters are marked by one dominant trait. Macbeth's ambition is frequently cited. Overweening ambition, it's claimed, makes Macbeth great. This theory is dead wrong. If Macbeth were merely ambitious, there'd be no play. He'd simply defeat the English and rule Scotland. Macbeth is a brilliantly realized character because of the contradiction between his ambition on one hand and his guilt on the other. From this profound inner contradiction springs his passion, his complexity, his poetry.

Dimension means contradiction: either within deep character (guilt-ridden ambition) or between characterization and deep character (a charming thief). These contradictions must be *consistent*. It doesn't add dimension to portray a guy as nice throughout a film, then in one scene have him kick a cat.

Consider Hamlet, the most complex character ever written. Hamlet isn't three-dimensional, but ten, twelve, virtually uncountably dimensional. He seems spiritual until he's blasphemous. To Ophelia he's first loving and tender, then callous, even sadistic. He's courageous, then cowardly. At times he's cool and cautious, then impulsive and rash, as he stabs someone hiding behind a curtain without knowing who's there. Hamlet is ruthless and compassionate, proud and self-pitying, witty and sad, weary and dynamic, lucid and confused, sane and mad. His is an innocent worldliness, a worldly innocence, a living contradiction of almost any human qualities we could imagine.

Dimensions fascinate; contradictions in nature or behavior rivet the audience's concentration. Therefore, the protagonist must be the most dimensional character in the cast to focus empathy on the star role. If not, the Center of Good decenters; the fictional universe flies apart; the audience loses balance.

BLADE RUNNER: Marketing positioned the audience to empathize with Harrison Ford's Rick Deckard, but once in the theatre, filmgoers were drawn to the greater dimensionality of the replicant Roy Batty (Rutger Hauer). As the Center of Good shifted to the antagonist, the audience's emotional confusion diminished its enthusiasm, and what should have been a huge success became a cult film.

Cast Design

In essence, the protagonist creates the rest of the cast. All other characters are in a story first and foremost because of the relationship they strike to the protagonist and the way each helps to delineate the dimensions of the protagonist's complex nature. Imagine a cast as a kind of solar system with the protagonist as the sun, supporting roles as planets around the sun, bit players as satellites around the planets—all held in orbit by the gravitational pull of the star at the center, each pulling at the tides of the others' natures.

Consider this hypothetical protagonist: He's amusing and optimistic, then morose and cynical; he's compassionate, then cruel; fearless, then fearful. This four-dimensional role needs a cast around him to delineate his contradictions, characters toward whom he can act and react in different ways at different times and places. These supporting characters must round him out so that his complexity is both consistent and credible.

Character A, for example, provokes the protagonist's sadness and cynicism, while Character B brings out his witty, hopeful side. Character C inspires his loving and courageous emotions, while Character D forces him first to cower in fear, then to strike out in fury. The creation and design of characters A, B, C, and D is dictated by the needs of the protagonist. They are what they are principally to make clear and believable, through action and reaction, the complexity of the central role.

Although supporting roles must be scaled back from the protagonist, they too may be complex. Character A could be two-dimensional: outwardly beautiful and loving/inwardly grotesque as choices under pressure reveal cold, mutated desires. Even one

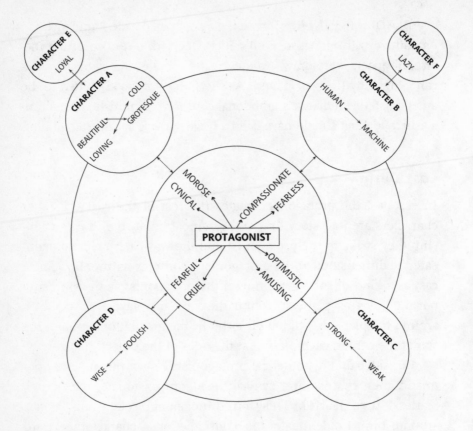

dimension can create an excellent supporting role. Character B could, like the Terminator, have a single yet fascinating contradiction: machine versus human. If the Terminator were merely a robot or a man from the future, he might not be interesting. But he's both, and his machine/human dimension makes a superb villain.

The physical and social world in which a character is found, his or her profession or neighborhood, for example, is an aspect of characterization. Dimension, therefore, can be created by a simple counterpoint: Placing a conventional personality against an exotic background, or a strange, mysterious individual within an ordinary, down-to-earth society immediately generates interest.

Bit parts should be drawn deliberately flat . . . but not dull. Give each a freshly observed trait that makes the role worth playing for the moment the actor's onscreen, but no more.

For example, suppose your protagonist is visiting New York City for the first time, and as she steps out of Kennedy Airport, she can't wait for her first ride with a New York taxi driver. How to write that role? Do you make him a philosophizing eccentric with a baseball cap sideways on his head? I hope not. For the last six decades every time we get in a cab in a New York movie, there he is, the kooky New York cab driver.

Perhaps you create the screen's first silent New York cab driver. She tries to start New York conversations about the Yankees, the Knicks, the mayor's office, but he just straightens his tie and drives on. She slumps back, her first New York disappointment.

On the other hand, the cab driver to end all cab drivers: a gravel-voiced but wonderfully obliging oddball who gives her a definitive tutorial in big-city survival—how to wear her purse strap across her chest, where to keep her mace can. Then he drives her to the Bronx, charges her a hundred and fifty bucks and tells her she's in Manhattan. He comes on helpful, turns into a thieving rat—a contradiction between characterization and deep character. Now we'll be looking all over the film for this guy because we know that writers don't put dimensions in characters they're not going to use again. If this cabby doesn't show up at least once more, we'll be very annoyed. Don't cause false anticipation by making bit parts more interesting than necessary.

The cast orbits around the star, its protagonist. Supporting roles are inspired by the central character and designed to delineate his complex of dimensions. Secondary roles need not only the protagonists but also one another, to bring out their dimensions. As tertiary characters (E and F on the diagram) have scenes with the protagonist or other principals, they also help reveal dimensions. Ideally, in every scene each character brings out qualities that mark the dimensions of the others, all held in constellation by the weight of the protagonist at the center.

The Comic Character

All characters pursue desire against forces of antagonism. But the dramatic character is flexible enough to step back from the risk and

382 ◆ ROBERT MCKEE

realize: "This could get me killed." Not the comic character. The comic character is marked by a blind obsession. The first step to solving the problem of a character who should be funny but isn't is to find his mania.

When the political satires of Aristophanes and farcical romances of Menander passed into history, Comedy degenerated into the ribald, peasant cousin of Tragedy and Epic Poetry. But with the coming of the Renaissance—from Goldoni in Italy to Molière in France (skipping Germany) to Shakespeare, Jonson, Wycherley, Congreve, Sheridan; through Shaw, Wilde, Coward, Chaplin, Allen, the crackling wits of England, Ireland, and America—it ascended into the gleaming art of today—the saving grace of modern life.

As these masters perfected their art, like all craftsmen, they talked shop and came to realize that a comic character is created by assigning the role a "humour," an obsession the character does not see. Molière's career was built on writing plays ridiculing the pro-tagonist's fixation—*The Miser, The Imaginary Invalid, The Misan-thrope*. Almost any obsession will do. Shoes, for example. Imelda Marcos is an international joke because she doesn't see her neu-rotic need for shoes, by some estimates over three thousand pairs. Although in her tax trial here in New York she said it was only twelve hundred . . . and none fit. They're gifts from shoe compa-nies, she claimed, who never get the size right.

In *All in the Family* Archie Bunker (Carroll O'Connor) was a blindly obsessed bigot. As long as he doesn't see it, he's a buffoon and we laugh at him. But if he were to turn to someone and say, "You know, I am a racist hate monger," the comedy is over.

A SHOT IN THE DARK: A chauffeur is murdered on the estate of Benjamin Ballon (George Saunders). Enter a man obsessed with being the world's most perfect detective, Captain Clouseau (Peter Sellers), who decides that Ballon did the deed and confronts the bil-lionaire in the billiards room. As Clouseau lays out his evidence, he rips the felt on the pool table and smashes the cues, finally sum-ming up with: ". . . and zen you killed him in a rit of fealous jage." Clouseau turns to leave but walks around the wrong side of the door. We hear THUMP as he hits the wall. He steps back and with cool contempt, says, "Stupid architects."

A FISH CALLED WANDA: Wanda (Jamie Lee Curtis), a master criminal, is obsessed with men who speak foreign languages. Otto (Kevin Kline), a failed CIA agent, is convinced he's an intellectual—although, as Wanda points out, he makes mistakes such as thinking that the London Underground is a political movement. Ken (Michael Palin) is so obsessed with a love of animals that Otto tortures him by eating his goldfish. Archie Leach (John Cleese) has an obsessive fear of embarrassment, a fear, he tells us, that grips the whole English nation. Midway through the film, however, Archie realizes his obsession and once he sees it, he turns from comic protagonist to romantic lead, from Archie Leach to "Cary Grant." (Archie Leach was Cary Grant's real name.)

Three Tips on Writing Characters for the Screen

1. Leave room for the actor.
This old Hollywood admonition asks the writer to provide each actor with the maximum opportunity to use his or her creativity; not to overwrite and pepper the page with constant description of behaviors, nuances of gesture, tones of voice:

> Bob leans on the lectern, crossing one leg over the other, one arm akimbo. He looks out over the heads of the students, arching an eyebrow thoughtfully:
>
>
>
> BOB
> (phlegmatically)
> Blaa, blaa, blaa, blaa, blaa
> . . .
>
>

An actor's reaction to a script saturated with that kind of detail is to toss it in the trash, thinking, "They don't want an actor, they want a puppet." Or if the actor accepts the role, he'll take a red pencil and scratch all that nonsense off the page. The details above are meaningless. An actor wants to know: What do I want? Why do I want it? How do I go about getting it? What stops me? What are the consequences? The actor brings a character to life from the subtext out: desire meeting forces of antagonism. On-camera he'll say and do what the scene requires, but characterization must be his work as much as or more than yours.

We must remember that, unlike the theatre where we hope our work will be performed in hundreds, if not thousands of productions, here and abroad, now and into the future, on screen there will be only one production, only one performance of each character fixed on film forever. Writer/actor collaboration begins when the writer stops dreaming of a fictional face and instead imagines the ideal casting. If a writer feels that a particular actor would be his ideal protagonist and he envisions her while he writes, he'll be constantly reminded of how little superb actors need to create powerful moments, and won't write this:

> BARBARA
> (offering Jack a
> cup)
> Would you like this cup of
> coffee, darling?

The audience *sees* it's a cup of coffee; the gesture says, "Would you like this?"; the actress is feeling "darling . . ." Sensing that less is more, the actress will turn to her director and say: "Larry, do I have to say 'Would you like this cup of coffee, darling?' I mean, I'm offering the damn cup, right? Could we just cut that line?" The line is cut, the actress sets the screen on fire silently offering a man a cup of coffee, while the screenwriter rages, "They're butchering my dialogue!"

2. Fall in love with all your characters.
We often see films with a cast of excellent characters . . . except one, who's dreadful. We wonder why until we realize that the writer hates this character. He's trivializing and insulting this role

at every opportunity. And I'll never understand this. How can a writer hate his own character? It's his baby. How can he hate what he gave life? Embrace all your creations, especially the bad people. They deserve love like everyone else.

Hurt and Cameron must have loved their Terminator. Look at the wonderful things they did for him: In a motel room he repairs a damaged eye with an Exacto knife. Standing over a sink, he pries his eyeball out of his head, drops it in the water, mops up the blood with a towel, puts on Gargoyle sunglasses to hide the hole, then looks in the mirror and smooths down his tangled hair. The stunned audience thinks, "He just pried his eyeball out of his head and he gives a damn what he looks like. He's got vanity!"

Then a knock at the door. As he looks up, the camera takes his POV and we see his computer screen super-imposed over the door. On it is a list of responses to someone knocking: "Go away," "Please come back later," "Fuck off," "Fuck off, asshole." His cursor goes up and down while he makes his choice and stops at "Fuck off, asshole." A robot with a sense of humor. Now the monster's all the more terrifying, for thanks to these moments we have no idea of what to expect from him, and therefore imagine the worst. Only writers who love their characters discover such moments.

A hint about villains: If your character's up to no good and you place yourself within his being, asking, "If I were he in this situation, what would I do?," you'd do everything possible to get away with it. Therefore, you would not act like a villain; you would not twist your mustache. Sociopaths are the most charming folks we ever meet—sympathetic listeners who seem so deeply concerned about our problems while they lead us to hell.

An interviewer once remarked to Lee Marvin that he'd played villains for thirty years and how awful it must be always playing bad people. Marvin smiled, "Me? I don't play bad people. I play people struggling to get through their day, doing the best they can with what life's given them. Others may think they're bad, but no, I never play bad people." That's why Marvin could be a superb villain. He was a craftsman with a deep understanding of human nature: No one thinks they're bad.

If you can't love them, don't write them. On the other hand, permit neither your empathy nor antipathy for a character to produce melodrama or stereotype. Love them all without losing your clearheadedness.

3. Character is self-knowledge.

Everything I learned about human nature I learned from me.
—Anton Chekhov

Where do we find our characters? Partly through observation. Writers often carry notepads or pocket tape recorders and as they watch life's passing show, collect bits and pieces to fill file cabinets with random material. When they're dry, they dip in for ideas to stir the imagination.

We observe, but it's a mistake to copy life directly to the page. Few individuals are as clear in their complexity and as well delineated as a character. Instead, like Dr. Frankenstein, we build characters out of parts found. A writer takes the analytical mind of his sister and pieces it together with the comic wit of a friend, adds to that the cunning cruelty of a cat and the blind persistence of King Lear. We borrow bits and pieces of humanity, raw chunks of imagination and observation from wherever they're found, assemble them into dimensions of contradiction, then round them into the creatures we call characters.

Observation is our source of characterizations, but understanding of deep character is found in another place. The root of all fine character writing is self-knowledge.

One of the sad truths of life is that there's only one person in this vale of tears that we ever really know, and that's ourselves. We're essentially and forever alone. Yet, although others remain at a distance, changing and unknowable in a definitive, final sense, and despite the obvious distinctions of age, sex, background, and culture, despite all the clear differences among people, the truth is we are all far more alike than we are different. We are all human.

We all share the same crucial human experiences. Each of us is suffering and enjoying, dreaming and hoping of getting through our days with something of value. As a writer, you can be certain that everyone coming down the street toward you, each in his own way, is having the same fundamental human thoughts and feelings that you are. This is why when you ask yourself, "If I were this character in these circumstances, what would I do?" the honest answer is always correct. You would do the human thing. Therefore, the more you penetrate the mysteries of your own humanity, the more you come to understand yourself, the more you are able to understand others.

When we survey the parade of characters that has marched out of the imaginations of storytellers from Homer to Shakespeare, Dickens, Austen, Hemingway, Williams, Wilder, Bergman, Goldman, and all other masters—each character fascinating, unique, sublimely human and so many, many of them—and realize that all were born of a single humanity . . . it's astounding.

18

THE TEXT

DIALOGUE

All the creativity and labor that goes into designing story and character must finally be realized on the page. This chapter looks at the text, at dialogue and description, and the craft that guides their writing. Beyond text, it examines the poetics of story, the Image Systems embedded in words that ultimately result in filmic images that enrich meaning and emotion.

Dialogue is not conversation.

Eavesdrop on any coffee shop conversation and you'll realize in a heartbeat you'd never put that slush onscreen. Real conversation is full of awkward pauses, poor word choices and phrasing, non sequiturs, pointless repetitions; it seldom makes a point or achieves closure. But that's okay because conversation isn't about making points or achieving closure. It's what psychologists call "keeping the channel open." Talk is how we develop and change relationships.

When two friends meet on the street and talk about the weather, don't we know that theirs isn't a conversation about the weather? What is being said? "I'm your friend. Let's take a minute out of our busy day and stand here in each other's presence and reaffirm that we are indeed friends." They might talk about sports, weather, shopping . . . anything. But the text is not the subtext. What is said and done is not what is thought and felt. The scene is not about what it seems to be about. Screen dialogue, therefore, must have the swing of everyday talk but content well above normal.

First, screen dialogue requires compression and economy. Screen dialogue must say the maximum in the fewest possible words. Second, it must have direction. Each exchange of dialogue must turn the beats of the scene in one direction or another across the changing behaviors, without repetition. Third, it should have purpose. Each line or exchange of dialogue executes a step in design that builds and arcs the scene around its Turning Point. All this precision, yet it must sound like talk, using an informal and natural vocabulary, complete with contractions, slang, even, if necessary, profanity. "Speak as common people do," Aristotle advised, "but think as wise men do."

Remember, film is not a novel; dialogue is spoken and gone. If words aren't grasped the instant they leave the actor's mouth, annoyed people suddenly whisper, "What did he say?" Nor is film theatre. We watch a movie; we hear a play. The aesthetics of film are 80 percent visual, 20 percent auditory. We want to see, not hear as our energies go to our eyes, only half-listening to the soundtrack. Theatre is 80 percent auditory, 20 percent visual. Our concentration is directed through our ears, only half-looking at the stage. The playwright may spin elaborate and ornate dialogue—but not the screenwriter. Screen dialogue demands short, simply constructed sentences—generally, a movement from noun to verb to object or from noun to verb to complement in that order.

Not, for example: "Mr. Charles Wilson Evans, the chief financial officer at Data Corporation in the 666 building on Fifth Avenue in Manhattan, who was promoted to that position six years ago, having graduated magna cum laude from Harvard Business School, was arrested today, accused by the authorities of embezzlement from the company's pension fund and fraud in his efforts to conceal the losses." But with a polish: "You know Charlie Evans? CFO at Data Corp? Ha! Got busted. Had his fist in the till. Harvard grad ought to know how to steal and get away with it." The same ideas broken into a series of short, simply constructed, informally spoken sentences, and bit by bit the audience gets it.

Dialogue doesn't require complete sentences. We don't always bother with a noun or a verb. Typically, as above, we drop the opening article or pronoun, speaking in phrases, even grunts.

Read your dialogue out loud or, better yet, into a tape recorder to avoid tongue twisters or accidental rhymes and alliterations such as: "They're moving their car over there." Never write anything that calls attentions to itself as dialogue, anything that jumps off the page and shouts: "Oh, what a clever line am I!" The moment you think you've written something that's particularly fine and literary—cut it.

Short Speeches

The essence of screen dialogue is what was known in Classical Greek theatre as *stikomythia*—the rapid exchange of short speeches. Long speeches are antithetical with the aesthetics of cinema. A column of dialogue from top to bottom of a page asks the camera to dwell on an actor's face for a talking minute. Watch a second hand crawl around the face of a clock for a full sixty seconds and you'll realize that a minute is a long time. Within ten or fifteen seconds the audience's eye absorbs everything visually expressive and the shot becomes redundant. It's the same effect as a stuck record repeating the same note over and over. When the eye is bored, it leaves the screen; when it leaves the screen, you lose the audience.

The literary ambitious often shrug this problem off, thinking the editor can break up long speeches by cutting to the listening face. But this only introduces new problems. Now an actor is speaking offscreen, and when we disembody a voice, the actor must slow down and overarticulate because the audience, in effect, lip-reads. Fifty percent of its understanding of what is being said comes from watching it being said. When the face disappears it stops listening. So offscreen speakers must carefully spit out words in the hope the audience won't miss them. What's more, a voice offscreen loses the subtext of the speaker. The audience has the subtext of the listener, but that may not be what it's interested in.

Therefore, be very judicious about writing long speeches. If, however, you feel that it's true to the moment for one character to carry all the dialogue while another remains silent, write the long speech, but as you do, remember that there's no such thing in life as a monologue. Life is dialogue, action/reaction.

If, as an actor, I have a long speech that begins when another character enters and my first line is "You've kept me waiting," how do I know what to say next until I see the reaction to my first words? If the other character's reaction is apologetic, his head goes down in embarrassment, that softens my next action and colors my lines accordingly. If, however, the other actor's reaction is antagonistic, as he shoots me a dirty look, that may color my next lines with anger. How does anyone know from moment to moment what to say or do next until he senses the reaction to what he just did? He doesn't know. Life is always action/reaction. No monologues. No prepared speeches. An improvisation no matter how we mentally rehearse our big moments.

Therefore, show us that you understand film aesthetics by breaking long speeches into the patterns of action/reaction that shape the speaker's behavior. Fragment the speech with silent reactions that cause the speaker to change the beat, such as this from AMADEUS as Salieri confesses to a priest:

> SALIERI
> All I ever wanted was to sing
> to God. He gave me that
> longing. And then made me
> mute. Why? Tell me that.

The Priest looks away, pained and embarrassed, so Salieri answers his own question rhetorically:

> SALIERI
> If he didn't want me to praise
> Him with music, why implant
> the desire . . . like a lust in

my body and then deny me
the talent?

Or put parentheticals within dialogue for the same effect, such
as this from later in the scene:

> SALIERI
> You understand, I was in love
> with the girl . . .
> > (amused by his own
> > choice of words)
> . . . or at least in lust.
> > (seeing the priest
> > look down at a
> > crucifix held in his
> > lap)
> But I swear to you, I never
> laid a finger on her. No.
> > (as the priest looks
> > up, solemn, judg-
> > mental)
> All the same, I couldn't bear
> to think of anyone else
> touching her.
> > (angered at the
> > thought of Mozart)
> Least of all . . . the creature.

A character can react to himself, to his own thoughts and emotions, as does Salieri above. That too is part of the scene's
dynamics. Demonstrating on the page the action/reaction patterns
within characters, between characters, between characters and the
physical world projects the sensation of watching a film into the
reader's imagination and makes the reader understand that yours
is not a film of talking heads.

The Suspense Sentence

In ill-written dialogue useless words, especially prepositional phrases, float to the ends of sentences. Consequently, meaning sits somewhere in the middle, but the audience has to listen to those last empty words and for that second or two they're bored. What's more, the actor across the screen wants to take his cue from that meaning but has to wait awkwardly until the sentence is finished. In life, we cut each other off, slicing the wiggling tails off each other's sentences, letting everyday conversation tumble. This is yet another reason why in production actors and directors rewrite dialogue, as they trim speeches to lift the scene's energy and make the cueing rhythm pop.

Excellent film dialogue tends to shape itself into the periodic sentence: "If you didn't want me to do it, why'd you give me that . . ." Look? Gun? Kiss? The periodic sentence is the "suspense sentence." Its meaning is delayed until the very last word, forcing both actor and audience to listen to the end of the line. Read again Peter Shaffer's superb dialogue above and note that virtually every single line is a suspense sentence.

The Silent Screenplay

The best advice for writing film dialogue is *don't*. Never write a line of dialogue when you can create a visual expression. The first attack on every scene should be: How could I write this in a purely visual way and not have to resort to a single line of dialogue? Obey the Law of Diminishing Returns: The more dialogue you write, the less effect dialogue has. If you write speech after speech, walking characters into rooms, sitting them in chairs and talking, talking, talking, moments of quality dialogue are buried under this avalanche of words. But if you write for the eye, when the dialogue comes, as it must, it sparks interest because the audience is hungry for it. Lean dialogue, in relief against what's primarily visual, has salience and power.

THE SILENCE: Ester and Anna (Ingrid Thulin and Gunnel Lindblom) are sisters living in a lesbian and rather sadomasochistic relationship. Ester is seriously ill with tuberculosis. Anna is bisexual, has an illegitimate child, and enjoys tormenting her older sister. They're traveling home to Sweden, and the film takes place in a hotel during their journey. Bergman has written a scene in which Anna goes down to the hotel restaurant and allows herself to be seduced by a waiter in order to provoke her sister with this afternoon affair. The "waiter seduces the customer" scene . . . how would you write it?

Does the waiter open a menu and recommend certain items? Ask her if she's staying at the hotel? Traveling far? Compliment her on how she's dressed? Ask her if she knows the city? Mention he's getting off work and would love to show her the sights? Talk, talk . . .

Here's what Bergman gave us: The waiter walks to the table and accidentally on purpose drops the napkin on the floor. As he bends to pick it up, he slowly sniffs and smells Anna from head to crotch to foot. She, in reaction, draws a long, slow, almost delirious breath. CUT TO: They're in a hotel room. Perfect, isn't it? Erotic, purely visual, not a word said or necessary. That's *screenwriting*.

Alfred Hitchcock once remarked, "When the screenplay has been written *and the dialogue has been added,* we're ready to shoot."

Image is our first choice, dialogue the regretful second choice. Dialogue is the last layer we *add* to the screenplay. Make no mistake, we all love great dialogue, but less is more. When a highly imagistic film shifts to dialogue, it crackles with excitement and delights the ear.

DESCRIPTION

Putting a Film in the Reader's Head

Pity the poor screenwriter, for he cannot be a poet. He cannot use metaphor and simile, assonance and alliteration, rhythm and rhyme, synecdoche and metonymy, hyperbole and meiosis, the grand tropes. Instead, his work must contain all the substance of literature but not be literary. A literary work is finished and complete within itself. A screenplay waits for the camera. If not literature, what then is the screenwriter's ambition? To describe in such a way that as the reader turns pages, a film flows through the imagination.

No small task. The first step is to recognize exactly what it is we describe—the sensation of looking at the screen. Ninety percent of all verbal expression has no filmic equivalent. "He's been sitting there for a long time" can't be photographed. So we constantly discipline the imagination with this question: What do I see on the screen? Then describe only what is photographic: Perhaps "He stubs out his tenth cigarette," "He nervously glances at his watch," or "He yawns, trying to stay awake" to suggest waiting a long time.

Vivid Action in the Now

The ontology of the screen is *an absolute present tense in constant vivid movement.* We write screenplay in the present tense because, unlike the novel, film is on the knife edge of the now—whether we flash back or forward, we jump to a new *now.* And the screen expresses relentless action. Even static shots have a sense of aliveness, because although the imagery may not move, the audience's eye constantly travels the screen, giving stationary images energy. And, unlike life, film is vivid. Occasionally, our daily routine may be broken by light glinting off a building, flowers in a shop window, or a woman's face in the crowd. But as we walk through our days we're more inside our heads than out, half-seeing, half-hearing the world. The screen, however, is intensely vivid for hours on end.

On the page vividness springs from the names of the things. Nouns are the names of objects; verbs the names of actions. To write vividly, avoid generic nouns and verbs with adjectives and adverbs attached and seek the name of the thing: Not "The carpenter uses a big nail," but "The carpenter hammers a *spike.*" "Nail" is a generic noun, "big" an adjective. The solid, Anglo-Saxon "spike" pops a vivid image in the reader's mind, "nail" a blur. How big?

The same applies to verbs. A typical line of nondescription: "He starts to move slowly across the room." How does somebody "start" across a room on film? The character either crosses or takes a step and stops. And "move slowly"? "Slowly" is an adverb; "move" a vague, bland verb. Instead, name the action: "He pads across the room." "He (ambles, strolls, moseys, saunters, drags himself, staggers, waltzes, glides, lumbers, tiptoes, creeps, slouches, shuffles, waddles, minces, trudges, teeters, lurches, gropes, hobbles) across the room." All are slow but each vivid and distinctively different from the others.

Eliminate "is" and "are" throughout. Onscreen nothing is in a state of being; story life is an unending flux of change, of becoming. Not: "There is a big house on a hill above a small town." "There is," "They are," "It is," "He/She is" are the weakest possible ways into any English sentence. And what's a "big house"? Chateau? Hacienda? A "hill"? Ridge? Bluff? A "small town"? Crossroads? Hamlet? Perhaps: "A mansion guards the headlands above the village." With a Hemingwayesque shunning of Latinate and abstrate terms, of adjectives and adverbs, in favor of the most specific, active verbs and concrete nouns possible, even establishing shots come alive. Fine film description requires an imagination and a vocabulary.

Eliminate all metaphor and simile that cannot pass this test: "What do I see (or hear) onscreen?" As Milos Forman observed, "In film, a tree is a tree." "As if," for example, is a trope that doesn't exist onscreen. A character doesn't come through a door "as if." He comes through the door—period. The metaphor "A mansion guards . . ." and simile "The door slams like a gunshot . . ." pass the test in that a mansion can be photographed from a foreground angle that gives the impression it shelters or guards a village below it; a door slam can crack the ear like a gunshot. In fact, in MISSING the sound effects of all door slams were done with gunshots to subliminally increase tension as the conscious mind hears a door slam but the unconscious reacts to a gunshot.

These, on the other hand, were found in submissions to the European Script Fund: "The sun sets like a tiger's eye closing in the jungle," and, "The road twists and knifes and gouges its way up the hillside, struggling until it reaches the rim, then disappears out of sight before bursting onto the horizon." They are director traps, seductive but unphotographable. Although the European writers of these passages lack screenwriting discipline, they are ingenuously trying to be expressive; whereas American writers, out of cynicism and laziness, often resort to sarcasm:

"BENNY, in his thirties, is a small, muscular Englishman with an air of mania that suggests that, at least once in his life, he's bitten the head off a chicken." And, "You guessed it. Here comes the sex scene. I'd write it, but my mother reads these things." Amusing, but that's what these writers want us to think so we don't notice that they can't or won't write. They've resorted to bald telling masked by sarcasm because they haven't the craft, talent, or pride to create a scene that acts out the simplest of ideas.

Eliminate "we see" and "we hear." "We" doesn't exist. Once into the story ritual, the theatre could be empty for all we care. Instead, "We see" injects an image of the crew looking through the lens and shatters the script reader's vision of the film.

Eliminate all camera and editing notations. In the same way actors ignore behavioral description, directors laugh at RACK FOCUS TO, PAN TO, TIGHT TWO SHOT ON, and all other efforts to direct the film from the page. If you write TRACK ON, does the reader see a film flowing through his imagination? No. He now sees *a film being made*. Delete CUT TO, SMASH CUT TO, LAP DISSOLVE TO, and other transitions. The reader assumes that all changes of angle are done on a cut.

The contemporary screenplay is a *Master Scene* work that includes only those angles absolutely necessary to the telling of the story and no more. For example:

INT. DINING ROOM—DAY

Jack enters, dropping his briefcase on the antique chair next to the door. He notices a note propped up on the dining room table. Strolling over, he picks up the note, tears it open, and reads. Then crumpling the note, he drops into a chair, head in hands.

If the audience knows the contents of the note from a previous scene, then the description stays on Jack reading and slumping into a chair. If, however, it's vital that the audience read the note with Jack or it wouldn't be able follow the story, then:

INT. DINING ROOM—DAY

Jack enters, dropping his briefcase on the antique chair next to the door. He notices a note propped up on the dining room table. Strolling over, he picks it up and tears it open.

INSERT NOTE:

Calligraphic handwriting reads: Jack, I've packed and left. Do not try to contact me. I have a lawyer. She will be in touch. Barbara

ON SCENE

Jack crumples the note and drops into a chair, head in hands.

Another example: If, as Jack sits, head in hands, he were to hear a car pull outside and hurry to a window, and it's critical to audience comprehension that they see what Jack sees at that moment, then continuing from above:

ON SCENE

Jack crumples the note and drops into a chair, head in hands.

Suddenly, a car PULLS UP outside. He hurries to the window.

JACK's POV

through the curtains to the curb. Barbara gets out of her station wagon, opens the hatch and takes out suitcases.

ON JACK

turning from the window, hurling Barbara's note across the room.

If, however, the audience would assume that car pulling up is Barbara coming back to Jack because she's done it twice before and Jack's angry reaction says it all, then the description would stay on the Master Shot of Jack in the dining room.

Beyond the essential storytelling angles, however, the Master Scene screenplay gives the writer a strong influence on the film's direction. Instead of labeling angles, the writer suggests them by breaking single-spaced paragraphs into units of description with images and language subtly indicating camera distance and composition. For example:

INT. DINING ROOM—DAY

Jack enters and looks around the empty room. Lifting his briefcase above his head, he drops it with a THUMP on the fragile, antique chair next to the door. He listens. Silence.

Pleased with himself, he ambles for the kitchen, when suddenly he's brought up short.

A note with his name on it sits propped against the rose-filled vase on the dinning table.

Nervously he twists his wedding ring.

Taking a breath, he strolls over, picks up the note, tears it open, and reads.

Rather than writing the above into a thick block of single spaced prose, lines of white split it into five units that suggest in order: A wide angle covering most of the room, a moving shot through the room, a close-up on the note, an even tighter close-up on Jack's ring finger, and a medium follow-shot to the table.

The briefcase insult to Barbara's antique chair and Jack's nervous gesture with his wedding ring express his shifts of feeling. Actor and director are always free to improvise new business of their own, but the miniparagraphs lead the reader's inner eye through a pattern of action/reaction between Jack and the room, Jack and his emotions, Jack and his wife as represented in her note. That's the life of the scene. Now director and actor must capture it under the influence of this pattern. How exactly will be their creative tasks. In the meantime, the effect of the Master Scene technique is a readability that translates into the sensation of watching a film.

IMAGE SYSTEMS

The Screenwriter As Poet

"Pity the poor screenwriter, for he cannot be a poet" is not in fact true. Film is a magnificent medium for the poet's soul, once the screenwriter understands the nature of story *poetics* and its workings within a film.

Poetic does not mean pretty. Decorative images of the kind that send audiences out of disappointing films muttering "but it's beautifully photographed" are not poetic. THE SHELTERING SKY: Its human content is aridity, a desperate meaninglessness—what was once called an *existential crisis*, and the novel's desert setting was metaphor for the barrenness of the protagonists' lives. The film, however, glowed with the postcard glamour of a tourist agency travelogue, and little or nothing of the suffering at its heart could be felt. Pretty pictures are appropriate if the subject is pretty: THE SOUND OF MUSIC.

Rather, poetic means an *enhanced expressivity*. Whether a story's content is beautiful or grotesque, spiritual or profane, quietistic or violent, pastoral or urban, epic or intimate, it wants full expression. A good story well told, well directed and acted, and perhaps a good film. All that plus an enrichment and deepening of the work's expressivity through its poetics, and perhaps a great film.

To begin with, as audience in the ritual of story, we react to every image, visual or auditory, symbolically. We instinctively sense that each object has been selected to mean more than itself and so we add a connotation to every denotation. When an automobile pulls into a shot, our reaction is not a neutral thought such as "vehicle"; we give it a connotation. We think, "Huh. Mercedes . . . rich. Or, "Lamborghini . . . foolishly rich." "Rusted-out Volkswagen . . . artist." "Harley-Davidson . . . dangerous." "Red Trans-Am . . . problems with sexual identity." The storyteller then builds on this natural inclination in the audience.

The first step in turning a well-told story into a poetic work is to exclude 90 percent of reality. The vast majority of objects in the world have the wrong connotations for any specific film. So the spectrum of possible imagery must be sharply narrowed to those objects with appropriate implications.

In production, for example, if a director wants a vase added to a shot, this prompts an hour's discussion, and a critical one. What kind of vase? What period? What shape? Color? Ceramic, metal, wood? Are there flowers in it? What kind? Where located? Foreground? Mid-ground? Background? Upper left of the shot? Lower right? In or out of focus? Is it lit? Is it touched as a prop? Because this isn't just a vase, it's a highly charged, symbolic object resonating meaning to every other object in the shot and forward and backward through the film. Like all works of art, a film is a unity in which every object relates to every other image or object.

Limited to what's appropriate, the writer then empowers the film with an *Image System*, or systems, for there are often more than one.

An IMAGE SYSTEM is a strategy of motifs, a category of imagery embedded in the film that repeats in sight and sound from beginning to end with persistence and great variation, but with equally great subtlety, as a subliminal communication to increase the depth and complexity of aesthetic emotion.

"Category" means a subject drawn from the physical world that's broad enough to contain sufficient variety. For example, a dimension of nature—animals, the seasons, light and dark—or a dimension of human culture—buildings, machines, art. This category must repeat because one or two isolated symbols have little effect. But the power of an organized return of images is immense, as variety and repetition drive the Image System to the seat of the audience's unconscious. Yet, *and most important*, a film's poetics must be handled with virtual invisibility and go consciously unrecognized.

An Image System is created one of two ways, via External or Internal Imagery. External Imagery takes a category that outside the film already has a symbolic meaning and brings it in to mean the same thing in the film it means outside the film: for example, to use the national flag—a symbol of patriotism and love of country—to mean patriotism, love of country. In ROCKY IV, for example, after Rocky defeats the Russian boxer, he wraps himself in a massive American flag. Or to use a crucifix, a symbol of love of God and religious feelings, to mean love of God, religious feelings; a spider's web to mean entrapment; a teardrop to mean sadness. External Imagery, I must point out, is the hallmark of the student film.

Internal Imagery takes a category that outside the film may or may not have a symbolic meaning attached but brings it into the film to give it an entirely new meaning appropriate to this film and this film alone.

LES DIABOLIQUE: In 1955 director/screenwriter Henri-Georges Clouzot adapted Pierre Boileau's novel, *Celle Qui N'etait Pas* to the screen. In it Christina (Vera Clouzot) is an attractive young woman but very shy, quiet, and sensitive. She has suffered from a heart condition since childhood and is never in the best of health. Years before she inherited an impressive estate in the suburbs of Paris that has been turned into an exclusive boarding school. She runs this school with her husband, Michel (Paul Meurisse), a sadistic, abusive, malignant bastard who delights in treating his wife like dirt. He's having an affair with one of the school's teachers, Nicole (Simone Signoret), and he's as vicious and cruel to his mistress as he is to his wife.

Everybody knows about this affair. In fact, the two women have become best friends, both suffering under the heel of this brute. Early in the film they decide that the only way out of their problem is to kill him.

One night they lure Michel to an apartment in a village well away from the school where they've secretly filled a bathtub full of water. He comes in, dressed in his three-piece suit, and arrogantly taunts and insults his two women while they get him as drunk as they possibly can, then try to drown him in the bathtub. But he's not that drunk and it's a hell of a struggle. The terror nearly kills the poor wife, but Nicole rushes into the living room and grabs a ceramic statue of a panther from the coffee table. She loads this heavy thing on the man's chest. Between the weight of the statue and her own strength she manages to hold him down under the water long enough to drown him.

The women wrap the body in a tarp, hide it in the back of a pickup truck, and sneak back to the campus in the middle of the night. The school's swimming pool hasn't been used all winter; an inch of algae covers the water. The women dump the body in and it submerges out of sight. They quickly retire and wait for the next day when the body will float up and be discovered. But the next day comes and goes and the body does not float up. Days go by and the body will not float up.

Finally, Nicole accidentally on purpose drops her car keys in the pool and asks one of the older students to retrieve them. The kid dives down under the scum and searches and searches and searches. He comes up, gulps some air, then goes down again and searches and searches and searches. He comes up to gulp air, then goes down a third time and searches and searches and searches. At last he surfaces . . . with the car keys.

The women then decide it's time to clean the swimming pool. They order the pool drained and stand at its edge, watching as the scum goes down and down and down and down . . . to the drain. But there is no body. That afternoon a dry cleaner's van drives out from Paris to deliver the cleaned and pressed suit that the man died in. The women rush into Paris to the cleaners where they find a receipt, and on it is the address of a boardinghouse. They head there and talk to a concierge who says, "Yes, yes, there was a man living here but . . . he moved this morning."

They go back to the school and even more bizarre things happen: Michel appears and disappears in the windows of the school. When they look at the senior class graduation photo, there he is standing behind the students, slightly out of focus. They can't imagine what's going on. Is he a ghost? Did he somehow survive the drowning and he's doing this to us? Did someone else find the body? Are they doing this?

Summer vacation comes and all the students and teachers leave. Then Nicole herself departs. She packs her bags, saying she can't take this anymore, abandoning the poor wife alone.

That evening Christina can't sleep; she sits up in bed, wide awake, her heart pounding. Suddenly in the dead of night she hears the sound of typing coming from her husband's office. She slowly gets up and edges down a long corridor, hand on her heart, but just as she touches the office doorknob, the typing stops.

She eases open the door and there, alongside the typewriter, are her husband's gloves . . . like two huge hands. Then she hears the most terrifying sound imaginable: dripping water. Now she heads toward the bathroom off the office, her heart raging. She creaks open the bathroom door and there he is—still in his three-piece suit, submerged in a bathtub full of water, the faucet dripping.

The body sits up, water cascades off. Its eyes open but there are no eyeballs. Hands reach out for her, she grabs her chest, has a fatal heart attack, and drops dead on the floor. Michel reaches under his eyelids and removes white plastic inserts. Nicole jumps out of a closet. They embrace and whisper, "We did it!"

The opening titles of LES DIABOLIQUE look as if they're over an abstract painting of grays and blacks. But suddenly, as titles end, a truck tire splashes from bottom to top of the screen and we realize we've been looking at the top angle view of a mud puddle. The camera comes up on a rainy landscape. From this first moment on, Image System "water" is continually and subliminally repeated. It's always drizzly and foggy. Condensation on windows runs in little drops to the sills. At dinner they eat fish. Characters drink wine and tea while Christina sips her heart medicine. When the teachers discuss summer vacation, they talk of going to the South of France to "take the waters." Swimming pool, bathtubs . . . it's one of the dampest films ever made.

Outside this film water is a universal symbol of all things positive: sanctification, purification, the feminine—archetype for life itself. But Clouzot reverses these values until water takes on the power of death, terror, and evil, and the sound of a dripping faucet brings the audience up out of its seats.

CASABLANCA weaves three Image Systems. Its primary motifs create a sense of imprisonment as the city of Casablanca becomes a virtual penitentiary. Characters whisper their "escape" plans as if the police were prison guards. The beacon on the airport tower moves through the streets like a searchlight scanning a prison compound, while window blinds, room dividers, stair railings, even the leaves of potted palms create shadows like the bars of prison cells.

The second system builds a progression from the particular to the archetypal. Casablanca starts as a refugee center but becomes a mini-United Nations filled with not only Arab and European faces but Asian and African ones as well. Rick and his friend Sam are the only Americans we meet. Repeated images, including dialogue in which characters speak to Rick as if he were a country, associate Rick to America until he comes to symbolize America itself and Casablanca the world. Like the United States in 1941 Rick is steadfastly neutral, wanting no part in yet another World War. His conversion to the fight subliminally congratulates America for finally taking sides against tyranny.

The third system is one of linking and separating. A number of images and compositions within the frame are used to link Rick and Ilsa, making the subliminal point that although these two are apart, they belong together. The counterpoint to this is a series of images and compositional designs that separate Ilsa from Laszlo, giving the opposite impression that although these two are together, they belong apart.

THROUGH A GLASS DARKLY is a multiplot film with six story lines—three positive climaxes devoted to the father, three negative endings to his daughter—in a point/counterpoint design that interweaves no fewer than four Image Systems. The father's stories are marked by open spaces, light, intellect, and verbal communication; the daughter's conflicts are expressed in closed spaces, darkness, animal images, and sexuality.

CHINATOWN also employs four systems, two of External Imagery, two of Internal Imagery. The primary internalized system is motifs of "blind seeing" or seeing falsely: Windows; rearview mirrors; eyeglasses, and particularly broken spectacles; cameras; binoculars; eyes themselves, and even the open, unseeing eyes of the dead, all gather tremendous forces to suggest that if we are looking for evil out in the world, we're looking in the wrong direction. It is in here. In us. As Mao Tse-tung once said, "History is the symptom, we are the disease."

The second internalized system takes political corruption and turns it into social cement. False contracts, subverted laws, and acts of corruption become that which hold society together and create "progress." Two systems of External Imagery, water versus drought and sexual cruelty versus sexual love have conventional connotations but are used with a sharp-edged effectiveness.

When ALIEN was released *Time* magazine ran a ten-page article with stills and drawings asking the question: Has Hollywood gone too far? For this film incorporates a highly erotic Image System and contains three vivid "rape" scenes.

When Gail Anne Hurd and James Cameron made the sequel, ALIENS, they not only switched genres from *Horror* to *Action/Adventure*, they reinvented the Image System to motherhood as Ripley becomes the surrogate mother of the child Newt (Carrie Henn), who in turn is the surrogate mother of her broken doll. The two are up against the most terrifying "mother" in the universe, the gigantic monster queen who lays her eggs in a womblike nest. In dialogue, Ripley remarks, "The monsters make you pregnant."

AFTER HOURS works on only one internalized refrain but with a rich variety: Art. But not as the ornament of life. Rather, art as a weapon. The art and artists of Manhattan's Soho district constantly assault the protagonist, Paul (Griffin Dunne), until he's encapsulated inside a work of art and stolen by Cheech and Chong.

Going back through the decades, Hitchcock's *Thrillers* combine images of religiosity with sexuality, while John Ford's *Westerns* counterpoint wilderness with civilization. In fact, traveling back through the centuries we realize that Image Systems are as old as story itself. Homer invented beautiful motifs for his epics, as did Aeschylus, Sophocles, and Euripides for their plays. Shakespeare submerged a unique Image System into each of his works, as did Melville, Poe, Tolstoy, Dickens, Orwell, Hemingway, Ibsen, Chekhov, Shaw, Beckett—all great novelists and playwrights have embraced this principle.

And who, after all, invented screenwriting? Novelists and playwrights who came to the cradles of our art in Hollywood, London, Paris, Berlin, Tokyo, and Moscow to write the scenarios of silent films. Film's first major directors, such as D. W. Griffith, Eisenstein, and Murnau, did their apprenticeship in the theatre; they too realized that, like a fine play, a film can be taken to the sublime by the repetition of a subliminal poetics.

And an Image System *must be* subliminal. The audience is not to be aware of it. Years ago as I watched Buñuel's VIRIDIANA, I noticed that Buñuel had introduced an Image System of rope: A child jump ropes, a rich man hangs himself with a rope, a poor man uses rope as a belt. About the fifth time a piece of rope came on the screen the audience shouted in unison, "Symbol!"

Symbolism is powerful, more powerful than most realize, as long as it bypasses the conscious mind and slips into the unconscious. As it does while we dream. The use of symbolism follows the same principle as scoring a film. Sound doesn't need cognition, so music can deeply affect us when we're unconscious of it. In the same way, symbols touch us and move us—*as long as we don't recognize them as symbolic*. Awareness of a symbol turns it into a neutral, intellectual curiosity, powerless and virtually meaningless.

Why, then, do so many contemporary writer/directors label their symbols? The hamhanded treatment of "symbolic" images in the remake of CAPE FEAR, BRAM STOKER'S DRACULA, and THE PIANO, to name three of the more barefaced examples. I can think of two likely reasons: First, to flatter the elite audience of self-perceived intellectuals that watches at a safe, unemotional distance while collecting ammunition for the postfilm ritual of cafe criticism. Second, to influence, if not control, critics and the reviews they write. Declamatory symbolism requires no genius, just egotism ignited by misreadings of Jung and Derrida. It is a vanity that demeans and corrupts the art.

Some argue that the film's Image System is the director's work and that he or she alone should create it. And I've no argument with that, for ultimately the director is responsible for every square inch of every shot in the film. Except . . . how many working directors understand what I've explained above? Few. Perhaps two dozen in the world today. Just the very best, while, unfortunately, the vast majority cannot tell the difference between decorative and expressive photography.

I argue that the screenwriter should begin the film's Image System and the director and designers finish it. It's the writer who first envisions the ground of all imagery, the story's physical and social world. Often, as we write, we discover that spontaneously we've already begun the work, that a pattern of imagery has found its way into our descriptions and dialogue. As we become aware of that, we devise variations and quietly embroider them into the story. If an Image System doesn't arrive on its own, we invent one. The audience won't care how we do it; it only wants the story to work.

TITLES

A film's title is the marketing centerpiece that "positions" the audience, preparing it for the experience ahead. Screenwriters, therefore, cannot indulge in literary, nontitle titles: TESTAMENT, for example, is actually a film about postnuclear holocaust; LOOKS AND SMILES portrays desolate lives on welfare. My favorite nontitle tile is MOMENT BY MOMENT. MOMENT BY MOMENT is the working title I always use until I figure out the title.

To title means *to name*. An effective title points to something solid that is actually in the story—character, setting, theme, or genre. The best titles often name two or all elements at once.

JAWS names a character, sets the story in the wilds, and gives us the theme, man against nature, in the *Action/Adventure* genre. KRAMER VS. KRAMER names two characters, a divorce theme, and *Domestic Drama*. STAR WARS titles an epic conflict of galactic warriors. PERSONA suggests a cast of psychologically troubled characters and a theme of hidden identities. LA DOLCE VITA places us in a decadent setting among the urban rich. MY BEST FRIEND'S WEDDING establishes characters, setting, and *Romantic Comedy*.

A title, of course, isn't the only marketing consideration. As the legendary Harry Cohn once observed, "MOGAMBO is a terrible title. MOGAMBO, starring Clark Gable and Ava Gardner, is a great f . . . ing title."

19

A WRITER'S METHOD

Professional writers may or may not receive critical acclaim, but they're in control of the craft, have access to their talent, improve their performance over the years, and make a living from the art. A struggling writer may at times produce quality, but from day to day he cannot make his talent perform when and as he wants, doesn't progress in quality from story to story, and receives little, if any, income from his efforts. On the whole, the difference between those who succeed and those who struggle is their opposed methods of work: inside out versus outside in.

WRITING FROM THE OUTSIDE IN

The struggling writer tends to have a way of working that goes something like this: He dreams up an idea, noodles on it for a while, then rushes straight to the keyboard:

EXT. HOUSE—DAY

Description, description, description. Characters A and B enter.

                    CHARACTER A
          Dialogue, dialogue, dialogue.

                    CHARACTER B
          Dialogue, dialogue, dialogue.

Description, description, description, description, description.

He imagines and writes, writes and dreams until he reaches page 120 and stops. Then he hands out Xerox copies to friends and back come their reactions: "Oh, it's nice, and I love that scene in the garage when they threw paint all over each other, was that funny or what? And when the little kid came down at night in his pajamas, how sweet! The scene on the beach was so romantic, and when the car blew up, exciting. But I don't know . . . there's something about the ending . . . and the middle . . . and the way it starts . . . that just doesn't work for me."

So the struggling writer gathers friends' reactions and his own thoughts to start the second draft with this strategy: "How can I keep the six scenes that I love and that everyone else loves and somehow pretzel this film through them in a way that'll work?" With a little more thought he's back at the keyboard:

INT. HOUSE—NIGHT

Description, description, description. Characters A and C enter while Character B watches from hiding.

CHARACTER A
Dialogue, dialogue, dialogue.

CHARACTER C
Dialogue, dialogue, dialogue.

Description, description, description, description, description.

He imagines and writes, writes and dreams, but all the while he clings like a drowning man to his favorite scenes until a rewrite comes out the other end. He makes copies and hands them out to friends and back come reactions: "It's different, decidedly different. But I'm so glad you kept that scene in the garage and with the kid in his pajamas and the car on the beach . . . great scenes. But . . .

there's still something about that ending and the middle and the way it starts that just doesn't work for me."

The writer then does a third draft and a fourth and a fifth but the process is always the same: He clings to his favorite scenes, twisting a new telling through them in hopes of finding a story that works. Finally a year's gone by and he's burned out. He declares the screenplay perfect and hands it to his agent, who reads it without enthusiasm, but because he's an agent, he does what he must. He too makes copies, papers Hollywood, and back come reader reports: "Very nicely written, good crisp, actable dialogue, vivid scene description, fine attention to detail, the story sucks. PASS ON IT." The writer blames the Philistine tastes of Hollywood and gears up for his next project.

WRITING FROM THE INSIDE OUT

Successful writers tend to use the reverse process. If, hypothetically and optimistically, a screenplay can be written from first idea to last draft in six months, these writers typically spend the first four of those six months writing on stacks of three-by-five cards: a stack for each act—three, four, perhaps more. On these cards they create the story's *step-outline*.

Step-Outline

As the term implies, a step-outline is the story told in steps.

Using one- or two-sentence statements, the writer simply and clearly describes what happens in each scene, how it builds and turns. For example: "He enters expecting to find her at home, but instead discovers her note saying she's left for good."

On the back of each card the writer indicates what step in the design of the story he sees this scene fulfilling—at least for the moment. Which scenes set up the Inciting Incident? Which is the Inciting Incident? First Act Climax? Perhaps a Mid-Act Climax? Second Act? Third? Fourth? Or more? He does this for Central Plot and subplots alike.

He confines himself to a few stacks of cards for months on end for this critical reason: He wants to destroy his work. Taste and experience tell him that 90 percent of everything he writes, regardless of his genius, is mediocre at best. In his patient search for quality, he must create far more material than he can use, then destroy it. He may sketch a scene a dozen different ways before finally throwing the *idea* of the scene out of the outline. He may destroy sequences, whole acts. A writer secure in his talent knows there's no limit to what he can create, and so he trashes everything less than his best on a quest for a gem-quality story.

This process, however, doesn't mean the writer isn't filling pages. Day after day a huge stack grows on the side of the desk: but these are biographies, the fictional world and its history, thematic notations, images, even snippets of vocabulary and idiom. Research and imaginings of all kinds fill a file cabinet while the story is disciplined to the step-outline.

Finally, after weeks or months, the writer discovers his Story Climax. With that in hand, he reworks, as needed, backward from it. At last he has a story. Now he goes to friends, but not asking for a day out of their lives—which is what we ask when we want a conscientious person to read a screenplay. Instead he pours a cup of coffee and asks for ten minutes. Then he pitches his story.

The writer never shows his step-outline to people because it's a tool, too cryptic for anyone but the writer to follow. Instead, at this critical stage, he wants to tell or pitch his story so he can see it unfold in time, watch it play on the thoughts and feelings of another human being. He wants to look in that person's eyes and see the story happen there. So he pitches and studies the reactions: Is my friend hooked by my Inciting Incident? Listening and leaning in? Or are his eyes wandering? Am I holding him as I build and turn the progressions? And when I hit the Climax, do I get a strong reaction of the kind I want?

Any story pitched from its step-outline to an intelligent, sensitive person must be able to grab attention, hold interest for ten minutes, and pay it off by moving him to a meaningful, emotional experience—just as my LES DIABOLIQUE pitch hooked, held, and moved you. Regardless of genre, if a story can't work in ten minutes, how will it work in 110 minutes? It won't get better when it gets bigger. Everything that's wrong with it in a ten-minute pitch is ten times worse onscreen.

Until a good majority of listeners respond with enthusiasm, there's no point going forward. "With enthusiasm" doesn't mean people leap up and kiss you on both cheeks, rather they whisper "Wow" and fall silent. A fine work of art—music, dance, painting, story—has the power to silence the chatter in the mind and lift us to another place. When a story, pitched from a step-outline, is so strong it brings silence—no comments, no criticism, just a look of pleasure—that's a hell of a thing and time is too precious to waste on a story that hasn't that power. Now the writer's ready to move to the next stage—the treatment.

Treatment

To "treat" the step-outline, the writer expands each scene from its one or two sentences to a paragraph or more of double-spaced, present-tense, moment by moment description:

Dining Room—Day Jack walks in and tosses his briefcase on the chair next to the door. He looks around. The room is empty. He calls her name. Gets no answer. He calls it again, louder and louder. Still no answer. As he pads to the kitchen, he sees a note on the table. Picks it up, reads it. The note says that she has left him for good. He drops in the chair, head in hands, and starts to cry.

> *In treatment the writer indicates what characters talk about—
> "he wants her to do this, but she refuses," for example—but
> never writes dialogue. Instead, he creates the subtext—the true
> thoughts and feelings underneath what is said and done. We
> may think we know what our characters are thinking and
> feeling, but we don't know we know until we write it down:*

Dining Room—Day The door opens and Jack leans on the jamb, exhausted from a day of failed and frustrating work. He looks around the room, sees she's not around, and hopes like hell she's out. He really doesn't want to have to deal with her today. To be sure he has the house to himself, he calls her name. Gets no answer. Calls out louder and louder. Still no answer. Good. He's finally alone. He lifts his briefcase high in the air drops it with a thud onto her precious Chippendale chair next to the door. She hates him for scratching her antiques but today he doesn't give a damn.

Hungry, he heads for the kitchen, but as he crosses the room he notices a note on the dining-room table. It's one of those damn, annoying notes that she's always leaving around, taped to the bath-room mirror or the refrigerator or whatever. Irritated, he picks it up and tears it open. Reading it, he discovers that she's left him for good. As his legs go weak, he drops into a chair, a knot twisting in his gut. His head falls into his hands and he starts to cry. He's sur-prised by his outburst, pleased he can still feel some emotion. But his tears are not grief; they're the dam breaking with relief that the relationship is finally over.

•   •   •

The forty to sixty scenes of a typical screenplay, treated to a moment by moment description of all action, underlaid with a full subtext of the conscious and unconscious thoughts and feelings of all characters, will produce sixty, eight, ninety, or more double-spaced pages. In the studio system from the 1930s to the 1950s when producers ordered treatments from writers, they were often two hundred to three hundred pages long. The strategy of studio writers was to extract the screenplay from a much larger work so nothing would be overlooked or unthought.

The ten- or twelve-page "treatments" that pass around show business today are not treatments but outlines given enough words that a reader can follow the story. A ten-page outline is not nearly enough material for a screenplay. Today's writers may not return to the vast treatments of the studio system, but when a step-outline is expanded to a treatment of sixty to ninety pages, creative achieve-ment expands correspondingly.

At the treatment stage, we inevitably discover that things we thought would work a certain way in the step-outline now want to change. Research and imagination never stop, and so the characters and their world are still growing and evolving, leading us to revise any number of scenes. We won't change the overall design of the story because it worked every time we pitched it. But within that structure scenes may need to be cut, added, or reordered. We rework the treatment until every moment lives vividly, in text and subtext. That done, then and only then does the writer move to the screenplay itself.

SCREENPLAY

Writing a screenplay from a thorough treatment is a joy and often runs at a clip of five to ten pages per day. We now convert treatment description to screen description and add dialogue. And dialogue written at this point is invariably the finest dialogue we've ever written. Our characters have had tape over their mouths for so long, they can't wait to talk, and unlike so many films in which all characters speak with the same vocabulary and style, dialogue written after in-depth preparation creates character-specific voices. They don't all sound like one another and they don't all sound like the writer.

At the first draft stage, changes and revisions will still be needed. When characters are allowed to speak, scenes in treatment you thought would work a certain way now want to alter direction. When you find such a fault, it can rarely be fixed with a simple rewrite of dialogue or behavior. Rather, you must go back into the treatment and rework the setups, then perhaps go beyond the faulty scene to redo the payoff. A number of polishes may be necessary until you reach the final draft. You must develop your judgment and taste, a nose for your own bad writing, then call upon a relentless courage to root out weaknesses and turn them into strengths.

If you shortcut the process and rush straight to screenplay from outline, the truth is that your first draft is not a screenplay, it's a surrogate treatment—a narrow, unexplored, unimprovised, tissue-thin treatment. Event choice and story design must be given free rein to consume your imagination and knowledge. Turning Points must be imagined, discarded, and reimagined, then played out in text and subtext. Otherwise you have little hope of achieving excellence. Now, how and when do you want to do that? In treatment or screenplay? Either may work, but, more often than not, screenplay is a trap. The wise writer puts off the writing of dialogue for as long as possible because *the premature writing of dialogue chokes creativity.*

Writing from the outside in—writing dialogue in search of scenes, writing scenes in search of story—*is the least creative method.* Screenwriters habitually overvalue dialogue because they're the only words we write that actually reach the audience. All else is assumed by the film's images. If we type out dialogue before we know *what happens,* we inevitably fall in love with our words; we're loath to play with and explore events, to discover how fascinating our characters might become, because it would mean cutting our priceless dialogue. All improvisation ceases and our so-called rewriting is tinkering with speeches.

What's more, the premature writing of dialogue is the slowest way to work. It may send you in circles for years before you finally realize that not all your children are going to walk and talk their way to the screen; not every idea is worth being a motion picture. When do you want to find that out? Two years from now or two months from now? If you write the dialogue first, you'll be blind to this truth and wander forever. If you write from the inside out, you'll realize in the outline stage that you can't get the story to work. Nobody likes it when pitched. In truth, you don't like it. So you toss it in the drawer. Maybe years from now you'll pick it up and solve it, but for now you go on to your next idea.

As I offer this method to you, I'm fully aware that each of us, by trial and error, must find our own method, that indeed some writers short-cut the treatment stage and produce quality screenplays, and that in fact a few have written very well from the outside in. But I'm also left to wonder what brilliance they might have achieved had they taken greater pains. For the inside-out method is a way of working that's both disciplined and free, designed to encourage your finest work.

FADE OUT

You have pursued *Story* to its final chapter, and, with this step, taken your career in a direction many writers fear. Some, dreading that awareness of how they do what they do would cripple their spontaneity, never study the craft. Instead, they march along in a lockstep of unconscious habit, thinking it's instinct. Their dreams of creating unique works of power and wonder are seldom, if ever, realized. They put in long, tough days, for no matter how it's taken, the writer's road is never smooth, and because they have a gift, from time to time their efforts draw applause, but in their secret selves they know they're just taking talent for a walk. Such writers remind me of the protagonist of a fable my father loved to recite:

> *High above the forest floor, a millipede strolled along the branch of a tree, her thousand pairs of legs swinging in an easy gait. From the tree top, song birds looked down, fascinated by the synchroniza-tion of the millipede's stride. "That's an amazing talent," chirped the songbirds. "You have more limbs than we can count. How do you do it?" And for the first time in her life the millipede thought about this. "Yes," she wondered, "how **do** I do what I do?" As she turned to look back, her bristling legs suddenly ran into one another and tangled like vines of ivy. The songbirds laughed as the millipede, in a panic of confusion, twisted herself into a knot and fell to the earth below.*

You too may sense this panic. I know that when confronted with a rush of insights even the most experienced writer can be knocked off stride. Fortunately, my father's fable had an Act Two:

On the forest floor, the millipede, realizing that only her pride was hurt, slowly, carefully, limb by limb, unraveled herself. With patience and hard work, she studied and flexed and tested her appendages, until she was able to stand and walk. What was once instinct became knowledge. She realized she didn't have to move at her old, slow, rote pace. She could amble, strut, prance, even run and jump. Then, as never before, she listened to the symphony of the songbirds and let music touch her heart. Now in perfect command of thousands of talented legs, she gathered courage and, with a style of her own, danced and danced a dazzling dance that astonished all the creatures of her world.

Write every day, line by line, page by page, hour by hour. Keep *Story* at hand. Use what you learn from it as a guide, until command of its principles becomes as natural as the talent you were born with. Do this despite fear. For above all else, beyond imagination and skill, what the world asks of you is courage, courage to risk rejection, ridicule and failure. As you follow the quest for stories told with meaning and beauty, study thoughtfully but write boldly. Then, like the hero of the fable, your dance will dazzle the world.

SUGGESTED READINGS

My education owes a debt to the writers of many hundreds of books and essays on the art of story. Below, however, is a shortlist of works that have been the most insightful, the most inspiring.

Aristotle's Poetics. Translation and commentary by Stephen Halli-well. Chapel Hill: University of North Carolina Press, 1986.

Bjorkman, Stig, Torsten Manns, and Jonas Sima. *Bergman on Bergman.* Translation by Paul Britten Austin. New York: Simon & Schuster, 1973.

Booth, Wayne C. *The Rhetoric of Fiction.* 2d ed. Chicago: University of Chicago Press, 1983.

Burke, Kenneth. *The Philosophy of Literary Form.* Berkeley: University of California Press, 1974.

Burnett, Hallie, and Whit Burnett. *The Fiction Writer's Handbook.* New York: Barnes & Noble, 1979.

Campbell, Joseph. *The Hero with a Thousand Faces.* 2d ed. Princeton, N.J.: Princeton University Press, 1972.

Friedman, Norman. *Form and Meaning in Fiction.* Athens: University of Georgia Press, 1975.

Gardner, John. *On Becoming a Novelist.* New York: Harper & Row, 1983.

James, Henry. *The Art of the Novel.* Edited by R. P. Blackmur. New York: Scribner's, 1932.

Koestler, Arthur. *The Act of Creation.* New York: Macmillan, 1964.

Langer, Susanne K. *Feeling and Form.* New York: Macmillan, 1977.

Lawson, John Howard. *Film: The Creative Process.* New York: Hill & Wang, 1964.

Lawson, John Howard. *The Theory and Technique of Playwriting and Screenwriting.* New York: G.P. Putnam's, 1949.

Mamet, David. *On Directing Film*. New York: Viking Press, 1981.

Rowe, Kenneth T. *Write That Play*. New York: Funk & Wagnalls, 1939, 1968.

Scholes, Robert, and Robert Kellogg. *The Nature of Narrative*. Oxford: Oxford University Press, 1966.

FILMOGRAPHY

THE ACCIDENTAL TOURIST (US/1988)
Screenplay by Frank Galati, Lawrence Kasdan.
Based on the novel by Anne Tyler.
ADAM's RIB (US/1949)
Written by Ruth Gordon and Garson Kanin.
ADDICTED TO LOVE (US/1997)
Written by Robert Gordon.
AFTER HOURS (US/1985)
Written by Joseph Minion.
AIRPLANE (US/1980)
Written by Jim Abrahams, David Zucker, Jerry Zucker.
ALICE DOESN'T LIVE HERE ANYMORE (US/1974)
Written by Robert Getchell.
ALICE IN WONDERLAND (US/1951)
Animated film based on *The Adventures of Alice in Wonderland* and
  Through the Looking Glass by Lewis Carroll.
ALIEN (US/1979)
Screenplay by Dan O'Bannon.
Based on a story by Dan O'Bannon, Ronald Shusett.
ALIENS (US/1986)
Screenplay by James Cameron.
Based on a story by James Cameron, David Giler, Walter Hill, and
  on characters created by Dan O'Bannon, Ronald Shusett.
ALIVE (US/1993)
Screenplay by John Patrick Shanley.
Based on the nonfiction account by Piers Paul Read.
ALL THAT JAZZ (US/1979)
Written by Robert Alan Aurther, Bob Fosse.

AMADEUS (US/1984)
Screenplay by Peter Shaffer.
Based on the original stage play by Peter Shaffer.
AMARCORD (It/Fr/1973)
Written by Federico Fellini, Tonino Guerra.
AND JUSTICE FOR ALL (US/1979)
Written by Valerie Curtin, Barry Levinson.
ANGEL HEART (US/1987)
Screenplay by Alan Parker.
Based on the novel *Falling Angel* by William Hjortsberg.
ANIMAL FARM (UK/1955)
Animated film based on the novel by George Orwell.
ANNIE HALL (US/1977)
Written by Woody Allen, Marshall Brickman.
APOCALYPSE NOW (US/1979)
Written by John Milius, Francis Ford Coppola.
Suggested by the novella *Heart of Darkness* by Joseph Conrad.
ARACHNOPHOBIA (US/1990)
Written by Dan Jakoby, Wesley Strick.
Based on a story by Don Jacoby, Al Williams.
BABE (Aust/1995)
Screenplay by George Miller, Chris Noonan.
Based on the children's book *The Sheep-Pig* by Dick King-Smith.
BABETTE'S FEAST (Den/1987)
Screenplay by Gabriel Axel.
Based on the story by Isak Dinesen.
BABY BOOM (US/1987)
Written by Nancy Meyers and Charles Shyer.
THE BAD AND THE BEAUTIFUL (US/1952)
Screenplay by Charles Schnee.
Based on the short stories by George Bradshaw.
BAD DAY AT BLACK ROCK (US/1955)
Screenplay by Millard Kaufman.
Based on the short story "Bad Time at Honda" by Howard Breslin.
BAD TIMING (UK/1980)
Written by Yale Udoff.

BAMBI (US/1942)
Animated film based on the story by Felix Salten.
BARRY LYNDON (UK/1975)
Screenplay by Stanley Kubrick.
Based on the novel by W.M. Thackeray.
BARTON FINK (US/1991)
Written by Ethan Coen and Joel Coen.
BASIC INSTINCT (US/1992)
Written by Joe Eszterhas.
THE BATTLE OF ALGIERS (Algeria/It/1966)
Written by Franco Solinas, Gillo Pontecorvo.
BATTLESHIP POTEMKIN (USSR/1925)
Written by Sergei Eisenstein.
BEING THERE (US/W.Ger/1979)
Screenplay by Jerzy Kosinski.
Based on the novel by Jerzy Kosinski.
BEN HUR (US/1959)
Screenplay by Karl Tunberg.
Based on the novel by Lew Wallace.
BETRAYAL (UK/1982)
Screenplay by Harold Pinter.
Based on the play by Harold Pinter.
BETTY BLUE (Fr/1986)
Screenplay by Jean-Jacques Beineix.
Based on the novel 37 2 *Le Matin* by Philippe Dijan.
BIG (US/1988)
Written by Gary Ross, Anne Spielberg.
THE BIG SLEEP (US/1946)
Screenplay by William Faulkner, Leigh Brackett, Jules Furthman.
Based on the novel by Raymond Chandler.
BILLY BUDD (UK/1962)
Screenplay by Peter Ustinov, Robert Rossen.
Based on the novel by Herman Melville.
THE BIRDS (US/1963)
Screenplay by Evan Hunter.
Based on the short story by Daphne Du Maurier.

BLACK WIDOW (US/1987)
Written by Ronald Bass
BLADE RUNNER (US/1982)
Screenplay by Hampton Fancher, David Peoples.
Based on the novel *Do Androids Dream of Electric Sheep?* by Philip
    K. Dick.
BLAZING SADDLES (US/1974)
Written by Norman Steinberg, Mel Brooks, Andrew Bergman,
    Richard Pryor, Alan Unger.
BLIND DATE (US/1987)
Written by Dale Launer.
THE BLOOD OF A POET (Fr/1930)
Written by Jean Cocteau.
BLOW UP (US/1966)
Written by Michelangelo Antonioni, Tonino Guerra.
Based on a short story by Julio Cortazar.
BLUE VELVET (US/1986)
Written by David Lynch.
BOB ROBERTS (US/1992)
Written by Tim Robbins.
BODY HEAT (US/1981)
Written by Lawrence Kasdan.
BONFIRE OF THE VANITIES (US/1990)
Screenplay by Michael Cristofer.
Based on the novel by Tom Wolfe.
BRAM STOKER'S DRACULA (US/1992)
Screenplay by James V. Hart.
Based on the novel by Bram Stoker.
BRAZIL (UK/1984)
Written by Terry Gilliam, Tom Stoppard, Charles McKeown.
THE BREAKFAST CLUB (US/1985)
Written by John Hughes.
BREAKING THE WAVES (Den/1996)
Written by Lar Von Trier.

BREATHLESS (Fr/1959)

Screenplay by Jean-Luc Godard.

Based on an original treatment by Francois Truffaut.

THE BRIDGES OF MADISON COUNTY (US/1995)

Screenplay by Richard LaGravenese.

Based on the novel by Robert James Waller.

BRIEF ENCOUNTER (UK/1945)

Screenplay by Noel Coward, Anthony Havelock-Allan, David Lean, Ronald Neame.

Based on the one-act play *Still Life* by Noel Coward.

BRINGING UP BABY (US/1938)

Screenplay by Dudley Nichols, Hagar Wilde.

Based on a story by Hagar Wilde.

BULL DURHAM (US/1988)

Written by Ron Shelton.

BULLETS OVER BROADWAY (US/1994)

Written by Woody Allen, Douglas McGrath.

BUTCH CASSIDY AND THE SUNDANCE KID (US/1969)

Written by William Goldman.

THE CABINET OF DR. CALIGARI (Ger/1920)

Screenplay by Carl Mayer, Hans Janowitz.

Based on an original story by Carl Mayer, Hans Janowitz.

CAMP NOWHERE (US/1994)

Written by Andrew Kurtzman, Eliot Wald.

CAPE FEAR (US/1991)

Screenplay by Wesley Strick.

Based on the screenplay by James R. Webb and the novel *The Executioners* by John D. MacDonald.

CARNAL KNOWLEDGE (us/1971)

Written by Jules Feiffer.

CASABLANCA (US/1942)

Screenplay by Julius J. Epstein, Philip G.Epstein, Howard Koch.

Based on an unpublished play *Everybody Comes to Rick's* by Murray Burnett and Joan Alison.

CASINO (US/1995)
Screenplay by Nicolas Pileggi, Martin Scorcese.
Based on the book by Nicholas Pileggi.
CHARIOTS OF FIRE (UK/1981)
Written by Colin Welland.
UN CHIEN ANDALOU (Fr/1928)
Written by Luis Bunuel, Salvador Dali.
CHINATOWN (US/1974)
Written by Robert Towne.
CHOOSE ME (US/1984)
Written by Alan Rudolph.
CHUNKING EXPRESS (HK/1994)
Written by Wong Kar-Wai.
CITIZEN KANE (US/1941)
Written by Herman J. Mankewicz, Orson Welles.
CLAIRE'S KNEE (Fr/1970)
Written by Eric Rohmer.
CLEAN AND SOBER (US/1988)
Written by Tod Carroll.
CLOWNS (It/1970)
Written by Federico Fellini, Bernardino Zapponi.
COMING HOME (US/1978)
Written by Waldo Salt, Robert C. Jones.
Based on a story by Nancy Down.
THE CONVERSATION (US/1974)
Written by Francis Ford Coppola.
THE COOK, THE THIEF, HIS WIFE AND HER LOVER
    (UK/Fr/1989)
Written by Peter Greenaway.
COOL HAND LUKE (US/1967)
Screenplay by Donn Pearce, Frank R. Pierson.
Based on the novel by Donn Pearce.
COP (US/1988)
Screenplay by James B. Harris.
Based on the novel *Blood on the Moon* by James Ellroy.

CRIES AND WHISPERS (Swe/1972)
Written by Ingmar Bergman.
CRIMES AND MISDEMEANORS (US/1989)
Written by Woody Allen.
THE CRYING GAME (UK/1992)
Written by Neil Jordan.
DANCE WITH A STRANGER (UK/1984)
Written by Shelagh Delaney.
DANCES WITH WOLVES (US/1990)
Screenplay by Michael Blake.
Based on the novel by Michael Blake.
DANGEROUS LIAISONS (US/1988)
Screenplay by Christopher Hampton.
Based on the play *Les Liaisons Dangereuses* by Christopher
    Hampton, adapted from the novel by Choderlos de Laclos.
DAVID AND LISA (US/1962)
Screenplay by Eleanor Perry.
Based on the novel by Theodore Isaac Perry.
DEAD RINGERS (Can/1988)
Screenplay by David Cronenberg, Norman Snider.
Based on the book *Twins* by Bari Wood and Jack Geasland.
DEATH BY HANGING (Japan/1968)
Written by Tsutomu Tamura, Mamoru Sasaki, Michinori Fukao,
    Nagisa Oshima.
Based on a newspaper story.
DEATH IN VENICE (It/1971)
Screenplay by Luchino Visconti, Nicholas Badalucco.
Based on the novel by Thomas Mann.
DEATH WISH (US/1974)
Screenplay by Wendell Mayes.
Based on the novel by Brian Garfield.
THE DEER HUNTER (US/1978)
Screenplay by Deric Washburn.
Based on a story by Deric Washburn, Quinn K. Redeker, Louis
    Garfinkle, and Michael Cimino.

LES DIABOLIQUES (Fr/1954)
Screenplay by Henri-Georges Clouzot, Jerome Geronimi, Frederick
    Grendel, Rene Masson.
Based on the novel *Celle qui n'etait plus* by Pierre Boileau and
    Thomas Narcejac.
DIARY OF A COUNTRY PRIEST (Fr/1950)
Screenplay by Robert Bresson.
Based on the novel by Georges Bernanos.
DIE HARD (US/1988)
Screenplay by Jeb Stuart, Steven E. de Souza.
Based on the novel *Nothing Lasts Forever* by Roderick Thorp.
DINER (US/1982)
Written by Barry Levinson.
THE DIRTY DOZEN (US/UK/1967)
Screenplay by Nunnally Johnson, Lukas Heller.
Based on the novel by E. M. Nathanson.
THE DISCREET CHARM OF THE BOURGEOISE (Fr/It/Sp/1972)
Written by Luis Bunuel, Jean-Claude Carriere.
DO THE RIGHT THING (US/1989)
Written by Spike Lee.
THE DOCTOR (US/1991)
Screenplay by Robert Caswell.
Based on the book *A Taste of My Own Medicine* by Ed Rosenbaum.
DR. STRANGELOVE; OR, HOW I LEARNED TO STOP
    WORRYING AND LOVE THE BOMB (UK/1964)
Screenplay by Stanley Kubrick, Terry Southern, Peter George.
Based on the novel *Red Alert* by Peter George.
LA DOLCE VITA (It/Fr/1960)
Written by Federico Fellini, Tullio Pinelli, Brunello Rondi, Ennio
    Flaiano.
DOMINICK AND EUGENE (UK/1988)
Written by Alvin Sargent, Corey Blechman.
Based on a story by Danny Porforio.
DONA FLOR AND HER TWO HUSBANDS (Braz/1978)
Screenplay by Bruno Barreto.
Based on the novel by Jorge Amado.

DRACULA (US/1931)

Screenplay by Garratt Ford, dialogue by Dudley Murphy, from
    Hamilton Deane's and John L. Balderston's stage adaptation of
    the novel by Bram Stoker.

DRUGSTORE COWBOY (US/1989)

Screenplay by Gus Van Sant, Jr., Damiel Yost.

Based on the novel by James Fogle.

E.T. THE EXTRA-TERRESTRIAL (US/1982)

Written by Melissa Matheson.

EARTHQUAKE (US/1974)

Written by George Fox, Mario Puzo.

EAT DRINK MAN WOMAN (Taiwan/1994)

Written by Hui-Ling Wang, James Schamus, Ang Lee.

L'ECLISSE (It/Fr/1962)

Written by Michelangelo Antonioni, Tonino Guerra with Elio
    Bartolini and Ottiero Ottieri.

$8^1/_2$ (It/Fr/1963)

Written by Federico Fellini, Ennio Flaiano, Tullio Pinelli, Brunello
    Rondi.

THE ELECTRIC HORSEMAN (US/1979)

Written by Robert Garland.

THE ELEPHANT MAN (US/1980)

Written by Christopher De Vore, Eric Bergren, David Lynch.

Based on the books *The Elephant Man and Other Reminiscences* by
    Sir Frederick Treves and *The Elephant Man: A Study in Human
    Dignity* by Ashley Montagu.

ELEPHANT WALK (US/1954)

Screenplay by John Lee Mahin.

Based on the novel by Robert Standish.

THE EMPIRE STRIKES BACK (US/1980)

Screenplay by Leigh Brackett, Lawrence Kasdan.

Based on an original story by George Lucas.

THE ENGLISH PATIENT (UK/1996)

Screenplay by Anthony Minghella.

Based on the novel by Michael Ondaatje.

EQUUS (UK/1977)
Screenplay by Peter Shaffer.
Based on the play by Peter Shaffer.
EVERYONE SAYS I LOVE YOU (US/1996)
Written by Woody Allen.
EVITA (US/1996)
Screenplay by Alan Parker, Oliver Stone.
Based on the musical play by Andrew Lloyd Webber and Tim Rice.
THE EXORCIST (US/1973)
Screenplay by Peter William Blatty.
Based on the novel by Peter William Blatty.
THE FABULOUS BAKER BOYS (US/1989)
Written by Steve Kloves.
FACES (US/1968)
Written by John Cassavetes.
FALLING DOWN (US/1993)
Written by Ebbe Roe Smith.
FALLING IN LOVE (US/1984)
Written by Michael Cristofer.
FAREWELL MY CONCUBINE (HK/China/1993)
Screenplay by Lilian Lee, Lu Wei.
Based on the novel by Lilian Lee.
FAREWELL MY LOVELY (US/1975)
Screenplay by David Zelag Goodman.
Based on the novel by Raymond Chandler.
FELLINI's ROMA (It/Fr/1972)
Written by Federico Fellini, Bernardino Zapponi.
LE FEU FOLLET (Fr/1963)
Screenplay by Louis Malle.
Based on the novel by Pierre Drieu La Rochelle.
THE FIFTH ELEMENT (Fr/1997)
Written by Luc Besson, Robert Mark Kamen.
FIRST BLOOD (US/1982)
Screenplay by Michael Kozoll, William Sackheim, Sylvester
    Stallone.
Based on the novel by David Morrell.

THE FIRST DEADLY SIN (US/1980)
Screenplay by Mann Rubin.
Based on the novel by Lawrence Sanders.
A FISH CALLED WANDA (UK/1988)
Written by John Cleese.
Based on a story by John Cleese and Charles Crichton.
THE FISHER KING (US/1991)
Written by Richard LaGravenese.
FITZCARRALDO (WGer/1981)
Written by Werner Herzog.
FIVE EASY PIECES (US/1970)
Screenplay by Adrien Joyce.
Based on a story by Adrien Joyce and Bob Rafelson.
THE FLIGHT OF THE PHOENIX (US/1965)
Screenplay by Lukas Heller.
Based on the novel by Elleston Trevor.
FORREST GUMP (US/1994)
Written by Eric Roth.
Based on the novel by Winston Groom.
FOUR WEDDINGS AND A FUNERAL (UK/1994)
Written by Richard Curtis.
THE FUGITIVE (US/1993)
Screenplay by Jeb Stuart, David Twohy.
Based on a story by David Twohy and on characters created by Roy
    Huggins for the television series.
FULL METAL JACKET (UK/1987)
Screenplay by Stanley Kubrick, Michael Herr, Gustav Hasford.
Based on the novel *The Short Timers* by Gustav Hasford.
GALLIPOLI (Aust/1981)
Written by David Williamson.
GANDHI (UK/1982)
Written by John Briley.
GHOSTBUSTERS (US/1984)
Written by Dan Aykroyd, Harold Ramis.

GLENGARRY GLEN ROSS (US/1992)
Screenplay by David Mamet.
Based on the play by David Mamet.
GLORY (US/1989)
Screenplay by Kevin Jarre.
Based on the books *Lay This Laurel* by Lincoln Kirstein and *One Gallant Rush* by Peter Burchard, and the letters of Robert Gould Shaw.
THE GODFATHER (US/1972)
Screenplay by Francis Ford Coppola, Mario Puzo.
Based on the novel by Mario Puzo.
THE GODFATHER, PART II (US/1974)
Screenplay by Francis Ford Coppola, Mario Puzo.
Based on the novel by Mario Puzo.
GOING IN STYLE (US/1979)
Written by Martin Brest.
THE GOLD RUSH (US/1925)
Written by Charles Chaplin.
THE GOOD SON (US/1993)
Written by Ian McEwan.
THE GRADUATE (US/1967)
Screenplay by Calder Willingham, Buck Henry.
Based on the novel by Charles Webb.
GRAND CANYON (US/1991)
Written by Meg Kasdan, Lawrence Kasdan.
GRAND HOTEL (US/1932)
Screenplay by William A. Drake.
Based on the novel by Vicki Baum.
LA GRANDE ILLUSION (Fr/1937)
Written by Jean Renoir, Charles Spaak.
THE GREAT GATSBY (US/1974)
Screenplay by Francis Ford Coppola.
Based on the novel by F. Scott Fitzgerald.
THE GREAT TRAIN ROBBERY (US/1903)
Directed and filmed by Edwin S. Porter.

GREED (US/1924)
Screenplay by Erich von Stroheim, June Mathis.
Based on the novel *McTeague* by Frank Norris.
GROSSE POINT BLANK (US/1997)
Written by Tom Jankiewicz, D. V. DeVincentis, Steve Pink, John Cusack.
GROUNDHOG DAY (US/1993)
Written by Danny Rubin, Harold Ramis.
THE HAND THAT ROCKS THE CRADLE (US/1992)
Written by Amanda Silver.
HANNAH AND HER SISTERS (US/1986)
Written by Woody Allen.
HAROLD AND MAUDE (US/1971)
Written by Colin Higgins.
HIGH HOPES (UK/1988)
Written by Mike Leigh.
HIS GIRL FRIDAY (US/1940)
Screenplay by Charles Lederer.
Based on the play *The Front Page* by Ben Hecht and Charles MacArthur.
HOOP DREAMS (US/1994)
Documentary produced by Frederick Marx, Peter Gilbert, and director, Steve James.
HOPE AND GLORY (UK/1987)
Written by John Boorman.
THE HOSPITAL (US/1971)
Written by Paddy Chayefsky.
THE HOUR OF THE WOLF (Swe/1967)
Written by Ingmar Bergman.
HOWARDS END (UK/1992)
Screenplay by Ruth Prawer Jhabvala.
Based on the novel by E. M. Forster.
THE HURRICANE (US/1979)
Screenplay by Lorenzo Semple, Jr.
Based on the novel by Charles Nordhoff and James Norman Hall.

HUSBANDS (US/1970)
Written by John Cassavetes.
HUSBANDS AND WIVES (US/1992)
Written by Woody Allen.
THE HUSTLER (US/1961)
Screenplay by Robert Rossen, Sidney Carroll.
Based on the novel by Walter Tevis.
I NEVER PROMISED YOU A ROSE GARDEN (US/1977)
Screenplay by Gavin Lambert, Lewis John Carlino.
Based on the novel by Hannah Green.
IF . . . (UK/1968)
Screenplay by David Sherwin.
Based on the original script *Crusaders* by David Sherwin and John
　　Howlett.
IN THE HEAT OF THE NIGHT (US/1967)
Written by Stirling Sillphant.
IN THE REALM OF THE SENSES (Fr/Jap/1976)
Written by Nagisa Oshima.
THE IN-LAWS (US/1979)
Written by Andrew Bergman.
INTERVIEW WITH A VAMPIRE (US/1994)
Screenplay by Anne Rice.
Based on the novel by Anne Rice.
INTOLERANCE (US/1916)
Scenario: D.W. Griffith.
ISADORA (UK/1968)
Written by Melvyn Bragg, Clive Exton.
JFK (US/1991)
Screenplay by Oliver Stone, Zachary Sklar.
Based on the books *Trail of the Assassins* by Jim Garrison and *Cross-
　　fire: The Plot That Killed Kennedy* by Jim Marrs.
JAWS (US/1975)
Screenplay by Peter Benchley, Carl Gottlieb.
Based on the novel by Peter Benchley.
JERRY MAGUIRE (US/1996)
Written by Cameron Crowe.

JESUS OF MONTREAL (Can/1988)
Written by Denys Arcand.
JOHN AND MARY (US/1969)
Screenplay by John Mortimer.
Based on the novel by Mervyn Jones.
THE JOY LUCK CLUB (US/1993)
Screenplay by Amy Tan, Ronald Bass.
Based on the novel by Amy Tan.
JU DOU (China/1990)
Screenplay by Liu Heng.
Based on the story *Fuxi Fuxi* by Liu Heng.
JURASSIC PARK (US/1993)
Screenplay by Michael Crichton, David Koepp.
Based on the novel by Michael Crichton.
THE KID (US/1921)
Written by Charles Chaplin.
KISS OF THE SPIDER WOMAN (Br/1985)
Screenplay by Leonard Schrader.
Based on the novel by Manuel Puig.
KOYAANISQATSI (US/1983)
Written by Ron Fricke, Godfrey Reggio, Michael Hoenig, Alton
    Walpole.
KRAMER VS. KRAMER (US/1979)
Screenplay by Robert Benton.
Based on the novel by Avery Corman.
THE LADY EVE (US/1941)
Screenplay by Preston Sturges.
Based on the play by Monckton Hoffe.
The LAST DAYS OF POMPEII (It/1913)
Based on the novel by Edward Bulwer Lytton.
THE LAST EMPEROR (It/HK/UK/1987)
Written by Mark Peploe, Bernardo Bertolucci with Enzo Ungari.
Based on the autobiography *From Emperor to Citizen* by Pu Yi.
THE LAST SEDUCTION (US/1994)
Written by Steve Barancik

LAST YEAR AT MARIENBAD (Fr/It/1961)
Written by Alain Robbe-Grillet
A LEAGUE OF THEIR OWN (US/1992)
Written by Lowell Ganz and Babaloo Mandel.
Based on a story by Kim Wilson, Kelly Candaela.
LEAVING LAS VEGAS (US/1995)
Screenplay by Mike Figgis.
Based on the novel by John O'Brien.
LENNY (US/1974)
Screenplay by Julian Barry.
Based on the play by Julian Barry.
LETHAL WEAPON (US/1987)
Written by Shane Black.
LIKE WATER FOR CHOCOLATE (Mex/1991)
Screenplay by Laura Esquivel.
Based on the novel by Laura Esquivel.
THE LION KING (US/1994)
Written by Irene Mecchi, Jonathan Roberts, Linda Woolverton.
LITTLE BIG MAN (US/1970)
Screenplay by Calder Willingham.
Based on the novel by Thomas Berger.
The LITTLE MERMAID (US/1989)
Written by John Mosher, Ron Clements.
LITTLE SHOP OF HORRORS (US/1986)
Screenplay by Howard Ashman.
Based on the musical play by Howard Ashman and Alan Menken
    which was based on the 1960 film written by Charles Griffith.
LONE STAR (US/1996)
Written by John Sayles.
THE LONELINESS OF THE LONG DISTANCE RUNNER
    (UK/1962)
Screenplay by Alan Sillitoe.
Based on the short story by Alan Sillitoe.
LORD JIM (UK/US/1965)
Screenplay by Richard Brooks.
Based on the novel by Joseph Conrad.

LOVE SERENADE (Aust/1997)
Written by Shirley Barrett.
THE LOVED ONE (US/1965)
Screenplay by Terry Southern, Christopher Isherwood.
Based on the novel by Evelyn Waugh.
M (Ger/1931)
Written by Thea von Harbou, Fritz Lang.
Based on a magazine article by Egon Jacobson.
MAN BITES DOG (Bel/1992)
Written by Remy Belvaux, Andre Bonzel, Benoit Poelvoorde,
    Vincent Tavier.
THE MAN WHO WOULD BE KING (US/1975)
Screenplay by John Huston, Gladys Hill.
Based on the short story "The Man Who Would Be King" by
    Rudyard Kipling.
THE MANCHURIAN CANDIDATE (US/1962)
Screenplay by George Axelrod.
Based on the novel by Richard Condon.
MANHATTAN (US/1979)
Written by Woody Allen, Marshall Brickman.
MANHUNTER (US/1986)
Screenplay by Michael Mann.
Based on the novel *Red Dragon* by Thomas Harris.
THE MARK (UK/1961)
Screenplay by Sidney Buchman, Stanley Mann.
Based on the novel by Charles Israel.
MARTY (US/1955)
Screenplay by Paddy Chayefsky.
Based on the teleplay by Paddy Chayefsky.
MASCULINE FEMININE (Fr/1966)
Written by Jean-Luc Godard.
M.A.S.H. (US/1970)
Screenplay by Ring Lardner, Jr.
Based on the novel by Richard Hooker.
MEAN STREETS (US/1973)
Written by Martin Scorcese, Mardik Martin.

MEN IN BLACK (US/1997)
Written by Ed Solomon.
MEPHISTO (Hun/WGer/1981)
Screenplay by Istvan Szabo, Peter Dobai.
Based on the novel by Klaus Mann.
MESHES OF THE AFTERNOON (US/1943)
Written by Maya Deren, Alexander Hammid.
MICHAEL COLLINS (UK/1996)
Written by Neil Jordan.
MIDNIGHT COWBOY (US/1969)
Screenplay by Waldo Salt.
Based on the novel by James Leo Herlihy.
MIDNIGHT RUN (US/1988)
Written by George Gallo.
A MIDSUMMER NIGHT'S DREAM (US/1935)
Arranged for the screen by Charles Kenyon, Mary C. McCall.
Based on the play by William Shakespeare.
THE MISFITS (US/1961)
Written by Arthur Miller.
MISSING (US/1982)
Screenplay by Costa-Gavras, Donald Stewart.
Based on the non-fiction book *The Execution of Charles Horman* by
  Thomas Hauser.
MISTER SMITH GOES TO WASHINGTON (US/1939)
Written by Sidney Buchman.
Based on a story by Lewis R. Foster.
MRS. PARKER AND THE VICIOUS CIRCLE (US/1994)
Written by Alan Rudolph, Randy Sue Coburn.
MRS. SOFFEL (US/1984)
Written by Ron Nyswaner.
MOBY DICK (UK/1956)
Screenplay by Ray Bradbury, John Huston.
Based on the novel by Herman Melville.
MODERN TIMES (US/1935)
Written by Charles Chaplin.

MONTY PYTHON AND THE HOLY GRAIL (UK/1974)
Written by Graham Chapman, John Cleese, Terry Gilliam, Eric
    Idle, Michel Palin.
MOONSTRUCK (US/1987)
Written by John Patrick Shanley
THE MORNING AFTER (US/1986)
Written by James Hicks.
MOULIN ROUGE (UK/US/1952)
Screenplay by John Huston, Anthony Veiller.
Based on the novel by Pierre La Mure.
MURIEL's WEDDING (Aust/1996)
Written by P. J. Hogan.
THE MUSIC ROOM (Ind/1958)
Screenplay by Satyajit Ray.
Based on the novel by Tarashankar Banerjee.
MY BEST FRIEND's WEDDING (US/1997)
Written by Ronald Bass.
MY DINNER WITH ANDRE (US/1981)
Written by Wallace Shawn, Andre Gregory.
MY FAVORITE SEASON (Fr/1996)
Written by Pascal Bonitzer and André Téchiné.
MY MAN GODFREY (US/1936)
Written by Morrie Ryskind, Eric Hatch, Gregory La Cava.
NAKED (UK/1993)
Written by Mike Leigh.
THE NAKED GUN FROM THE FILES OF POLICE SQUAD
    (US/1988)
Written by Jerry Zucker, Jim Abrahams, David Zucker, Pat Proft.
NANOOK OF THE NORTH (Can/1922)
Written by Robert Flaherty.
NASHVILLE (US/1975)
Written by Joan Tewkesbury.
NASTY HABITS (UK/1976)
Screenplay by Robert Enders.
Based on the novel *The Abbess of Crewe* by Muriel Spark.

NATIONAL LAMPOON's ANIMAL HOUSE (US/1978)
Written by Harold Ramis, Douglas Kenney, Chris Miller.
NETWORK (US/1976)
Story and Screenplay by Paddy Chayefsky.
NIGHT AND FOG (Fr/1955)
Written by Alain Resnais.
A NIGHT AT THE OPERA (US/1935)
Written by George S. Kaufman, Morrie Ryskind.
THE NIGHT PORTER (It/1973)
Written by Liliana Cavani, Italo Moscati.
NIXON (US/1995)
Written by Stephen J. Rivele, Christopher Wilkinson, Oliver Stone.
LA NOTTE (It/Fr/1960)
Written by Michelangelo Antonioni, Ennio Flaiano, Tonino
    Guerra.
NOW, VOYAGER (US/1942)
Screenplay by Casey Robinson.
Based on the novel by Olive Higgins Prouty.
AN OFFICER AND A GENTLEMAN (US/1982)
Written by Douglas Day Stewart.
OH! WHAT A LOVELY WAR (UK/1969)
Screenplay by Len Deighton.
Based on the stage play by Joan Littlewood and Charles Chilton.
THE OLD MAN AND THE SEA (US/1958)
Screenplay by Peter Viertel.
Based on the novella by Ernest Hemingway.
ON GOLDEN POND (US/1981)
Screenplay by Ernest Thompson.
Based on the play by Ernest Thompson.
ON THE WATERFRONT (US/1954)
Screenplay by Budd Schulberg.
Based on the novel by Budd Schulberg.
ORDINARY PEOPLE (US/1980)
Screenplay by Alvin Sargent.
Based on the novel by Judith Guest.

OUT OF AFRICA (US/1985)

Screenplay by Kurt Luedtke.

Based on *Out of Africa* by Isak Dinesen, *Isak Dinesen: The Life of a Story-Teller* by Judith Thurman, and *Silence Will Speak* by Errol Trzebinski.

OUTBREAK (US/1995)

Written by Lawrence Dworet, Robert Roy Pool.

PAISAN (It/1946)

Written by Sergio Amidei, Federico Fellini, Roberto Rossellini.

THE PAPER CHASE (US/1973)

Screenplay by James Bridges.

Based on the novel by John Jay Osborn, Jr.

PARENTHOOD (US/1989)

Written by Lowell Ganz, Babaloo Mandel.

PARIS, TEXAS (WGer/Fr/1984)

Written by Sam Shepard.

PASCALI'S ISLAND (UK/1988)

Screenplay by James Dearden.

Based on the novel by Barry Unsworth.

THE PASSION OF JOAN OF ARC (Fr/1928)

Written by Carl Dreyer, Joseph Delteil.

Based on a book by Joseph Delteil.

PASSION FISH (US/1992)

Written by John Sayles.

PAT AND MIKE (US/1952)

Written by Ruth Gordon and Garson Kanin.

PATHS OF GLORY (US/1957)

Screenplay by Stanley Kubrick, Calder Willingham, Jim Thompson.

Based on the novel by Humphrey Cobb.

PELLE THE CONQUEROR (Den/Swe/1987)

Screenplay by Bille August.

Based on the novel by Martin Andersen Nexo.

THE PEOPLE VS. LARRY FLYNT (US/1996)

Written by Scott Alexander, Larry Karaszewski.

PERSONA (Swe/1966)
Written by Ingmar Bergman.
THE PHANTOM OF LIBERTY (Fr/It/1974)
Written by Luis Bunuel, Jean-Claude Carriere.
THE PIANO (Aust/1993)
Written by Jane Campion.
THE PLAYER (US/1992)
Screenplay by Michael Tolkin.
Based on the novel by Michael Tolkin.
POLICE ACADEMY (US/1984)
Written by Neal Israel, Pat Proft, Hugh Wilson.
THE POSEIDON ADVENTURE (US/1972)
Screenplay by Stirling Silliphant, Wendell Mayes.
Based on the novel by Paul Gallico.
POSTCARDS FROM THE EDGE (US/1990)
Screenplay by Carrie Fisher.
Based on the novel by Carrie Fisher.
THE POSTMAN (IL POSTINO) (It/Fr/Bel/1995)
Screenplay by Anna Pavignano, Michael Radford, Furio Scarpelli,
    Giacomo Scarpelli, Massimo Troisi.
Based on the novel *Burning Patience* by Antonio Skarmeta.
PRIVATE BENJAMIN (US/1980)
Written by Nancy Meyers and Charles Shyer, Harvey Miller.
PRIZZI'S HONOR (US/1985)
Screenplay by Richard Condon, Janet Roach.
Based on the novel by Richard Condon.
THE PRODUCERS (US/1968)
Written by Mel Brooks.
LA PROMESSE (Bel/Fr/Lux/1996)
Written by Luc Dardenne, Jean-Pierre Dardenne.
PSYCHO (US/1960)
Screenplay by Joseph Stefano.
Based on the novel by Robert Bloch.
PULP FICTION (US/1994)
Written by Quentin Tarantino.
Based on stories by Quentin Tarantino and Roger Avary.

Q & A (US/1990)
Screenplay by Sidney Lumet.
Based on the novel by Edwin Torres.
QUEST FOR FIRE (US/1982)
Screenplay by Gerard Brach.
Based on the novel *La Guerre du Feu* by J. H. Rosny, Sr.
QUIZ SHOW (US/1994)
Screenplay by Paul Attanasio.
Based on the book *Remembering America: A Voice from the Sixties*,
     by Richard N. Goodwin.
RADIO DAYS (US/1987)
Written by Woody Allen.
RAGING BULL (US/1980)
Screenplay by Paul Schrader, Mardik Martin.
Based on the book by Jake La Motta with Peter Savage.
RAIDERS OF THE LOST ARK (US/1981)
Screenplay by Lawrence Kasdan.
Based on a story by George Lucas and Phillip Kaufman.
RAIN (US/1932)
Screenplay by Maxwell Anderson.
Based on the play by John Colton and Clemence Randolph from
     the story by W. Somerset Maugham.
RAIN MAN (US/1988)
Written by Ronald Bass, Barry Morrow.
THE RAINMAKER (US/1956)
Screenplay by N. Richard Nash.
Based on the play by N. Richard Nash.
RASHOMON (Jap/1950)
Screenplay by Akira Kurosawa, Shinobu Hashimoto.
Based on two short stories by Ryunosuke Akutugawa.
RED (Fr/Pol/Swi/1994)
Written by Krzysztof Piesiwicz, Krzysztof Kieslowski.
THE RED DESERT (It/Fr/1964)
Written by Michelangelo Antonioni, Tonino Guerra.
REGARDING HENRY (US/1991)
Written by Jeffrey Abrams.

THE REMAINS OF THE DAY (UK/US/1993)
Screenplay by Ruth Prawer Jhabvala.
Based on the novel by Kazuo Ishiguro.
REPULSION (UK/1995)
Written by Roman Polanski, Gerard Brach.
RESERVOIR DOGS (US/1992)
Written by Quentin Tarantino.
THE RETURN OF THE JEDI (US/1983)
Written by Lawrence Kasdan, George Lucas.
Based on an original story for the screen by George Lucas.
REVERSAL OF FORTUNE (US/1990)
Screenplay by Nicholas Kazan.
Based on the nonfiction book by Alan Dershowitz.
RISKY BUSINESS (US/1983)
Written by Paul Brickman.
A RIVER RUNS THROUGH IT (US/1992)
Screenplay by Richard Friedenberg.
Based on the novella by Norman Maclean.
THE ROAD TO MOROCCO (US/1942)
Written by Frank Butler, Don Hartman.
THE ROAD WARRIOR (Aust/1981)
Written by Terry Hayes, George Miller, Brian Hannant.
ROBOCOP (US/1987)
Written by Edward Neumeier, Michael Miner.
ROCKY (US/1976)
Written by Sylvester Stallone.
ROGER & ME (US/1989)
Written by Michael Moore.
ROMY AND MICHELLE'S HIGH SCHOOL REUNION (US/1997)
Written by Robin Schiff.
THE ROSE (US/1979)
Screenplay by Bill Kerby, Bo Goldman.
Based on a story by Bill Kerby.
ROSEMARY'S BABY (US/1968)
Screenplay by Roman Polanski.
Based on the novel by Ira Levin.

THE RULING CLASS (UK/1972)
Screenplay by Peter Barnes.
Based on the play by Peter Barnes.
THE RUNNING, JUMPING AND STANDING STILL FILM
    (UK/1959)
"Devised" by Peter Sellers and Dick Lester.
RUNNING ON EMPTY (US/1988)
Written by Naomi Foner.
RUTHLESS PEOPLE (US/1986)
Written by Dale Launer.
THE SACRIFICE (Swe/Fr/1986)
Written by Andrei Tarkovsky.
SALVADOR (US/1986)
Written by Oliver Stone, Richard Boyle.
SATURDAY NIGHT FEVER (US/1977)
Screenplay by Norman Wexler.
Based in part on a magazine article "Tribal Rites of the New
    Saturday Night" by Nik Cohn.
THE SCARLET LETTER (US/1995)
Screenplay by Douglas Day Stewart.
Based on the novel by Nathaniel Hawthorne.
THE SCENT OF GREEN PAPAYA (Fr/Vietnam/1993)
Written by Tran Anh Hung.
SCHINDLER'S LIST (US/1993)
Screenplay by Steven Zaillian.
Based on the novel by Thomas Keneally.
SCOTT OF THE ANTARCTIC (UK/1948)
Written by Ivor Montagu, Walter Meade, Mary Hayley Bell.
SEA OF LOVE (US/1989)
Written by Richard Price.
SERPICO (US/1973)
Screenplay by Waldo Salt, Norman Wexler.
Based on the nonfiction book by Peter Maas.
SEVEN (US/1995)
Written by Andrew Kevin Walker.

THE SEVEN SAMURAI (Jap/1954)
Written by Shinobu Hashimoto, Akira Kurosawa, Hideo Oguni.
THE SEVENTH SEAL (Swe/1957)
Written by Ingmar Bergman.
SHALL WE DANCE (Jap/1996)
Written by Masayuki Suo.
THE SHELTERING SKY (UK/It/1990)
Screenplay by Mark Peploe, Bernardo Bertolucci.
Based on the novel by Paul Bowles.
SHINE (Aust/1996)
Screenplay by Jan Sardi.
Based on a story by Scott Hicks.
THE SHINING (US/1980)
Screenplay by Diane Johnson, Stanley Kubrick.
Based on the novel by Stephen King.
SHIP OF FOOLS (US/1965)
Screenplay by Abby Mann.
Based on the novel by Katherine Anne Porter.
A SHOT IN THE DARK (UK/US/1964)
Screenplay by Blake Edwards, William Peter Blatty.
Based on the stage play by Harry Kurnitz from the play by Marchel
     Achard.
SHORT CUTS (US/1993)
Screenplay by Robert Altman, Frank Barhydt.
Based on stories by Raymond Carver.
THE SILENCE OF THE LAMBS (US/1991)
Screenplay by Ted Tally.
Based on the novel by Thomas Harris.
SINGLE WHITE FEMALE (US/1992)
Screenplay by Don Roos.
Based on the novel *SWF Seeks Same* by John Lutz.
SLEEPING WITH THE ENEMY (US/1991)
Screenplay by Ronald Bass.
Based on the novel by Nancy Price.
SLEEPLESS IN SEATTLE (US/1993)
Written by Nora Ephron, David S. Ward, Jeff Arch.

SLING BLADE (US/1996)
Screenplay by Billy Bob Thornton.
THE SNAKE PIT (US/1948)
Screenplay by Frank Partos, Millen Brand.
Based on the novel by Mary Jane Ward.
SNOW WHITE AND THE THREE STOOGES (US/1961)
Written by Noel Langley, Elwood Ullman.
SOLARIS (USSR/1972)
Screenplay by Andrei Tarkovsky, Friedrich Gorenstein.
Based on the novel by Stanislaw Lemm.
SOMEBODY UP THERE LIKES ME (US/1956)
Screenplay by Ernest Lehman.
Based on the autobiography by Rocky Graziano with Rowland
   Barber.
SOMEWHERE IN TIME (US/1980)
Screenplay by Richard Matheson.
Based on the novel *Bid Time Return* by Richard Matheson.
THE SOUND OF MUSIC (US/1965)
Screenplay by Ernest Lehman.
Based on the stage musical by Richard Rodgers and Oscar
   Hammerstein II.
SPARTACUS (US/1960)
Screenplay by Dalton Trumbo.
Based on the novel by Howard Fast.
SPEED (US/1994)
Written by Graham Yost.
STAND BY ME (US/1986)
Screenplay by Raynold Gideon, Bruce A. Evans.
Based on the novella *The Body* by Stephen King.
STAR 80 (US/1983)
Screenplay by Bob Fosse.
Based in part on the magazine article "Death of a Playmate" by
   Teresa Carpenter.
STAR WARS (US/1977)
Written by George Lucas.

STEEL MAGNOLIAS (US/1989)
Screenplay by Robert Harling.
Based on the play by Robert Harling.
THE STOLEN CHILDREN (It/Fr/1992)
Written by Sandro Petraglia, Stefano Rulli, Gianni Amelio.
STORM OVER ASIA (USSR/1928)
Written by Osip Brik.
LA STRADA (It/1954)
Written by Federico Fellini, Tullio Pinelli with Ennio Flaiano.
STRANGER THAN PARADISE (US/1984)
Written by Jim Jarmusch.
STRANGERS WHEN WE MEET (US/1960)
Screenplay by Evan Hunter.
Based on the novel by Evan Hunter.
STRAW DOGS (UK/1971)
Screenplay by David Zelag Goodman, Sam Peckinpah.
Based on the novel *The Siege of Trencher's Farm* by Gordon M.
    Williams.
A STREETCAR NAMED DESIRE (US/1951)
Screenplay by Tennessee Williams.
Based on Oscar Saul's adaptation of the play by Tennessee
    Williams.
STRIPES (US/1981)
Written by Len Blum and Dan Goldberg, Harold Ramis.
SUDDEN IMPACT (US/1983)
Written by Joseph C. Stinson.
SULLIVAN's TRAVELS (US/1941)
Written by Preston Sturges.
SUNRISE (US/1927)
Scenario by Carl Mayer.
Based on the novel *The Journey to Tilsit* by Hermann Sudermann.
SUNSET BOULEVARD (US/1950)
Screenplay by Charles Brackett, Billy Wilder, D.M. Marshman, Jr.
Based on the story "A Can of Beans" by Charles Brackett and Billy
    Wilder.

SUPERMAN (UK/1978)
Written by Mario Puzo, David Newman, Leslie Newman, Robert
  Benton.
THE SWEET SMELL OF SUCCESS (US/1957)
Screenplay by Clifford Odets, Ernest Lehman.
Based on the short story "Tell Me About It Tomorrow" by Ernest
  Lehman.
THE SWIMMER (US/1968)
Screenplay by Eleanor Perry.
Based on the short story by John Cheever.
THE SWORD IN THE STONE (US/1963)
Screenplay by Bill Peet.
Based on the novel *The Once and Future King* by T. H. White.
SYBIL (US/1977)
Screenplay by Stewart Stern.
Based on the book by Flora Rheta Schreiber.
TAXI DRIVER (US/1976)
Written by Paul Schrader.
10 (US/1979)
Written by Blake Edwards.
THE TENANT (Fr/1976)
Screenplay by Gerard Brach, Roman Polanski.
Based on the novel by Roland Topor.
TENDER MERCIES (US/1983)
Written by Horton Foote.
THE TERMINATOR (US/1984)
Written by James Cameron, Gale Anne Hurd.
TERMS OF ENDEARMENT (US/1983)
Screenplay by James L. Brooks.
Based on the novel by Larry McMurtry.
THAT OBSCURE OBJECT OF DESIRE (Fr/Sp/1977)
Screenplay by Luis Bunuel, Jean-Claude Carriere.
Based on the novel *La Femme et le Pantin* by Pierre Louys.
THELMA & LOUISE (US/1991)
Written by Callie Khouri.

THEY SHOOT HORSES, DON'T THEY? (US/1969)
Screenplay by James Poe, Robert E. Thompson.
Based on the novel by Horace McCoy.
THIS IS SPINAL TAP (US/1984)
Written by Christopher Guest, Michael McKean, Harry Shearer,
    Rob Reiner.
3 WOMEN (US/1977)
Written by Robert Altman.
THROUGH A GLASS DARKLY (Swe/1961)
Written by Ingmar Bergman.
TIGHTROPE (US/1984)
Written by Richard Tuggle.
TO DIE FOR (US/1995)
Screenplay by Buck Henry.
Based on the novel by Joyce Maynard.
TO LIVE (China/1994)
Screenplay by Yu Hua, Lu Wei.
Based on the novel *Lifetimes* by Yu Hua.
TOOTSIE (US/1982)
Written by Larry Gelbart, Murray Schisgal.
TOP HAT (US/1935)
Written by Dwight Taylor and Allan Scott.
TOTAL RECALL (US/1990)
Written by Ronald Shusett, Dan O'Bannon, Gary Goldman.
Based on a story by Ronald Shusett, Dan O'Bannon, Jon Povill.
    Inspired by the short story "We Can Remember It for You" by
    Phillip K. Dick.
TRADING PLACES (US/1983)
Written by Timothy Harris, Herschel Weingrod.
TRANS-EUROPE EXPRESS (Fr/1966)
Written by Alain Robbe-Grillet.
THE TREASURE OF THE SIERRA MADRE (US/1948)
Screenplay by John Huston.
Based on the novel by B. Traven.

TWELVE ANGRY MEN (US/1957)
Written by Reginald Rose.
Based on the teleplay by Reginald Rose.
TWENTY BUCKS (US/1993)
Written by Leslie Bohem, Endre Bohem.
2001: A SPACE ODYSSEY (UK/US/1968)
Written by Stanley Kubrick, Arthur C. Clarke.
Based on a short story by Arthur C. Clarke.
UMBERTO D (It/1952)
Written by Cesare Zavattini, Vittorio De Sica.
THE UNBEARABLE LIGHTNESS OF BEING (US/1988)
Screenplay by Jean-Claude Carriere, Philip Kaufman.
Based on the novel by Milan Kundera.
UNFORGIVEN (US/1992)
Written by David Webb Peoples
UNLAWFUL ENTRY (US/1992)
Written by Lewis Colick.
AN UNMARRIED WOMAN (US/1978)
Written by Paul Mazursky.
THE USUAL SUSPECTS (US/1995)
Written by Christopher McQuarrie.
THE VERDICT (US/1982)
Screenplay by David Mamet.
Based on the novel by Barry Reed.
VERTIGO (US/1958)
Screenplay by Alec Coppel, Samuel Taylor.
Based on the novel D'Entre les Morts by Pierre Boileau and Thomas
    Narcejac.
VIRIDIANA (Sp/Mex/1961)
Written by Luis Bunuel, Julio Alejandro.
Based on story by Luis Bunuel.
I VITELLONI (It/Fr/1953)
Written by Federico Fellini, Ennio Flaiano, Tullio Pinelli.
VIVA ZAPATA (US/1952)
Written by John Steinbeck.

WALL STREET (US/1987)
Written By Stanley Weiser, Oliver Stone.
THE WAR OF THE ROSES (US/1989)
Screenplay by Michael Leeson.
Based on the novel by Warren Adler.
WATERSHIP DOWN (UK/1978)
Screenplay by Martin Rosen.
Based on the novel by Richard Adams.
WAYNE'S WORLD (US/1992)
Written by Mike Myers, Bonnie Turner, Terry Turner.
A WEDDING (US/1978)
Written by John Considine, Patricia Resnick, Allan Nicholls, Robert
    Altman.
WEEKEND (Fr/It/1967)
Written by Jean-Luc Godard.
WELFARE (US/1975)
Documentary produced and directed by Frederick Wiseman.
WHEN HARRY MET SALLY (US/1989)
Written by Nora Ephron.
WHISPERS IN THE DARK (US/1992)
Written by Christopher Crowe.
WHITE HEAT (US/1949)
Written by Ivan Goff, Ben Roberts.
Based on a story by Virginia Kellogg.
WHITE MEN CAN'T JUMP (US/1992)
Written by Ron Shelton.
WHO FRAMED ROGER RABBIT (US/1988)
Screenplay by Jeffrey Price, Peter S. Seaman.
Based on the novel *Who Censored Roger Rabbit?* by Gary K. Wolf.
WILD STRAWBERRIES (Swe/1957)
Written by Ingmar Bergman.
WINTER LIGHT (Swe/1962)
Written by Ingmar Bergman.
THE WITCHES OF EASTWICK (US/1987)
Screenplay by Michael Cristofer.
Based on the novel by John Updike.

WITNESS (US/1985)
Written by Earl W. Wallace, William Kelley.
Based on a story by Earl W. Wallace, William Kelly, Pamela
    Wallace.
The WIZARD OF OZ (US/1939)
Screenplay by Noel Langley, Florence Ryerson, Edgar Allen Woolf.
Based on the novel *The Wonderful Wizard of Oz* by L. Frank Baum.
THE YELLOW SUBMARINE (UK/1968)
Screenplay by Lee Minoff, Al Brodax, Jack Mendelsohn, Erich
    Segal.
Based on the song by John Lennon and Paul McCartney.
YOUNG FRANKENSTEIN (US/1974)
Written by Gene Wilder, Mel Brooks.
YOUNG MISTER LINCOLN (US/1939)
Written by Lamar Trotti.
A ZED AND TWO NOUGHTS (GB/Neth/1985)
Written by Peter Greenaway.
ZELIG (US/1983)
Written by Woody Allen.
ZERO DE CONDUITE (Fr/1933)
Written by Jean Vigo.

INDEX

Accidental Tourist, The, 6,
36, 49, 50, 55, 59
Action/Adventure Genre,
36, 61, 82, 85,
91–92, 107, 216,
406, 409. *See also*
Survival Films
heroes of, 213
Actors
as artists, 253
and subtext, 254–55
Acts, 41. *See also* Climax;
Endings; Inciting
incident; Scenes
design, 217–22
design variations,
222–25
false ending, 224–25
five or more act
structure, 219–22
last, climax, kinds of,
42, 118–21
last, final condition, 41,
42
Mid-Act Climax, 220
and pacing, 289–91,
294
and progression,
118–19, 208–16,
294–301
reversal, 217–18, 220,
222–24
rhythm, 225–27
subplot/multiplot,
219–22, 226–32
three-act story, 218–17,
218–19
Adam's Rib, 223
Adaptation, 364–70
first principle of, 367
Addicted to Love, 125
Aesthetic emotion,
110–12
After Hours, 47, 52, 359,
406–7

Airplane, 360
*Alice Doesn't Live Here
Anymore,* 198
Alice in Wonderland, 85
Alien, 186–89, 224, 406
Aliens, 224, 406
Alive, 82, 124
All in the Family (TV
series), 382
All That Jazz, 85, 128
Allen, Woody, 4, 123, 344
Altman, Robert, 9, 56, 65
Amadeus, 366–67, 369,
391–92
Amarcord, 65
And Justice for All, 126,
321–22
Angel Heart, 94
Animal Farm, 68, 85
Animal House, 320, 360
Animation, 85
Annie Hall, 125, 256–57,
362, 366
Anouilh, Jean, 12
Antagonism, Principle of,
317–18
contradictory value in,
318
design for story
analysis, 318–33
negation of the
negation, 318–19
Antiplot, 45–47, 64, 66
change versus stasis,
57–58
coincidence in, 52–53
ending, 60
and film budget, 63
inconsistent realities
in, 54–57
invention of, 350
quasi, 56
time in, 51–52
Apocalypse Now, 121
Arachnophobia, 124

Arc of the film, 41
Archer, William, 16
Archetypal story, 3–4
Archplot, 45–46, 64–65
and audience, 62–64
causality, 52
closed ending, 47–48
consistent realities,
53–57
external conflict,
48–49
protagonist, 49–51
scenes, number of, 210
time, 51
Aristotle, 5, 11, 13, 79,
100, 109, 110, 186,
217, 338, 357–58,
376–77
Art Film, 7, 59–61, 63,
86, 88–89
false ending, 225
and inciting incident,
204
Asian filmmaking, 14, 62
Astaire, Fred/Ginger
Roger films, 332
Audience
and act design, 217–18
bond, 141–43
Elizabethan, 90
emotional experience
of, 243–48
and entertainment as
ritual, 12
and gap, 179–80,
270–71
intelligence of, 6–7
and Obligatory Scene,
198–200
positioning the, 89–90
principles controlling
(empathy/authen-
ticity), 186–89
reaction, 135–36,
179–80

Audience (cont.)
  shrinking, vis-à-vis
    choice of story
    structure, 62–64
  target, 240
August, Bille, 50
Authenticity in film,
  186–89
Authorship, 185–89
Autobiography, 84
Avant-garde film-making,
  64–65

Babe, 137
Babette's Feast, 59
Baby Boom, 126
Backstory, 183, 231,
  340–41, 348, 350
Bad & the Beautiful, The,
  55
Bad Day at Black Rock, 55,
  119
Bad Timing, 47, 51–52, 55
Bambi, 81
Barry Lyndon, 344
Barton Fink, 55, 56–57
Basic Instinct, 97
Battle of Algiers, 84
Battleship Potemkin, The,
  20, 46, 68–69, 136,
  366
Beat, 37–38, 258–59, 270,
  286–87
Beckett, Samuel, 54
Being There, 327
Ben Hur, 366
Benchley, Peter, 196, 202
Bergman, Andrew, 319
Bergman, Ingmar, 4, 9,
  65, 72, 112, 203, 394
Betrayal, 352
Betty Blue, 250
Big, 46, 55, 81, 330
Big Wednesday, 84
Big Sleep, The, 119
Billy Budd, 257
Biography, 84, 85, 183
Birds, The, 125
Black Comedy, 82, 88,
  321
Black Comedy (Shaffer),
  217
Black Widow, 229
Blade Runner, The, 366,
  379

Blazing Saddles, 64, 93
Blind Date, 107
Blocking Characters,
  95–96
Blood of the Poet, 47
Blow Up, 55
Blue Velvet, 59
Bob Roberts, 59, 84
Body Heat, 97
Bond, James, 103–4, 195,
  213, 214, 306
Bonfire of the Vanities,
  The, 369
Bostonians, The (James),
  369
Bram Stoker's Dracula,
  408
Brazil, 224
Breakfast Club, The, 136
Breathless, 65
Bridge on the River Kwai,
  The (Boulle), 367–68
Bridges of Madison County,
  96
Brief Encounter, 46, 97
Bringing Up Baby, 46,
  300
Buddy Salvation Plot, 80,
  85
Budget, and story
  structure, 63–64
Bugs Bunny, 85, 137
Bull Durham, 85
Bullets Over Broadway,
  126
Bunker, Archie, 382
Buñuel, Luis, 407
Burke, Kenneth, 1
Burnett, Hallie and Whit,
  21
Burroughs, William S., 54

Cabinet of Dr. Caligari,
  The, 46, 93
California scenes, 336
Cameron, James, 406
Camp Nowhere, 360
Cape Fear, 408
Caper Genre, 82
Carnal Knowledge, 193,
  196, 337, 338
Carpenter, John, 43–44
Casablanca, 20, 201, 223,
  228, 229, 260–70,
  287, 288–89, 306,

310, 333, 342–43, 353,
  371–72, 375, 377,
  405–6
Casino, 128
Cassavetes, John, 9
Cast design, 183–85,
  379–81
  size of, 213, 214
Cavani, Liliana, 348–49
Center of Good, 347–49,
  378–79
Chaplin, Charlie, 4
Character. See also
    Protagonist
  arc, 104–5
  backstory, 183
  biography of, 84, 85,
    183
  cast design, 183–85,
    379–81
  climax and, 107–6
  comic, 381–83
  and contradiction,
    379–80
  dimension, 378–80
  first step in creating,
    143–45
  and the gap, 147–49,
    151–52, 177–79,
    270–71
  revelation, 103–4
  and risk/maturity,
    149–51
  screenplay of
    Chinatown, 154–76,
    178
  structure and character
    functions, 105–7
  three levels of conflict,
    146
  three tips for writing,
    383–87
  true, 101, 375–77
  versus characterization,
    100–102
  world of, 145–47
"Character as destiny," 52
Character-driven story,
  107
Chariots of Fire, 85
Chase sequence, 366
Chayefsky, Paddy, 118,
  257
Cheap Surprise, 354, 355
Chekhov, Anton, 386

Chien Andalou, Un, 47
Chinatown, 55, 56, 97, 98, 119, 124–25, 154–76, 178, 201, 228, 236–37, 239, 240, 241, 256, 296, 301, 331–32, 336, 341, 351, 371, 406
Choose Me, 358
Christie, Agatha, 350
Chungking Express, 47
Citizen Kane, 46, 359–60
Claire's Knee, 47
Classical Design, 44–46, 49, 52
  and audience, 62–64
  and writer's craft, 64–65
Clean and Sober, 126
Cliché, 7, 67–68
  action genre, 61
  and Hollywood films, 61
  and multiplication of act climaxes, 221
  overcoming, 76–78
  and scenes leading to climax, 293–94
  and thriller, 87
  transition, 301
Climax, 42, 220–22, 309–12. *See also* Acts; Controlling Idea; Endings
  and character, 107–6
  difficulty of writing, 206
  and irony, 128–29
  last act, 42, 206
  Mid-Act Climax, 220
  and mystery, 350–51
  Penultimate, 224–25
  positive/negative, 304
  and reversal, 42, 309
  rhythm and tempo, 291–94
  and self-recognition, 118
  Sequence Climax, 234
  and Turning Point, 286–87, 304–5, 311–12
Clouzot, Henri-Georges, 402, 405
Clowns, 47

Cocktail Party, The (Eliot), 367
Cocteau, Jean, 177
Cohn, Harry, 409
Coincidence, 356–59
Coleridge, Samuel Taylor, 186
Columbo (TV series), 117, 350
Comedy
  comic character, 381–83
  design, 361–62
  genre, 19–20, 82, 87–88, 247
  hybrids (Dramedy, Crimedy), 362
  problem of, 359–62
Coming Home, 328
Commercial films, bad script, 23, 24
Composition
  expressing progression, 294–300
  pacing, 289–91, 294
  rhythm and tempo, 291–94
  third thing, 301
  transition, 301
  unity and variety, 288–89
Computer Generated Images (CGI), 24–25
Conflict, Law of, 210–13. *See also* Antagonism, Principle of
  complication through complexity, 213–15
  conflict at three levels, 215
  and scene analysis, 261, 268
Controlling Idea, 112, 114–17
  and climax, last act, 119–21. *See also* endings
  components of, 115–16
  in creative process, 117–18
  and *The Deer Hunter*, 297
  ironic, 125–28

  and *Kiss of the Spider Woman*, 231
  and society, 129–31
  and subplot, 219–22, 226–32
  versus counter idea, 118–21
Conversation, The, 12, 87, 312
Cook, the Thief, His Wife & Her Lover, The, 220
Cool Hand Luke, 81
Cop, 94
Courtroom Drama, 82, 84, 181, 229
Creative choices, 76–78
Creative limitation, 90–92
Crichton, Charles, 87
Cries and Whispers, 72
Crime and Punishment, 71, 323
Crimes and Misdemeanors, 97
Crime Story, 82, 86, 87, 92, 114, 116, 119, 181, 229
Crimedy, 362
Crisis, 303–4, 309
  decision, 304, 308
  design of, 307–9
  placement, 306–7
Creative limitation, 71–72
Crying Game, The, 20, 55, 56, 96, 194, 196

Dance with a Stranger, 124
Dances with Wolves, 93
Dangerous Liaisons, 3, 59, 83, 96, 116, 117, 311, 369
David and Lisa, 94
Dead Ringers, 94
Death by Hanging, 47
Death in Venice, 207
Death Wish, 130
Deer Hunter, The, 126, 296–97, 308
Detective Genre, 82
  on TV, 320–21
Diabolique, 402–4, 413
Dialogue, 388–90
  description, 394–400
  image systems, 400–408

Dialogue (*cont.*)
short speeches, 390–92
silent screenplay, 393–94
suspense sentence, 393
when to begin writing, 417
Dickens, Charles, 98
Didacticism, 121–23
Die Hard, 3, 36, 92, 119
Diner, 136, 228
Dirty Dozen, The, 136
Dirty Harry, 116–17
Disaster/Survival Film, 82
Discreet Charm of the Bourgeoisie, 57, 58, 222
Disillusionment Plot, 80, 81, 84, 85, 86, 87, 114
Do the Right Thing, 50, 59, 136, 228
Doctor, The, 126
Docu-Drama, 84
Documentaries, 47
Domestic Drama, 74, 82, 214, 356, 409
Dominick and Eugene, 189
Dona Flor and Her Two Husbands, 46, 251
Dr. Strangelove, 55, 71, 122, 360
Dracula, 324
Dramedy, 362
Dream Sequence, 343
Drugstore Cowboy, 59, 81
DuBois, Blanche, 137–38

Earthquake, 125
Eat Drink Man Woman, 20, 50, 136, 228
Eco-Drama, 82
Education Plot, 36, 80, 81, 85, 107, 116, 178, 292
8 1/2, 20, 47, 55, 65
Eisenstein, Sergei, 369, 407
Electric Horseman, The, 126, 127
Elephant Man, The, 125
Elephant Walk, 358
Eliot, T.S., 133, 365

Empire Strikes Back, The, 236, 239, 241, 305, 336, 341
Endings. *See also* Acts; Climax
climax and character, 107–9, 310
closed versus open, 47–48
deus ex machina, 357–58, 361
down-ending films, 311
false, 224–25
idealistic, 123
ironic, 125–28
keys to, 310, 312
Obligatory Scene, 198–99
pessimistic, 124–25
placement of crisis and climax at, 306–7
reversal, 217–18, 220, 309
English Patient, The, 61, 311
Equus, 94
Espionage Drama, 82
Esquivel, Laura, 4
E.T., 42, 224
Ethics (Aristotle), 11
European filmmaking, 14, 59–60, 204
European screenwriting, education, 16–17
European Script Fund, 396
Everybody Says I Love You, 59
Evita, 85
Exposition, 328–29
California scenes, 336
pace, 336
withholding information, 336

Fabulous Baker Boys, The, 55, 56
Faces, 57, 58
Falling Down, 81
Falling in Love, 96
False Mystery, 354–55
Fantasy Genre, 53–54, 70, 85, 355
Farce, 64, 82, 85, 107, 213

Farewell My Concubine, 337, 338
Farewell, My Lovely, 119
Faulkner, William, 375
Feiffer, Jules, 193
Fellini, Federico, 65
Fields, Verna, 203
Fifth Element, The, 61
Film Noir, 82, 84
First Blood, 103
First Deadly Sin, The, 94, 230
First Deadly Sin, The (Sanders), 230
Fish Called Wanda, A, 20, 46, 55, 72, 88, 360, 361–62, 383
Fisher King, The, 59, 92, 126
Fitzcarraldo, 81, 124
Five Easy Pieces, 47, 55, 56
Flashback, 341–42, 352
Flaubert, Gustave, 369
Flight of the Phoenix, 124
Foote, Horton, 9, 32, 44, 199
Forced Entry, 94
Ford, Harrison, 92
Ford, John, 407
Foreman, Carl, 368
Foreshadowing, 200
Forman, Milos, 369, 396
Forrest Gump, 25, 81
Forster, E. M., 369
400 Blows, The, 129
Four Weddings and a Funeral, 46, 220
Fowler, Gene, 108
French Scenes, 292–93
Friedman, Norman, 80
Frost, Robert, 90
Frye, Christopher, 365
Fugitive, The, 36, 49–50, 119, 220, 290
Full Metal Jacket, 122

Gallipoli, 121
Gallo, George, 92
Gandhi, 84
Gangster Genre, 82
Gap
Casablanca, 270–71
and character development, 147–49

Chinatown, 154–76
and comedy, 362
creating within, 177–79
and energy of story,
179–80
Love Serenade, 311–12
and point of no return,
208
Genres
and audience
expectations, 89–90
conventions, 87–89,
178
creative limitations,
90–82
history, 79
lists and film examples,
80–86
mastery of, 89–90
mixing and
reinventing, 92–98
and setting, 183
and Shakespeare, 90
shift in, 225
Ghost, 96
Ghostbusters, 12
Glengarry Glen Ross, 72
Glory, 83, 309
Godard, Jean-Luc, 54, 65
Godfather, The, 348
Godfather, The: Part II,
46, 207, 311
Goethe, von, Johann, 79
Going in Style, 126
Gold Rush, The, 361
Goldman, William, 310
Good Son, The, 94
Graduate, The, 95
Grand Canyon, 126
Grand Hotel, 50, 137
Grand Illusion, 46
Great Gatsby, The, 81
Great Train Robbery, The,
46
Greed, 20, 46, 81, 109, 312
Griffith, D. W., 293, 366,
407
Gross Pointe Blank, 81
Groundhog Day, 3, 116, 117
Guest, Judith, 205

Hamburger Hill, 121
Hamlet (character of),
105, 111, 378
Hampton, Christopher, 83

*Hand That Rocks the
Cradle, The,* 94
Hannah and Her Sisters,
17, 123, 126, 136, 344
Harold and Maud, 81
Hart, Moss, 352
Heidegger, Martin, 211
Hemingway, Ernest, 98,
321
High Adventure Genre,
82, 85
High Hopes, 137
His Girl Friday, 360
Historical Drama, 83
Hitchcock, Alfred, 88–89,
225, 394, 407
Holes, 370–72
Hollywood films, 3
"big hook," 198
budget, 63–64
and clichés, 61
and inciting incident,
204
number distributed per
year, 13
rebellion against, 66
script development,
cost, 13–14
story analyst, 17–18
story submissions
accepted yearly, 13
studio system, 17
versus art film, 59–61
Hope and Glory, 136
Horror Film, 80, 213, 406
and Cheap Surprise,
355
Supernatural, 80
Super-Uncanny, 80
Uncanny, 80
Hospital, 257
Hour of the Wolf, 80
Hurd, Gail Anne, 406
Hurricane, 358
Husbands, 57
Husbands and Wives, 96,
344
Husserl, Edmund, 66
Hustler, The, 46, 55, 81

*I Never Promised You a
Rose Garden,* 93–94
I Vitioni, 65
Idea. *See* Controlling Idea
Il Postino, 59, 81

Image Systems,
400–408
Imaginary Invalid, The
(Molière), 382
In-Laws, The, 313
In the Heat of the Night,
116, 117
In the Realm of the Senses,
47, 55, 307
Inciting Incident, 181,
189–94, 208, 311,
318, 356
and act design, 217–24
creating, 206–7
design of, 198–200
and flashback, 341
locating, 200–204
and Marx Brothers
film, 361
quality of, 204–7
Inner monologues, 177
Interview with a Vampire,
143
Intolerance, 50
Irony, 128–29
dramatic, 351–55
in endings/climax,
125–28
ironic ascension,
298–300
negative, 128, 129
Isadora, 84

James, Henry, 206, 369
Jaws, 112, 124, 190–91,
197, 198, 199,
202–203, 288, 303,
356–57, 409
Jerry Maguire, 126
Jesus of Montreal, 225
JFK, 59, 345
Jhabvala, Ruth Prawer,
369
John and Mary, 76
Joy Luck Club, The, 222
Joyce, James, 54
Ju Dou, 46
Jurassic Park, 358

Kasdan, Lawrence, 92
Kaufman, Phillip, 352
Key Images, 312
Kid, The, 312
King Lear (Shakespeare),
376–77

Kiss of the Spider Woman, 107–8, 231–32
Kiss of the Spider Woman (Puig), 231
Koyaanisqutsi, 47
Kramer vs. Kramer, 112, 125, 126, 198, 202, 206, 215–16, 221, 236, 288, 307–8, 409
Kubrick, Stanley, 122

La Dolce Vita, 87, 129, 312, 409
La Notte, 198
La Promesse, 81
La Strada, 65
Lady Eve, The, 360
Last Days of Pompeii, The, 46
Last Emperor, The, 337, 338
Last Seduction, The, 97
Last Year at Marienbad, 47, 57, 63, 68
Law of Diminishing Returns, 244, 293, 393
Lawson, John Howard, 16
Le Feu Follet, 81
League of Their Own, A, 85
Lean, David, 368
Leaving Las Vegas, 3, 96, 198, 222, 307
L'Eclisse, 81
Lenny, 87
Les Diabolique. See Diabolique
Lethal Weapon, 94, 362
Life Story, 31–32
Like Water for Chocolate, 4
Limitation of story, 71
Lion King, The, 3, 85
Little Big Man, 337, 338
Little Mermaid, The, 85
Little Shop of Horrors, 361
Lone Star, 96, 294
Loneliness of the Long Distance Runner, The, 85
Longing Story, 96
Looks and Smiles, 408
Lord Jim, 81
Lost Highway, 47
Love Serenade, 311–12

Love Story, 80, 84, 85, 86, 92, 95–98, 114, 116, 178, 214, 226, 229, 289, 310, 352
Loved One, The, 88
Lumet, Sidney, 292

M, 46, 55
Macbeth (Shakespeare), 81, 142–43, 378
Maltese Falcon, The, 87
Mamet, David, 72
Man Bites Dog, 20, 59, 84
Man Who Would Be King, The, 55, 82
Manchurian Candidate, The, 325
Manhattan, 125
Manhunter, 94
Mark, The, 94
Marty, 46, 55
Marvin, Lee, 385
Marx Brothers films, 361
Masculine Feminine, 57, 58
*M*A*S*H*, 360
Maturation Plot, 81, 85, 90, 120
McQuarrie, Christopher, 70
Mean Streets, 80
Medical Drama, 82, 181
Melodrama, 370
Men in Black, 25, 295
Mephisto, 81, 326
Merrily We Roll Along (Kaufman & Hart), 352
Meshes of the Afternoon, 47, 55
Metamorphosis (Kafka), 202
Metz, 80
Michael Collins, 83
Midnight Cowboy, 189
Midnight Run, 92
Midsummer's Night Dream, A (Shakespeare), 137, 227
Mike's Murder, 90
Mind Worm, 374–75
minimalism. *See* miniplot
miniplot, 45–47, 64–65, 66
  change versus stasis, 57–58

  and film budget, 63
  inconsistent realities, 53–57
  internal conflict, 49
  multiplot variation, 49, 56
  negative ending, 59
  open ending, 48, 57
  protagonist, 49–51
  and reversals, 222–24
Misanthrope, The (Molière), 382
Miser, The (Molière), 382
Misfits, The, 87
Miss Julie (Strindberg), 217
Missing, 116, 117, 321, 396
Moby Dick, 195
Mockumentary, 56, 84
Modern Epic, 81, 84, 85
Modern Times, 20
Mogamo, 409
Molière, 98, 382
Moment by Moment, 408
Montage, 343–44
Monty Python and the Holy Grail, 19, 47, 57, 64
Moonstruck, 197
Morning After, The, 94
Moulin Rouge, 299–300
Mr. Smith Goes to Washington, 81
Mrs. Parker and the Vicious Circle, 81
Mrs. Soffel, 95–96, 193–94, 196, 226
Multiplot, 49, 56, 123–24, 226–32, 406
Murder Mystery, 82, 97, 342
Muriel's Wedding, 81
Murnau, F. W., 407
Music Room, The, 47, 198
Musical, 84, 289
Musical Horror Film, 92–93
My Best Friend's Wedding, 81, 409
My Dinner with Andre, 68, 292–93
My Favorite Season, 356
My Man Godfrey, 362
Mystery, 349–51
  and backstory, 350

cliffhanger, 355
closed, 350
false, 354–55
open, 350
and red herrings, 350

Naked, 57, 58
Naked Gun, 360
Naked Lunch, 214
Nanook of the North, 47
Nash, Richard, 35
Nashville, 55, 56, 128, 137
Nasty Habits, 360
Network, 128, 360
Newspaper Drama, 82
Night and Fog, 47
Night at the Opera, 360
Nightporter, The, 348–49
1984, 81
Nixon, 84, 128
North Dallas Forty, 85,
    126, 127

O'Bannon, Dan, 187–89
Objective correlative, 66
Obligatory Scene,
    198–200, 303, 308
Officer and a Gentleman,
    An, 126
Oh! What a Lovely War,
    121
Old Man and the Sea, The,
    81
On the Waterfront, 201
Ordinary People, 6, 126,
    189, 204–5, 295–96,
    309, 323
Othello, 226, 298–99
Out of Africa, 126, 127
Outbreak, 340

Pacing, 289–91, 294
Paisan, 47
Paper Chase, The, 126
Parenthood, 3, 20, 49, 136,
    228
Paris, Texas, 47, 48, 55
Parody, 82
Pascal, Blaise, 5
Pascali's Island, 329
Passion de Jeanne D'Arc,
    La, 47
Passion Fish, 80
Pat and Mike, 198
Paths of Glory, 122

Pelle the Conqueror, 47,
    50, 136, 369
People vs. Larry Flint, The,
    81
Persona, 20, 47, 65, 112,
    409
Personal story, bad script,
    22–23, 24
Phantom of Liberty, 58
Piano, The, 408
Pitch, 413–14
Plato, 129, 130
Player, The, 13
Plot, 43. See also Archplot;
    Antiplot; Climax,
    Crisis; Inciting
    Incident; Miniplot;
    Structure; Subplot
Poetics, The (Aristotle), 5,
    217
Point of View (POV)
    character's, 363–64
    shots, 362–63
"Pointless pace killer,"
    179
Points of no return,
    208–10
Police Academy, 360
Political Drama/Allegory,
    82, 85, 229, 289, 310
Political Thriller, 116
Politics
    of story design, 58–66
    of story's world, 182
Polti, 79–80
Poseidon Adventure, The,
    82, 124
Posse, 93
Postcards from the Edge, 3,
    59
Postman Always Rings
    Twice, The, 358
Premise, 112–13
Prison Drama, 82
Prizzi's Honor, 88, 360
Producers, The, 360
Progression, 118–23, 209
    complication versus
        complexity, 213–16
    ironic, 298–300
    law of conflict, 210–13,
        261, 268
    personal, 295–96
    points of no return,
        208–10

social, 294–95
symbolic ascension,
    296–98
Protagonist, 136–41. See
    also Character
    and audience bond,
        141–43
    and gap, 147–49,
        151–52, 177–79,
        270–71
    and inciting incident,
        181, 191–94,
        198–207
    Multiprotagonist,
        136–37
    Plural, 136
    and quest, 196–97
    screenplay of
        Chinatown, 154–76,
        178
    single versus multiple,
        49–50
    and spine of story,
        194–96
    switch during story, 137
Private Benjamin, 360
Psycho, 137, 225
Psycho-Drama, 82, 92,
    93–95
Psycho-Thriller, 75,
    94–95, 114, 230
Puig, Manuel, 231
Pulp Fiction, 50, 136
Punitive Plot, 81, 84, 85,
    128
Puzo, Mario, 312

Q & A, 59, 97, 119
Quartet, 369
Quest, 196–97
Quest for Fire, 124
Quiz Show, 126

Raging Bull, 85
Raiders of the Lost Ark, 19,
    92, 220
Rain, 300
Rain Man, 126
Rainmaker, The, 34–35
Rambo, 103
Rashomon, 20
Ray, Satyajit, 4
Red, 96
Red Desert, The, 12, 47, 55,
    250

Redemption Plot, 80, 81, 85, 92, 107, 126
Redford, Robert, 205
Regarding Henry, 126
Reiner, Rob, 56
Remains of the Day, 36, 96
Research, 72–76
 and birth of characters, 74
 fact, 73–74
 imagination, 73
 memory, 72–73
 and progressive complications, 213
Reservoir Dogs, 20, 342
Resnais, Alain, 47
Resolution, 312–14
Return of the Jedi, 236, 341
Revenge Tale, 82
Reversal, 217–18, 220, 225–27
Reversal of Fortune, 3, 20, 59
Rhys, Jean, 369
Rhythm, 291–93
Risky Business, 81
River Runs Through It, A, 47
River, The, 191
Road to Morocco, 64
Road Warrior, The, 49
Robbe-Grillet, Alain, 63
Robocop, 119
Rocky, 201–2, 223, 229
Rocky IV, 402
Roma, 84
Romantic Comedy, 82, 360
Romy and Michele's High School Reunion, 80
Room With a View, A (Forster), 369
Rose, The, 128
Rosemary's Baby, 324
Rossen, Robert, 257
Rowe, Kenneth, 16
Ruling Class, The, 360
Running, Jumping, and Standing Still Film, The, 47
Running on Empty, 59
Ruthless People, 299

Sacrifice, The, 47

Salt, Waldo, 189
Salvador, 59
Sanders, Lawrence, 230
Sargent, Alvin, 189, 205
Sartre, Jean-Paul, 211, 212
Satire, 82
Saturday Night Fever, 81
Scarlet Letter, The, 369
Scenes, 35–37. *See also* Composition
 and beats, 217, 258–59, 270, 286–87
 closing value, 259, 270, 286
 crisis, 303–9
 emotional transitions, 243–48
 French Scenes, 292–93
 Law of Diminishing Returns, 244, 293
 length of, 291–92
 mood, 247–48
 number of in Archplot, 210
 number of in three-act story, 218–19
 number of in two-hour film, 291, 415
 Obligatory, 199–200, 303, 308
 opening value, 258, 259, 261, 270, 272, 286
 "pointless pace killer," 179
 Sequence Climax, 234
Setups/Playoffs, 238–43, 271–72
 text and subtext, 252–57
 transition/Third Thing, 301–2
 Turning Points, 74, 209, 217, 233–38, 243, 248–51, 259, 270–71, 286–87
 writing, specifics to do, 395–400
Scene analysis, 257–59
 Casablanca, 260–70, 287
 Through a Glass Darkly, 271–87
 Scent of Green Papaya, The, 56

Science Fiction, 85
Schiller, von, Johann, 79
Schindler's List, 81, 126
Schrader, Leonard, 231–32
Scott of the Antarctic, 125
Screwball Comedy, 82
Sea of Love, 120, 229
Sequence, 38. *See also* act three scene example, 38–41
Serpico, 189
Setting, 68–72, 181–85, 217
 and creative limitation, 71–72
 duration, 68
 and genre, 183
 level of conflict, 69
 location, 69
 and mood, 247–48
 period, 68
 place, 69
 politics of setting world, 182
 rituals of setting world, 182–83
 values of setting world, 183
 versus story, 72
Setups/Playoffs, 238–43, 271–72
Seven, 94, 97, 119
Seven Samurai, The, 46, 55, 56, 136
Seventh Seal, The, 46, 312
Shaffer, Peter, 369, 391–92, 393
Shakespeare, William, 90, 95, 365, 369, 407
 filmed works, 366
 five act structure, 220–21
Shall We Dance, 47, 81
Sheltering Sky, The, 400
Shine, 12, 46, 120, 220, 323, 337
Shining, The, 80
Ship of Fools, 50
Shortcuts, 50, 57, 58, 137, 227, 228
Shot in the Dark, A, 382–83
Silence of the Lambs, The, 119, 349

Silence, The, 65, 393–94
Silent Era of film, 366
Single White Female, 94
Sitcom, 82
Six Guns and Society
    (Wright), 81
Sleeping with the Enemy,
    94
Sleepless in Seattle, 96
Slice-of-life works, 58
Sling Blade, 312
Snake Pit, The, 93
Snow White and the Three
    Stooges, 129
Soap Opera, 213, 214, 216
Social Drama, 82, 84–85,
    92, 121–22
Solaris, 85
Somebody Up There Likes
    Me, 85
Somewhere in Time, 85
Sound of Music, The, 400
Spartacus, 81
Speed, 119, 222
Spielberg, Steven, 202–3
Spine (through-
    line/superobjective)
    of story, 194–96, 338
Sports Genre, 85, 201,
    229
Stand by Me, 81
Stanislavski, Konstantin,
    65, 112
Star '80, 128
Star Wars, 85, 256, 305,
    341, 409
Steel Magnolias, 314
Step-outline, 412–15
    expansion of, 415
Stereotypical story, 4–5
Stolen Children, 47
Stone, Oliver, 345
Storm Over Asia, 366
Story event, 33–35, 37. *See*
    also scene
Story values, 34
Storytelling, 113
Stranger Than Paradise,
    47
Strangers in Paradise, 359
Strangers When We Meet,
    96–97
Straw Dogs, 36
Stream of Consciousness
    work, 213, 214, 216

Streetcar Named Desire, A,
    137–38, 324
Strindberg, August, 54,
    217
Stripes, 360
Structure of story, 32–33.
    See also Acts;
    Character; Climax;
    Endings; Inciting
    Incident
    active versus passive
        protagonist, 50–51
    Archplot, Miniplot,
        Antiplot, 43–47
    causality versus
        coincidence, 52–53
    change versus stasis,
        57–58
    and character
        functions, 105–7
    classical design,
        44–46, 52
    closed versus open
        endings, 47–49
    consistent versus
        inconsistent
        realities, 53–57
    creative limitation,
        90–92
    design, five-part,
        181–85
    external versus internal
        conflict, 48–49
    and film budget, 63–64
    and genre, 86–89,
        90–98
    linear versus nonlinear
        time, 51–52
    nonplot, 58, 60
    "pointless pace killer,"
        179
    politics of story design,
        58–66
    quest theme, 196–97
    as rhetoric, 113–14
    setting, 68–72, 181–85
    single versus multiple
        protagonists, 49–50
    subplot/multiplot,
        219–22, 226–32
Sturges, Preston, 9
Style, adding vividness to,
    395–97
Subplot, 219–22, 226–32
    and resolution, 312–14

Sudden Impact, 119
Sullivan's Travels, 201,
    239–40, 241, 301
Sunrise, 366
Sunset Boulevard, 84, 352
Superman, 318
Surprise, 355–56
    Cheap, 354, 355
Survival Films, 124, 125
Suspense sentence, 393
Suspense story, 351
Sweet Smell of Success,
    The, 326
Swimmer, The, 227–28
Sword in the Stone, The, 85
Sybil, 93

Tarantino, Quentin, 342
Tarkovsky, Andrei, 85
Taxi Driver, 201
Technical advances in
    film, and story,
    24–25
Tempo, 293–94
10, 126
Tenant, The, 80, 326
Tender Mercies, 19, 32, 43,
    44, 47, 55, 81, 197,
    199–200, 290, 303
Terminator, 20, 224–25,
    297–98, 372, 379,
    385
Terms of Endearment, 126,
    127
Testament, 408
Testing Plot, 81, 85
Text and subtext, 252–57
That Obscure Object of
    Desire, 47, 55
Thelma & Louise, 46, 55,
    136, 306, 308
They Shoot Horses, Don't
    They?, 128
Third Thing, 301
This is Spinal Tap, 3, 84,
    360
Thoreau, Henry David,
    139
Three Faces of Eve, The,
    93
3 Women, 55, 56
Thriller Genre, 82, 87,
    178, 226, 229, 247,
    353–54, 355, 407. *See*
    also Psycho-Thriller

Through a Glass Darkly,
    50, 203, 271–86,
    406
Tightrope, 94
Titles, 408–9
    poor, 90
To Die For, 84
Toller, Ernst, 54
Tootsie, 126, 300
Top Hat, 46, 55
Total Recall, 85
Towne, Robert, 154
    screenplay of
        Chinatown, 154–76
Trading Places, 234, 235,
    360
Trainspotting, 6
Trans-Europ-Express, 57
*Treasure of the Sierra
    Madre, The*, 81, 312
Treatment, 413–16
Truffaut, François, 9, 312
Turning Points, 74, 209,
    217, 233–37
    and backstory, 340, 341
    and characters' choices,
        248–51
    and climax, 311–12
    and comedy, 362
    and emotional
        transitions, 243–48
    and flashback, 341
    and problem of
        interest, 346
    and question of self-
        expression, 237–38
    scene analysis, 270–71,
        286–87
Twelve Angry Men, 292
Twenty Bucks, 227
2001: A Space Odyssey, 46

Ulysses (Joyce), 367
Umberto D, 57, 58

Un Chien Andalou, 64
*Unbearable Lightness of
    Being, The*, 358
Unforgiven, 20, 83, 93
Unmarried Woman, An,
    126, 206–7
Usual Suspects, The, 70,
    351

Verdict, The, 104, 222,
    229
Vertigo, 20, 119, 225
Viridiana, 407
Viva Zapata!, 81
Voice-over narration,
    344–45
Von Stroheim, Erich,
    109

Wall Street, 81, 128, 234,
    235, 325
War and Peace, 71
War and Peace (Tolstoy),
    137
War Genre, 81
War of the Roses, The, 88,
    125, 128, 311
Watership Down, 68
Wayne's World, 47, 55, 64
Wedding, A, 137
Weekend, 47, 54, 55, 64,
    65, 359
Welfare, 47
West Side Story, 85
Western Genre, 81, 86,
    93, 192, 407
Wild Strawberries, 47
When Harry Met Sally, 55,
    56, 96, 360
Whispers in the Dark, 94
White Men Can't Jump, 85
Who Framed Roger Rabbit,
    20, 53–54
Wild Strawberries, 343

Winter Light, 55, 81
Witches of Eastwick, The,
    124, 136
Witness, 95, 226
Wizard of Oz, The, 70,
    129, 223–24
Woman's Film, 82
Woolf, Virginia, 54
Wright, Will, 81
Writers Guild of America,
    script registration
    service, 15
Writing for film
    authorship, 185–89
    believing in what you
        write, 65–66
    earning a living,
        61–64
    endurance, 98–99
    from the inside out,
        152–76, 412–17
    from the outside in,
        410–12
    mastering classical
        form, 64–65
    and Mind Worm, 374
    as poet, 400–408
    and risk/maturity,
        149–51
    screenplay length, 415
    step outline, 412–15
    style, tips on, 395–97
    treatment, 406–8

Yeats, William Butler, 13
Yellow Submarine, The, 85
Young Frankenstein, 360
Young Mr. Lincoln, 84

Zed & Two Noughts, A, 47,
    55
Zedung, Mao, 406
Zelig, 84
Zero de Conduite, 47